Equality and Human Rights

Equality and Human Rights

Sachin Verma

RANDOM

RANDOM PUBLICATIONS

NEW DELHI (INDIA)

Equality and Human Rights

ISBN 978-93-5111-223-5

Published in 2014 in India by

RANDOM PUBLICATIONS

4376-A/4B, Gali Murari Lal, Ansari Road
New Delhi-110 002
Phone : +91-11-43580356, +91-11-23289044
e-mail: randomexports@gmail.com, sales@randompublications.com, info@randompublications.com

Reprinted 2026

Type Setting by : Keystoneprintads, Delhi-110051

Preface

The fundamental fights are guaranteed to protect the basic human rights of all citizens of India and are put into effect by the courts, subject to some limitations. One of such fundamental rights is the Right to Equality. Right to Equality refers to the equality in the eyes of law, discarding any unfairness on grounds of caste, race, religion, place of birth sex. It also includes equality of prospects in matters of employment, abolition of untouchability and abolition of titles. Articles 14, 15, 16, 17 and 18 of the Constitution of India highlight the Right to Equality in detail. This fundamental right is the major foundation of all other rights and privileges granted to Indian citizens. It is one of the chief guarantees of the Constitution of India. Thus, it is imperative that every citizen of India has easy access to the courts to exercise his/her Right to Equality.

Equality before law is well defined under the Article 14 of the Constitution which ensures that every citizen shall be likewise protected by the laws of the country. It means that the State will not distinguish any of the Indian citizens on the basis of their gender, caste, creed, religion or even the place of birth. The state cannot refuse equality before the law and equal defense of the law to any person within the territory of India. In other words, this means that no person or groups of people can demand for any special privileges. This right not only applies to the citizens of India but also to all the people within the territory of India.

The right of Social Equality and Equal Access to Public Areas is clearly mentioned under the Article 15 of the Constitution of India stating that no person shall be shown favoritism on the basis of color, caste, creed language, etc. Every person shall have equal admittance to public places like public wells, bathing ghats, museums, temples etc. However, the State has the right to make any special arrangement for women and children or for the development of any socially or educationally backward class or scheduled castes or scheduled tribes. This article applies only to citizens of India.

Article 16 of the Constitution of India clearly mentions that the State shall treat everyone equally in the matters of employment. No citizen shall be discriminated on the basis of race, caste, religion, creed, descent or place of birth in respect of any employment or office under the State. Every citizen of India can apply for government jobs. However, there are some exceptions to this right. The Parliament may pass a law mentioning that specific jobs can only be filled by candidates who are residing in a particular area. This requirement is mainly for those posts that necessitate the knowledge of the locality and language of the area. Apart from this, the State may also set aside some posts for members of backward classes, scheduled castes or scheduled tribes which are not properly represented in the services under the State to uplift the weaker sections of the society. Also, a law may be passed which may entail that the holder of an office of any religious institution shall also be a person professing that specific religion. Though, this right shall not be granted to the overseas citizens of India as directed by the Citizenship (Amendment) Bill, 2003.

I thank all members of my team who have helped in the preparation of the book. My special thanks go to "Random Publications" who have published the book.

– ***Sachin Verma***

Contents

1

Meaning of Human Rights

INTRODUCTION

Fundamental rights which humans have by the fact of being human, and which are neither created nor can be abrogated by any government. Supported by several international conventions and treaties, these include cultural, economic, and political rights, such as right to life, liberty, education and equality before law, and right of association, belief, free speech, information, religion, movement, and nationality.

Promulgation of these rights is not binding on any country, but they serve as a standard of concern for people and form the basis of many modern national constitutions. Although they were defined first by the UK philosopher John Locke as absolute moral claims or entitlements to life, liberty, and property, the best-known expression of human rights is in the US Declaration of Rights in 1776 which proclaims that "All men are by nature equally free and independent and have certain inherent natural rights of which when they enter a society they cannot by an compact deprive or divest their posterity." Called also fundamental rights.

See also civil rights and natural rights. Also, its said that a right is not what someone gives you; its what no one can take from you. Yet, in India, basic human rights have somehow been taken from a vast section of the population. With a million scavengers, thousands of cases of domestic violence and dowry deaths, and an appalling number of child labourers.

HUMAN RIGHTS—THE MODERN INVENTION

The term *"human rights"* is a relatively modern invention.

It covers under its umbrella three different types of rights:

1. The fundamental freedoms or classical civil liberties,
2. Ethnic and religious rights
3. Socio-economic rights.

Some constitutions have enumerated the first or the first and the second and attempted to set up judicial enforcement of such rights. The third category has not been stated in a constitution in an enforceable form, but some constitutions refer to them as directive principles of state policy.

The more important rights may be said to include the right of each individual to:

- Freedom of speech and expression,
- Freedom from arrest or detention except under authority of law,
- Freedom from cruel, inhumane or degrading punishments and the right to a fair trial by a competent and independent court,
- Freedom to enjoy lawfully acquired property,
- Equality of persons before the law,
- Freedom of assembly and association (including public meeting and withdrawal of labour),
- Freedom of thought, conscience and religion,
- Freedom to contract,
- freedom to engage in a trade, profession or occupation,
- Freedom of movement within a nation and across national borders.

The idea of these rights has arisen in multi-linguistic, multi-cultural, multi-racial and multi-religious populations. The notion of equality before the law and equal protection of the law underlies the rights and is generally included in constitutions which have bills of rights, though in a particular situation it may be available in conjunction with some other right. The idea of equality before the law implies that persons or groups must not be discriminated against without justification. The words "*without justification*" are relevant. Discrimination is both inevitable and proper in human affairs because of the differences between human beings, accidents (both natural and man induced) and many factors which affect the nurture and development of individuals. These by their nature are not justiciable in the courts.

ALLEGED DUTIES OF THE STATES

In this category are alleged duties of the state: to secure full employment for all people of working age, to provide adequate standards of living and education to all citizens, to rapidly develop the country, to distribute the social product equitably, to eliminate economic and social privilege and disparity, to ensure social security and welfare, to develop the culture and languages of ethnic groups, to protect the environment, to safeguard the independence, sovereignty, unity and territorial integrity of the, country and to promote international peace and co-operation.

Past History of Human rights in Different Countries

The analysis refers to three types of rights:

1. The traditional rights primarily involving protection of individuals from government,
2. Ethnic and religious rights and
3. Social welfare rights.

It is important to distinguish between the different historical and conceptual bases of these three categories of rights which are loosely termed *"human rights"*. Such differences between them are often blurred or ignored, with serious consequences for the operation of fundamental freedoms. Since the second world war, there has been a great emphasis on human rights other than the classical civil liberties: on socio-economic rights, and on the rights of groups or classes or nations.

The recognition that the promotion of socio-economic rights, as rights to benefit from the state, stand in great tension with civil liberties may be often deliberately obscured, but it is nevertheless widespread and it is, of course, a correct recognition. The traditional civil liberties, many have correctly recognised, require institutional settings, historical traditions, a sense of community. The socio-economic rights can, in principle, be granted by the state, even by a state which suppresses all non-state organisations and institutions. Very different kinds of societies may be involved....

The attempt to elevate human rights, in any particular formulation, uncritically, as urgent, unhistorical, abstract demands is not only based on intellectual error but is like most propaganda and moral indoctrination inherently unstable and unable to cope with genuine criticism. Human rights can only be understood, and therefore must be taught, in the concrete contexts in which they arise and have to be implemented. This is the social context of concrete history and real politics. There is also, in an important sense, a concrete human context. This is best portrayed by world literature, or at least by the great literature of the world, and not by shallow declarations and proclamations.

The third category commonly included within the term *"human rights"*, namely *"socio-economic rights"*, raises basic questions regarding the meaning and operation of human rights. The recognition of this category as rights has created certain contradictions within the concept, leading to the weakening of civil liberties. The consequences of such recognition and the conflict that arises between civil liberties and socio-economic *"rights"* creates many problems. There are human needs. Yet where a need exists, however compelling, a right cannot be said to automatically spring into existence.

Restrictions on Rights

In countries which have bills of rights there is a basic statement of freedoms subject to permitted abridgment of such freedoms. Freedoms are restricted in the public interest on grounds of national security, to preserve public order, to protect public health, to maintain moral standards, to secure due recognition and respect for the rights and freedoms of others or to meet the just requirements of the general welfare of a democratic society. The United States Supreme Court has over the years qualified the rights in the constitution. Any statement of rights is not absolute and must of necessity be subject to limitations on the Above lines. The right of free speech and expression does not extend to sedition, slander, defamation and obscenity. The principle of equality before the law cannot deny a legislature the power to classify persons for legislative purposes and to legislate affecting them, provided that the classification is not arbitrary and is based on a real and substantial distinction bearing a reasonable and just relation to the objects sought to be achieved.

Thus the legislature could enact legislation regulating the activities of money lenders. This would amount to a singling out of money lenders and would be prima facie in conflict with the principle of equality before the law. But provided the classification is reasonable and there is a legitimate object to be achieved the legislation would nonetheless be valid. The instances of legitimate restrictions of rights. They are intended to illustrate that no right available to an individual or group is or can be absolute. This seems obvious but is often not appreciated.

The Clash of Rights

The reality that human rights are not absolute, and are subject to reasonable restrictions, does not mean that the rights can be arbitrarily curtailed just as to legislative or bureaucratic discretion. The manner in which restrictions are to be determined and imposed and the criteria which apply to the formulation of restrictions are crucial. If human rights are to be meaningful they cannot be subject to crude majoritarian dictates.

What distinguishes a human right from any other right is that a human right is available to and enforceable by a minority, however small, even against the wishes of a majority. If human rights were to become subject to ordinary parliamentary control they would be no different from any other statutory right which parliament is free to confer and withdraw at its pleasure. The restriction of human rights is therefore a crucial and delicate question. They cannot be based on ideological perceptions of parliamentarians, bureaucrats or the Human Rights Commission but must be grounded on objectively ascertained and comprehended criteria.

The *National Times*, week ending 25 August, 1979, referred to *"the right to march demonstrations"* and by way of example: *"Senator George Georges was gaoled yet again for upholding the principle of the right to democratic protest in Brisbane streets"*. What are these rights? There is no absolute right to democratic protest or to march. There are rights of speech and expression and assembly. But these rights are subject to limitations. The right to freedom of association must be exercised so as not to interfere with the rights of others to move about the streets or go about their business. Where there is a clash of rights, methods must be devised through rational analysis, political avenues and the courts so that the rights of all parties could be exercised so as not to inconvenience each other. If this is not possible (as it often is not) there must be a compromise or one must be restricted and give way to the other.

The clash of rights is a factor which the United States courts and citizens are very familiar with. An example of a conflict of rights is where the right of free expression of the press to coverage of news stories may clash with the right of an accused in a criminal case not to be prejudiced by adverse publicity of allegations made against him prior to trial or in a pre-trial hearing.

American journalists generally would not show such an obvious lack of understanding of the basic principles underlying fundamental rights as is demonstrated by the quotation. The is just one of numerous examples in contemporary Australia where so called rights are claimed without reference to conflicting rights and basic common sense.

Exaltation of Particular Rights

One of the real problems in the human rights arena today is the failure by the Human Rights Commission and many who profess to be concerned about human rights to appreciate that human rights are complementary to each other. The pursuit of one particular right without regard to others is self defeating and destructive of the overall framework of rights which is essential to the operation of specific rights.

Human rights activists overlook this dimension. Some rights such as the right to equality of persons before the law, freedom of speech and freedom of person and property are more important than other rights. If one right must prevail over another a rational basis must be provided. This involves an examination of the two rights, an evaluation of the importance of each and the context within which they operate.

2

Movements Conducted by Indian Government

EMERGENCE OF CIVIL LIBERTIES MOVEMENTS

In India, the last quarter of the 20th century has been witness to a growing recognition of the place and relevance of human rights. It is axiomatic that this interest in human rights is rooted in the denial of life and liberty that was a pervasive aspect of the Emergency. The mass arrests of the leaders of the opposition, and the targeted apprehension of those who could present a challenge to an authoritarian state, are one of the dominant images that have survived. The involuntary disappearance of Rajan in Kerala is more than a symbol of the excesses of unbridled power.1 Forced evictions carried out in Delhi in what is known as 'Turkman Gate' conjures up visions of large scale razing of dwellings of those without economic clout, and of their displacement into what were the outlying areas of the city. The catastrophic programme of mass sterilisation is an indelible part of emergency memory. The civil liberties movement was a product of the emergency. Arbitrary detention, custodial violence, prisons and the use of the judicial process were on the agenda of the civil liberties movement.

WOMEN'S MOVEMENT

The same period also saw the emergence of a nascent women's movement. In December 1974, the Committee on the Status of Women in India submitted its report to the Government of India preceding the heralding in of the International Women's Year in 1975.

The Status Report, in defiance of standard expectations:

- Set out almost the entire range of issues and contexts as they affected women. Basing their findings, and revising their assumptions about how women live, on the experiences of women and communities that they met, the Committee redrew the contours of women's position, problems and priorities.
- Gave a fillip to the re-nascent women's movement.

The women's movement has been among the most articulate, and heard, in the public arena. The woman as a victim of dowry, domestic violence, liquor, rape and custodial violence has constituted one discourse. Located partly in the women's rights movement, and partly in the campaign against AIDS,3 women in prostitution have acquired visibility. The question of the practice of prostitution being considered as 'sex work' has been variously raised, while there has been a gathering unanimity on protecting the women in prostitution from harassment by the law.

The Uniform Civil Code debate, contesting the inequality imposed on women by 'personal' laws has been resurrected, diverted and re-started. Representation, through reservation, of women in parliament and state legislatures has followed the mandated presence of women in panchayats. Population policies have been contested terrain, with the experience of the emergency acting as a constant backdrop. 'Women's rights are human rights' has demanded a re-construction of the understanding of human rights as being directed against action and inaction of the state and agents of the state. Patriarchy has entered the domain of human rights as nurturing the offender.

PUBLIC INTEREST LITIGATION

In the late '70s, but more definitively in the early '80s, the Supreme Court devised an institutional mechanism in public interest litigation (PIL). PIL opened up the court to issues concerning violations of rights, and non realization of even bare non-negotiables4 by diluting the rule of *locus standi*; any person could move the court on behalf of a class of persons who, due to indigence, illiteracy or incapacity of any other kind were unable to reach out for their rights. In its attempt to make the court process less intimidating, the procedure was simplified, and even a letter to the court could be converted into a petition.

In its early years, PIL was a process which:

- Recognised rights and their denial which had been invisibilised in the public domain. Prisoners, for instance, hidden amidst high walls which confined them, found a space to speak the language of fundamental and human rights.
- Led to 'juristic' activism, which expanded the territory of rights of persons. The fundamental rights were elaborated to find within them the right to dignity, to livelihood, to a clean environment, to health, to education, to safety at the workplace. The potential for reading a range of rights into the fundamental rights was explored.

Individuals, groups and movements have since used the court as a situs for struggle and contest, with varying effect on the defining of what constitutes human rights, and prioritising when rights appear to be in conflict.

STRUGGLE AGAINST PERVASIVE DISCRIMINATION

Dalit movements have kept caste oppression, and the oppression of caste, in public view. Moving beyond untouchability, which persists in virulent forms, the movement has had to contend with increasing violence against dalits even as dalits refuse to suffer in silence, or as they move beyond the roles allotted to them in traditional caste hierarchy. The growth of caste armies in Bihar, for instance, is one manifestation. The assassination of dalit panchayat leaders in Melmazhuvur in Tamil Nadu is another. The firing on dalits by the police forces when they were seen to be rising their oppression in the southern tip of Tamil Nadu is a third.

The scourge of manual scavenging has been brought into policy and the law campaigns; there have been efforts to break through public obduracy in acknowledging that untouchability exists. In the meantime, there are efforts by groups working on dalit issues to internationalise deep discrimination of caste by influencing the agenda of the World Conference Against Racism.

RESISTING DISPLACEMENT INDUCED BY 'DEVELOPMENT' PROJECTS

There has been widespread contestation of project-induced displacement. The recognition of inequity, and of violation of the basic rights of the affected people, has resulted in growing interaction between local communities and activists from beyond the affected region, and the articulation of the rights and the injuries has been moulded in the process of this interaction.

Resource rights were agitated in the early years of protest in the matter of forests; conservation and the right of the people to access forest produce for their subsistence and in acknowledgment of the traditional relationship between forests and dwellers in and around forests. Environmentalists and those espousing the dwellers' and forest users' causes have spoken together, parted company and found meeting points again, over the years. The right to resources is vigorously contested terrain.

COMMUNALISM

The 1980s, but more stridently in the 1990s, communalism has become a part of the fabric of politics. The anti- Sikh riots following Indira Gandhi's assassination was a ghastly reminder that communalism could well lurk just beneath the surface. The Bhagalpur massacres in 1989 represent another extreme communal manifestation. The demolition of the Babri Masjid on December 6, 1992 is an acknowledged turning point in majoritarian communalism, and impunity.

The complicity of the state is undeniable. The killing of Graham Staines and his sons in Orissa was another gruesome aspect of communalism. The questioning of conversions in this climate is inevitably seen as infected with the communal virus. The forcible 're-conversion' in the Dangs area in Gujarat too has communal overtones. Attacks on Christians are regularly reported in the press, and the theme of impunity is being developed in these contexts.

NEW MOVEMENTS AND CAMPAIGNS

The professionalising of the non-governmental sector has had an impact on finding public space for certain issues and in making work on the issues sustainable. Child labour, AIDS-related work, the area of devolution and aiding women's participation in panchayat institutions, and battling violence against women have found support and sustainability in funding infrastructure development and support. These have existed alongside civil liberties groups and initiatives, grassroots campaigns such as the Campaign for the Right to Information based in Rajasthan, the development struggle which has the Narmada Bachao Andolan at its helm, or the fish workers' forum that has combated, sometimes successfully, the encroachments by the large-scale and capital-intensive into the livelihoods of traditional fishing communities. Movements for self-determination, militancy, dissent and the naxalite movement have provoked various extraordinary measures which have, in turn, prompted human rights groups into protest and challenge. The Terrorist and Disruptive Activities (Prevention) Act (TADA) is an instance.6 The Armed Forces Special Powers Act (AFSPA) continues.

Encounter killings, disappearances and the ineffectiveness of the judicial system in places where 'extraordinary' situations of conflict prevail, characterise the human rights-related scenario. A jurisprudence of human rights has emerged in these contexts. Networking, and supporting each other through conflicts and campaigns, is not infrequent. There are glimmerings of the emergence of, or existence of a human rights community in this. This has had groups and movements working on tourism, forest dwellers rights, civil liberties, displacement, women's rights and environment, for instance, finding a common voice in protesting the nuclear blasts in May 1999, or in condemning the attacks on the filming of 'Water' which had undisguised communal overtones.

There has also been a building of bridges across causes and the emergence of an inter-woven community of interests. As the vista of rights has expanded, conflicts between rights have begun to surface. There has been a consequent prioritisation of rights. The determination of priorities has often depended on the agency which engages in setting them- sometimes this has been environmental groups, at others workers, and yet other times, it has been the court, for instance.

In this general setting, we embarked on a mapping of:

- Human rights issues
- Responses – state and non-state – to human rights situations
- Conflicts between rights and prioritisation of rights, and
- A miscellany of issues including the treatment, and the place of state and non-state violence, and the question of who speaks for whom, and the relationship between the advocate of an interest and the persons or classes of persons affected by the advocacy.

3

Different Movements Conducted by the Indian Government

MOVEMENT ABOUT DEATH PENALTY

There was an audible objections from women's groups; some women's groups extended it support. It was when the issue was raised again in 1998, that there was an avalanche of protest from women's groups. The NCW too released a report of a study it had done which showed that most of their respondents opposed the prescription of death penalty for rape. For some in the women's movement, the opposition to death penalty for rape appears to have been a pragmatic position - since it would only make the women more vulnerable if the penalty were so severe. For others, the pragmatic argument was a means of opposing the spread of death penalty into areas where it is not, already. What is disturbing is the persistence of the Home Minister in holding out the death penalty as a promise to women, as a statement of seriousness about the problem. In this context the failure to challenge the prescription of the death penalty for offences in the Commission of Sati (Prevention) Act 1987 also becomes an area that needs to be re-visited.

- Shifting the onus of proof. This has already been introduced into the Evidence Act 1872 in 1983 and 1986. Section 113A raises a presumption as to abetment of suicide by a married woman where she commits suicide within seven years of her marriage, and it is shown that her husband or in-laws or a relative of her husband had subjected her to cruelty. Section.113 B raises a presumption of dowry death where it is shown that soon before her death she had been subjected to cruelty or harassment by the accused for, or in connection with, any demand for dowry. Section114 A presumes absence of consent in certain prosecutions for rape. A respondent reasoned that she had opposed this shifting of onus of proof because it would open the gates for the state to extend the shifting of onus to other areas. Also, while the violations are certainly heinous, the criminal justice system is structured to require the prosecution to prove guilt; it is often not possible for an accused to rebut an accusation, she said, even where the accused may be innocent. Further it is a dilution of fair trial standards. The contrary position is that there are offences where such a presumption is not necessary if justice is to be done to the woman.

- A separate criminal code for women. This was a proposal that emanated from the NCW and was widely discussed in 1995-96. This was intended to make the trial less traumatic for women, speed up the criminal judicial process, and it was expected to raise the conviction rate. There were discussions of making some inroads into the rights given to an accused under the law. This proposal, however, appears to have been shelved. It was suggested to us that child sexual abuse being of an extraordinary nature, there should be a relaxation of fair trial standards in dealing with it.

HIV, AIDS AND DISCLOSURE

The two conflicting positions on disclosure by a hospital/doctor about the HIV+ status of a person has been set out *supra* while mapping human rights issues. To that discussion of the issue may be added that the view on disclosure seems to have been influenced by the context of the proposed marriage of the petitioner in that case. It may be appropriate to consider the reach of the principle of disclosure while weighing the rights content of the court's decision.

AIDS AND HIGH RISK GROUPS

The AIDS campaign has given visibility to women in prostitution who had so far been unable to requisition public spaces. There are few who deny that women in prostitution need to be empowered to prevent their becoming ready victims of HIV transmission, as also of passing the virus on. However, the programme of intervention to protect from AIDS has re-introduced the idea of high risk groups, and women in prostitution as constituting such a group - a notion that was contested in the 1980s as discriminatory, and with the potential of leading to victimisation oftargetted groups.

ABORTION IN THE CONTEXT OF WOMEN'S HEALTH AND SEX SELECTIVE ABORTION

When Parliament passed the 1971 law legalising abortion under certain conditions, the statement of objects and reasons listed three reasons for passing the law:

1. *As a health measure*: When there is danger to the life or risk to the physical or mental health of the woman;
2. *On humanitarian grounds*: Such as when pregnancy arises from a sex crime like rape or intercourse with a lunatic woman, etc.; and

3. *Eugenic grounds*: Where there is substantial risk that the child, if born, would suffer from deformities and diseases.

By 1995, when the Maternity Benefit Act 1961 was amended, the insertion of population control provisions into the law was being acknowledged, and resisted. The 1995 amendment, however, did give a renewed emphasis to placing the onus for family size on the woman when it incorporated 'leave with wages for tubectomy operation' as a 'maternity benefit', even as it gave medical termination of pregnancy the same position in law as miscarriage. This is a statement of the adoption of abortion as state supported policy. The question of abortion as a right, and abortion as a population control measure may need to be re-visited. There was also a proposal to limit the provision of maternity benefit under the Act to women workers up to the second child; this however seems to have been dropped, perhaps because of the protest that met the proposal at almost every turn.

The Pre-natal Diagnostic Techniques (Regulation and Prevention of Misuse) Act 1994, which was modelled on an earlier Maharashtra law, was enacted expressly 'to prohibit pre-natal diagnostic techniques for determination of sex of the foetus leading to female foeticide. Such abuse of techniques is discriminatory against the female sex and affects the dignity and status of women.'64 The punishment for transgressing the prohibition of the law is intended to be deterrent. Yet, in the seven years since the law was enacted, there have been no prosecutions of which any of our respondents made mention. The conflict inherent in asking for abortion as a matter of right, and believing that sex selective abortion needs tobe curbed requires to be squarely addressed.

FREEDOM OF EXPRESSION, PRIVACY AND CENSORSHIP

The depiction of women, as also of violence against women, has raised difficult questions of censorship and of free speech and expression. The control that capital has over the media has been recognised, and it is not the free speech rights of corporations that is in issue here. Feminists worry that the power to determine what is 'obscene' or 'indecent' could curtail the use of media to interrogate, for instance, rape: for the depiction of rape could be viewed as 'obscene' and explicitly addressing the issue proscribed. Even as feminists, and women, find public spaces for their speech and expression, the space could get restricted and reconstructed by censorship. The Miss World contest organised in Bangalore in 1996 gave rise to similar, uneasily quietened questions.

The responsibility of the researcher, and the impact of publishing research findings, has been in issue in the Almora case, where research published in September 1999 became a subject of singular controversy in April2000. The research, on AIDS and the local community, used the responses from a sample of respondents who spoke about the sexual practices in the area, from where male migration for work is very high. Promiscuity and adultery were spoken of. The protesters were angry at the depiction of the community in the report. That the research was funded by a foreign donor agency added a dimension to the protest. The NGO later apologised, and withdrew the report. By then, three activists had spent 45 days in jail.

In the meantime the state had moved in to impose the NSA on them. This last deed was roundly condemned, and much of the human rights community spoke as one to attack the state action. The questions raised by the research and the report, however, continue to hang in the air.

PROSTITUTION

There has been considerable movement in public perception. Most significant though has been the openness with which the practice, proliferation and problems of prostitution are now discussed. Inevitably, perhaps, there have been conflicts that have surfaced in this area of women's rights. On the one hand is the demand that sex work be recognised as real work. In the mid-'90s this was articulated as sex work being seen as labour. There was also a demand that labour laws be applied to sex work. That appears to have been gradually amended to the demand that sex work be accepted as labour in terms of the dignity that labour commands. A collective of women in prostitution identified three R's - Respect, Recognition and Reliance. The women in the collective also spoke about the right to say 'No' in the course practice of their profession, and said they had to be given the right of 'self-determination'.

While there was no demurring about the need to protect women from exploitation - from the police, the pimp, the madam and the client - there were dissenting voices on recognising prostitution as sexual labour. As one respondent said it: 'Feminists are being included in a much larger agenda. They are giving patriarchy and sexual exploitation a sugar coating by calling it work. Earlier patriarchy oppressed women by calling them 'mother goddess' and curbing her freedom. Today patriarchy oppresses her by calling her the 'bread winner'. She continued: 'I accept that today the state is doing little to stop trafficking. But the day sex work is seen as work under law, that will be the end of all efforts to stop trafficking.(Trafficking-While trafficking in women is rampant in many parts of the country, and also across borders, it is Kerala that the sexual exploitation of women and trafficking has been exposed, and the accused brought to trial and conviction.

The *Surinelli* case, the *Ice Cream Parlour* case and the *Vidhura* case are undiluted narratives of sexual exploitation. In the *Surinelli* case, forty persons, including prominent political figures and persons from the establishment among them, were convicted after a prolonged trial in 2000. They are now on bail while their appeal is pending. Some women's activists have been studying the issue of migration and trafficking - whether for prostitution, labour in sweat shops, domestic work which is often ill-paid and oppressive, or as mail order brides — while recognizing that while migration makes women vulnerable to exploitation - and violence, migration is often not wholly involuntary. Women, for instance, migrate to escape violent domestic situations too. Shorn of its moral content, activists say, the law regarding trafficking could actually help women trafficked into situations for which they did not bargain.)

A woman from the collective, however, said: 'Trafficking can only be stopped by us. Only we know what is happening in our areas. We are telling the government they should give us the right to act.' She however conceded that not all areas where prostitution is practised and trafficking occurs were yet capable of being so monitored. We see ourselves as workers, she said, and we want a union that will give us a base.

A 'mela' which was organised by the collective in Calcutta in March 2001 reportedly met with stiff resistance from some women activists, while others stood up for the rights of the women to organise themselves. It is sometimes depicted as an issue of 'agency' of the woman as against those who see women in prostitution as victims, and subjects of exploitation.

Six aspects which a woman in the collective adverted to if they were to be considered to be 'labour', and their association recognised, were:

- Police raids would not happen.
- Mental torture in the rescue homes would cease. Also, when the girls are released by pimps, they say they have paid huge amounts when they actually pay far less in bond. Bonded labour is therefore rampant in the present dispensation, she said.
- A self-regulatory examination board, with a multi-sectoral member composition would be able to prevent the entry of minors into prostitution. The two criteria of age and willingness would be applied by them. Now, we don't have even the right to stay where we are, she said.
- The right to say 'No' would get established.
- Teasing to demean women in prostitution would reduce.
- When they retire, they are not even able to go back home; once they are declared to be labour, that will change. That would be real rehabilitation, she said.

There was some conceptual confusion about 'decrimina-lising' and 'legalising' prostitution. While most of our respondents saw a need to decriminalise to prevent them from being a vulnerable group, the mix up with legalizing prostitution - which many among our respondents were unable to accept– dogged our discussion. A proposal that the travel of single women across political borders be controlled, which was under discussion with the NCW, was dismissed by some respondents as being a prescription for obstructing freedom of movement of women and as likely to serve no other end. The children of women in prostitution are seen by the law as being potentially in 'moral danger'. The Juvenile Justice Act 1986 and its successor legislation - the Children in Need of Care and Protection Act 2000 - allow for their children to be taken over by the state. A judge of the Supreme Court had even said that the women should be 'coaxed, cajoled or coerced' to give up their children. This clash of a complex of rights and of perceptions needs to be more fully understood.

ENVIRONMENT

In the past fifteen years, environmental concerns have acquired a dominance which, it seems, have re-prioritised, and sometimes dislodged, rights.

REDUCED POLLUTION AND HAZARDS V. WORKERS' LIVELIHOOD

The issue was most starkly represented in the Delhi Relocation case. When 168 industries in the first instance, and thereafter all 'hazardous' industry in Delhi, were ordered to be closed or relocated, the conflict between the right to reduced pollution and hazards, and workers' jobs exploded into prominence. The matter arose out of a PIL filed by an environmental lawyer. The condition in which such an order would leave the workers - whether the industries closed down or relocated - was not considered till after the decision was made. The order, coming from the Supreme Court, has had an effect of finality and narrow negotiability which has pushed workers' rights very low in the hierarchy of rights into a residuary position.

In Kerala, the Grasim industries pollution case has engaged the environmentalists since the 1970s, and the workers from even earlier. Between 1985 and 1988, the industry closed down for reasons unconnected with the pollution. Environmentalists and workers then fought on the same side to have the industry re-started; the loss of jobs was then the primary concern. Since it re-started in 1988, the environmentalists have been gradually moving away from an appreciation of labour's concerns, since they do not see that environmental concerns and workers' jobs can be accommodated in a single solution. The environmentalists have voted for battling the pollution at all costs, even as they are chagrined at having to leave labour out of the reckoning. In Trivandrum, we heard of people whose livelihoods had been dislocated by the pollution of the coastal waters demanding that either the industry close down, or they be absorbed into the industry in replacement of livelihood lost due to the pollution.

In Tuticorin in Tamil Nadu, among the salt pans is located a chemical industry. A drying pond stands mute testimony to the potent pollution being caused by the industry. The salt workers' cooperative is maintaining a stoical silence about the pollution, since any protest from them may result in loss of jobs for about 1800 workers employed in the industry. In Vellore in Tamil Nadu, when the Supreme Court ordered that tanneries be closed, around 8000 workers were reportedly laid off. On the one hand, a labour activist said that it is time that workers developed a position which takes public health, pollution and environmental issues into account. On the other, the practice of using the court system, in PIL, to project a uni-dimensional view of the issue by environmentalists was attacked. The present priority accorded to environmental issues was seen as allowing the environmentalists to get away without having to reconcile conflicting concerns.

Shelter v. Conservation

The displacement, by court order, of residents of slums bordering, and encroaching in some measure, into the Borivili National Park in Mumbai has raised similar concerns. The clash between environmentalists and those espousing the cause of the slum dwellers has been violent, and the positions apparently irreconcilable.

Shelter v. Beautification

A petition asking for garbage disposal in Delhi has allowed the Supreme Court to order demolition of slum dwellings. While doing so, the court has likened giving land for rehabilitation to 'an encroacher' to 'rewarding a pickpocket'. In this vein, there has been a mass-scale illegalising of structures which house the poor. In the same order, the court has directed that garbage disposal being a public purpose, land should be released to the municipal corporation, free of cost. The court has been re-working priorities, and groups approaching the court increasingly recognise that environment, as expansively defined, is likely to take precedence over other rights such as shelter and workers' livelihood. There has been greater scope for negotiation, however, when the survival of an industry is concerned– clean-up technology (particularly ETPs and CETPs) which, at best, is recognised to be a partial answer, have been accepted as an answer to the charge of pollution.

Tribals v. Forests

The presenting of the conflict in these terms, *i.e.*, tribals vs. forests, has tended to marginalise the tribal communities. There has been denudation of the rights of tribals who habitually reside in forests and live off forest produce. The creation of national parks and sanctuaries has led to installing the concept in law of exclusion of the tribal from the forest. Where they are being allowed access, their rights are severely circumscribed– by identity cards, timings, numerous checkpoints and a very limited range of permitted activity - leaving them often at the mercy of the forest officer. A distinct school of thought has emerged which advocates against the exclusion of tribals, and which sees a role for tribal and forest dependent communities in the conservation of forests.

The reconstructing of the rights of tribal communities is, largely, except for the rare exception, being done without the participation of the affected communities.

Anti-smoking law v. Workers

The workers in the tobacco industry have found their jobs threatened by the anti-smoking legislation that has been introduced in some states. Trade unions find themselves impelled to oppose the ban because it will cause reduced sale of beedis and, consequently, reduced employment. They also argued that it was a ploy by large tobacco companies to snuff out the beedi industry since it is the class which smokes beedis which will have difficulty in finding spaces which are not public and where they may smoke legally. Yet, this would present workers as selfcentred and anti-health. The conflict defies easy solution.

TRIBAL LAND ALIENATION

The law, generally prohibits the transfer of land from a tribal to a non-tribal in agency areas, or scheduled areas, except for reasons recognised by law, and by procedure prescribed therein. While this is usually respected as fair and legitimate protection extended to scheduled tribes, and to prevent exploitation of the tribal by the non-tribal, the situation in Kerala has been somewhat complicated.

In 1975, the state legislature enacted the Kerala Scheduled Tribes (Restriction on Transfer of Lands and Restoration of Alienated Lands) Act 1975. The law has had a chequered career, with the government attempting to dilute the effect of the law, by amendment, and the courts demanding its implementation in its 1975 guise.

The question of alternative land rather than restoration has also been mooted – but it is not clear that such alternative land exists. While tribal activists have been campaigning for enforcing the 1975 law, others have been muted in their reactions. The reason, our respondents say, is because the land appears to have been transferred for a price to settlers who are themselves only marginalised populations.

It would be unjust and iniquitous to dislodge them from lands for which they have paid as much as they can afford, it was said. This was represented as a case of conflicting interests, but of two equally, if differently, affected communities. Rehabilitation of the already displaced adivasi community appears to be one way of resolving the issue - a view with which tribal activists do not concur, considering it as an erosion, even a denial of the right against alienation of land.

DALIT MOVEMENT AND THE CASTE AS RACE REPRESENTATION

The effort by NGOs to get caste on the race agenda at the Conference for the Elimination of Racial Discrimination has been an attempt to internationalize the issue of caste. Some activists and leaders in the dalit movement have also been involved. While some of them have got on board as in Gujarat, the dalit activists/leaders in Andhra Pradesh and Tamil Nadu have been consulted but have chosen not to enter the arena themselves. This is how a dalit activist leader explained it: 'We need international pressure. So far we have treated it as an internal matter. This will help the issue get focus.... This has been raised by NGOs, not by the movement. I don't know about donor politics. We only tried to get some control by putting some of our academicians in it. But we are not sure what it means.'

A Dalit leader who had not heard of this move objected to the caste-as-race representation. Race is not our politics, he said. Our fight is against brahmanism and casteism, he said. Even if it were to be considered that NGOs may not be able to consult with *all* affected or concerned persons, groups, organizations or movements before espousing causes, the conflict that could exist where the NGO position and that of movement politics do not converge has to be addressed.

SPEEDY DISPOSAL OF CASES V. OPEN CRIMINAL JUSTICE PROCESS

Overcrowding in prisons has been partly attributed to the problem of transporting undertrials to the courts, and of finding police escort to perform this task. In response there is an emerging practice of magistrates holding court within prison premises. This reportedly happens in Delhi and in Bangalore, for instance.

The prison is patently a closed premise, as also beyond the beat of the persons who make the judicial process an open system, including lawyers, reporters and observers. In a different context, the virtues of in camera trials in cases of rape to protect the interests of the victim of rape has also been debated, inconclusively.

HUMAN RIGHTS LAWYERING

In approaching the court, or when an activist is drawn into the judicial process, a question of representation of a political or an ideological position often rises. Illustratively, a feminist litigating for getting custody of her child may be faced with two choices: either to assert the stereotype– the mother as the primary career of the child, and the child needing the care and attention that only the mother can give - and increase the probability of getting custody, or staying within the politics of feminism and reject such stereotyping which, in turn, may drastically reduce the chances of getting a favourable order from the court.

An instance, again, is in matters of contempt of court, where activists may be advised to tone down their honest opposition to a court order which is patently unjust, even unconstitutional, or perhaps to tender an apology which would serve the requirement of the court, but which may compromise the politics of the contemnor. Difficulties abound where activists are picked up by the police, and there are apprehensions that they may be subjected to torture, or even be killed in a fake encounter - does politics stop at the doorstep of the courtroom?

Is it necessary to get the consent of the activist before taking a position in court, in a habeas corpus petition, for instance? And what is to be done where the activist is unreachable?

4

Mapping of Human Rights Issues

CUSTODIAL VIOLENCE

Custody death, torture in custody and custodial rape have been subjects of much concern. Custodial violence has been on the agenda of civil rights groups for over two decades, and reports documenting instances of violence and its systemic occurrence, have been instrumental in the campaigns against custodial violence. Although custody deaths have found an acknowledgment from the state, and the NHRC has issued directions to the states,

- To report of the NHRC any death in custody within 24 hours of the occurrence, and
- To videotape the post-mortem proceedings,

It is difficult to assess if this has resulted in any reduction in the incidence of custody deaths. NHRC reports show a marked increase in the reported cases of custody deaths each year. This is attributed, by the NHRC, to increased reporting and not to increased incidence of the crime; this, however, needs to be further investigated.

The incidence of custody deaths demonstrates more undeniably the brutalisation of the processes of law enforcement by the police and armed forces. However, custodial torture (not resulting in death) is not at the focus of campaigns to reduce custodial violence. There are few places which have taken up the treatment of the victims of torture as victims of torture. The Indian state, in the meantime, has resisted attempts (including that of the NHRC) to have it ratify the Torture Convention In recent reported cases from the Gauhati High Court, it is 15 and 16-year olds who are found to have been victims of state violence, and the defence of the state has been that they were hardened militants.

Custodial rape has found an expanded definition - in terms of power rape - in the Penal Code, 1860.8 However, these provisions have hardly been invoked. In the meantime, most often, judicial perceptions of the victim of custodial rape have in significant measure, discredited the victim's version, and blamed the victim resulting in reduction of sentence for policemen convicted of rape to less than the minimum prescribed in law. From Mathura to Rameeza Bi to Maya Tyagi to Suman Rani - these women have become symbols of patriarchal prejudices. Campaigns in the matter of custodial rape have invoked their name, and they are now names that are etched into the history and legend of the women's movement. In the meantime, the legal dictum that the identity of a victim of rape be not disclosed to protect her privacy has been set in place.

PROJECT DISPLACEMENT

Project displacement, for the construction of large dams or for power projects, for instance, have led to protest movements directly involving the affected people. The NBA has utilised strategies and tactics of protest – including *jal samarpan,* human chains, working on the funders and the contractors to withdraw, participating in the proceedings before, and surrounding, the World Commission on Dams - which have refused to let the issue be drowned out. This has also seen the manufacturing of conflicting forces, such as the pro-dam lobby which is believed to be largely state-sponsored.

Human rights issues that arise include:

- Displacement, *per se*
- The poverty of rehabilitation, and often, the impossibility of rehabilitation
- The impoverishment that results from displacement
- The non-reckoning of cultural and community identity and of rights.

What constitutes development has come into severe question in this arena. The Land Acquisition Act 1894 has been at the centre of protests. Among the strategies adopted to deal with the coercive nature of the law has been the drafting of alternative legislation. The obduracy of the state in not approving a policy for rehabilitation of the displaced has also been cause for protest.

THE INTERNALLY DISPLACED DUE TO CONFLICTS

The large-scale internal migration caused by political violence has created classes of internal refugees. During the years of militancy in the Punjab, after the anti-Sikh riots in 1984, and the movement of Kashmiri Pandits out of the valley have provided visible evidence of such migration. While the violence that preceded the migration has been squarely addressed in human rights terms, the rehabilitation and return of the migrants after displacement appears to have been only on the margins of the human rights movement.

REFUGEES

India has not ratified the 1951 UN Convention on Refugees, nor has it signed the 1967 protocol. The Indian state has generally resisted visits from the UNHCR to camps where refugees are housed. Activists say that the Indian state has been relatively benign towards refugees. One non-governmental source, in 1999, India hosted more than 2,92,000 refugees; which includes more than 16,000 persons from Afghanistan, 65,000 Chakmas from Bangladesh, 30,000 Bhutanese of Nepali origin, 50,000 Chin indigenous people from Myanmar and about 39,000 pro-democracy student activists from Rangoon and the Mandalay region, 1,10,000 Sri Lankan Tamils of whom 70,000 are in camps and 40,000 outside, 1,10,000 Tibetans and around 7000 persons from other countries.

The assassination of Rajiv Gandhi in 1991 has reportedly altered the treatment meted out to the Sri Lankan refugees. A fact-finding report of a civil liberties organisation in Tamil Nadu, Sri Lankan refugees fall into three categories: those who are in the 133 refugee camps; refugees who maintain themselves outside the camps; and those who have been identified as belonging to militant groups who were kept in virtual rigorous confinement in the three special camps. In August 1995, 43 inmates of the Special Camp at Tippu Mahal, Vellore escaped and a one-man commission set up by the state describes the structure and administration of the camps.

The refugees were found to be prisoners in these camps and, as even the state appointed commission had remarked, 'admittedly these inmates or most of them are in rigorous confinement in the special camps for five or six years continuously.' The testimony of the two inmates to the fact-finding team also revealed that the camp in Vellore had among its inmates at least 12 disabled persons.

The Government of India does not appear to have any policy on how to deal with refugee-prisoners in their camps. The protection of Chakma refugees in the state of Arunachal Pradesh, and their right to have their claim for citizenship considered, was canvassed by a civil liberties group before the NHRC. The Supreme Court, approached by the NHRC, directed that the threats held out to the Chakmas by the local citizens be dealt with by the state. It also asserted that their applications for being granted citizenship be considered under the Citizenship Act. The difficulties besetting refugees even after long years of residence in a state, with state acquiescence, were in evidence here.

LAND ALIENATION

The loss to communities of right over land is widespread, and various movements to recover control over land and related resources have been active particularly in the past decade and a half, though some movements go back many decades. The issue of tribal land alienation was linked with that of displacement, and the judicial system was used to get an order declaring unconstitutional the transfer of land from a tribal to a non-tribal through the medium of the state (in its land acquisition capacity).Recent efforts to delete this constitutional protection given in Schedule V of the Constitution are being resisted as a denial of basic protection given to tribals, paving the way for their displacement and impoverishment. The issue of land alienation was one of the primary issues in the struggle for separate statehood for Uttaranchal, and till today is identified as one of the main rights violations occurring in the state.

In Kerala, the issue is differently positioned. While the loss of land to the tribal is viewed as a violation of their rights and protection of those rights, the settlers are largely people who are themselves on the economic margins. While groups from within the tribal communities have been demanding restoration of alienated land, and the High Court has supported their stand, other human rights advocates maintain an uneasy silence since the contest appears to be between two vulnerable communities.

RIGHT OVER RESOURCES

The right of the forest dwellers to reside in forests, and for those dependent on forest produce to have access to forests, is contested terrain. Till recently, there were conservation groups which demanded that removing tribals from within forest areas was necessary in the interest of conservation. This stand has softened somewhat, and a more symbiotic relationship between the forest and the dweller recognised as possible. The problems are now spoken of in terms of overpopulation, and over-grazing, in the forest area.

State policy is, however, widely perceived as being inimical to the continuance of the forest dweller within the forest. 'Settling' of rights and interests is therefore met with deep suspicion, as is happening in Madhya Pradesh.

Activists have therefore been mobilising the grassroots - in MP, it was through a *padayatra* over a period of six months –to resist the conservation projects which may end up pauperising the dwellers, and, further, may denude the forest too. There have been attempts in the early '90s to prepare a new Forest Bill that will contain within it the interests of conservation, and of the people. Efforts such as this have stalled the legislation proposed by the state which groups and movements see as being opposed to rights - including the right to livelihood, to culture, to security, to shelter, among others - even while the alternative bills have hardly ever been adopted.

An activist identified the problem of land and resources being related to how possession and ownership of land are perceived.

There are three kinds of property he said:

1. Private property
2. Public property
3. Common property

What is held as 'public property' by the state, he said, has been treated as property owned by the state, and not held in trust by the state. It is the notion of common property that has to be resurrected and advanced. The entry of mining interests into Orissa has, for instance, brought into the open the problem that is inherent in globalisation when it comes into conflict with local interest. The unequal, triangular contest between multinational mining interests, the state which binds itself to protecting the multinational interest on Indian territory, and the local dwellers–in the case of mining, it is often tribals - manifests itself as a human rights issue.

Aquaculture, which brings in corporations to exploit resources through prawn culture, for instance, has been resisted on grounds of loss of livelihood, long-term destruction of marine life and consequent degradation of the environment. Corporatised aquaculture and shrimp farms have been banned. Deep-sea trawlers have also been banned, and the livelihood and lives of fisher communities salvaged. So, too, with prawn culture. Human rights activists see setbacks to these efforts at preservation of community livelihoods and of the environment in the Aquaculture Bill that has been presented to the Parliament in 2000.

The Aruvari Sansad (Water Parliament) in Ajmer district in Rajasthan, which, with the help of the Tarun Bharat Sangh, an NGO, has wrested control over the river, the check dams it has built along it, the revived rivers and the fish that have sprung into being in the river is an uncommon assertion over water and water resources to the exclusion of agencies of the state. The issue of land reforms and the redistribution of land was encountered in Andhra Pradesh. The Peoples War Group, for instance, avers that land reform is at the root of their attacks against the state. The problem of professional land grabbers, and the response of land invasion to take possession of land which should rightly belong to the invading community, was also seen in Andhra Pradesh. State response has been to treat the attacks, and invasion, as public order, or law and order, problems.

The loss of tribal land through land alienation - something that the law limits - has raised other issues in Kerala, for instance. The land had been bought from the tribals by settlers who are themselves economically and socially marginalised. A prolonged legal battle, where the court had directed the return of the land to the tribals, has not seen a solution to the contending interests of two communities, each in need of protection from expropriation.

URBAN SHELTER AND DEMOLITION

There has been a routinising of the emergency visible in the matter of cleaning up of the cities. In 2000-2001, Delhi has seen a spate of demolitions of 'slums'. The slum dwellers have been divided up into eligible and ineligibles, with the eligible being given very small plots of land on which they are required to construct houses within six months on a license basis. The size of the plot ensures that it is only a 'slum' that develops. The 'ineligibles' are not thereafter considered by state policy. Housing rights activists too do not appear to have been able to identify what happens to the ineligibles when demolition occurs. In Bangalore, housing rights groups have been attempting to demonstrate the effort and money that 'encroachers' expend on the land on which they settle; and that they have worked for their entitlement to alternative plots. In Bombay, and to a lesser extent elsewhere, there have been attempts to involve the slum dwellers in reconstructing the area in a manner which will let the slum disappear, while they are given places in high-rise tenements in the same area with the rest of the space to be used commercially.

In Patna, an order of the High Court in a PIL, requiring the municipal corporation to demolish encroachments, resulted in a demolition spree that an embarrassed court had to step in to stop. The illegal status of the urban dweller who cannot afford to purchase legality has been aggravated by B.N. Kirpal, J saying: 'Establishing or creating slums, it seems, appears to be good business and is well organised...Large areas of public land, in this way, are usurped for private use free of cost... The promise of free land, at the taxpayers' cost, in place of a jhuggi, is a proposal which attracts more land grabbers. *Rewarding an encroacher on public land with free alternate site is like giving a reward to a pickpocket.*'

Unlike South Africa, where the state's obligation to provide shelter before destroying even an illegal habitat was recognised, drawing upon international law, there is no such recognition in Indian law or judicial decisions. Activists and campaigners therefore face an unenviable, if unavoidable, task of combating the anti-poor stand of the state. Pavement dwelling, and houselessness, was raised in the '80s and, though it may never really have disappeared, it has resurfaced more rigorously since the demolitions have begun in Delhi.

Migrant workers living on pavements have been particularly vulnerable to random attacks in areas of militant violence. Newspapers have reported such occurrences in the '90s. This issue affecting migrant labour particularly needs to be addressed. The 'clearing' of pavements by removing hawkers has been a phenomenon visible in most cities. Eviction of hawkers, and of dwellers, is a significant issue, and the demands include recognition not only of shelter, land and monetary compensation, but of livelihood too.

LIVELIHOOD

Apart from issues of rights over resources, and in the context of displacement and relocation, the death of cotton farmers has, for instance, raised questions about protection of livelihood. Liberalisation has resulted in loss of jobs to large numbers in the workforce, and we hear of deaths among the working classes.

This is an area that seems to demand closer attention. The withdrawing of protective labour legislation, which is proposed, such as the 'abolition' part of the Contract Labour (Prohibition and Regulation) Act 1970, or the prohibition of night work for women except where specifically attempted, it is feared, is likely to shrink the rights of workers to a great degree. Freedom of association is also being re-cast in a new Trade Unions Bill, which labour leaders and activists believe is meant to stifle the powers of labour to group together and be heard. The casualisation of labour which the changes portend are expected to drastically reduce the bargaining power of labour.

In 1989, a PIL filed by two social/political activists from Orissa, led to the express recognition of starvation as a violation of fundamental rights. In 1994, the NHRC acknowledged that starvation is a violation of human rights and ordered the state to pay compensation to the families of victims of starvation in Kalahandi in Orissa.In March/April 2001, academics/researchers from the Delhi School of Economics and the Madras Institute of Development Studies have asked for distribution of buffer stocks that the government has stored in its godowns, to stem the tide of hunger among those with low purchasing power.

The juggling with the public distribution system, and the defining and re-defining of the poverty line and consequently of 'below poverty line' is causing particular concern. The death of 17 protesters chased by the police into the Tamaraparani river, and over 200 injured in the incident has been compared to the killing of innocent persons by the British at Jallianwallabagh 80 years ago.

On July 23, 1999, a solidarity procession organised by several political parties proceeded to the Collectorate in Tirunelveli Town in South Tamil Nadu, demanding an early solution of the wage dispute that had been the cause of discontent and agitation among tea workers in the Manjolai Tea Estate. The also demanded the immediate and unconditional release of 652 tea estate workers who had been kept in the Tiruchi jail for six weeks following a demonstration before the same Collectorate on June 7 and 8, 1999.

Talks on the labour dispute having failed, the political parties decided to present a charter of demands to the Collector. As the processionists neared the Collectorate, the police attempted to prevent the jeep which had the leaders of the agitation in it from proceeding further. As the crowd milled around, the events that ensued included a lathi charge by the police, the lobbing of tear gas and the police also opened fire. A video footage shows an injured person, bleeding, being carried away by four policemen. This injured person remains unaccounted for.

The police then chased the people down the banks of the river Tamaraparani forcing the people to jump into the water to save themselves from the police force. Photographs graphically reveal the pursuit of the people by the police into the river, even pushing the people back into the water. People drowned. There were injuries on the person of the drowned victims, testifying to ante-mortem police brutality. This episode constitutes a new threshold to police violence and brutality in labour related agitation and protest. The 'clearing' of pavements by removing hawkers has been a phenomenon visible in most cities. Eviction of hawkers, and of dwellers, is a significant issue, and the demands include recognition not only of shelter, land and monetary compensation, but of livelihood too.

SEXUAL HARASSMENT AT THE WORKPLACE

This issue acquired visibility with the decision of the Supreme Court in *Vishaka*. Earlier efforts at having the problem addressed, as, for instance, in the Delhi University, has drawn strength from the guidelines set out in the judgment. It was widely reported, however, that it was still proving difficult to get institutions to adopt the guidelines and act upon it. The Madras High Court, for instance, was reportedly averring that the guidelines did not apply to the court; and allegations of sexual harassment by a senior member of the Registry were given short shrift. The process of setting up a credible grievance redressal mechanism was reportedly being watered down in the recommendation of a committee to the Delhi University.

In Kerala, a Commission of Inquiry was set up after Nalini Netto, a senior official of the Indian Administrative Service, pursued her complaint of sexual harassment against a serving minister of the state cabinet - which is seen as a diversion from a representative investigative and redressal forum. P E Usha, in Kerala, faced hostility in her university when she followed up on her complaint of sexual harassment. There have been allegations of sexual harassment of women employees by senior persons within institutions working on human rights, and in progressive publications, which too have shown up the inadequacy of the redressal mechanisms.

- Translating the guidelines into norms in different institutions and workplaces;
- Finding support systems for women who are sexually harassed
- Breaking through thick walls of disbelief are reckoned to be the priorities. This has also been introduced into programmes on gender sensitisation for judicial officers.

Sexual harassment accompanied by violence has become a common feature with cases of acid throwing where there is unrequited love, and harassment which has culminated in the murder of a hounded girl.

RAPE

In the '80s and into the early '90s:

- The definition of rape
- The meaning of consent in the context of rape
- Marital rape was widely discussed, and alternative drafts and definitions essayed. While following *Tukaram and Ganpat's* case, 'power' rape was partially introduced into the law. The definition of rape, consent and the status of marital rape in law has however not been altered. Again, while the campaign's gains are witnessed

in the Supreme Court holding that, as a rule, the victim's version should not require corroboration and that it should be given credence

- The trauma of the trial continues,
- The law's sanction to delving into character evidence concerning the victim remains in the Evidence Act despite the flood of criticism and protest it has provoked.

In Uttaranchal, an issue not uncommon in investigations into, and trial of, rape surfaced. It was reported that women who were raped at Muzaffarnagar are being pressurised not to testify in the criminal cases not only by the police but also by their own community and political leaders, particularly since monetary compensation has been paid.

In 1994, the National Commission for Women (NCW) was asked by the Supreme Court to propose a scheme for establishing Rape Crisis Centres, and for a Criminal Injuries Compensation Board, which could care for victims of crime. This is yet to materialise. In the meantime, the women's movement in Rajasthan has got the administration to provide monetary relief to victims of rape, unconnected with trial and conviction. Though this has, at least occasionally, resulted in the veracity of the accusation being challenged as having been made so as to obtain the sum in compensation, it is seen as a move to helping the woman recover.

Rape as reprisal was symbolised in Bhanwari Devi's experience. Bhanwari Devi, a *saathin* working in Rajasthan in and around her village, was part of a wider network of women who were involved in a state-sponsored programme of empowerment particularly of women and girls. Her intervention to thwart the practice of child marriage in the community around her is commonly acknowledged as having resulted in the gang rape that was inflicted on her - as punishment, by men of the dominant community who were outraged by her intervention. The acquittal of the alleged rapists, more especially the reasoning of the court, based on caste and hierarchies of belief, accentuates the re-victimising of the woman.

The low rate of conviction for rape, and the protest from women's groups, were held out to justify a proposed amendment to criminal law to provide death penalty for the offence of rape. The conflict between provisions of the death penalty and human rights has surfaced, even if gradually, and the groups we met, as well as the National Commission for Women, have rejected the proposal for death penalty for the offence of rape.

DEATH PENALTY

The civil liberties movement has been consistent in its opposition to the death penalty. For a brief while, there were some sections in the women's movement who supported - either vocally, or by their silence - the imposition of death penalty for rape. This too has been retracted, and death penalty for rape opposed. After the period in the early '80s, when the Supreme Court drew up the `rarest of rare' rule, there has been a downward slide, particularly discernible in the 1990s.

- Multiple death sentences,
- Death penalty to minors, and
- Death sentence while reversing acquittal are not uncommon.

The campaign against execution of two youths in Andhra Pradesh who had been convicted of burning a bus which killed 23 passengers saw concerted action, which resulted in their sentence being commuted by the President.

The confirmation of the sentence of death on women is a relatively recent phenomenon. Ramashri's sentence was reduced to life by the Supreme Court, even as the court rejected the right of the NCW to intervene. The sentence of death imposed upon Nalini, convicted in the Rajiv Gandhi assassination case, has been opposed by human rights groups, along with the sentence of death meted out to three others in the same matter. Death sentence confirmed despite dissent among judges of benches of the Supreme Court on the sentence that should be imposed is another, disturbing, occurrence. Even doubts about the age of the accused - whether he had been less than 16 years of age and therefore a juvenile - were not sufficient to dispense with death sentence where death was awarded by a majority of judges. That the young accused was defended by legal aid lawyers and that 'It is reasonable to presume, in such circumstances, that the amicus curiae or advocate appointed on State brief, would not have been able even to see the petitioner, much less collect instructions from him, during the second and third tiers' was noticed only by the minority judge. Dearth of data, and difficulty of access to data is one obstacle to effectively countering the retentionists. In the meantime, the proliferation of death penalty in recent statutes, *viz..*,

- The Narcotic Drugs and Psychotropic Substances Act 1985 (and as amended in 1988),
- National Security Guards Act 1986,
- TADA 1987 (which lapsed in 1995, but trials under which continue),
- Arms Act 1950 (as amended in 1988),
- Indo-Tibetan Border Police Act 1992,
- The Scheduled Castes and Scheduled Tribes (Prevention of Atrocities) Act 1989,
- Commission of Sati (Prevention) Act 1987,
- Section 364 A IPC as introduced in 1993– 'kidnapping for ransom, etc.'

There has been a deafening silence from the NHRC on the issue of the death penalty.

FAKE ENCOUNTERS (EXTRA-JUDICIAL KILLINGS)

In India, extra-judicial killings by the police or the security forces are called 'encounter killings', meaning that the killing occurred during an armed encounter between the police or security forces and the victim. The killing by the state forces is most often declared to be defensive, cases of attempted murder and other related offences are registered against the victims, and the cases closed without further investigation since criminal cases come to an end upon the death of the accused.

Despite being 'unnatural deaths', and the victim having being killed, no investigation ensues to determine whether the death was in fact in an actual encounter, nor whether the use, and the extent of use, of force was justified. This is an acknowledged strategy of the state for eliminating certain kinds of opposition to the state and the established order. In Andhra Pradesh, for instance, the naxalites have been the targets; in Punjab, it was the militant; in Mumbai, it is those who are alleged to be part of the underworld. Civil liberties groups, journalists and lawyers have consistently challenged this practice over the past two decades.

The demand as it has been articulated after recent episodes has been:

- For doing away with state violence in the form of killings in fake encounters, and
- That all cases of encounter killings ought to be registered as first information reports (FIRs) and investigated before the case is closed. The practice of registering cases against the deceased and terminating the proceedings even before it begins is being vigorously challenged. The NHRC too has issued directions endorsing this recommended practice, but to little effect. These court, and out-of-court, battles have carried on throughout the '80s and the '90s to the present.

The Committee of Concerned Citizens (CCC), a group of individuals in Andhra Pradesh, has approached encounter killings differently. Addressing both naxalite groups and the state, the CCC has been working at de-escalation of violence. While the naxalite response has taken the CCC to the issue of land reforms as being fundamental in understanding violence of the opposition, the state, it is widely believed, is pursuing the path of unbridled unleashing of the use of encounters. The numbers killed in encounters have increased in the two years when the process of reconciliation was being negotiated by the CCC, making some of them ask if intervention by the human rights actors was actually prompting the state to escalate the violence. The human rights community has had to contend with the issue of impunity which is immediately seen as arising from thee non-registration and the non-investigation of cases.

INVOLUNTARY DISAPPEARANCES

The Punjab disappearances were brought into the open by two human rights defenders, Khalra and Kumar. Khalra was himself thereafter 'disappeared'. Investigations into these disappearances - which were uncovered when mortuary records in three districts of the Punjab were scrutinised and 'unidentified' and partially identified persons were found to have been cremated without informing the families of the deceased - was handed over by the Supreme Court to the NHRC.

The manner in which the matter was reduced to a point where the State of Punjab agreed to pay compensation of ₹ 1 lakh *(without admitting liability)* to the families of 18 persons who had been disappeared and the NHRC's tolerance of this stand of the state, is striking in the *general denial of the phenomenon of disappearances*. This was after the CBI had found that bodies of several persons had been cremated surreptitiously in the late '80s and early '90s–585 persons who had been subsequently identified had been cremated after being labelled as unidentified. Around 330 of them had been partially identified and over 1200 remained to be identified. The deficiency of compensation as a measure of reconciliation is also evident.

Disappearances appear to be a pattern where there is militant resistance to the state. Case law speaks of this phenomenon in the Northeast. In fact, the first major case of compensation for disappearance after being picked up by the armed forces was from the Northeast.33 On February 27, 2001, newspapers reported that it was alleged in the Lok Sabha, without being effectively countered, that the number of persons missing from the custody of the security forces and the police has risen to 2174 in Jammu and Kashmir; 76 cases had been registered and only one person had been challaned so far.

- Acknowledgment of involuntary disappearances
- Investigation, and seeking to establish what happened to the disappeared so that families and the community can finally know
- Prosecution and punishment, for reasons of deterrence too, and
- Compensation as a measure of atonement are being sought to be worked into the system. It was also reiterated that reconciliation would be impossible to achieve without such acknowledgment, identification of the disappeared and reparation.

That Khalra disappeared even while the matter was being taken to the Supreme Court is a statement on impunity. The theme of impunity was laid out when K.P.S. Gill, the policeman in-charge in Punjab through the waning years of militancy, lashed out in protest when a policeman, Sandhu, committed suicide while facing multiple charges of excesses committed during the years of militancy. The schizophrenic attitude of the process which rewarded him when he killed 'terrorists', and later sought to prosecute him for abuse of power even amounting to murder, stood exposed. Gill;

- Blamed the judiciary for having been inactive, or of playing safe, when captured terrorists were brought before it, and
- Held out the threat that if pursued by prosecution, the police would be unavailable to deal with militancy another time.

PREVENTIVE DETENTION

When the Constitution came into being in 1950, preventive detention laws were avowedly intended to be a transient measure. During the emergency, the Maintenance of Internal Security Act 1971 (MISA) was among the more infamous laws which allowed for preventive detention of persons in the avowed interest of maintenance of internal security. There are now a number of legislations which permit preventive detention, in the states and at the centre.

The National Security Act 1980 (NSA) is an instance of the latter. The A.P Prevention of Dangerous Activities of Bootleggers, Dacoits, Drug Offenders, Goondas, Immoral Traffic Offenders and Land Grabbers Act 1986 is an example of the former.

Public protest against the continuance of these laws is almost inaudible despite:

- The long periods, sometimes up to two years, that a person may be kept in preventive detention
- The tardiness of the procedure prescribed - *e.g.*, the executive may be given up to three months to get the opinion of the Advisory Board which may effectively have a person in custody under executive order up to ninety days
- The range of activities that are allowed to be covered by preventive detention laws that are unconnected with public order or law and order.

Unlike the challenge to the TADA, preventive detention laws have not engaged the human rights community in any sustained manner.

DETENTION

A range of detentions including those that were plainly illegal came to light during the course of our work:

- The incarceration of persons deemed to be 'non-criminal lunatics' (NCLs) or the wandering mentally ill in jails was investigated in a PIL before the Supreme Court. These are persons picked up under the Police Acts of the states, or under police powers in other laws such as the Indian Lunacy Act 1912, or its successor law, the Mental Health Act 1987.

  They are treated as `nuisances', or bracketed as being dangerous, this providing the rationale for putting them away. The term NCL is in contradistinction to `criminal lunatics', that is, those accused of crime but found to be mentally ill or suffering from mental disorder. For years NCLs were received in jails as places of 'safe custody' under the Indian Lunacy Act 1912 and later under the Mental Health Act 1987.

  In the states of West Bengal and Assam, where the Supreme Court sent Commissioners to investigate, it was found that many of those in jails as NCLs were in fact not mentally ill at all, but had been placed there deviously, to serve some completely unrelated purpose. For instance, a 70-year woman was found to have been put away as an NCL apparently because her landlord was using it as a means of evicting her. We heard resonances of this reasoning from a lawyer-activist in Chennai.

- The Supreme Court declared, in August 1993, that using jails as places of safe custody to house non-criminal mentally ill persons (NCMI) is unconsti-tutional. Apart from the state of Assam, which admitted in an affidavit in the Supreme Court to continuing the practice, the NHRC has intermittently reiterated that NCMI should be housed in places other than jails. It is plain that the practice continues.
- This is an area that has not been widely addressed within the human rights community. NHRC's recognition of the issue too has been desultory.
- There is evidence in law reports, and activists have admitted to have knowledge of, the practice of hostage taking by the police where the person to be apprehended is not within reach of the police. Relatives of the person sought are then picked up and kept in custody till he surrenders. This appears to have happened with some regularity in Punjab, but we also heard of it in Delhi and Andhra Pradesh, for instance. This breach of the law needs further investigation and response.
- There have been reports of people spending long years in jail, which could have been averted if prisons were not as inaccessible as they are. *Rudul Sah,*37 the man who spent fourteen years in jail because he had been considered unfit to stand trial, and continued to remain untried despite having been declared fit, is one wellknown instance. Recent instances from Bihar38 and West Bengal reveal that the neglect that occasions such illegal incarceration continues. The incapacity of a person to follow up on his trial and sentence, and to procure orders in time has been known to keep him in prison long after he was due to have been released.

The inability to furnish bail or sureties was reportedly one such reason for the large undertrial population.

- It is evident that systemic changes are imperative if these questions of personal liberty are to be addressed.
- In custodial institutions other than prisons - in 'protective homes' for women, for instance, the problem of custody versus shelter has been raised. Protective homes are established under the Immoral Traffic (Prevention) Act 1956 (ITPA). Since they are the only statutory institutions that can house women for 'protection' as also for

'correction',41 they act as places of custody, operating within the executive-magistracy system. We met women in 'protective custody' in the Agra Protective Home, who were witnesses in a case to be tried in Jhansi; they desired to leave and they had been in the institution for nearly two years. But the law would not let them. 'Rescued' women were placed in these institutions, but the purpose of 'rehabilitation' was found to be too inadequate to make the difference.

- Prison jurisprudence since the late '60s recognises that prisoners do not lose all their rights because of imprisonment. Yet, there is a loss of rights within custodial institutions which continue to occur. For instance, it was found that the HIV status of all the women in the Agra Protective Home was public knowledge, and there was no confidentiality attaching to this information. There was segregation within the institutions of those found to be HIV positive, and, for a while, the Supreme Court too endorsed this. The rules governing women in these institutions uncannily resemble prison rules - such as those concerning visitors, letters, and even punishment for conduct within the institutions.
- Persons working in this area said that this was an area which called for an injection of human rights experience and perspectives.
- The non-release of persons cured of mental illness from institutions was also reported to be a problem. We repeatedly met the need for halfway homes and support services which could help a person be restored to liberty.
- In Delhi, we heard of persons who had been picked up as being persons of Bangladeshi origin, who were kept in custody in a night shelter till they could be repatriated if they were, in fact, found to belong to Bangladesh and the Foreigners Act 1946 could be invoked to effect this move. There was concern that even the basis of identifying them as possible foreigners was not clear and that dispelling suspicion of nationality could well be more difficult for the poor and the dispossessed.

It is also found that it is common practice to pick up people for questioning, and not record their presence in the police station till the police is ready to present them before a magistrate - a way of thwarting the constitutional requirement that every person taken into custody be produced before a magistrate within 24 hours.

Apart from the illegality of such detention, it also makes difficult proving torture in custody during the period of illegal, unrecorded, detention. Human rights activists suggest that telegrams be dispatched to the Chief Minister, the Director General of Police, the Superintendent of Police, and the Governor for instance, when information about such illegal detention is obtained, to establish the time of detention. The conditions of persons with mental illness in institutions have been cause for human rights concern. In Gwalior Mental hospital, for instance, it was found that persons with mental illness were left in nakedness; the explanation was that they tore their clothes if they were given them. The press raised the issue. Chaining of mentally ill patients was also a practice, and this was outlawed by an order of the court.

One difficulty in ensuring that such violations do not occur, and in getting the law implemented, is access. The human rights community has not engaged with the problems faced within the walls of custodial institutions. Imaginative answers which will make open institutions of what are now bureaucratic, and closed, institutions is an imperative. The hysterectomy controversy in the early 1990s in Pune represents another aspect of the control and decisionmaking within custodial institutions. The hysterectomy of girls below 18 years of age, who were mentally retarded, raised controversy about the decision made by the professionals.

The professionals involved in making the decision neither denied that the hysterectomy was being done, nor did they did see it as a violation. It was justified as being in the best interests of the hygiene of the mentally retarded girl, as making practicable the care of the mentally retarded. The response did not rule out the possibility of sexual abuse when within the institutions, but said it would protect the girls from pregnancy in the event of such an encounter.

The persons responsible for the decision responded angrily to the charges of human rights violations. The Medical Council of India, however, distanced itself from this position, and declared the practice as being against their norms. The intervention of the media and the human rights community precluded further hysterectomies from being done.

MISSING WOMEN

There are various situations which throw up the issue of 'missing' women. The lopsided sex ratio in many states, and the juvenile sex ratio in even a state such as Kerala (which is held out by planners and economists as the model performer on the population front), is one area where women, and girls, go `missing'. In Orissa, we heard of the phenomenon of 'Jhansi' marriages and 'Gwalior' marriages. Girls from very poor homes were escorted by a 'broker' to be married to men in Jhansi or Gwalior, and he would bring back a bride price of ₹10,000 to ₹25,000 to be given to the girl's family. While some of these marriages had been found to be genuine, the possibility of some of these women being trafficked was not ruled out.

Also, what a girl/woman did if deserted or ill-treated was not clear. There was therefore an attempt by activists to keep track of women who had not been heard from for over a period of three months, so that their whereabouts could be verified and their safety ascertained. In July 1999, activists had begun the process of documenting the 'missing' woman. In Delhi, we were informed that missing persons reports when women go missing from their marital homes were hardly ever related with unidentified bodies of women who were declared to have committed suicide by drowning, for instance-The paucity of information, and the difficulties in follow up, has kept this issue in the margins of human rights concerns.

HOMICIDE IN THE MATRIMONIAL HOME

Often identified as being dowry-related deaths, unnatural deaths of women in their marital home has acquired prominence. Like encounter killings, acknowledgment has not led to a reduction in the incidence of such homicide. In Andhra Pradesh in 1990 a civil liberties organisation raised the issue of violation of women's rights as a human rights issue by comparing the number of dowry deaths and the number of encounter killings during one time period - about 2000 dowry deaths, and 300 deaths in encounters. In Bangalore, a women's group keeps a watch in the Burns Ward of the leading government hospital, and also scrutinises newspapers for reports of deaths of young women, which they then follow up.

They also had a 'Truth Commission' where a tribunal heard the narratives of the families of girls/women who had been the victims of dowry deaths. The inadequacies of investigation, and the many slips in the judicial process which results in a low rate of prosecution and a lower rate still of conviction, was observed everywhere. The definition of 'dowry death' in the Penal Code, based on preponderance of probability and a shifting of onus represents a significant shift in criminal law and jurisprudence. In the meantime, the Dowry Prohibition Act has been hardly at all implemented. Most states still have no Dowry Prohibition Officers. The maintenance of list of things given and received is still not mandatory. S.498 A, which was brought in to deal with cruelty in the matrimonial home, has suffered criticism as being abused, sending the family of the man to prison till bail is procured.

Some women's groups, however, contended that the abuse was only marginal, and that this was the only provision in law which could hold the perpetrator of domestic cruelty accountable. Some also spoke of bringing into law the notions of right to matrimonial home and matrimonial property as other approaches of protecting women on whom cruelty is practised.

DOMESTIC VIOLENCE

In locating domestic violence in the terrain of human rights, one point of view was that it is not the identity of the perpetrator alone which can be allowed to determine whether a victim has been subjected to a human right violation or not: that it is a man or his family who exercises their power to harass, assault and injure a woman, and not the state which is the perpetrator, should then make no difference to the place for this violence in human rights discourse. Also, it is state practice, and endorsement, of patriarchy that keeps such violence in the home, we were told.

- Crime against women cells in police stations
- Counselling centres
- Help lines
- Short stay homes - which, though, are few in number have been set up in many cities.

There has also been a concerted effort to bring in a law to deal with domestic violence. A Bill prepared, debated and presented to the government by a women's organisation has been adopted by Parliament for discussion, which is a significant step in a non-governmental role in law making. S.498 A was introduced into the Penal Code in 1983. It makes cruelty to a woman within the matrimonial home punishable with imprisonment up to three years and fine. It is a cognisable, non-bailable, offence. Widespread violence against women, and increasing evidence of women dying unnatural deaths in the matrimonial homes provoked the women's movement to demand a change in the criminal law.

The offence is non-bailable, that is a complaint under sextion 498 A, once registered as an FIR, would result in the arrest of the members of the matrimonial family of the woman. They would have to be granted bail by a court before release, and this could keep them in custody for varying periods of time. In matters of remission of sentence, too, offenders convicted under s.498 A may be excluded. On the one hand, there have been complaints of the misuse of this provision, and the consequent harassment, often incarceration, of many members of the family complained against. On the other, there is little scope to deny that the incidence of cruelty, including physical cruelty, which leads even to death, is extraordinarily high.

This is an issue yet unresolved; the Domestic Violence Bill may have some impact on it. In the meantime, an activist lawyer asserts that the phenomenon of violence and death in the matrimonial home should not need to be linked invariably with the phenomenon of dowry; violence and cruelty are independent entities within many homes. An activist also told us: when a man beats his wife regularly, and the wife gets him soundly thrashed by the police, civil liberties groups are sometimes confused on what stand to take.

CHILD LABOUR

Apart from the employment of children in work, including those classified as hazardous, it was reported that:

- Children continue to be sold into labour. The parents of a young girl from Assam were paid a sum of money for the girl to be brought to Delhi as a domestic worker. Her plight came to light when she ran away from the ill-treatment she suffered, and she was given shelter by a social activist.

- Child workers employed in homes and in commercial workplaces, were subjected to ill-treatment. The chaining of bonded child labour in the carpet industry near Varanasi so that they could not escape was reported. Injuries on the person of domestic child workers in Delhi sometimes resulting in death, have been reported intermittently in the press. In Maharashtra, a civil liberties organization took the state and a contractor to court when the latter ill-treated, resulting in death, one of the young boys he had brought with him from Tamil Nadu.

These manifestations of violence against the child disguised as child labour calls to be addressed. The vulnerability of the child has also been seen in Delhi, for instance, where child domestic workers have been accused of killing their employers, or in being accomplices to outsiders. The 'social clause' on child labour does not result in doing away with child labour, we were told, but causes segregation.

There were dissenting voices on the ILO Convention on the Elimination of the Worst Forms of Child Labour. The provisions which speak of child prostitution and child pornography as labour are unacceptable, they said. 'These are crimes, not labour,' we were told. Further, when Indian law is so strict that it says that non-payment of minimum wages amounts to bonded labour - a provision that is not found in any international convention – what use is one more convention, we were asked.

In 1993, the Supreme Court declared that education is a fundamental right till a child reaches the age of 14 years. Education for the child has got tangled with the issue of child labour; sending the child to school is projected as a necessary step to ending the practice of child labour. In Andhra Pradesh, an organization working in the area of education for children has done away with the uncertainties of definition by working on the premise that every child out of school is child labour. They have therefore arrived at a non-negotiable: that every child must belong in a school. In this view, NFE (non-formal education) centres, for instance, would be a means of perpetuating child labour. So, too, with the adjusting of school timings to accommodate the working child. In the meantime, this 1999 Convention is being canvassed for signature, and ratification by the Indian State.

The convention defines 'the worst forms of child labour' as comprising:

- All forms of slavery or practices similar to slavery, such as the sale and trafficking of children, forced or compulsory labour, debt bondage and serfdom;
- The use, procuring or offering of a child for prostitution, for the production of pornography or for pornographic performances;
- The use, procuring or offering of a child for illicit activities, in particular for the production and trafficking of drugs as defined in the relevant international treaties;

- Work which, by its nature or the circumstances in which it is carried out, is likely to jeopardize the health, safety or morals of children.'

This is in consonance with the recent trend among UN organizations to directly involve human rights in standard-setting, and the creating of binding obligations of states in their area of operation.

THE 'NEGLECTED' CHILD

Street children have their peculiar vulnerability. In Bangalore, a study reveals that almost every street child has been sexually violated at some time or another. They are also specially susceptible to drugs. Street children, however, take care of themselves, and often of each other. It does not appear that institutionalising them is an answer to their needs, nor do they seem willing to trade their liberty for a life off the streets. In Bangalore, Bombay and Delhi, we heard of drop-in centres: places where children could drop in for a wash to keep their savings and to discuss their problems with others, if they so chose. They were, however, reported to be vulnerable to being 'rounded up' and sent periodically into state institutions from where they would need help to emerge, or from where they would 'escape'.

Women in prostitution have faced the possibility of their children being forcibly separated from them, following an order of the Supreme Court in *Gaurav Jain v. Union of India.* A 'raid' conducted by Delhi Police in 1990 (a year after the first *Gaurav Jain* order), in which 112 'children' were picked up from the GB Road area was an indication of what such a power being given to the police could mean to the women and their children. The recent changed law on 'children in need of care and protection' even prescribes adoption as an option that may be enforced by the state.

CHILD ABUSE

There has been increasing evidence of child abuse, and more particularly child sexual abuse, being pervasive. The perpetrator is often a near relative or someone close to the family. This adds to the vulnerability of the abused child, and, apart from the confusion and sense of shame which the child experiences, it is also that there is a problem with a refuge which the child can access. The dependence on the family as a support structure in times of abuse breaks down when the offending event occurs in the home.

Following what is widely considered as a useful intervention in the Supreme Court in the *Vishaka* guidelines regarding sexual harassment in the workplace, the matter of child abuse has also been taken to the court, and the Law Commission has been inducted into setting the parameters for care and action in cases of child sexual abuse.

THE 'UNWANTED' GIRL CHILD

The declining sex ratio, particularly the declining juvenile sex ratio, even in Kerala which is celebrated in economic writings and in state policy for having achieved a high rate of literacy and negative population growth, has begun to seriously engage, among others, researchers and women activists.

The low status of women continues to be reflected in:

- The practice of infanticide including in some parts of Tamil Nadu,
- Foeticide,
- Sex-selective abortion which the amniocentesis technology has made common, and
- Mal-nourishment among girl children.

In Usilampatti Taluk, reportedly, the ratio of female: male is 879:1000. Since 1986, the issue of female infanticide has been in focus in this area. More recently, scanning centres have mushroomed in the area, and female foeticide is rampant among those who are able to afford it. We were told that, in Tamil Nadu, there are around 2000 scan centres, most of which are unregistered.

A researcher reported his encounter with the sale of girl children by communities in Andhra Pradesh to persons who then placed them for adoption. He drew attention to the astonishing fact that there is, as of now, no law to control, or punish, the sale of children. The involvement of adoption agencies in A.P. in what is allegedly the sale of children has since come to public attention, in April 2001.

PROSTITUTION

The fear of AIDS, it is perceived, has given the issue of prostitution a visibility. This has, however, led to attributing to women in prostitution the trait of being a 'high risk group', even as it has been contended that it is high risk behaviour and not high risk groups that should be targeted. It appears that patterns of funding have impacted on this identification of the prostitute woman as belonging to a high-risk group.

The demand for prostitution to be recognised as 'sex work' has been raised, with dignity of the woman in prostitution as its basis. There are differing perceptions about prostitution - one which sees it as exploitative of women, and another that views it as representing the 'agency' of the women in the profession. There are various shades of meaning given to 'exploitation' and 'agency' which lies in the spaces between these two positions.

Decriminalisation is also proposed, and disputed, on differing understandings of what decriminalising will mean, and do. Most of the people we spoke to on the issue of prostitution, however, felt after a discussion emphasizing the difference, that the practice of prostitution should be delinked from the issue of trafficking. In this context, trafficking is seen to be the sale and purchase of women and girls, and, more recently, boys, into prostitution.

While 'voluntariness' is a term with graded meanings, especially since economic compulsions and social exclusion are not uncommon causes for entering into the practice of prostitution, it is the distinctly involuntary nature of trading in human beings that is at the hub of trafficking. Trafficking in minors is a scourge that is commonly referred to as a crime to be curbed. We encountered the issue of organising women in prostitution in two different ways. In Calcutta, a 'samiti' of sex workers are articulating their position, and taking a pro-active lead in matters of preventing the entry of minors into the profession in their area of operation. They also said that, if trafficking be seriously dealt with, they be allowed to, legally, participate in curtailing trafficking - for who else was more likely than the people already in the profession to know when women and girls were bought and sold, they asked.

In Mumbai, a respondent working among prostitute women for over a decade, advocated 'collectivisation' but had a problem with adopting the norm of forming unions of women in prostitution. While she did find that the state was doing very little about trafficking, she was convinced that if sex work were seen as 'real work' under the law, all efforts to curb trafficking would cease. It was also suggested that 'sex work is real work' is a funderdriven agenda, and, that those who do not adopt this line were being deliberately excluded.

In Kerala, however, a different perspective emerged where a distinction was drawn between the demand that persons in sex work should get all labour rights and the rights based approach. As a feminist, our respondent espoused the rights based approach. There was a recognition that most feminist ideologies oppose commercial sex workers coming together; the commercialization of the body was identified as the problem. Also, most people do not believe in the agency of commercial sex workers, it was explained. There was an opposition to licensing since that would only lead to further exploitation.

The issue has been in visibilised over the years, and with people in high places being involved, it has helped to send it further underground. The *Surinelli* and *Vidhura* cases have however increased confidence to complain; and people are now listening differently. Another women's activist opposed the use of the term 'commercial sex worker': prostitution is not productive work, she said. But her main problem was that she saw prostitution as reinforcing patriarchy, and that endorsing prostitution as work would fall into the snare patriarchy has set for the women's movement.

In the matter of trafficking, it was pointed out that proposals for checking all women travelling on their own, particularly across borders was a move detrimental to the interests of women and could end up curbing their right to free movement and achieve little else.

Prisons

The conditions in jails; solitary confinement; the refusal to make condoms available in Tihar jail on the ground that homosexuality is an offence in law, and this would be seen as fostering an illegality; the inhuman treatment of prisoners, including their being kept in leg irons, for instance; overcrowding of prisons; the right of prisoners, including undertrials, to vote are issues that have been raised repeatedly over the years. The courts have been the arena of contest. The inadequacy of medical services in prisons, often resulting in the death of prisoners has been much in evidence. Apart from the inconclusive enquiry into the death of Rajan Pillai, when he was in jail, High Courts and the NHRC have been confronted repeatedly with this issue. Statistics in the Annual Reports of the NHRC reveal that there are a much larger number of deaths in judicial custody than there is in police custody. Given the frequency and seriousness of the complaints about medical services in prisons, it would bear investigation to find out how many of the deaths in judicial custody are, in fact, occasioned by medical negligence. The condition of persons on death row does not appear to have been investigated so far. Nor the effect that execution of prisoners has on their families.

The inaccessibility to legal services that is endemic in most prisons, has been identified as a human rights issue, but has not been resolved yet. There are reports of prison riots which were allegedly caused by the poor conditions in prisons including insufficient provision of food, and the maltreatment, including the brutalising, of prisoners. On November 17, 1999, for instance, a riot broke out in Chennai Central Prison. It left at least nine persons dead, and one more succumbed to injuries on November 19, 1999. There were at least seven prisoners with bullet injuries who were referred to the government general hospital. The injured and dead in the riots varies, but it appears to be around 100 prisoners. The deputy jailor was killed in the riots.

The simmering discontent seems to have had to do with inadequate food, the meagre water supplied to the prisoners, and the torture meted out to them by the prison staff. The death of a prisoner tortured and killed in the Central Prison in July 1999, which was explained away without an enquiry as being a suicide, seems to have caused resentment and anger among the prisoners. It was the death of Boxer Vadivel, a prisoner believed to have been tortured for over three days between 12th and 15th of November, and the torture of two other prisoners by the Deputy Jailor which sparked off the riots. Jeyakumar was burned alive.

The prisoners claimed to a fact-finding team that the rebellion had already come under control when antiriot police were brought in and prisoners were indiscriminately targeted. For instance, a prisoner who was physically disabled, and could not have posed any threat to the police, was shot at point blank range. The anatomy of a prison riot, and what it means in the context of human rights, and of punishment, calls to be investigated in full, and addressed. Prison riots have been erupting sporadically, leaving little reason to doubt that they are symptomatic of a systemic malaise. The condition of medical care in prisons is woeful, and cases before the High Courts and the NHRC testify to this fact. The inordinately large number of deaths in judicial custody is also an indicator. That prisons are death traps becomes apparent. Overcrowding of prisons, with a large population of undertrial prisoners spending extended periods in jail – a recent press report cites a survey conducted by the State (Jail) Department in Bihar which shows 154 undertrial prisoners in Bhagalpur jail for over 20 years awaiting trial and they are now over 70 years old - only strains the system further. Systemic changes and bold initiatives are imperative. So far, the Supreme Court's directive in 1979 to release undertrial prisoners on personal recognisance bonds, and periodic intervention thereafter by the Supreme Court, has provided ad hoc relief. There is little to indicate that there has been any fundamental re-thinking on this matter. On the other hand, recent legislation is severe in matters of bail, and persons arrested under the NDPS Act 1985, for instance, regardless of the nature of their participation in the offence, are not entitled to bail.

In Mumbai, social workers reported that they have been allowed access to prisoners to help them re-establish, and maintain, contact with their families, and to provide related support services to the prisoners. They admitted to shutting their eyes to human rights violations in prisons (and in lock-ups) since any intervention of that nature would jeopardise even the services they are now able to provide. In Chennai and in Mumbai, the '80s and a part of the '90s saw active provision of legal aid to prisoners; in Chennai, the High Court legal aid board was engaged in this process. In Delhi, legal literacy, literacy, meditation and yoga and legal aid has reached Tihar jail. The setting up of the NHRC appears to have had some impact on the accessibility of prisons, as have the many PILs which challenged the conditions within.

Wages to Prisoners

The work that prisoners do has been devalued in a decision of the Supreme Court in *State of Gujarat v. High Court of Gujarat*.48 A judge in the case has held that

- Prisoners are not entitled to minimum wages, particularly where they have been sentenced to rigorous imprisonment, and it is part of their sentence to do hard labour
- The non-payment of wages in prison will not amount to a violation of the constitutional dictum on the right against exploitation
- Where they do earn a wage, apart from deductions for their maintenance in the prison, monies may be taken from it to pay to the victim as compensation.

There is a complete negation of the rehabilitative potential of work and wages, and a re-introduction of the purely punitive in this judgment of the court that human rights advocates and activists will have to contest.

Sexuality

Discrimination against, and harassment of, those with a sexual orientation different from the heterosexual is being more openly addressed in the past ten years than it was earlier. Yet, coming out openly is still an act of courage. And we were told how homosexual couples were susceptible to arrest and extortion. Just the knowledge that a person is a homosexual would render him vulnerable, they said. The lesbian groups that we met spoke about the difficulty of coming out, and the support services that were needed to help resist, principally, the families. One of the ways of providing that support is in the initiation of 'help lines'.

Freedom of Expression

The rise of communalism has been accompanied by an assault on free expression. The vandalising of M.F. Hussain's paintings because he had painted a nude Saraswati many years ago; the destruction of the exhibition organised by SAHMAT in Varanasi because it depicted Rama differently from how the vandals believed he should be depicted; the protests, and their vulgarisation when the protesters paraded in their underwear in front of Dilip Kumar's house, against the film 'Fire'; the concerted attacks on the filming of 'Water' - all these are instances of intolerance, which have denied free expression, with the implicit - sometimes explicit - support of the state. The banning of the play on Nathuram Godse following protests and disturbances are part of a pattern.

More recently, there have been reports of a government circular that conferences, seminars, workshops...which include participants from abroad require clearance from the government, including the External Affairs Ministry. Human rights are specifically in the list. And it is particularly applicable to people from Pakistan, China, Bangladesh, Sri Lanka and Afghanistan.

Dalits

The practice of untouchability has persisted, and dalit activists and unions have been making efforts to demonstrate its pervasiveness and variety, even while they contest its practice. In Andhra Pradesh, in a study done by dalit activists, 46 ways of practising untouchability have been documented. In Kerala, there was collaboration underway between caste groups and dalits in combating caste and brahmanism. In Gujarat, a study of the practice of untouchability has been recently done.

Some groups working among dalits, and including some dalit groups, have been lobbying to place caste as an agenda in the World Conference against Racism. The definition evolving in the conference, which includes discrimination based on descent and occupation is seen as an acknowledgment of caste discrimination. This is an avowed effort to internationalise the issue of caste-based discrimination and oppression. This issue permits an exploration into the relationship between a movement - in this case, the dalit movement - and groups working with dalits and/or dalit issues in terms of their respective politics and priorities. Police firing on a group of dalit villagers in Nadunalumoo-laikkinaru in Tamil Nadu in 1991 is believed to have occurred to put down a young leadership that was emerging in the village. A chain of circumstances from the support given to the villagers by activists, to filing the matter as a case in the Supreme Court, to three committees which investigated the matter, to the awarding and disbursement of compensation to the injured villagers and the court order which prohibited the indicted policemen from being posted in the vicinity appears to have empowered the village. It has also bolstered their confidence that help could well come from beyond the village. In Melavalavur it was a different story. This is a panchayat which is reserved for dalit leadership within the panchayat system.

When elections were first to be held:

- The dalits were chastised, subjected to a community fine of ₹2000 and warned to withdraw their nominations.
- In the second round, the administration urged the dalits to file nominations, which they did. The ballot boxes were taken away by the non-dalit villagers.
- The third time around, the administration promised protection and conducted the elections amidst threats and tight security. About a month after the elections, the dalit panchayat leader, Murugesan, and five of his comrades were waylaid when they were travelling in a public bus, and brutally hacked to death on the highway.

This was in June 1997. Since then, another election has nominally installed a dalit as panchayat head. But the village lives in a state of permanent terror. A police outpost has been set up, but in that part of the village from where the threat to the dalits emanates. A memorial has been constructed to the memory of the six dead men. The Scheduled Castes and Scheduled Tribes (Prevention of Atrocities) Act has been on the statute books since 1989. There are however hardly any convictions under this Act. Dalit activists say that there are many loopholes in the law which help offenders slip out of both the Atrocities Act as well as the Penal Code. An activist madeparticular mention of section 3 (iv) and (v) of the Act49 in illustrating the non-user of this law. Studies on the working of this Act have been started in some states.

Manual scavenging, and the disinterest of the state in putting an end to this inhuman practice which involves the carrying of excreta manually, and which additionally aggravates caste-based exclusion has been identified as a priority for action in Andhra Pradesh and Tamil Nadu.

Medical Research

The connection between abortion, in vitro fertilisation and gene manipulation was drawn to ask how the question of human rights could be considered in this context. The poser was: ought it not to be the primary question whether neo-eugenics through gene manipulation should be resisted, or was it to be asked in terms of the mother's choice to have a 'blue-eyed baby girl'? Depo Provera, a contraceptive drug, was introduced into the Indian market without conducting Phase IV trials, which meant that the Indian state conducted no research specific to Indian users before deciding to introduce the drug in the market. The issue in Phase IV trials of Net-oen was of informed consent. In the pre-liberalisationphase, we were informed, all research was to be undertaken by the ICMR. But post-liberalisation, there has been a dramatic change, and the trend has been for pharmaceutical companies, or the NGOs funded for the purpose, to conduct research; their agenda is not beyond suspicion. Pharmaceutical companies have been attempting to dilute the guidelines for scientific research on human subjects. The Nuremberg Code was very strict. The later Helsinki declaration, we were told, relaxed these rules. And efforts are underway to further relax the notion of informed consent for the greater common good. These efforts have been stalled at the international level. But ICMR's 'Ethical Guidelines for Biomedical Research on Human Subjects' has been amended in 2000 to allow proxy consent in some cases, such as in epidemiological situations or in the larger public good. In 1997, the Indian government signed an agreement with the USA that would allow Indian citizens to be used as research subjects in an international research project on human genome for furthering 'international good'. Since this became known, there have been protests - that the bodies of Indian citizens do not belong to the state that it can sign them away.

Court battles around banned drugs being sold in the Indian market have sometimes resulted in prospective banning. But the plea of the pharmaceutical company that the stocks be not destroyed, but that they be allowed to transport it to another jurisdiction outside India has been allowed.50 Sharing information with other potential markets becomes of importance, and ways of doing this may have to be established.

Population Policies

There has been a deliberate re-introduction of 'incentives' and 'disincentives', and of punitive measures into state policy.

- The birth of a third child beyond a period of gestation from the commencement of state laws on the subject (including Himachal Pradesh, Rajasthan and Haryana) will disqualify a person from standing for elections to the panchayat, or to continue in office.
- Medical termination of pregnancy and tubectomy has been included in the Maternity Benefit Act 1961 (in 1995) for 'benefit' under the law. The threatened denial of 'maternity benefit' for the birth of the third child and thereafter was, however, shelved after concerted protest, The new provision puts an onus on the woman to keep the size of her family low.

- There are private proposals pending in various state legislatures including Delhi and Andhra Pradesh to disentitle the third child to ration under the Public Distribution System, and for the parent to be penalised in their jobs if they hold a government job. The Delhi proposal even included provisions that the family could not be allowed to procure a house if there was a third child! These have not yet become law, but they have not disappeared from the public debate altogether.
- 'Social marketing' of contraceptive drugs, supported in Uttar Pradesh by large grants from funders, has been the subject of protest from, particularly, women activists. Social marketing, which includes across-the-counter sales, would inevitably lead to ill-informed use of the contraceptives, without an understanding of the side effects, or of the meaning of symptoms that may manifest upon use. The prioritising of reducing population at the cost of women's health is being stoutly resisted.

Organ Transplant

A racket in the sale of kidneys was exposed in Karnataka in the late 1980s and early '90s. There were allegations that the 'donor' was duped and his kidneys were removed and 'donated'; or that the donor had sold his kidneys as a commodity may be sold to raise resources - poverty was the characteristic that distinguished the donor. A series of exposés confirmed that there was a pattern to the sale and purchase of kidneys, which implicated, among others, doctors and hospitals.

The dust refused to settle, and in 1994, Parliament enacted the Transplantation of Human Organs Act 1994, which allowed organ donation either only after death, or where the receiver was a near relative of the donor, or it is actuated by 'affection, or attachment towards the recipient.' An Authorization Committee has to approve the donation.

The Act, in its prefatory text, says it is 'to provide for the regulation of removal, storage and transplantation of human organs for therapeutic purposes and for the prevention of commercial dealings in human organs.' The issue seems to have acquired a subterranean residence since. This may be an area which must be regularly revisited to prevent exploitation, and worse. In a different context, the issue of surrogacy has entered Indian parlance; but the human rights, and legal, implications have not been pursued with much rigour.

Bonded Labour

Though the Bonded Labour Act is of 1976 vintage, it was not till the Supreme Court's judgment in December 1983 that the recognition of bonded labour acquired a national reach.

As the champion of the bonded labour said it, it is that needs to be dealt with to get people an experience of human rights:

- Minimum wages,
- Minimum guarantees of employment,
- Child labour,
- Land rights and
- Alcohol

Identification, release and rehabilitation of bonded labour have happened essentially by court supervision. In Tamil Nadu, there is a separate ministry that has been set up to deal with bonded labour; this was following a report given to the Supreme Court of the extent of bonded labour prevalent in the state. The issue of bonded labour has been handed over by the court to the NHRC, which has set up a committee including activists, advocates and bureaucrats with experience, to find a means of dealing with the issue. We watched while a political activist working among bonded labour discoursed with a body of bonded labourers from Rajasthan.

They were seeking his help in getting free, and getting land which could help them retain their liberty. The advice was that they get together a mass of similarly positioned people before launching a campaign in their district. The confidence they exuded that bringing together 25,000 people in the district would not be an unmanageable task was an indication of the dimensions of the problem of bonded labour.

Anti-liquor Movements

There is a connection that seems to exist between liquor and violence, particularly domestic violence. Many parts of the country have witnessed anti-liquor movements in assertion of the women's right to be free of violence. This includes Andhra Pradesh, Himachal Pradesh and Orissa. Apart from the factor of state interest - particularly in terms of revenue - in the proliferation of liquor, the liquor mafia also has a long reach. There have been reports of women leading anti-liquor movements being killed, in an apparent attempt to stifle protest and resistance.

Illicit liquor and the deaths of those who drink the brew – the 'hooch tragedy', as it is termed – is oft-experienced, and it is common to find people wielding state power, including ministers, being implicated. Last year, for instance, Kerala reverberated with reports of deaths in just such a hooch tragedy. In Uttarakhand, the demand for prohibition was closely linked to the struggle for statehood and is a challenge before the new government.

HIV and AIDS

The right have been issues that have been raised in the context of AIDS, particularly since the AIDS Bill which was in circulation in the mid-1980s. The identification as 'high risk groups' or as 'high risk activity' has been considered both in pragmatic and rights-related terms. While categorizing people as 'high risk' on the basis of the class to which they belong has been rejected by rights activists, it has in fact been adopted in practice.

- To privacy
- To confidentiality between doctor and patient
- To informed consent
- Against discrimination

The question of confidentiality has been adjudicated in the 'right to marry' case in which the Supreme Court held that the right to marry is not an absolute right. Referring to the provisions in the Penal Code, the court held that, apart from making a person punishable under the law if he marries and transmits AIDS to a woman, there was duty upon him not to marry. And the doctor, aware of the HIV status of the patient had not disclosed it to persons he knew were likely to be affected by it, he would be a participant in the crime,' the court said. Till a disease/ condition is cured, the right to marry will be 'suspended', the court has held. There are two points of view in this position of the court on the 'right to marry'. A rights group advocating the cause of people with HIV/AIDS, and of persons with a positive status, contend that the right to marry is part of the right to life. A woman activist lawyer has taken the stand that the disclosure mandated by the court is necessary to protect the interests of women. The former group contests this expectation, and holds that this will result in denial of rights to positive people without empowering women.

A respondent further located it in the context of 'personhood' - that even while conceding that there may be no right to marry, there would be a violation of the rights of the HIV+ person where there is disclosure without any of the protections that an HIV+ person may need, and to which they would be entitled - particularly given the rejection and discrimination that is known to ensue.

The right to treatment, and discrimination - in the workplace, in custodial institutions and in places like hospitals of positive people are centrally in the human rights arena.

Denotified Tribes

British India notified specified tribes as 'criminal tribes', with all members of the tribe tarred by the same brush, and all of them classed as criminals or potential criminals. The Indian Parliament passed a law in the early years after independence repealing this categorization of tribes. The 'ex-criminal tribes' are now referred to as 'denotified tribes'. While the status of these tribes has changed in law, the prejudices attaching to treatment of these tribes seems relatively unchanged. The attribution of criminal characteristics to a tribe has not abated. That they continue to be called `denotified tribes' freezes their status. Rampant discrimination, and criminalisation (different from criminality) was reported. The neglect of land reforms, and of improving their conditions of life, was reportedly allowing for the perpetuation of stereotypes about these communities. The very construction of identity was said to be responsible for the human rights violations that they faced, and was acknowledged as a violation on its own.

Tourism

Tourism's contribution to the violation of human rights has become an area of increasing concern:

- The growth of the sex industry, including the use of children for sexual pleasure, is associated by activists with tourism.
- The displacement and exclusion of people from forest areas, and the introduction of elite tourism is said to be passed off as 'eco-tourism'; activists find this contradictory
- The taking over of agricultural land to create hotel resorts, as is happening in the Diamond Harbour area in West Bengal, is opposed as being inherently unjust and environmentally unfriendly.
- The images of the reservoir in the Tehri and at the Sardar Sarovar being converted into lake resorts, militates particularly against equity. These instances merely illustrate a point. Destruction of culture, sometimes through showcasing culture, is another issue. An instance is the Todas in Tamil Nadu. The non-involvement of local communities in making choices about whether, and what kind of, tourism would be brought into their midst was also reported.

Right to Information

A concerted, and effective, campaign for the right to information has been underway in Rajasthan, spearheaded by the Mazdoor Kisan Sangharsh Samiti (MKSS). It has caught the imagination of activists and groups across the country, particularly as a tool for preventing and challenging violations as well as asserting the right to development.

A norm of transparency has been given prominence, including transparency of the government as well as the group working in the area. The irresistible force it has generated has moved the government, albeit reluctantly, to table a Freedom of Information Bill 2000.

Meanwhile, the right to information has been introduced into the law following the Bhopal Gas disaster. Among the persons now entitled to receive information about potential hazards in a factory are,

- The workers,
- The local authority,
- People living in the vicinity of the factory as also the Inspector appointed under the Factories Act 1948.

The information is to include the means of disposal of hazardous substances, and the arrangements for their storage or transportation.

Information on what should be done to limit damage in the event of a disaster is also to be disseminated; the onus is on those running the factory. We did not, however, hear of anyone having used these provisions. The rights inherent in these provisions demand to be asserted.

Bhopal

Sixteen years after the Bhopal Gas disaster occurred, and Methyl Iso cyanate (MIC) leaked from the Union Carbide plant in Bhopal on 2/3rd December 1984, the victims still wait for justice.

- The payments of pitifully small amounts as compensation
- The shrinking of their remedies, including the way the appeals system has been worked to reduce the entitlement of the victims;
- The difficulties in access to medical care
- The disbelief, even all these years later, that they were indeed victims of the disaster52
- The absence of a legal aid system
- The immobility of the state in the matter of the extradition of Warren Anderson of the UCC; the reduced gravity of the charges against the Indian accused; and the snail's pace progress of the trial
- The vanishing corporation, where mergers result in the original corporation pretending to a civil death, and the vanishing liability. The recent takeover of UCC by Dow Chemicals is an instance.
- The absolving of liability which has been introduced into the law53 and which is reportedly being used by MNCs coming into the country in the liberalised era.

The difficulties in bringing an MNC before Indian courts have not yet found answers. Neither has the problem posed by the state often being a tort-feasor itself.

There are also reports of continuing harm to the people in the vicinity, and to water sources, emanating from the plant site, where chemicals continue to be stored in vats.

- Continued care of the victims of Bhopal
- Access to the information gathered by ICMR, and
- Monitoring and research connected with the Bhopal Gas disaster, at least over a period of fifty years have been set out as priorities owed to the victims of the disaster.

A Draft Code of Conduct for Corporations was discussed by a group of persons brought together in Geneva by the Office of the High Commissioner for Human Rights on March 30- 31, 2001.

The First Draft Code envisages:

- Social responsibility of corporations, and
- Corporations as human rights watchdogs.

These could be difficult roles to reconcile with the experience of Union Carbide in Bhopal, Enron in Maharashtra and with the shadow of corruption and the unviability of the Power Purchase Agreement, Cogentrix in Karnataka and the allegations of corruption and the anxieties about environmental degradation55, in Kashipur in Orissa and the dominance given to mining interests, to name a few instances. The introduction of genetically modified cotton where corporations experiment on Indian soil, and take no responsibility for the consequences of use of genetically modified (GM) technology, is another instance. The resistance to the 'terminator' seeds reflects the concern of farmers and others about the destructive power of corporate profit-seeking on their autonomy and self-sustenance. The various, even if failed, attempts to use the international patenting regime to appropriate the use of *haldi, neem* and *basmati,* for instance, to serve multinational corporate interest has raised questions of rights of people over resources in contest with the profit motive. Issues of liability are weak in the Draft Code's first version. The importance of involving persons from jurisdictions of corporate conduct which may have to be accounted for in a code may have to be recognised, and participation in the settling of international standards and making of international law facilitated.

Environment and Pollution

Environmental litigation has been among the visible aspects of contending with pollution. The courts, particularly the Supreme Court, have been accorded primacy in the matters concerning the environment, by environmentalists as well as the state.

The court has used:

- Closure
- Relocation
- Clean-up technologyas remedial tools, and
- The polluter pays principle and
- Pollution fine as reparative and sanctioning measures.

There has also been an induction of the precautionary principle, and a statement of the acceptance of the norm of sustainable development, including within it the concept of inter-generational equity. The preventive principle does not find similar spaces in judicial dicta.

The loss of livelihood, and the denudation of the resources of land and water, were witnessed, for instance, in:

- Limestone quarrying in Dehradun, where the court ordered closure of the mines, rehabilitation of mine owners, and afforestation and restoration of the land (1980s),
- Tanneries in Kanpur (1980), Vellore and Calcutta (1990s) which were located along rivers, and where the court ordered closure, and the establishment of effluent treatment plants before reopening the units
- A complex of industries in Andhra Pradesh, where the court ordered clean-up technology, and compensation to affected farmers (1990s),

- The Bichhri (Rajasthan) case of hazardous waste negligently disposed on premises of four industries which had been closed down and left after being in operation without requisite environmental clearances; the court set out the polluter pays principle. But the difficulties besetting restoration where toxic damage has occurred was also evident in this matter.

Conservation of forest resources and the right of the tribal to live in, and live off, the forest is set out elsewhere in this report. The relocation of industries from within Delhi, and the consequent closure and loss of employment of large numbers in the workforce has emerged from within an environmental context. It is related later in this report while dealing with conflicts and the prioritising of rights. The locating of a nuclear power plant in the Sunderbans is another instance of the anomalies that 'development' is imposing on a people and on the environment.

Political violence by Non-state Actors

Variously termed as 'militancy', 'terrorism', 'non-state violence', the use of violence in pursuing political ends has been in existence for over a couple of decades at least, in a number of states.

The state response has been varied including:

- The enactment of the TADA, and other extraordinary laws, including the treatment of political violence as 'organised crime' as has happened in Andhra Pradesh, Madhya Pradesh and Maharashtra.
- The identification of such political activists as 'enemy' of military forces - as in the ITBP Act which defines 'enemy' as including 'all armed mutineers, armed rebels, armed rioters, pirates and any person in arms against whom it is the duty of any person subject to this Act to take action.'
- The unleashing of state violence, as happened in the Punjab particularly in the late '80s, and the beginning of the '90s. Or, again, as being witnessed in the encounter killings in Andhra Pradesh.
- The implicit equation of state violence with non-state violence in placing both in the agenda of the NHRC,while yet leaving violations by the Armed Forces beyond the NHRC's direct reach.

The question of political violence has gone through phases in the civil liberties movement. In the 1970s, a political journalist told us, he had walked out of a civil liberties organisation because they had taken a decision to focus on state violence, and not speak to condemn violence by non-state actors. In the 1980s, silence about the violence of the militants in Punjab, which included the deliberate and often indiscriminate killing of civilian targets, was held out as evidence of the partial and one-sided image that the civil liberties movement conjured up; there was an uncertainty that crept in among civil liberties groups too.

In the 1990s, there was an open debate, most specifically in the context of Andhra Pradesh, where one point of view held that political violence to overpower and alter systemic violence could not be condemned; and another point of view emerged that revolutionary violence was not equal to, or the same as, people's response, and that sustained violence over decades injured the weak and the vulnerable the most. 'Systematic and calculated violence begins with the enemy, ' a civil liberties activist says, 'but soon turns to agents of the enemy within and among one's friends.' There is also the question of congruence between means and ends, he adds.

The abduction and disappearance of Sanjay Ghosh at the hands of the ULFA in 1997 did lead to re-appraisal of the presumptions about revolutionary violence and the latitude that should be permitted it.

A civil liberties group, for instance, spoke of its position as opposition to 'systematic, significant and sensitive killing by armed opposition groups.' An activist said: 'unless a revolutionary movement develops a tradition of human rights, there is a problem.'

The ranks of 'surrendered' militants (SULFA in Assam, Surrendered PWG in AP) has raised human rights issues - not only in terms of their rehabilitation but also for how they are used by the state. Caught between the cadres that they have walked away from, and the police or security forces who are now their protectors, it has been noticed that an inordinately large number of 'surrendered' militants die violent deaths.

It also appeared evident to civil liberties groups that the surrendered militants are set up as stooges to carry out 'executions, which would then be passed off as a clash between the cadres and the deserters. Their position is plainly vulnerable. In Andhra Pradesh, we heard that cases against surrendered naxalites are never dropped, leaving them open to blackmail and to being manipulated.

Recent brutal killings of civil liberties activists, often in broad daylight and open to public gaze, are suspected to have been engineered on order of the state government, using surrendered naxalites. Political violence in North Kerala and West Bengal seems to claim victims with regularity. It is an occurrence about which activists in both states spoke. In West Bengal, activists spoke of 140 CPM workers having died in 1999-2000 (over one and half years). This is concentrated mainly in the Hooghly, they said, but had spread to Calcutta too. It has percolated to the grassroots and, they said, it has ceased to have ideological basis. Peace talks, and mediation, seem to be ways in which intervention has been attempted by human rights activists.

Clamping Down on Protest

Protest, dissent and resistance are most often treated as 'law and order' problems and the state responds Accordingly. This not merely reduces matters of development choices, economic and physical displacement and political difference into a case of law and order, but, in the process, it results in employment of aggression in putting down protestors or those who challenge the decision or the authority of the state. The protests against reservation in educational institutions, and the demand for a separate state in the hill areas of Uttar Pradesh came to a close with the formation of a new state–Uttaranchal. The 'Uttaranchal' movement was accompanied by violence when the state attempted to quell the protests and agitations that took place. The crackdown on the protestors on their way to holding a public rally in Delhi on October 2, 1994 'resulted in a lot of bloodshed including loss of many lives, infliction of injuries on persons belonging to both sides, outraging the modesty of women ranging to ravishments.' Activists in Uttarakhand refer to it as the 'Muzaffarnagar' happenings (*Kaand).*

Approached, the Allahabad High Court had the CBI enquire into the allegations of violations. Prosecution was launched, but the accused officers subsequently discharged. In the meantime, the High Court had given directions for payment of damages and compensation. On appeal, the Supreme Court set aside this order in May 1999.

While castigating the High Court for stepping beyond its brief, the Supreme Court made no observation on the excesses committed by the police.

The clamping down takes many forms:

- The imposition of prohibitory order under section.144 Cr.P.C.
- The refusal to grant permissions to take out processions.
- The arrest of protesters.
- Implicating protestors in criminal cases.
- Tear gas, lathi charge, firing on protesters.
- The branding of speech and action of protesters as seditious, or as obstructing development and therefore being against the national interest.
- The forcible removal of protesters from the site of protest.
- Forcible breaking of hunger strikes.

The disappearance of Khalra who, along with Kumar, investigated mass cremations in three districts in Punjab is one of the startling instances of attacks on human rights defenders. Lawyers appearing for naxalites are regularly intimidated and threats held out to them. Anti-liquor activists have been killed, and there is little doubt that the liquor mafia is behind the killings. Organising or supporting people in resisting displacement, and the taking away of land or water resources for mineral exploitation or prawn culture, has led to cases being lodged against activists. The killing of Shankar Guha Niyogi by assassins paid by industry is another attempt at killing the leader to weaken a movement.

The contempt jurisdiction of courts, which has been used liberally particularly in recent years, constitutes a potent threat to free speech, expression and to protest. The conflict between the Supreme Court and the

Narmada Bachao Andolan and its members and allies in the matter of contempt has resurfaced after the judgment of the court allowing the raising of the height of the dam. Truth, incidentally, is no defence in a matter of contempt. The device of 'subjudice' is also often used to still discussion, and to refuse to share information with those seeking access to it.

In the more extreme manifestations of clamping down, there is custodial violence and encounter killings. It is also evident that civilians often get caught in the crossfire. They may be subjected to harassment including body searches, detention, rough questioning by security forces and routinely treated with suspicion. Search and seizure of private dwellings, even of whole villages are common. Caught between militants and the security forces, civilians face the dual threat of either being punished by the former for being 'informers', or punished by the latter for harbouring or aiding militants.

Disability

The 1990s has seen a visibility, and position for the disabled in public spaces. The emergence of disability groups seems definitely to have made a difference. The enactment of Persons with Disabilities (Equal Opportunities, Protection of Rights and Full Participation) Act, 1995, which was received by law persons with a certain scepticism as soft law, has acquired a significance with disability groups activating the law. The 'disability audit' of public buildings and spaces undertaken by the physically disabled in Delhi in April 2001, is an illustration of the potential of the law to help those who can use it.60 The introduction of 'disability' into the census is seen as another step ahead for the disabled.

A disability activist in Hyderabad spoke of the trauma that those disabled by accidents experience. He said it was not uncommon that accident victims would call, seeking help from depression and the push to commit suicide caused by the loss of limb or faculty. Those physically disabled from birth would use their experience with disability to help the recently disabled to cope, he said.

Even when the First Citizen's Report was produced in 1985, the effect of fluorosis on the people in parts of Nalgonda in Andhra Pradesh was described. In the intervening years, it appears some efforts have been made by a non-state agency to provide 'filters' to the people living in the fluoride-affected areas; a cursory visit was sufficient to reveal that most people have, but don't often use, these filters. The visit was to Mada Yedevelly at Narkatpalli Mandal in Nalgonda district. A school teacher who led the way said that it is known to have the highest fluorosis rate in India.

There are about 1600 people in the village now, said our respondents. 200 or so have moved out, they said. Till ten years ago, they used to drink the water, they said. Then, when they realised its devastating effects, they started getting water from other areas, where they go to work, for instance. There is a tank where water from another village, Puthurenipalli, is brought, but that is not free of fluoride either; only less so than their village water. There is a defluoridation plant established by the Dutch government in Yellareddigudam gram panchayat, but that is a littleway away. The connection between the plant and the village water supply was not evident. And there are still distended limbs, prematurely aged bodies and a range of milder signs of the persistence of fluorosis.

These illustrations of the causing of disability, as a result of accidents or by inadequate attention to public health issues, is accompanied by the absence of state policy to take preventive or reparative steps. There have been some attempts at making easier the securing of an amount in compensation, but there is very little in evidence to deal with the post-accident trauma, or rehabilitation of these victims.

Corruption and Criminalisation of Politics

Corruption has been at the centre of attention in various arenas in public life. The harassment of prostitute women for the policeman's 'hafta',61 and the endemic problems in filing FIRs and having investigations done are instances of one manner of human rights violations represented in corruption. The Enron issue, which had allegations of corruption at its centre is an instance of distorted priorities which can deepen debt, even while re-ordering the priorities in decision-making– the local people's voices were not even heard by those in power, and it is presumed that money exchanging hands had a lot to do with it.

Largesse and abuse of public office was much in evidence. In the Supreme Court, it was seen in the cases of allotment of petrol pumps and gas retail outlets under the charge of one central minister, and the allotment of commercial plots and shops by another. These serve to illustrate.

The criminalisation of politics brought out in the Vohra Committee report (1997), only confirmed what is commonly known to be a fact. The everyday corruption of the petty potentate will have to be understood in this larger context of institutionalized corruption and crime. The extent to which such corruption leads to every day violations of rights is popular knowledge; documenting instances, and the effect of such corruption, would help understand the human rights dimension of corruption as it affects the everyday person.

'Natural' Disasters

Earthquakes, floods and droughts have recurred with rigorous frequency. While some of these happenings have indeed been 'acts of God' or 'force majeure', a relationship between land and water use and droughts, for instance, has been drawn by activists and researchers. The post-disaster treatment of the affected population has given rise to rights issues. The relative neglect of those devastated by the Orissa cyclone in October 1999 is contrasted by development workers with the relatively improved treatment of those afflicted by the Gujarat earthquake in January 2001. The victims of the Uttarkashi earthquake in 1991, in the meantime, have said that they were yet to see anything beyond aid in the immediate aftermath of the earthquake reach them. The development of a rights perspective in the context of such disasters may shift the emphasis from welfare to rights.

Even when the First Citizen's Report was produced in 1985, the effect of fluorosis on the people in parts of Nalgonda in Andhra Pradesh was described. In the intervening years, it appears some efforts have been made by a non-state agency to provide 'filters' to the people living in the fluoride-affected areas; a cursory visit was sufficient to reveal that most people have, but don't often use, these filters. The visit was to Mada Yedevelly at Narkatpalli Mandal in Nalgonda district. A school teacher who led the way said that it is known to have the highest fluorosis rate in India. There are about 1600 people in the village now, said our respondents. 200 or so have moved out, they said. Till ten years ago, they used to drink the water, they said.

Then, when they realised its devastating effects, they started getting water from other areas, where they go to work, for instance. There is a tank where water from another village, Puthurenipalli, is brought, but that is not free of fluoride either; only less so than their village water. There is a defluoridation plant established by the Dutch government in Yellareddigudam gram panchayat, but that is a little way away. The connection between the plant and the village water supply was not evident. And there are still distended limbs, prematurely aged bodies and a range of milder signs of the persistence of fluorosis.

These illustrations of the causing of disability, as a result of accidents or by inadequate attention to public health issues, is accompanied by the absence of state policy to take preventive or reparative steps. There have been some attempts at making easier the securing of an amount in compensation, but there is very little in evidence to deal with the post-accident trauma, or rehabilitation of these victims.

5

Status of Human Rights in India

INTRODUCTION

The situation of human rights (Human rights are "rights and freedoms to which all humans are entitled." Proponents of the concept usually assert that everyone is endowed with certain entitlements merely by reason of being human. Human rights are thus conceived in a universalist and egalitarian fashion. Such entitlements can exist as shared norms of actual human moralities, as justified moral norms or natural rights supported by strong reasons, or as legal rights either at a national level or within international law. However, there is no consensus as to the precise nature of what in particular should or should not be regarded as a human right in any of the preceding senses, and the abstract concept of human rights has been a subject of intense philosophical debate and criticism.

The human rights movement emerged in the 1970s, especially from former socialists in eastern and western Europe, with major contributions also from the United States and Latin America. The movement quickly jelled as social activism and political rhetoric in many nations put it high on the world agenda. By the 21st century, Moyn has argued, the human rights movement expanded beyond its original anti-totalitarianism to include numerous causes involving humanitarianism and social and economic development in the Third World. Many of the basic ideas that animated the movement developed in the aftermath of the Second World War, culminating in its adoption by the *Universal Declaration of Human Rights* by the United Nations General Assembly in 1948. While the phrase "human rights" is relatively modern the intellectual foundations of the modern concept can be traced through the history of philosophy and the concepts of natural law rights and liberties as far back as the city states of Classical Greece and the development of Roman Law.

The true forerunner of human rights discourse was the enlightenment concept of natural rights developed by figures such as John Locke and Immanuel Kant and through the political realm in the *United States Bill of Rights* and the *Declaration of the Rights of Man and of the Citizen*. All human beings are born free and equal in dignity and rights. They are endowed with reason and conscience and should act towards one another in a spirit of brotherhood) in India is a complex one, as a result of the country's large size and tremendous diversity, its status as a developing country and a sovereign, secular, democratic republic, and its history as a former colonial territory. The Constitution of India provides for Fundamental rights (Fundamental Rights is a charter of rights contained in the Constitution of India. It guarantees civil liberties such that all Indians can lead their lives in peace and harmony as citizens of India.

These include individual rights common to most liberal democracies, such as equality before law, freedom of speech and expression, freedom of association and peaceful assembly, freedom to practice religion, and the right to constitutional remedies for the protection of civil rights by means of writs such as habeas corpus.

Violations of these rights result in punishments as prescribed in the Indian Penal Code, subject to discretion of the judiciary. The Fundamental Rights are defined as basic human freedoms which every Indian citizen has the right to enjoy for a proper and harmonious development of personality. These rights universally apply to all citizens, irrespective of race, place of birth, religion, caste, creed, colour or Gender. They are enforceable by the courts, subject to certain restrictions. The Rights have their origins in many sources, including England's Bill of Rights, the United States Bill of Rights and France's Declaration of the Rights of Man.

THE DIFFERENT RIGHTS RECOMMENDED BY DIFFERENT GOVERNMENTS

The six fundamental rights recognised by the constitution are:

1. Right to equality, including equality before law, prohibition of discrimination on grounds of religion, race, caste, sex or place of birth, and equality of opportunity in matters of employment
2. Right to freedom of speech and expression, assembly, association or union, movement, residence, and right to practice any profession or occupation (some of these rights are subject to security of the State, friendly relations with foreign countries, public order, decency or morality)
3. Right against exploitation, prohibiting all forms of forced labour, child labour and traffic in human beings;
4. Right to freedom of conscience and free profession, practice, and propagation of religion;
5. Right of any section of citizens to conserve their culture, language or script, and right of minorities to establish and administer educational institutions of their choice; and
6. Right to constitutional remedies for enforcement of Fundamental Rights.

Rights mean those freedoms which are essential for personal good as well as the good of the community. The rights guaranteed under the Constitution of India are fundamental as they have been incorporated into the "fundamental Law of the land" and are enforceable in a court of law. However, this does not mean that they are absolute or that they are immune from Constitutional amendments.

Fundamental rights for Indians have also been aimed at overturning the inequalities of pre-independence social practices. Specifically, they have also been used to abolish untouchability and hence prohibit discrimination on the grounds of religion, race, caste, sex, or place of birth. They also forbid trafficking of human beings and forced labour.

They also protect cultural and educational rights of ethnic and religious minorities by allowing them to preserve their languages and also establish and administer their own education institutions.), which include freedom of religion. Clauses also provide for Freedom of Speech, as well as separation of executive and judiciary and freedom of movement within the country and abroad.

HUMAN RIGHT WATCHES OF DIFFERENT COUNTRIES

In its report on human rights in India during 2010, Human Rights Watch (Human Rights Watch is an international non-governmental organization that conducts research and advocacy on human rights. Its headquarters are in New York City and it has offices in Berlin, Beirut, Brussels, Chicago, Geneva, Johannesburg, London, Los Angeles, Moscow, Paris, San Francisco, Tokyo, Toronto, and Washington.

Human Rights Watch was founded in 1978, under the name of Helsinki Watch, to monitor the former Soviet Union's compliance with the Helsinki Accords.[2] Helsinki Watch adopted a methodology of publicly "naming and shaming" abusive governments through media coverage and through direct exchanges with policymakers. By shining the international spotlight on human rights violations in the Soviet Union and its vassal states in Eastern Europe, Helsinki Watch contributed to the democratic transformations of the region in the late 1980s.

Americas Watch

Americas Watch was founded in 1981 while bloody civil wars engulfed Central America. Relying on extensive on-the-ground fact-finding, Americas Watch not only addressed perceived abuses by government forces but also applied international humanitarian law to investigate and expose war crimes by rebel groups. In addition to raising its concerns in the affected countries, Americas Watch also examined the role played by foreign governments, particularly the United States government, in providing military and political support to abusive regimes.

Asian Watch, African Watch And Middle East Watch

Asia Watch (1985), Africa Watch (1988), and Middle East Watch (1989) were added to what was then known as "The Watch Committees." In 1988, all of the committees were united under one umbrella to form Human Rights Watch.), stated India had "significant human rights problems".[1] They identified lack of accountability for security forces and impunity for abusive policing including "police brutality, extrajudicial killings, and torture" as major problems. An independent United Nations expert in 2011 expressed concern that she found human rights workers and their families who "have been killed, tortured, ill-treated, disappeared, threatened, arbitrarily arrested and detained, falsely charged and under surveillance because of their legitimate work in upholding human rights and fundamental freedoms.

CHRONOLOGY OF EVENTS REGARDING HUMAN RIGHTS IN INDIA

1829 – The practice of sati was formally abolished by Governor General William Bentick after years of campaigning by Hindu reform movements such as the Brahmo Samaj of Ram Mohan Roy against this orthodox Hindu funeral custom of self-immolation of widows after the death of their husbands.

1929– *Child Marriage Restraint Act*, prohibiting marriage of minors under 14 years of age is passed.

1947– India achieves political independence from the British Raj.

1950– The Constitution of India establishes a sovereign democratic republic with universal adult franchise. Part 3 of the Constitution contains a Bill of Fundamental Rights enforceable by the Supreme Court and the High Courts. It also provides for reservations for previously disadvantaged sections in education, employment and political representation.

1952– Criminal Tribes Acts repealed by government, former "criminal tribes" categorized as "denotified" and Habitual Offenders Act (1952) enacted.

1955– Reform of family law concerning Hindus gives more rights to Hindu women.

1958– Armed Forces (Special Powers) Act, 1958-

1973– Supreme Court of India rules in *Kesavananda Bharati case* that the basic structure of the Constitution (including many fundamental rights) is unalterable by a constitutional amendment.

1975–77– State of Emergency in India – extensive rights violations take place.

1978– SC rules in *Menaka Gandhi v. Union of India* that the right to life under Article 21 of the Constitution cannot be suspended even in an emergency.

1978– Jammu and Kashmir Public Safety Act, 1978.

1984– Operation Blue Star and the subsequent 1984 Anti-Sikh riots

1985-6– The Shah Bano case, where the Supreme Court recognised the Muslim woman's right to maintenance upon divorce, sparks protests from Muslim clergy. To nullify the decision of the Supreme Court, the Rajiv Gandhi government enacted The Muslim Women (Protection of Rights on Divorce) Act 1986

1987– Hashimpura massacre during communal riots in Meerut.

1989– *Scheduled Caste and Scheduled Tribe (Prevention of Atrocities) Act, 1989* is passed.

1989– Present – Kashmiri insurgency sees ethnic cleansing of Kashmiri Pandits, desecrating Hindu temples, killing of Hindus and Sikhs, and abductions of foreign tourists and government functionaries.

1992– A constitutional amendment establishes Local Self-Government (Panchayati Raj) as a third tier of governance at the village level, with one-third of the seats reserved for women. Reservations were provided for scheduled castes and tribes as well.

1992– Babri Masjid demolished by Hindu mobs, resulting in riots across the country.

1993– National Human Rights Commission is established under the *Protection of Human Rights Act.*

2001– Supreme Court passes extensive orders to implement the right to food.

2002– Violence in Gujarat, chiefly targeting its Muslim minority, claims many lives.

2005– A powerful *Right to Information Act* is passed to give citizen's access to information held by public authorities.

2005– *National Rural Employment Guarantee Act (NREGA)* guarantees universal right to employment.

2006– Supreme Court orders police reforms in response to the poor human rights record of Indian police.

2009– Delhi High Court delcares that Section 377 of the Indian Penal Code, which outlaws a range of unspecified "unnatural" sex acts, is unconstitutional when applied to homosexual acts between private consenting individuals, effectively decriminalising homosexual relationships in India.

6

Socio-economic Issues in Indian Human Rights

Since India's Independence in 1947, country has faced several social and economic issues.

SOCIAL ISSUES

VIOLENCE

The 16th Century [[Babri Mosque], (built by destroying Ram Mandir - birth place of God Ram) was destroyed by the members of Hindu nationalist VHP and Bajrang Dal in 1992, resulting in nationwide religious riots) Constitutionally India is a secular state, but large-scale violence have periodically occurred in India since independence. In recent decades, communal tensions and religion-based politics have become more prominent..Although India is generally known for religious pluralism, the Hindutva ideology propagates that India belongs to the Hindus, and the Christians and the Muslims are "aliens", and many proponents of this ideology portray violence against Muslims and Christians as a form of "self-defence" against "invaders".

The Hindutva ideology is at the core of Sangh Parivar politics and its expression in violence against religious minority. Throughout the history of post-Independence India, both Muslim and Christian communities have faced repeated attacks from Hindu activists. As the Hindutva ideology has grown more powerful over the years, many Hindutva activists have partaken in riots against minority communities. Over the last decade, religious violence in India has increasingly become what academics believe to be organized pogroms to eliminate minority communities. Some state governments in India have been accused of not effectively prosecuting those who attack religious minorities. Major religious violent incidents include Ayodhya debate, Bombay Riots, 1993 Bombay bombings, 2002 Gujarat violence. Although related, Hinduism and Hindutva are different. Hinduism is a religion while Hindutva is a political ideology. The Hindutva movement is not supported by majority of Hindus.

Some tolerant or "secular" Hindus use the term "Hindu Taliban" to describe the supporters of the Hindutva movement. In Jammu and Kashmir, Since March 1990, estimates of between 250,000 to 300,000 pandits have migrated outside Kashmir due to persecution by Islamic fundamentalists in the largest case of ethnic cleansing since the partition of India.The proportion of Kashmiri Pandits in the Kashmir valley has declined from about 15 per cent in 1947 to, by some estimates, less than 0.1 per cent since the insurgency in Kashmir took on a religious and sectarian flavour Many Kashmiri Pandits have been killed by Islamist terrorists in incidents such as the Wandhama massacre and the 2000 Amarnath pilgrimage massacre.

In recent years, there has been a sharp increase in violent attacks on Christians in India, often perpetrated by Hindu Nationalists.The acts of violence include arson of churches, re-conversion of Christians to Hinduism, distribution of threatening literature, burning of Bibles, raping of nuns, murder of Christian priests and destruction of Christian schools, colleges, and cemeteries.The Sangh Parivar and related organisations have stated that the violence is an expression of "spontaneous anger" of "vanvasis" against "forcible conversion" activities undertaken by missionariesa claim described as "absurd" and rejected by scholars. Between 1964 and 1996, thirty-eight incidents of violence against Christians were reported.n 1997, twenty-four such incidents were reported.In 2007 and 2008 there was a further flare up of tensions in Orissa, the first following the Christians' putting up a Pandhal in land traditionally used by Hindus and the second after the unprovoked murder of a Hindu Guru and four of his disciples while observing Janmashtami puja. This was followed by an attack on a 150-year-old church in Madhya Pradesh, and more attacks in Karnataka.

TERRORISM

The regions with long term terrorist activities today are Jammu and Kashmir, Central India (Naxalism) and Seven Sister States (independence and autonomy movements). In the past, the Punjab insurgency led to militant activities in the Indian state of Punjab as well as the national capital Delhi (Delhi serial blasts, anti-Sikh riots). As of 2006, at least 232 of the country's 608 districts were afflicted, at differing intensities, by various insurgent and terrorist movements. Terrorism in India has often been alleged to be sponsored by Pakistan. After most acts of terrorism in India, many journalists and politicians accuse Pakistan's intelligence agency, the Inter-Services Intelligence of playing a role. Recently, both the US and Afghanistan have accused Pakistan of carrying out terrorist acts in Afghanistan.

NAXALISM

Naxalism is an informal name given to communist groups that were born out of the Sino-Soviet split in the Indian communist movement. Ideologically they belong to various trends of Maoism. Initially the movement had its centre in West Bengal. In recent years, they have spread into less developed areas of rural central and eastern India, such as Chattisgarh and Andhra Pradesh through the activities of underground groups like the Communist Party of India (Maoist)·The CPI (Maoist) and some other Naxal factions are considered terrorists by the Government of India and various state governments in India.

CASTE RELATED VIOLENCE

Caste-related violence and hate crimes in India have occurred despite the gradual reduction of casteism in the country. Independent India has witnessed considerable amount of violence and hate crimes motivated by caste. Ranvir Sena, a caste-supremacist fringe paramilitary group based in Bihar, has committed violent acts against Dalits and other members of the scheduled caste community.

Phoolan Devi, who belonged to *Mallah* lower-caste, was mistreated and raped by upper-caste Thakurs at a young age. She then became a bandit and carried out violent robberies against upper-caste people. In 1981, her gang massacred twenty-two Thakurs, most of whom were not involved in her kidnapping or rape. Phoolan Devi went on to become a politician and Member of Parliament. Over the years, various incidents of violence against Dalits, such as Kherlanji Massacre have been reported from many parts of India. At the same time, many violent protests by Dalits, such as the 2006 Dalit protests in Maharashtra, have been reported as well.

The Mandal Commission was established in 1979 to "identify the socially or educationally backward",and to consider the question of seat reservations and quotas for people to redress caste discrimination. In 1980, the commission's report affirmed the affirmative action practice under Indian law whereby members of lower castes were given exclusive access to a certain portion of government jobs and slots in public universities. When V. P. Singh Government tried to implement the recommendations of Mandal Commission in 1989, massive protests were held in the country. Many alleged that the politicians were trying to cash in on caste-based reservations for purely pragmatic electoral purposes.

In 1990s, many parties Bahujan Samaj Party (BSP), the Samajwadi Party and the Janata Dal started claiming that they are representing the backward castes. Many such parties, relying primarily on Backward Classes' support, often in alliance with Dalits and Muslims, rose to power in Indian states.At the same time, many Dalit leaders and intellectuals started realizing that the main Dalit oppressors were so-called Other Backward Classes,and formed their own parties, such as the Indian Justice Party. The Congress (I) in Maharashtra long relied on OBCs' backing for its political success.Bharatiya Janata Party has also showcased its Dalit and OBC leaders to prove that it is not an upper-caste party. Bangaru Laxman, the former BJP president (2001–

2002) was a former Dalit. Sanyasin Uma Bharati, former CM of Madhya Pradesh, who belongs to OBC caste, was a former BJP leader. In 2006 Arjun Singh cabinet minister for MHRD of the UPA government was accused of playing caste politics when he introduced reservations for OBCs in educational institutions all around.

5EDUCATION INITIATIVES

Since the Indian Constitution was finalized in 1949, education has remained one of the priorities of the Indian government. The first education minister Maulana Azad founded a system of education which aimed to provide free education at the primary level. Primary education was made free and compulsory for children from 6-14, and child labour was banned. The government introduced incentives to education and disincentives for not receiving education – for instance, the provision of mid-day meals in schools were introduced.

Many similar initiatives echoed, and the largest of such initiatives is Sarva Shiksha Abhiyan, which actively promoted "Education for All". In line with this, the United Progressive Alliance (UPA) aimed to increase their expenditure on education to 6 per cent of its Gross Domestic Product (GDP) from values fluctuating about 3 per cent through their National Common Minimum Programme (NCMP) in 2004. The Right of Children to Free and Compulsory Education Act was also imposed in 2009. Despite these initiatives, education continues to persist as an impediment to development.

ISSUES

While many schools were built, they had poor infrastructure and inadequate facilities. Schools in the rural areas were especially affected. District Information System for Education (DISE) in India in 2009, only about 51.5 per cent of all schools in India have boundary walls, 16.65 per cent have computers and 39 per cent have electricity. Of which, only 6.47 per cent of primary schools and 33.4 per cent of secondary schools have computers, and only 27.7 per cent of primary schools have electricity. Learning in poorly furbished schools was not conducive, resulting in poor quality education.

Furthermore, the absence rates of teachers and students were high, while their retainment rates low. The incentives for going to school were not apparent, while punishment for absence was not enforced. Despite the government's decree on compulsory education and the child labour ban, many children were still missing classes to go to work. The government did not interfere even when children missed school.

Also, online country studies publications by the Federal Research Division of the Library of Congress stated that "it was not unusual for the teacher to be absent or even to subcontract the teaching work to unqualified substitutes". This exacerbates the problems of the lack of qualified teachers. Currently, the student-teacher ratio remains high at around 32, which is not much of an improvement since 2006 when the ratio was 34.

ECONOMIC ISSUES

Poverty

One-third of India's population (roughly equivalent to the entire population of the United States) lives below the poverty line and India is home to one-third of the world's poor people. Though the middle class has gained from recent positive economic developments, India suffers from substantial poverty. The new World Bank's estimates on poverty based on 2005 data, India has 456 million people, 41.6 per cent of its population, living below the new international poverty line of $1.25 (PPP) per day. The World Bank further estimates that 33 per cent of the global poor now reside in India. Moreover, India also has 828 million people, or 75.6 per cent of the population living below $2 a day, compared to 72.2 per cent for Sub-Saharan Africa.

Wealth distribution in India is fairly uneven, with the top 10 per cent of income groups earning 33 per cent of the income.Despite significant economic progress, 1/4 of the nation's population earns less than the government-specified poverty threshold of $0.40/day. Official figures estimate that 27.5 per cent of Indians lived below the national poverty line in 2004–2005. A 2007 report by the state-run National Commission for Enterprises in the Unorganised Sector (NCEUS) found that 25 per cent of Indians, or 236 million people, lived on less than 20 rupees per day[with most working in "informal labour sector with no job or social security, living in abject poverty."

Corruption

Corruption is widespread in India. India is ranked 72 out of a 179 countries in Transparency International's Corruption Perceptions Index, although its score has improved consistently from 2.7 in 2002 to 3.5 in 2007. Corruption has taken the role of a pervasive aspect of Indian politics and bureaucracy.

In India, corruption takes the form of bribes, evasion of tax and exchange controls, embezzlement, etc. A 2005 study done by Transparency International (TI) India found that more than 50 per cent had firsthand experience of paying bribe or peddling influence to get a job done in a public office.The chief economic consequences of corruption are the loss to the exchequer, an unhealthy climate for investment and an increase in the cost of government-subsidised services.

The TI India study estimates the monetary value of petty corruption in 11 basic services provided by the government, like education, healthcare, judiciary, police, etc., to be around ₹ 21,068 crores. India still ranks in the bottom quartile of developing nations in terms of the ease of doing business, and compared to China and other lower developed Asian nations, the average time taken to secure the clearances for a startup or to invoke bankruptcy is much greater.

Economic and social disparities also plague the fundamentals of the education system. Rural children are less able to receive education because of greater opportunity costs, since rural children have to work to contribute to the family's income. The Annual Status of Education in 2009, the average attendance rate of students in the rural states is about 75 per cent. Though this rate varies significantly, states like Uttar Pradesh and Bihar had more than 40 per cent absentees during a random visit to their schools. In the urban states, more than 90 per cent of the students were present in their schools during a visit.

7

Caste System and Human Rights

CASTE SYSTEM IN INDIA

Caste system in India is a composite structure of different social classes in the Hindu religion. Caste system in India has a long history dating back to the ancient past. It dates back to that era when people used to believe that people were born into a particular social status. They also believed that experiences in past lives and good deeds can actually reincarnate one into higher social strata in the next life. The Indian caste system has gone places with the changes that have taken place in the society.

Education has been massively instrumental in bringing a change in the state of mind though a large section of a society, mostly the older generation is still under the curse of this social ostracism. In the present times, rural India is still under the restraints of the caste system, where still one's caste influences their food habits, their clothing and even their occupation. The 'dalits' are those, who are customarily poor households and they may be peasants, labourers, or servants doing menial jobs and also certain 'unclean' jobs like disposing of the dead. Urban areas today have been modified quite a great deal.

HISTORY OF THE DEVELOPMENT OF CASTE SYSTEM

The development of the caste system in India never seems to be having any universally accepted history as such. Though there is a general speculative faith that the earliest settlers to this land, the Indo-Aryans might have actually established the caste system, gradually placing them in the higher ladder of the society. There is a whole lot of controversy regarding the theory of the Indo-Aryan migration.

The Hindu scriptures can also be taken into consideration in this regard, which has some passages that can be interpreted to sanction the caste system. This also indicates that the caste system is not an essential part of the Hindu religion. The Vedas or the most ancient 'shruti' texts emphasise very less on the caste system, same is maintained in a hymn from the Rig Veda. Later scriptures like Bhagavad Gita and Manu Smriti propounds four Varnas, to be

God's creation. There is a general idea believed by scholars that may be in the initial phases the caste system was a bit flexible. Migration from one caste to the other was possible by switching jobs. Various passages from Manu Smriti and other scriptures emphasise that the caste system in India was originally non-hereditary. Therefore, through these facts one gets an impression how the caste system developed in the later stages into a firm intricate structure from a bendable one in the earlier Vedic age.

VARNA AND JATI IN INDIA

Ancient Hindu scriptures have the citations of four varnas or colour, which is the basic social class in the caste system in India. Bhagavad-Gita says that varnas are decided on the grounds of Guna which is the amalgamation of the five elements of ether, air, fire, water and earth, and Karma which is the concept of action. In accordance with the powers of the born nature, works of Brahmins, Kshatriya, Vaishya, and Sudras differ.

Four varnas that are mentioned by other shastras are the Brahmins destined as teachers, scholars and priests, the Kshatriyas as kings and warriors, the Vaishyas were the trading class and the Shudras were agriculturists, service providers, and some artisan groups. These are further classified into jatis. Another group excluded from the main society was called Parjanya or Antyaja. This is the group of former untouchables who were considered either the lower section of Sudras or beyond the caste system altogether. Varna and jati are two different concepts. Varna actually unifies the Hindu sub communities or jatis into the four groups. Jati or community is an endogamous group where the members marry within themselves. There is a further division of the sub communities into exogamous groups in terms of gotras. There are exactly thousands of sub castes or jatis in India, often with particular ecological ranges and a governmental or corporate structure. Jatis are the way in which caste is embodied for most practical purposes.

INDIAN CASTE AND SOCIAL STATUS

India is a multicultural, multilingual country which adopts a liberal attitude towards its diverse religious practices. One can find the prevalence of the caste system more in Hinduism than any other religion. Caste system in India has a history and it defines how caste has evolved through the ages. Caste and social status has always been quite puzzling. In the British era, they tried to equalise the caste system in India with the class system. Castes are the divisions, into which a certain section of the community belongs, which also enjoy social status accordingly.

What is generally meant by the social status is the prestige or the honour that is being attached to one's position in the society. An individual might acquire more power and privilege due to a characteristic; this puts him among the privileged group of the people who enjoy high status. Brahmins are the priestly class, the protector of religion while the Kshatriyas hold the political power. Therefore caste and social status were inter-related. A higher caste individual was always looked with awe and reverence.

BRITISH IMPACT OVER CASTE SYSTEM IN INDIA

Some scholars are of the view that the caste system in India was never so rigid until the British interfered in the caste related issues in India. They almost equated caste with the class system that exist in their country and in the process tampered with the long established caste system. Even among the Dalits there were the distinctions of high and low, and conflicts often took place. Caste system was seen as a pointer of social standing, intellectual ability and occupation. Hence the British wanted to include it in the census. Moreover, it becomes obvious that British notions of cultural purity were interwoven with these judgments of people based on caste when reactions to censuses are examined. The British policies of 'divide and rule' were again a step towards breaking up of the unity in which caste played an important role.

The listing of the population into rigid categories during the 10 year census led to the stiffening of caste identities. Caste system in India is a complex system of several distinctions, which have divided the society into the high and low strata. Lots of measures at present have been taken up by the government for the upliftment of the backward castes who do not have a social standing. There are disputes and complications regarding the caste system in India, which sometimes takes the shape of a sensitive issue. From the ancient times till the present day caste system has gone through a vast shift from how it was considered by the people and its rigidity.

ECONOMIC SOCIAL EXCLUSION AND THE AMBEDKAR PRINCIPLES OF EMPLOYMENT

An increasing number of international companies and banks are investing in the countries of South Asia, particularly in India. This may have positive consequences for those countries. However the Dalit Solidarity Network UK believes it is increasingly important that foreign investors look carefully at their recruitment and employment policies in South Asia. Especially in India, there is a distinct and all-pervasive system of discrimination based on caste. The United Nations and its agencies refer to it as "discrimination based on work and descent". What it means is that people who are born into specific groups, trades or castes are unable to escape from the stigma of their background or their origins. Hence those born as leatherworkers, barbers, agricultural workers or manual scavengers will remain in those employment sectors all their lives. Sometimes people escape from the system by moving to the large towns or cities, but overall the system remains heavily in place. "Dalit" is a term which has had increasing currency in recent years. Literally, it means "the oppressed". It encompasses peoples who used to be called "untouchables", or "Harijans"; who are often also referred to as "Scheduled Castes", because the way they are referred to in the constitution of India. "Adivasi" is a term which refers to those who are members of "Scheduled Tribes".

That is, individuals who are racially distinct, as indigenous peoples, in contradistinction to the Caucasian peoples who invaded and settled India centuries ago. There is legislation stemming from the Indian Constitution which outlaws caste discrimination. The Chair of the committee which wrote the constitution of the Republic of India was Dr. Ambedkar. He was a highly educated Dalit who was admitted into Gray's Inn and was called to the Bar. He also completed his second Doctoral studies in the London School of Economics and his thesis was subsequently published as 'The problem of the rupee'. Ambedkar became an all-India figure and the undisputed leader of the Dalits. He used this vantage-point successfully to question with blunt and militant doggedness the claim of Gandhi to represent all of India and especially the Dalits.

He died in 1956 having served as India's first Law Minister. Under the constitution, the Republic of India is empowered1 to "promote with special care the educational and economic interests of the weaker sections of the people, and, in particular, of the Scheduled Castes2 and the Scheduled Tribes3, and shall protect them from social injustice and all forms of exploitation". To achieve this aim, the State has used a two-fold approach: the provision of legal safeguards against discrimination4; and a "Reservation Policy5" in the State sector and State Supported Sector Subsequently, there has been further legislation, which has introduced penalties for specific examples of caste discrimination. These include the 1989 Prevention of Atrocities Act, the 1993 Protection of Human Rights Act, and the 1993 Employment of Manual Scavengers Act.

However, these laws are far from effective. The Reservation Policy allocates 17 per cent of public sector jobs to Scheduled Castes, and a further 8 per cent to Scheduled Tribes. This approximately reflects their respective percentages in the population as a whole. Since the inception of the Reservation Policy following independence in 1947, there has been a significant increase in the number of Dalit and Adivasi government employees, but this is for a population of between about 250 million Dalits and Adivasis. 60 years after Independence, the raw percentages in government employment and public sector undertakings now do very roughly reflect the percentages of the population which are Dalit and Advasi. Because the Reservation Policy does not extend to the private sector recruitment is not done according to quota systems. Therefore, it is not possible to get comparative figure for the proportion of Dalits and Adivasi employed in the private sector, nor - most importantly - the seniority of jobs they hold. This is unfortunate, because the private sector, in relation to the State Sector and State Supported Sector, is rather a big player. 76 per cent of the workforce is engaged in the private sector and only 24 per cent is employed in the State Sector and the State Supported Sector6. The present context is also that the State Sector and the State Supported Sector are shrinking, while the private sector is expanding. It is estimated that 90 per cent of the Dalit and Adivasi workforce is engaged in menial jobs in the Private Sector.

In practice, they have very little - and sometimes no - protection against discrimination. It remains extremely difficult for the 25 per cent of the population referred to by the government as Scheduled Castes and Scheduled Tribes, to overcome the discrimination they face. This is a negative situation, both in terms of human rights, and in terms of economic potential. An article in the New York Times recently described the typing competition, in English, the journalist had with an eight-year-old Dalit girl in a village "about an hour's drive – and ten centuries – from Bangalore, India's Silicon Valley". The eightyear- old, he said, "left me in the dust, to the cheering delight of her classmates". It is important to examine the potential which is being lost because of the caste system. The United Progressive Alliance government in New Delhi is committed to exploring the expansion of the reservation system, into the private sector. According to a recent article in the Indian Express, the state government of Maharashtra is already preparing such legislation. Foreign investment in India is high, and increasing, not the least because it is viewed as a stable country with a high growth rate.

Economically, India is a "happening" country. The caste system has specific effects, when it comes to recruitment of workers for industries which are being developed with outside capital and technological know-how. To respond to this situation DSN-UK, a member of the International Dalit Solidarity Network, is proposing a set of employment principles for foreign investors in South Asia. After a series of consultations spread over a year with the private, public, and charities sectors, we have finalised what we shall call the Ambedkar Principles, and are pleased to be launching them formally on the 20 July 2006.

CASTE AND SOCIAL STATUS

Traditionally, although the political power lay with the Kshatriyas, historians portrayed the Brahmins as custodians and interpreters of Dharma, who enjoyed much prestige and many advantages. Fa Hien, a Buddhist pilgrim from China, visited India around 400 AD. "Only the lot of the Chandals he found unenviable; outcastes by reason of their degrading work as disposers of dead, they were universally shunned... But no other section of the population were notably disadvantaged, no other caste distinctions attracted comment from the Chinese pilgrim, and no oppressive caste 'system' drew forth his surprised censure.". In this period kings of Sudra and Brahmin origin were as common as those of Kshatriya varna and caste system was not wholly prohibitive and repressive. The castes did not constitute a rigid description of the occupation or the social status of a group. Since British society was divided by class, the British attempted to equate the Indian caste system to their own social class system.

They saw caste as an indicator of occupation, social standing, and intellectual ability. Intentionally or unintentionally, the caste system became more rigid during the British Raj, when the British started to enumerate castes during the ten year census and codified the system under their rule. The Harijans, or the people outside the caste system, had the lowest social status. The Harijans, earlier referred to as untouchables by some, worked in what were seen as unhealthy, unpleasant or polluting jobs. In the past, the Harijans suffered from social segregation and restrictions, in addition to extreme poverty.

They were not allowed temple worship with others, nor water from the same sources. Persons of higher castes would not interact with them. If somehow a member of a higher caste came into physical or social contact with an untouchable, the member of the higher caste was defiled, and had to bathe thoroughly to purge him or herself of the impurity. Social discrimination developed even among the Harijans; sub-castes among Harijans, such as the dhobi and nai, would not interact with lower-order Bhangis, who were described as "outcastes even among outcastes".Sociologists have commented on the historical advantages offered by a rigid social structure as well as its drawbacks.

While caste is now seen as anachronistic, in its original form the caste system served as an instrument of order in a society where mutual consent rather than compulsion ruled; where the ritual rights and the economic obligations of members of one caste or sub-caste were strictly circumscribed in relation to those of any other caste or sub-caste; where one was born into one's caste and retained one's station in society for life; where merit was inherited, where equality existed within the caste, but inter-caste relations were unequal and hierarchical.

A well-defined system of mutual interdependence through a division of labour created security within a community. In addition, the division of labour on the basis of ethnicity allowed immigrants and foreigners to quickly integrate into their own caste niches. The caste system played an influential role in shaping economic activities, where it functioned much like medieval European guilds, ensuring the division of labour, providing for the training of apprentices and, in some cases, allowing manufacturers to achieve narrow specialisation. For instance, in certain regions, producing each variety of cloth was the speciality of a particular sub-caste. Additionally, some philosophers have argued that the majority of people would be comfortable in stratified endogamous groups, as they were in ancient times.

CASTE MOBILITY

Some scholars believe that the relative ranking of other castes was fluid or differed from one place to another prior to the arrival of the British. Sociologists such as Bernard Buber and Marriott McKim describe how the perception of the caste system as a static and textual stratification has given way to the perception of the caste system as a more processual, empirical and contextual stratification. Other sociologists such as Y.B Damle have applied theoretical models to explain mobility and flexibility in the caste system in India.

According to these scholars, groups of lower-caste individuals could seek to elevate the status of their caste by attempting to emulate the practices of higher castes. Flexibility in caste laws permitted very low-caste religious clerics such as Valmiki to compose the Ramayana, which became a central work of Hindu scripture. There is also precedent of certain Shudra families within the temples of the Sri Vaishnava sect in South India elevating their caste.

The following is a list of changes in varna cited in Hindu texts:

- Manu eldest son [Priyavrata] became king, a Kshatriya. Out of his ten sons seven became kings while three became Brahman. Their names were Mahavira, Kavi and Savana.
- Kavash –ailush was born to a Sudra and attained varn of a Rishi. He became mantra-drashta to numerous Vedic mantras in Rig-Veda 10th Mandal.
- Jabala's son [Satyakama] born from unknown father became Rishi by his qualities.
- [Matanga] became a Rishi after his birth in low Varna.

According to some psychologists, mobility across broad caste lines may have been "minimal", though sub-castes (jatis) may have changed their social status over the generations by fission, re-location, and adoption of new rituals. Sociologist M. N. Srinivas has also debated the question of rigidity in Caste. In an ethnographic study of the Coorgs of Karnataka, he observed considerable flexibility and mobility in their caste hierarchies. He asserts that the caste system is far from a rigid system in which the position of each component caste is fixed for all time; instead, movement has always been possible, especially in the middle regions of the hierarchy. It was always possible for groups born into a lower caste to "rise to a higher position by adopting vegetarianism and teetotalism" *i.e.* adopt the customs of the higher castes. While theoretically "forbidden", the process was not uncommon in practice. The concept of sanskritization, or the adoption of upper-caste norms by the lower castes, addressed the complexity and fluidity of caste relations.

The fact that many of the dynasties were of obscure origin suggests some social mobility: a person of any caste, having once acquired political power, could also acquire a genealogy connecting him with the traditional lineages and conferring Kshatriya status. A number of new castes, such as the Kayasthas (scribes) and Khatris (traders), are mentioned in the sources of this period.

According to the Brahmanic sources, they originated from intercaste marriages, but this is clearly an attempt at rationalizing their rank in the hierarchy. Khatri appears to be unquestionably a Prakritised form of the Sanskrit Kshatriya. Many of these new castes played a major role in society. The hierarchy of castes did not have a uniform distribution throughout the country.

REFORMS

There have been challenges to the caste system from the time of Buddha, Mahavira and Makkhali Gosala. Opposition to the system of varG◎a is regularly asserted in the Yoga Upanic◎ad-s and is a constant feature of Cîna-âcâra tantrism, a Chinese-derived movement in Asom; both date to the medieval era. The Nâtha system, which was founded by Matsya-indra Nâtha and Go-rakc◎a Nâtha in the same era and spread throughout India, has likewise been consistently opposed to the system of varna. Many Bhakti period saints rejected the caste discriminations and accepted all castes, including untouchables, into their fold. During the British Raj, this sentiment gathered steam, and many Hindu reform movements such as Brahmo Samaj and Arya Samaj renounced caste-based discrimination.

The inclusion of so-called untouchables into the mainstream was argued for by many social reformers. Mahatma Gandhi called them "Harijans" (children of God) although that term is now considered patronizing and the term Dalit (downtrodden) is the more commonly used. Gandhi's contribution towards the emancipation of the untouchables is still debated, especially in the commentary of his contemporary Dr. B.R. Ambedkar, an untouchable who frequently saw Gandhi's activities as detrimental to the cause of upliftment of his people. The practice of untouchability was formally outlawed by the Constitution of India in 1950, and has declined significantly since then, to the point of a society allowing former untouchables to take high political office, like former President K. R. Narayanan, who took office in 1997, and former Chief Justice K. G. Balakrishnan.

MODERN STATUS OF THE CASTE SYSTEM

In some rural areas and small towns, the caste system is still very rigid. Caste is also a factor in the politics of India. The Government of India has officially documented castes and sub-castes, primarily to determine those deserving reservation (positive discrimination in education and jobs) through the census. The Indian reservation system, though limited in scope, relies entirely on quotas.

The Government lists consist of Scheduled Castes, Scheduled Tribes and Other Backward Classes:

- *Scheduled castes* (SC): Scheduled castes generally consist of "Dalit". The present population is 16 per cent of the total population of India (around 160 million). For example, the Delhi state has 49 castes listed as SC.

- *Scheduled tribes* (ST): Scheduled tribes generally consist of tribal groups. The present population is 7 per cent of the total population of India *i.e.* around 70 million.
- *Other Backward Classes* (OBC): The Mandal Commission covered more than 3000 castes under OBC Category and stated that OBCs form around 52 per cent of the Indian population. However, the National Sample Survey puts the figure at 32 per cent. There is substantial debate over the exact number of OBCs in India; it is generally estimated to be sizable, but many believe that it is lower than the figures quoted by either the Mandal Commission or the National Sample Survey. The caste-based reservations in India have led to widespread protests, such as the 2006 Indian anti-reservation protests, with many complaining of reverse discrimination against the forward castes (the castes that do not qualify for the reservation). Many view negative treatment of forward castes as socially divisive and equally wrong.

CASTE SYSTEM AMONG NON-HINDUS

In some parts of India, Christians are stratified by sect, location, and the castes of their predecessors, usually in reference to upper class Syrian Malabar Nasranis. Christians in Kerala are divided into several communities, including Syrian Christians and the so-called "Latin" or "New Rite" Christians. Syrian Christians derive status within the caste system from the tradition that they are converted Namboodiris and Jews, who were evangelized by St. Thomas. Writers Arundhati Roy and Anand Kurian have written personal accounts of the caste system at work in their community. Syrian Christians, especially Knanaya Christians, tend to be endogamous and not to intermarry with other Christian castes. The Latin Rite Christians were among the scheduled castes in the coastal belt of Kerala, where fishing was the primary occupation. They were actively converted by missionaries in the 16th and 19th centuries.

These missionary activities were carried out by Western Latin Rite missionaries who did not understand the significance of the caste system in India; none of the Syrian churches had participated in such activities among the scheduled castes of India because they were aware of the prejudices of the caste system. The government of India later granted this group OBC status. Very rarely are there intermarriages between Syrian Christians and Latin Rite ChristiansAnthropologists have noted that the caste hierarchy among Christians in Kerala is much more polarized than the Hindu practices in the surrounding areas, due to a lack of jatis. Also, the caste status is kept even if the sect allegiance is switched (*i.e.* from Syrian Catholic to Syrian Orthodox). In the Indian state of Goa, mass conversions were carried out by Portuguese Latin missionaries from the 16th century onwards. The Hindu converts retained their caste practices. The continued maintenance of the caste system among the Christians in Goa is attributed to the nature of mass conversions of entire villages, as a result of which existing social stratification was not affected. The Portuguese colonists, even during the Goan Inquisition, did not do anything to change the caste system. Thus, the original Hindu Brahmins in Goa now became Christian Bamons and the Kshatriya became Christian noblemen called Chardos. The Christian clergy became almost exclusively Bamon.

Vaishyas who converted to Christianity became Gauddos, and Shudras became Sudirs. Finally, the Dalits or "Untouchables" who converted to Christianity became Maharas and Chamars, the latter an appellation of the anti-Dalit ethnic slur Chamaar. Units of social stratification, termed "castes" by many, have developed among Muslims in some parts of South Asia. Sources indicate that the castes among Muslims developed as the result of close contact with Hindu culture and Hindu converts to Islam. The Sachar Committee's report commissioned by the government of India and released in 2006 documents the continued stratification in Muslim society. Among Muslims, those who are referred to as Ashrafs are presumed to have a superior status derived from their foreign Arab ancestry, while the Ajlafs are assumed to be converts from Hinduism, and have a lower status. In addition, the Arzal caste among Muslims was regarded by anti-caste activists like Ambedkar as the equivalent of untouchables. In the Bengal region of India, some Muslims stratify their society according to 'Quoms'.

While many scholars have asserted that the Muslim castes are not as acute in their discrimination as those of the Hindus, some like Ambedkar argued that the social evils in Muslim society were "worse than those seen in Hindu society". The Buddhists also had a caste system. In Sri Lanka, the Rodis might have been outcast by the Sri Lankan Buddhists due to the absence of ahimsa (non-violence), a central tenet of Buddhism, among their beliefs. The writer Raghavan notes, "That a form of worship in which human offerings formed the essential ritual would have been anathema to the Buddhist way of life goes without saying; and it needs no stretch of imagination that any class of people in whom the cult prevailed or survived even in an attenuated form would have been pronounced by the sangha (*i.e.* the Buddhist clergy) as exiles from the social order." Savarkar believed that the status of the backward castes (*e.g.* Chamar) that performed non-violence only worsened.

When Ywan Chwang traveled to South India after the period of the Chalukyan Empire, he noticed that the caste system had existed among the Buddhists and Jains. Jains also had castes in places such as Bihar. For example, in the village of Bundela, there were several "jaats" (groups) amongst the Jains. A person of one "jaat" cannot intermingle with a Jain or another "jaat". They also could not eat with the members of other "jaats". The Sikh Gurus criticized the hierarchy of the caste system. While some castes were widely perceived as being better or higher than others (*e.g.* Brahmins being higher than others), they preached that all sections of society were valuable and that merit and hard-work were essential aspects of life. In the Shiromani Gurdwara Prabandhak Committee, out of 140 seats, 20 are reserved for low caste Sikhs. However, the quota system has attracted much criticism due to the lack of meritocracy, since merit is considered the single most important component of winning a seat. Baha'i Faith has grown to prominence in India, since its philosophy of the unity of humanity attracted many of the lower castes.

CASTE-RELATED VIOLENCE

Caste-related violence and hate crimes in India have occurred despite the gradual reduction of casteism in the country. According to a report by Human Rights Watch, "Dalits and indigenous peoples (known as Scheduled Tribes or adivasis) continue to face discrimination, exclusion, and acts of communal violence. Laws and policies adopted by the Indian government provide a strong basis for protection, but are not being faithfully implemented by local authorities."

IN 2006 DALIT PROTESTS IN MAHARASHTRA

In November-December 2006, the desecration of a Ambedkar statue in Kanpur (Uttar Pradesh) triggered violent protests by Dalits in Maharashtra. Several people remarked that the protests were fueled by the Kherlanji Massacre. During the violent protests, the Dalit protestors set three trains on fire, damaged over 100 buses and clashed with police. At least four deaths and many more injuries were reported. Later, the Kanpur Police arrested a Dalit youth Arun Kumar Balmiki for desecrating the Ambedkar statue. According to the police, the youth had "admitted to having damaged the statue in a drunken state along with two friends". Earlier in a similar case, a Dalit youth was held for desecrating an Ambedkar statue in Gulbarga, Karnataka. In response to these protests, Raj Thackeray drew attention to another incident in Kherlanji, in which a Dalit allegedly raped a girl and killed her. Thackeray demanded action on those responsible for the rape and the subsequent death of the girl, and also remarked that nobody helped the girl's family.

ANDHRA PRADESH

This state is considered to be one of the most caste-crime infested places of India which has had many Dalit Massacres like Chundur Massacre, Neerukonda Massacre etc,.

RAJASTHAN

In the Indian province of Rajasthan, between the years 1999 and 2002, crimes against Dalits average at about 5024 a year, with 46 killings and 138 cases of rape.

TAMIL NADU

The state of Tamil Nadu has witnessed several caste-based incidents both against Dalits and Brahmins. In 2000, three young men belonging to the Dalit undercaste were killed in the Cuddalore district of Tamil Nadu. This fuelled some localized violence in the caste-sensitive region, which has seen numerous caste-related incidents in which the majority of the victims have been Dalits. Six of the killings have been registered as murders under the Indian Penal Code and others as "Deaths under suspicious circumstances". No arrests have been made in these cases. However, several Dalits have been arrested as goondas (hoodlums). The Chief minister of Tamil-Nadu, M. Karunanidhi, has been accused of having an "anti-Dalit" bias by the radical organization "Dalit Panthers of India". Theories concerning these crimes against Dalits range from "alcohol bootleggers opposing prohibition movements among Dalits" to "inter-caste relations between an Vanniya boy and a Dalit girl". Political parties sympathetic to the Dalits have protested against these incidents and have alleged systemic biases against Dalits in several parts of the country.

PUNJAB

On 25 May 2009, violence and rioting broke out when thousands of protesters took to the streets in almost all major towns and cities in the Indian state of Punjab after a dalit preacher, Sant Ramanand, was attacked in a temple in Vienna, Austria. He was among 16 people injured, including another preacher Sant Nirajnan Dass, and later died in hospital. Both the preachers were from a low-caste Sikh sect which has a large following in parts of Punjab and had travelled to Vienna to conduct a special service. Several high-caste Sikh groups had apparently opposed his presence and threatened violence. This happened after the preacher had reportedly made remarks about the Sikh groups.

Bant Singh case of Punjab

On the evening of January 5, 2006 Bant Singh, a poor Sikh Dalit, was attacked by unknown assailants. His injuries necessitated medical amputation. He alleges that this was in retaliation for actively working to secure justice for his daughter, who was gang raped by upper caste members of his village in Punjab five years earlier. A 55-year-old Dalit Sikh woman, Sawinder Kaur has been tortured, stripped and tied to a tree in Ram Duali village of Punjab because her nephew eloped with a girl from the same community. The police arrested four persons for allegedly committing the crime on 9 September 2007. In January, 1999 four members of the village panchayat of Bhungar Khera village in Abohar paraded a handicapped Dalit woman naked through the village. No action was taken by the police, despite local Dalit protests. It was only on July 20 that the four pancha yat members were arrested, after the State Home Department was compelled to order an enquiry into the incident. A Dalit Sikh woman, Sukhwinder Kaur of Sumel Kheri village was molested and beaten up by an octroi contractor of Malaudh when she resisted his attempt to sexually exploit her.

KHERLANJI MASSACRE

On September 29, 2006, four members of the Bhotmange family belonging to the Dalit underclass were slaughtered in Kherlanji, a small village in Bhandara district of Maharashtra. The women of the family, Surekha and Priyanka, were paraded naked in public, then allegedly gang-raped before being murdered . Although initially ascribed by the media and by the Human Rights Watch to upper castes, the criminal act was actually carried out by Kunbi caste (classified as Other Backward Classes by Government of India) farmers for having opposed the requisition of the Dalit land to have a road built over it. On November 23, 2006, some members of the Dalit community in the nearby district of Chandrapur staged a protest regarding this incident.The protesters allegedly turned violent and threw stones. The police resorted to baton-charging the protestors to control the situation. Dalit leaders, however, denied that they had first resorted to violent and stated that they had been "protesting in peace".

CASTE POLITICS IN INDIA

Identity Politics has become a prominent subject in the Indian politics in the past few years. Rise of low castes, religious identities, linguistic groups and ethnic conflicts have contributed to the significance of identity politics in India. The discourse on Identity, many scholars feel, is distinctly a modern phenomenon. Craig Calhoun aptly describes the situation when he argues that it is in the modern times we encounter intensified efforts at consolidating individual and categorical identities and reinforce self-sameness. This is primarily a modern phenomenon because some scholars feel that emphasis on identity based on a central organising principle of ethnicity, religion, language, gender, sexual preferences, or caste positions, etc, are a sort of "compelling remedy for anonymity" in an otherwise impersonal modern world. It is thus said to be a "pattern of belonging, a search for comfort, an approach to community."

However, the complex social changes and the imbrications of various forces, factors and events in this modern world have rendered such production and recognition of identities problematic. This is to say that any search for an 'authentic self or identity' is not an innocent and unnuanced possibility; it involves negotiating other, often overlapping and contested, heterodox or multiple 'selves'. Cascardi succinctly elucidates this by observing, "the modern subject is defined by its insertion into a series of separate value-spheres, each one of which tends to exclude or attempts to assert its priority over the rest", thereby rendering identity-schemes problematic. Nonetheless, the concerns with individual and collective identity that simultaneously seeks to emphasise differences and attempt to establish commonality with others similarly distinguished, have become a universal venture.

WHAT IS IDENTITY POLITICS

But the question is how do discourses on identity fit into the political landscape? What are the political underpinnings of these discourses on identity? What are the organising principles of movements that characterise themselves as those based on identity concerns? Can we define movements of workers as an instance of identity politics? In short what is the politics of identity and what are its organising principles? Identity Politics is said to "signify a wide range of political activity and theorising founded in the shared experiences of injustice of members of certain social groups". As a political activity it is thus considered to signify a body of political projects that attempts a "recovery from exclusion and denigration" of groups hitherto marginalised on the basis of differences based on their 'selfhood' determining characteristics like ethnicity, gender, sexual preferences, caste positions, etc.

Identity politics thus attempts to attain empowerment, representation and recognition of social groups by asserting the very same markers that distinguished and differentiated them from the others and utilise those markers as an assertion of selfhood and identity based on difference rather than equality. Contrastingly placed, it is to imply that adherents of identity politics essentialise certain markers that fix the identities of social groups around an ensemble of definitional absolutes. These markers may be those of language, culture, ethnicity, gender, sexual preferences, caste positions, religion, tribe, race, etc. institutionalised in jargons, metaphors, stereotypes, and academic literature and reinforced through practices of positive discrimination or affirmative action. The proponents of identity politics thus, assign the primacy of some "essence" or a set of core features shared only by members of the collectivity and no others and accepts individual persons as singular, integral, altogether harmonious and unproblematic identities. These core markers are different from associational markers like those of the workers who are defined more by their common interests rather than by certain core essential naturally 'given' identity attributes of the groups engaged in identity politics.

Though many would argue that "worker" was an identity deserving legitimacy and as a group, its movements can be referred to as identity Politics, but probably the term "identity politics" as a body of political projects implied to in contemporary discourses refers to certain essential, local and particular categorical identities rather than any universalising ideals or agenda. The adherents of identity politics utilise the power of myths, cultural symbols and kinship relations to mould the feeling of shared community and subsequently politicise these aspects to claim recognition of their particular identities. The strongest criticism against Identity Politics is that it often challenged by the very same markers upon which the sense of self or community is sought to be built.

It is despite the fact that identity politics is engaged in numerous aspects of oppression and powerlessness, reclaiming and transforming negative scripts used by dominant groups into powerful instruments for building positive images of self and community. In other words the markers that supposedly defines the community are fixed to the extent that they harden and release a process of ingroup essentialism that often denies internal dialogicality within and without the group and itself becomes a new form of closure and oppression. Identity Politics as a field of study can be said to have gained intellectual legitimacy since the second half of the twentieth century, *i.e.*, between 1950s and 1960s in the United States when large scale political movements of the second wave-feminists, Black Civil Rights, Gay and Lesbian Liberation movements and movements of various Indigenous groups in the U.S. and other parts of the world were being justified and legitimated on the basis of claims about injustices done to their respective social groups. However, as scholars like Heyes point out that although "'Identity Politics' can draw on intellectual precursors from Mary Wollstonecraft to Frantz Fanon, writing that actually uses this specific phrase—Identity Politics—is limited almost exclusively to the last 15 years.

IDENTITY POLITICS IN INDIA

In India we find that despite adoption of a liberal democratic polity after independence, communities and collective identities have remained powerful and continue to claim recognition. In fact, Beteille has shown that the Indian polity has consistently tried to negotiate the allegiance to a liberal spirit and the concerns and consciousness of community. According to Bikhu Parekh this process has recognised a wide array of autonomous and largely selfgoverning communities. It has sought to reconcile itself as an association of individuals and a community of communities, recognising both individuals and communities as bearer of rights. It was probably this claim for and granting of recognition of particular identities by the postindependence state of India that led many scholars to believe that a material basis for the enunciation of identity claims has been provided by the post-independent state and its structures and institutions.

In other words the state is seen as an "active contributor to identity politics through the creation and maintenance of state structures which define and then recognise people in terms of certain identities". Thus, we find identity politics of various hues abound in India, the most spectacular however, are those based on language, religion, caste, ethnicity or tribal identity. But having said this it would be wrong on our part to assume that each of these identity markers operate autonomously, independent of the overlapping influence of the other makers. In other words a homogenous linguistic group may be divided by caste affiliations that may be sub-divided by religious orientations or all may be subsumed under a broader ethnic claim.

Caste

Caste-based discrimination and oppression have been a pernicious feature of Indian society and in the post-independence period its imbrications with politics have not only made it possible for hitherto oppressed caste-groups to be accorded political freedom and recognition but has also raised consciousness about its potential as a political capital. In fact Dipankar Gupta has poignantly exposed this contradiction when he elaborates the differences between Ambedkar and Mandal Commission's view of caste. While the former designed the policy of reservations or protective discrimination to remove untouchability as an institution from Indian social life and polity, the latter considered caste as an important political resource. Actually, the Mandal commission can be considered the intellectual inspiration in transforming castebased identity to an asset that may be used as a basis for securing political and economic gains. Though it can also be said that the upper castes by virtue of their predominant position were already occupying positions of strengths in the political and economic system, and when the Mandal heightened the consciousness of the 'Dalits' by recognisisng their disadvantage of caste-identity as an advantage the confrontation ensues. The caste system, which is based on the notions of purity and pollution, hierarchy and difference, has despite social mobility, been oppressive towards the Shudras and the outcastes who suffered the stigma of ritual impurity and lived in abject poverty, illiteracy and denial of political power. The origin of confrontational identity politics based on caste may be said to have its origin on the issue of providing the oppressed caste groups with state support in the form of protective discrimination.

This groupidentity based on caste that has been reinforced by the emergence of political consciousness around caste identities is institutionalised by the caste-based political parties that profess to uphold and protect the interests of specific identities including the castes. Consequently, we have the upper caste dominated BJP, the lower caste dominated BSP (Bhaujan Samaj Party) or the SP (Samajwadi Party), including the fact that left parties (for example use of caste idioms for mobilising agricultural labourers in Andhra Pradesh elections in 1950) have tacitly followed the caste pattern to extract mileage in electoral politics. The Cumulative result of the politicisation can be summarised by arguing that caste-based identity politics has had a dual role in Indian society and polity. It relatively democratised the caste-based Indian society but simultaneously undermined the evolution of class-based organisations. In all, caste has become an important determinant in Indian society and politics, the new lesson of organised politics and consciousness of caste affiliations learnt by the hitherto despised caste groups have transformed the contours of Indian politics where shifting caste-class alliances are being encountered. The net effect of these mobilisations along caste-identities have resulted not only in the empowerment of newly emerging groups but has increased the intensity of confrontational politics and possibly leading to a growing crisis of governability.

Religion

Another form of identity politics is that effected through the construction of a community on the shared bond of religion. In India, Hinduism, Islam, Sikhism, Christianity, and Zoroastrianism are some of the major religions practised by the people. Numerically the Hindus are considered to be the majority, which inspires many Hindu loyalist groups like the RSS (Rashtriya Swayam Sevak Sangh) or the Siva Sena and political parties like the BJP (Bharatiya Janata Party) or the Hindu Mahasabha to claim that India is a Hindu State. These claims generate homogenising myths about India and its history. These claims are countered by other religious groups who foresee the possibility of losing autonomy of practise of their religious and cultural life under such homogenising claims. This initiates contestations that have often resulted in communal riots. The generally accepted myths that process the identity divide on religious lines centre on the 'appeasement theory', 'forcible religious conversions', general 'anti-Hindu' and thus 'anti-India' attitude of the minority religious groups, the 'hegemonic aspirations' of majority groups and 'denial of a socio-cultural space' to minority groups.

Historically, the Hindu revivalist movement of the 19th century is considered to be the period that saw the demarcation of two separate cultures on religious basis—the Hindus and the Muslims that deepened further because of the partition. This division which has become institutionalised in the form of a communal ideology has become a major challenge for India's secular social fabric and democratic polity. Though communalism for a major part of the last century signified Hindu-Muslim conflict, in recent years contestations between Hindus and Sikhs, Hindus and Christians have often crystallised into communal conflict. The rise of Hindu national assertiveness, politics of representational government, persistence of communal perceptions, and competition for the socio-economic resources are considered some of the reasons for the generation of communal ideologies and their transformation into major riots. Identity schemes based on religion have become a major source of conflict not only in the international context but since the early 1990s it has also become a challenge for Indian democracy and secularism. The rise of majoritarian assertiveness is considered to have become institutionalised after the BJP, that along with its 'Hindu' constituents gave political cohesiveness to a consolidating Hindu consciousness, formed a coalition ministry in March 1998. However, like all identity schemes the forging of a religious community glosses over internal differences within a particular religion to generate the "we are all of the same kind" emotion. Thus differences of caste groups within a homogenous Hindu identity, linguistic and sectional differences within Islam are shelved to create a homogenous unified religious identity. In post-independence India the majoritarian assertion has generated its own antithesis in the form of minority religions assertiveness and a resulting confrontational politics that undermines the syncretistic dimensions of the civil society in India. The process through which this religious assertiveness is being increasingly institutionalised by a 'methodical rewriting of history' has the potential to reformulate India's national identity along communal trajectories.

Language

Identity claims based on the perception of a collectivity bound together by language may be said to have its origin in the pre-independence politics of the Congress that had promised reorganisation of states in the post-independent period on linguistic basis. But it was the "JVP" (Jawaharlal Nehru, Vallabhbai Patel and Pattabhi Sitaramayya) Committee's concession that if public sentiment was "insistent and overwhelming", the formation of Andhra from the Teluguspeaking region of the then Madras could be conceded which as Michael Brecher mentions was the "opening wedge for the bitter struggle over states reorganisation which was to dominate Indian Politics from 1953 to 1956". Ironically, the claim of separate states for linguistic collectivities did not end in 1956 and even today continues to confront the concerns of the Indian leadership. But the problem has been that none of the created or claimed states are mono-ethnic in composition and some even have numerically and politically powerful minorities.

This has resulted in a cascading set of claims that continue to threaten the territorial limits of existing states and disputes over boundaries between linguistic states have continued to stir conflicts, as for instance the simmering tensions between Maharastra and Karnataka over the district of Belgaum or even the claims of the Nagas to parts of Manipur. The linguistic divisions have been complicated by the lack of a uniform language policy for the entire country. Since in each state the dominant regional language is often used as the medium of instruction and social communication, the consequent affinity and allegiance that develops towards one's own language gets expressed even outside one's state of origin.

For instance the formation of linguistic cultural and social groups outside one's state of origin helps to consolidate the unity and sense of community in a separate linguistic society. Thus language becomes an important premise on which group identities are organised and establishes the conditions for defining the 'in-group' and 'out-group'. Though it is generally felt that linguistic states provide freedom and autonomy for collectivities within a heterogeneous society, critics argue that linguistic states have reinforced regionalism and has provided a platform for the articulation of a phenomenal number of identity claims in a country that has 1,652 'mother tongues' and only fourteen recognised languages around which states have been reorganised. They argue that the effective result of recognition for linguistic groups has disembodied the feelings of national unity and national spirit in a climate where 'Maharastra for Marathis, Gujrat for Gujratis, etc" has reinforced linguistic mistrust and defined the economic and political goods in linguistic terms.

Ethnicity

You will study in detail about the ethnicity in unit 26 of the book 2 of this course. There are two ways in which the concept of ethnic identity is used; one, it insiders the formation of identity on the basis of single attribute - language, religion, caste, region, etc; two, it considers the formation of identity on the basis, of multiple attributes cumulatively. However, it is the second way formation of identity on the basis of more than one characteristics - culture, customs, region, religion or caste, which is considered as the most common way of formation of the ethnic identity.

The one ethnic identity is formed in relation to the other ethnic identity. The relations between more than one ethnic identities can be both harmonious and conflictual. Whenever there is competetion among the ethnic identities on the real or imaginary basis, it expressed in the form of autonomy movements, demand for session or ethnic riots.

CRITICISM

There has been criticism of the caste system from both within and outside of India. Criticism of the Caste system in Hindu society came both from the Hindu fold and Dalit.

HISTORICAL CRITICISM

Many bhakti period saints, including Nanak, Kabir, Caitanya, Dnyaneshwar, Eknath, Ramanuja and Tukaram, rejected all caste-based discrimination and accepted disciples from all the castes. Many Hindu reformers such as Swami Vivekananda believe that there is no place for the caste system in Hinduism. The 15th century saint Ramananda accepted all castes, including untouchables, into his fold. Most of these saints subscribed to the Bhakti movements in Hinduism during the medieval period that rejected casteism. Nandanar, a low-caste Hindu cleric, also rejected casteism and accepted Dalits. Some other movements in Hinduism have also welcomed lower-castes into their fold, the earliest being the Bhakti movements of the medieval period. Early Dalit politics involved many reform movements; these arose primarily as a reaction to the advent of Christian missionaries in India and their attempts to convert Dalits, who were attracted to the prospect of escaping the caste system. In the 19th Century, the Brahmo Samaj under Raja

Ram Mohan Roy actively campaigned against untouchability and casteism. The Arya Samaj founded by Swami Dayanand also renounced discrimination against Dalits. Sri Ramakrishna Paramahamsa and his disciple Swami Vivekananda founded the Ramakrishna Mission that participated in the emancipation of Dalits.

Upper-caste Hindus such as Mannathu Padmanabhan participated in movements to abolish untouchability against Dalits; Padmanabhan opened his family temple to Dalits for worship. Narayana Guru, a pious Hindu and an authority on the Vedas, also criticized casteism and campaigned for the rights of lower-caste Hindus within the context of Hinduism. The first upper-caste temple to openly welcome Dalits into their fold was the Laxminarayan Temple in Wardha in the year 1928; the move was spearheaded by reformer Jamnalal Bajaj. The caste system has also been criticized by many Indian social reformers. Some reformers, such as Jyotirao Phule and Iyothee Thass, argued that the lower caste people were the original inhabitants of India, who had been conquered in the ancient past by "Brahmin invaders." Mahatma Gandhi coined the term Harijan, a euphemistic word for untouchable, literally meaning Sons of God. B. R. Ambedkar, born in Hindu Dalit community, was a heavy critic of the caste system. He pioneered the Dalit Buddhist movement in India, and asked his followers to leave Hinduism, and convert to Buddhism. India's first Prime Minister, Jawaharlal Nehru, based on his own relationship with Dalit reformer Ambedkar, supported the eradication of untouchability for the benefit of the Dalit community. In 1936, the Maharaja proclaimed that "outcastes should not be denied the consolations and the solace of the Hindu faith". Even today, the Sri Padmanabhaswamy temple that first welcomed Dalits in the state of Kerala is revered by the Dalit Hindu community.

CONTEMPORARY CRITICISM

Organizations such as the Rashtriya Swayamsevak Sangh have actively criticized the caste system. Some activists consider the caste system a form of racial discrimination. At the United Nations Conference Against Racism in Durban, South Africa in March 2001, participants condemned discrimination based on the caste system and tried to pass a resolution declaring caste as a basis for segregation and oppression a form of apartheid. However, no formal resolution was passed.

The alleged maltreatment of Dalits in India has been described by some authors as "India's hidden apartheid". Critics of the accusations point to substantial improvements in the position of Dalits in post-independence India, consequent to the strict implementation of the rights and privileges enshrined in the Constitution of India, as implemented by the Protection of Civil rights Act, 1955. They also note that India has had a Dalit president, K.R. Narayanan, and argue that the practise had disappeared in urban public life. According to William A. Haviland, however:

- Although India's national constitution of 1950 sought to abolish cast discrimination and the practice of untouchability, the caste system remains deeply entrenched in Hindu culture and is still widespread throughout southern Asia, especially in rural India. In what has been called India's "hidden apartheid", entire villages in many Indian states remain completely segregated by caste. Representing about 15 percent of India's population—or some 160 million people—the widely scattered Dalits endure near complete social isolation, humiliation, and discrimination based exclusively on their birth status. Even a Dalit's shadow is believed to pollute the upper classes. They may not cross the line dividing their part of the village from that occupied by higher castes, drink water from public wells, or visit the same temples as the higher castes. Dalit children are still often made to sit in the back of classrooms.

Sociologists Kevin Reilly, Stephen Kaufman and Angela Bodino, while critical of casteism, conclude that modern India does not practice any apartheid since there is no state-sanctioned discrimination. They write that casteism in India is presently "not apartheid. In fact, untouchables, as well as tribal people and members of the lowest castes in India benefit from broad affirmative action programmes and are enjoying greater political power."</ref> The Constitution of India places special emphasis on outlawing caste discrimination, especially the practice of untouchability.

CASTE AND RACE

Allegations that caste amounts to race were addressed and rejected by B.R. Ambedkar, an advocate for Dalit rights and critic of untouchability. He wrote that "The Brahmin of Punjab is racially of the same stock as the Chamar of Punjab. The Caste system does not demarcate racial division. The Caste system is a social division of people of the same race", Such allegations have also been rejected by sociologists such as Andre Béteille, who writes that treating caste as a form of racism is "politically mischievous" and worse, "scientifically nonsensical" since there is no discernible difference in the racial characteristics between Brahmins and Scheduled Castes.

He states, "Every social group cannot be regarded as a race simply because we want to protect it against prejudice and discrimination". The Indian government also rejects the claims of equivalency between caste and racial discrimination, pointing out that the caste issues are essentially intra-racial and intra-cultural. Indian Attorney General Soli Sorabjee insisted that "he only reason India wants caste discrimination kept off the agenda is that it will distract participants from the main topic: racism. Caste discrimination in India is undeniable but caste and race are entirely distinct". Many scholars dispute the claim that casteism is akin to racism. Sociologist M. N. Srinivas has debated the question of rigidity in caste. Others have applied theoretical models to explain mobility and flexibility in the caste system in India.

According to these scholars, groups of lower-caste individuals could seek to elevate the status of their caste by attempting to emulate the practices of higher castes.

In her book Democracy and Authoritarianism in South Asia, Pakistani-American sociologist Ayesha Jalal writes, "As for Hinduism, the hierarchical principles of the Brahmanical social order have always been contested from within Hindu society, suggesting that equality has been and continues to be both valued and practiced." In India, some observers felt that the caste system must be viewed as a system of exploitation of poor low-ranking groups by more prosperous high-ranking groups. In many parts of India, land is largely held by high-ranking property owners of the dominant castes, who economically exploit low-ranking landless labourers and poor artisans. Matt Cherry claims that karma underpins the caste system, which traditionally determines the position and role of every member of Hindu society.

Caste determines an individual's place in society, the work he or she may carry out, and who he or she may marry and meet. According to him, Hindus believe that the karma of previous life will determine the caste an individual will be (re)born into. On 29 March 2007, the Supreme Court of India, as an interim measure, stayed the law providing for 27 per cent reservation for Other Backward Classes in educational institutions. This was done in response to a public interest litigation — Ashoka Kumar Thakur vs. Union of India. The Court held that the 1931 census could not be a determinative factor for identifying the OBCs for the purpose of providing reservation. The court also observed, "Reservation cannot be permanent and appear to perpetuate backwardness". However, the Supreme Court later upheld the reservation.

8

Human Rights and Dalit Women

All human beings have the right to live as human beings. Human rights are not conferred or given. They already exist in society. The concept of human rights aims at protection of rights like right to life, liberty and property. These rights are attributed to human beings irrespective of class, caste, gender, colour and religion. The Universal Declaration of Human Rights was unanimously adopted by the UN General Assembly on December 10th, 1948. The preamble of Indian constitution adequately empowers the central and state government to eliminate human rights violation in the country. Inspite of these international and national declarations and resolutions, human rights are violated in different countries all over the world.

In Indian society, due to the social barriers such as castetism, untouchability, patriarchy, disparity, superstition, religious exploitation and class variations, specific groups are becoming weaker and marginalised. These groups are facing the problems of identity crisis, deprivation, discrimination and atrocities. These marginalised groups are also identified and recognised as dalits, SC (scheduled castes) ST (scheduled tribes), OBC (other backward castes) NT (nomadic tribes) DT (denotified tribes) religious and linguistic minorities. Violence on human beings in any form results in violation of human rights. Human rights of dalits and women in general are normally violated by high castes and powerful communities to practice and exhibit patriarchy and castetism. But human rights of dalit women are violated extremely and in peculiar form. Dalit women are in worst position than dalits in general, in terms of sex ratio, wages, employment, occupation, assets, education, health, social mobility and political participation. Hence, it is important to discuss the status of dalit women and various problems they face even after 60 years of independence. This article makes an attempt to discuss basic facts, issues and concerns related to dalit women to suggest some alternatives to combat violation of their rights for social justice and equality. Explanation of relevant terms such as 'dalit', 'dalitism', and 'dalit women', is given below to broaden understanding about the issue. Further, the vulnerable situation of dalit women is also discussed in detail.

DALIT

Dalit is not a new word. Apparently it was used in the 1930's as a Hindi and Marathi translation of 'depressed classes'. The British used this term for what are now called the scheduled caste. Dr. Ambedkar chose the term 'broken men', as English translation of 'Dalit', to refer to the original ancestors of the untouchables. Dalit Panthers, the youth activists from dalit community revived the term and in their 1973 manifesto expanded its reference to include the scheduled tribes, neo Buddhists, the working people, the landless and poor peasants, women and also those who are being exploited politically, economically in the name of religion.

DALITISM

Dalitism essentially implies conditions of subjugation; economic, political, social and cultural. Dalitism also embodies different degrees of marginalisation. It includes not only marginalized status in the economic sphere but also in cultural, political, religious and social domains. That means Dalitism symbolizes marginalisation. It is a well known fact that marginalisation denies basic human rights and social justice.

DALIT WOMEN

Dalit women are one of the most marginalized segments in the society. The condition of dalit women is more vulnerable than non-dalit women.

Dalit women are suffering from multi-disadvantages:

- of being dalit *i.e* socio-economically and culturally marginalized section,
- being women and sharing the gender based inequalities and subordination

To explore these and other crucial issues concerning dalit women there is need to discuss some basic facts concerning the vulnerable situation of dalit women.

VULNERABLE STATUS OF DALIT WOMEN

It is easy for the historically dominating caste and gender to violate human rights of dalit women who are at the lowest rung of the hierarchical ladder. The type of violence inflicted on dalits is in the form of severest violation of human rights. Dalit and tribal women are raped as part of an effort by upper caste leaders, land lords and police to suppress movements to demand payment of minimum wages, to settle share cropping disputes or to reclaim lost lands.

The recent incident of Khairlanji Massacare is not something new. A dalit family had refused to let upper caste villagers built a road through their fields. Hence on September, 29th, 2006, Bhaiyalal Bhotmange's family, – wife Surekha, daughter Prinyanka and two sons were killed by the villagers of

Khairlangi in Bhandra district of Maharashtra. They were first attacked with huge iron chains and than abused by the other caste women of the village. Surekha and Priyanka were paraded naked and raped, and later, their bodies were mutilated and thrown into a pond.

This shows that dalit women are easy targets for any perpetrator Upper caste considers them to be sexually available. Hence they are largely unprotected by the state machinery. Further, there is prevalence of violence, making dalit women eat human excreta, parading them naked, gang- rape, murder, dacoity, robbery and burning of their huts or communities. These are the types of crime, which violate their human rights. According to SC/ST commission report between 1981 and 1986 about 4000 dalit women became victim of rape. In 1993 –94 this figure rose to 798 and 992 respectively. This means annually about 700 dalit women fall prey to sexual assault by high caste people. The main complaints of the poorer dalit women are that they have no good houses. In urban areas most of them stay in unhygienic slums and in rural areas their houses are away from main stream society. Under conditions of grinding poverty and severe exploitation at work place, dalit women also suffer caste specific ban on water access from upper castes and may be beaten up in their own houses as well. At the outset, prevailing caste and secondary status of women in the society is largely responsible for violation of human rights of dalit women. To understand the root cause of the situation it is essential to examine basic factors responsible for their vulnerability.

SOCIO-CULTURAL AND RELIGIOUS FACTORS

First and foremost dalit women are victims of social, religious and cultural practices like Devdasis and Jogins. In the name of these practices, village girls are married to God by their helpless parents. These girls are then sexually exploited by the upper caste landlords and rich men and directed in to trafficking and prostitution. In his autobiography, Kale has described a ritual called 'chira'. The literal meaning of the word 'chira', is to cut or break. In this ritual when a girl from the lower caste community reaches the age of puberty, an elderly prestigious man from the higher caste breaks the hymen of the girl child by sexual act. This ritual is performed in a way to make the girl accept this fact as a routine practice.

The 28th report of SC/ST commission reported that in February 1986 there were about ten thousand Jogins belonging to SC in Nizamabad district of Andhra Pradesh. The survey submitted by the district collector to Schedule Caste Finance Corporation revealed prevalence of 15,850 cases. Eighty percent of these Jogins belonged to SC. This data is just an example of one district of the country. Practices such as Chira, Jogins, Devdasi which are prevalent even today are harmful and threaten the dignity of dalit women and violate their human rights.

EDUCATIONAL STATUS

Low level of education is a problem in itself and in turn gives rise to many other problems.. In 1991, literacy among the dalit women was indeed quite low. In rural areas only 19.46 percentage women were literate. A report published by Ministry of Welfare, Government of India in 1998 showed that there is much difference in the literacy rate of dalits and non-dalits in general, and gender specific.

Literacy rate of non-dalits is 64.13 per cent and literacy rate of women is 39.29 per cent, where as dalit women's literacy rate is only 23.76 per cent. There is a large disparity in the literacy rate due to wide spread prejudice based on castetism and patriarchy against dalits and women in general and dalit women in particular.

ECONOMIC DEPRIVATION AND UNEMPLOYMENT

A careful look at the economic situation of dalit women reveals that their workforce structure is such that they rarely own any land. A large majority of them are agricultural labourers. The rate of unemployment among them is also quite high. About 90 per cent of women working in unorganized sector are mainly from lower castes. In 1991, about 71 per cent of dalit women workers in rural area were agricultural labourers. Only 19 per cent of them owned land.

A prominent researcher and sociologist while sharing her experience from a research on gender and land issue, informed that, when she enquired with dalit women about land owned by them in their names, they wondered about permissibility of owning land in their name. This indicates that neither do they own any land nor are they aware of their rights on land. When enquiries were made with Stri-mukti sanghatana and Prerana, Mumbai based organizations working on the issue of rag picking and prostitution respectively, to ascertain the proportion of dalit women in these occupations, it was learnt that NGOs usually do not keep record of caste.

However, Human Rights Watch Report mentioned that a large number of dalit women are engaged in unclean, inferior occupation such as sweeping, scavenging and working in dumping grounds, rag picking and also in prostitution. These women have to face steep discrimination in the matters of social relation and employment due to their engagement in these occupations.

HEALTH AND NUTRITION STATUS

Dalit women's daily diet is the leftover of family meals, inadequate in quantity and quality. Health services are either not available in case of illness or unaffordable even if available. In addition to that, due to early marriage and too many pregnancies their health is always at risk. If birth control is practiced at all, 91 per cent cases of tubetomy are performed on the women who have to carry the burden of family planning. In an overall situation where dalits are prone to ailments in general, women suffer from more serious and more varied kind of sickness. More than 80 per cent of women in reproductive age group (15 to 45) are anemic. Poor health status of dalit women pushes her then into more vulnerable situation

POLITICAL STATUS

Women constitute half of total population, but are unable to get equal share in active politics. Their socio-economic status directly depends on their participation in politics. Political parties in India speak much about equality of women but have totally ignored the dalit women. Traditionally, leadership in the village was confined to 'rural elites', who were aged and belonging to higher castes. In the year 1993, 73rd amendment in the constitution granted reservation to dalits, tribals and women in local government.

This amendment made it compulsory that one third of the seats reserved for dalits be filled by dalit women. In some states, there has been little or no acceptance of reservation for the lower castes and dalit women by the upper castes. This has resulted in atrocities against panchayat members including women. Dalits who stood for election were beaten, and dalit women were raped and ill-treated. The members of the higher castes, who are not prepared to relinquish power to the lower castes, grabbed their land. An easier method to retain power is to put-up proxy candidates but keep the control in the hands of the dominant castes, always men.

The incapacity of women, particularly dalit women, to assert their rights is at the root of the problem. The reservation for dalits, particularly for women, is accepted in form but seldom in substance. Any change in the status quo is resisted. Dalit women's sitting on chairs is seen as threat to social hierarchy. So, the upper castes in the village vetoed chairs in the panchayat office Dalit women also faced many problems in performing their duties due to illiteracy, lack of information and dependency on the male members of their families. An important obstacle is the no-confidence motion against dalit women as pradhan by the dominant sections.

Rural elites are unable to accept the power, which has been given into the hands of the poorer and disadvantaged women. Despite recognition and legal sanction for political rights, rigid caste system and patriarchy directly and indirectly has been suppressing dalit women and violating their political rights. This proves that human rights of dalit women are violated right from her family to the society at large by one and all.

All these factors are largely responsible for the precarious position of dalit women as far as their social, cultural, religious, economic, health and political status in the society is concerned. These factors force them to mutely allow violation of their civic and human rights. Thus they become victims of universal violence.

EFFORTS TO PROTECT HUMAN RIGHTS OF DALIT WOMEN

With the realization that violence is one of the potent threats to the peaceful existence of human beings, whole hearted and all round efforts are made at international, national and local level. The preamble to the Universal Declaration of Human Rights (UDHR) serves as a foundation and philosophy of Human rights.

There are a host of international conventions including those for prevention and punishment of genocide and elimination of all forms of racial and gender based discrimination. The World Conference Against Racism (WCAR) related to racial discrimination, xenophobia and intolerance held in Durban, South Africa in 2001, brought the issue of caste and untouchability based discrimination on the agenda of UN Conference in Durban. Among the several organisations, the National Campaign on Dalit Human Rights (NCDHR) – a collective of dalit NGOs, other NGOs, academicians', activists and large number of supporters spearheaded the national campaign in India for inclusion of the issue of caste and untouchability based discrimination in the Durban Conference.

The preamble of Indian constitution adequately empowers the central and state government to eliminate human right violation in the country Article 17 of the constitution provides for removal of untouchability. Based on this article Protection of Civil Rights Act' (PCR), was passed in 1955. However, there was no conviction/ under this Act hence, Thirtyfour years after the introduction of PCR Act, the Scheduled Caste and Schedule Tribes (Prevention of Atrocities) Act 1989 was enacted to bring various forms of atrocities to an end. In this Act the complainant is given more weightage. There are stringent provisions against the police for negligence (Pandit)

EMERGING IDENTITY OF DALIT WOMEN AND FORMATION OF DALIT WOMEN'S ORGANIZATIONS

The focus on education of low caste women is one of the important factors responsible for the emerging identity of Dalit women. Reformist intervention by Savitribai and Mahatma Phule of opening school for untouchable girls way back in 1848 was a turning point for changing status of dalit women.. Dr. Ambedkar's thought and action made important differences in the lives of dalit women. His movement and especially his organisations encouraged many dalit women to become educated to be active in public life and to gain leadership, self respect in the contemporary period encouraged women to participate in organisation for dalit women at regional, state and national level..

After independence in 1960's and 70's, the dalit movement and women's movement emerged to demand their rights against caste and gender respectively. However, specific problems of dalit women were not acknowledged by these movements. Hence in 1990's there were several special, independent and autonomous assertions of dalit women's identity; a case in point is the formation of National Federation for Dalit Women (NFDW) and All India Dalit Women's Forum (AIDWF) at the state level. The Maharashtra Dalit Mahila Sanghatana (MDMS) was formed in 1995. A year earlier, the women's wing of Bhartiya Republican Party (BRP) and the Bahujan Mahila Sangha (BMS) was set up the Bahujan Mahila Parishad. In December 1996, at Chandrapur, a Vikas Vanchit Dalit Mahila Parishad (VVDMP) was organised and a proposal to commemorate 25th December (the day on which Ambedkar had set Manu smriti on fire) as Bhartiya Smriti Divas was advanced. The Christi Mahila Sanghatana, an organisation of Dalit Christian Women was established in 1997.

These organisations have come together on several issues such as celebration of Bhartiya Stree Mukti Divas and on the issue of reservation for OBC women in parliament bodies. Indian Association of Women Studies (IAWS) network with dalit feminist across different regions had brought special issues on problems and identity of dalit women. Several efforts have been made since independence to secure human rights of women in general and dalit women in particular. Despite this, human rights of dalit women are seen to be violated in different forms. Such infringement of human rights echoes the need of evolving suitable mechanism to empower dalit women to assert for equal rights and justice in order to live a dignified life.

MECHANISM TO STRENGTHEN THE CAPACITY OF DALIT WOMEN

To be human is to respond to human sufferings and pain with compassion and effective concern. It is not enough to feel with the dalit women in their pain, There is more need for effective action, otherwise it would be just sentimentalism' says Sequeira in his article 'Human Response to Dalit Women. The needs and the problems of dalit women differ with city, village, area and caste.

It is essential to keep in mind that dalit women are not mere individuals but belong to a sociological and dialectical system. Therefore to recognise the system and to prohibit violation, first and foremost proper perspectives about the issues has to be developed among all by considering following suggestions:

AWARENESS FOR ASSERTION

Extensive reading of available literature can be done by young generation to understand the profile and problems of dalit women. Factual incidents and success stories of dalit women namely, 'We made History Too' by Meenakshi Moon and Urmila Pawar can be included in the educational texts.

ACCESS AND EXPOSURE VISITS

Special exposure visits to dalit localities can be organised for school and college students to assess basic amenities accessible to dalit women namely, water, electricity, health and hygiene. Similarly dalit women's visit to urban structured colonies can be arranged to impress upon the importance of standard of living of non-dalits. Such purposeful visits will broaden their horizons resulting in improved living of marginalised section.

ACADEMIC ACTIVITIES

Academic institutions need to be encouraged to undertake studies to assess the problems of violence and atrocities against dalit women as also the reasons therefore and to work out ways to overcome them. Thought provoking sessions on harmful social religions practices namely, Chira, Devdasi, Jogin need to be held for basic understanding and effective interventional strategies.

CAMPAIGNS AND SESSIONS

Campaigns for equal and rational distribution of natural resources among weaker sections can be organised to secure their rightful means of livelihood. Proper rehabilitation and shelter can be provided to those communities, which are out of the social periphery (NT/DT) to protect them from the risk of sexual abuse.

INCLUSION OF DALIT WOMEN IN VARIOUS SYSTEM

More dalit women in their population proportion (16.5 per cent SC, 7.5 per cent ST) should be given chance to enter in the system like police, judiciary, education, health and politics. Sessions can be organised for dalit activist and women activists to sensitize them about the magnitude of torture and oppression faced by the dalit women. Legal education dealing with protection of human rights of dalits and Prevention of Atrocities Act (1989) can be organised to prevent the problems of castism.

DALIT WOMEN'S RIGHT TO POLITICAL PARTICIPATION IN PANCHAYATI RAJ

Direct political participation of Dalit women in local governance is a central human right in itself and enables the realisation of a host of other human rights. Political voice and decision-making power concerning basic services, economic development and social justice are critical factors in challenging and transforming structural caste-class-gender discrimination, and enabling Dalit women to realise their fundamental rights.

Political participation also demands accountability from state and non-state actors to guarantee and respect these women's equal political voice and development. This requires a transformation of power relationships both within institutions of governance and in the women's social environment. Recent legal and policy reforms in India to ensure the representation of marginalised social groups in decentralised governance, including Dalits and specifically Dalit women, through constitutionally mandated reservations in Panchayati Raj institutions bring these issues to the fore. They demand analysis to determine how Dalit women are enabled to claim their right to political participation in local governance, and the extent to which this participation is an effective tool for empowerment and realisation of human rights for excluded social groups. Annammal, quoted above, calls on Dalit women to persevere with the 'social revolution' that the panchayat system and reservations therein have started in India. At the same time, the more tempered words by the Dalit women panchayat representatives from Ahmedabad district are an assessment of the present political situation and indicate where change is required: formal authority does not equal political power.

Key questions therefore posed in this research are:

1. Are Dalit women able to access panchayat posts and, once elected, exercise freely political power and authority for the welfare of their constituency, Dalits and women in particular?
2. What factors and structures facilitate or inhibit Dalit women's access, participation and impact in Panchayati Raj?
3. What is the role of various state institutions in preventing and responding to obstructions against Dalit women in Panchayati Raj?

ACCESS TO PANCHAYAT POSTS

Only a minority of the 200 Dalit women in this research, approximately one-third, were able to act with independence and freedom to win the panchayat elections. Both personal factors such as education, experience on social issues, motivation to bring development to their community and others, prior performance in panchayats, political negotiation skills, as well as external factors including family support, good relations with other villagers, economic stability and family's political contacts, all played a supportive role in enabling women to access panchayat positions. Given the low social, educational, economic and gender status of these women, however, they could be challenged and overpowered relatively easily by dominant forces.

For the majority of Dalit women, the panchayat election process masks strong, caste-based patriarchal control over them and the enjoyment of their rights. Around 85 per cent of Dalit women were pushed into panchayat politics primarily by dominant castes or their husbands, the former often working through the women's husbands. Dominant castes also for the most part sought to directly engineer elections by consensus, thereby making the reservation policy redundant. The primary tool for this, and the most significant factor drawn from this research, was benami or proxy politics.

TACTICS OF CONTROL

The effective use of proxy candidature provided legitimised political space for primarily dominant caste men and secondarily Dalit men to exploit Dalit women, and reinforce their own interests and the suppression of these women. At the same time, this denied Dalit women's right to independent and empowered participation in local governance. For example, a dominant caste man in Anand district in Gujarat named Dalit woman Gangaben a consensus candidate for the panchayat President's post, alongside determining the entire panchayat membership and making his wife the Vice President. The night before the news of this consensus panchayat became public, the man came to Gangaben's house to tell her that she had been elected President while threatening to stop her husband's work if she did not allow him to control the panchayat administration through her.

To ensure success in proxy politics, various strategies were employed drawing on Dalit women's vulnerabilities: their low gender status in the family; their low gender, caste and class status in society; their old age or widowhood status; exploiting and deepening intra-Dalit divisions through supporting one sub-caste against another, often to prevent a more assertive or vocal sub-caste member from being elected.

Livelihood dependency and lack of sufficient financial resources to meet election expenses also made the women vulnerable to proxy politics especially from dominant castes and political parties. Further, traditional, and in Gujarat state supported, consensus politics was used to uphold the caste-class-gender hierarchical status quo. According to Dalit women elected representatives in Ahmedabad district in Gujarat, "Consensus candidates who get selected are usually illiterate, poor people who are influenced by dominant castes on whom they depend for employment.

Whoever becomes President through consensus always has to act as a pawn of the village." Similarly, Dalit women elected representatives in Cuddalore district in Tamil Nadu stated, "It is completely wrong to be elected unopposed or unanimously. This way of election is an instrument to strengthen the power of the dominant castes. Not only this, it is against democratic rights, freedom and equality. This is another kind of violence that dominant castes use against us."

ACTIVE OBSTRUCTIONS DURING ELECTORAL PROCESS

Control over the election process was also achieved through other means, aiming to prevent or discourage the Dalit women from filing nominations or to force or push them to withdraw their nominations. This included pressure in the forms of caste and sexually-based abuse, allegations of immoral behaviour, threats, bribes and vilifying campaigns against women's capacity to govern, physical assaults and property destruction. It further included restrictions on freedoms through social norms preventing movement outside the home for campaigning, livelihood demands and compulsions of household responsibilities.

Obstructions also arose as a result of Dalit caste or sub-caste assertion, with identity politics playing a major role in the electoral process. A clear example was when dominant castes put up candidates from a smaller Dalit sub-caste, or divided the Dalit vote by supporting multiple candidates from one Dalit sub-caste to contest. This was done in order to obstruct independent and active Dalit women supporting Dalits' interests from nominating for panchayat posts, thereby challenging the norms of dominant caste authority and control.

As a result of mainly dominant caste efforts, therefore, 34 women failed to secure a panchayat seat. Likewise, rival Dalit women candidates and their families sometimes obstructed women in their efforts to secure the reserved seat for their own sub-caste or other interests, or to ensure that Dalit interests were represented in the panchayat rather than dominant caste interests through proxy Dalit candidates.

The obstructions 10.5 per cent of the women faced – primarily from dominant castes and other Dalit candidates/families – were heightened on the election day, when widespread breaches of the rule of law and electoral process were evident. Illegal voting practices included threatening or physically preventing the women candidates or other Dalits from voting or entering the election booths, attempted bogus voting, bribes given to voters to vote for rival candidates, and harassment or assault against the women. Further, 15.1 per cent of Dalit women also faced problems following the release of election results, thus being denied their right to post-election safety and security.

Overall then, out of the 200 Dalit women interviewed, 166 women entered into the panchayats as either presidents or members. Out of these women, 83.7 per cent did so through elections, 13.9 per cent were nominated as consensus candidates and 2.4 per cent were elected unopposed. The predominance of Dalit women entering through seats reserved specifically for them worked on the caste and gender biased assumption that general women reserved seats are for dominant caste women and SC reserved seats are for Dalit men. Dalit women then are effectively ghettoised into those seats specifically reserved for them.

PARTICIPATION IN THE PANCHAYATS

Once elected, dominant caste male control over panchayat resources and ingrained discriminatory attitudes continued to govern to a large extent the experiences of Dalit women panchayat representatives. At least three-quarters of these women were either proxies or faced strong opposition and obstructions while attempting to work for the benefit of their community.

The study findings confirm the Concluding Observations of the CERD Committee on the Indian Government's Report in 2007 that: "Dalit candidates, especially women, are frequently forcibly prevented from standing for election or, if elected, forced to resign from village councils or other elected bodies or not to exercise their mandate."

FULFILMENT OF PANCHAYAT ROLES

Only one-third of 119 Dalit women presidents were able to discharge their official responsibilities with freedom and independence. Taking three basic presidential roles, only 35.3 per cent of women called panchayat meetings, 31.9 per cent chaired them, and 27.7 per cent voluntarily signed resolutions. Only 26.1 per cent of women voluntarily authorised panchayat payments. Similarly, only 23.5 per cent of women approved contracts for panchayat development works. Instead, a number of women spoke of rubber-stamping panchayat decisions and signing cheques at the behest of others. The motive for these actions by dominant caste panchayat members, according to a group of Dalit women villagers in Madurai district in Tamil Nadu, is: "[They] think that if they allow [the Dalit woman President] to function in the panchayat, she will work for the welfare of Dalits. And if they allow this once, it will become a tradition in future, so she should continue to be subjugated under them. Thus they take away all responsibilities from her."

Power politics thus meant that dominant caste males, and to a lesser extent Dalit males and political parties controlled by dominant castes, were the real authority bearers in the majority of Dalit women headed panchayats. Data on proxy representation reveals that a little less than one-fifth of elected Dalit women functioned as proxies for their husbands and/or male relatives out of a total of 59 per cent proxy representatives, as compared to the one-third of elected women who were proxies for dominant castes and less than one-tenth for others including political parties. Thus the generally accepted assumption that Dalit women are mostly proxies for their husbands, like other caste women, was disproved through this research.

Further, while over half of the 166 elected presidents and members attended many or all of the panchayat meetings held during their term in office, only around half these women were vocal in terms of raising development-related and other issues in meetings. The remainder, most of them presidents, did not raise any new issues during meetings. For just over half of the 90 Dalit women who raised issues in panchayat meetings, however, their issues were never or only a few times discussed and approved. Moreover, what must be borne in mind is the number of women directed by dominant castes or their husbands as to what issues to discuss in meetings, essentially serving others' interests. Otherwise, especially Dalit women panchayat presidents often faced opposition and had to struggle to get their proposals discussed and approved.

ACTIVE OBSTRUCTIONS AND OTHER DISABLING FACTORS FOR PARTICIPATION

Around one-quarter of Dalit women elected representatives were restricted by others from active participation in panchayat council meetings. For example: they were prevented from attending; their right to speak was opposed; others spoke in their place; they faced caste or sexually charged abuse; others reinforced gender and caste norms on them in order to restrict their space for participation. Women who asserted their right to freely express their views in meetings were often negatively labelled as 'outspoken'. Dominant castes and men also refused to share knowledge that would enhance the women's administrative capabilities.

This was what a dominant caste Clerk did to village panchayat President Kowsalya from Coimbatore district in Tamil Nadu, in addition to which he wrote caste abusive words against her on the walls of the panchayat office, and along with dominant caste panchayat members tried to silence her in the panchayat. More internal reasoning for low participation of the women elected representatives, mentioned by 120 Dalit women elected representatives, concerned a number of interconnecting factors: their proxy status, fear, lack of self-confidence and knowledge connected to their poor educational status, and compliance with imposed traditional caste and gender roles.

Less than one-third of women came from families with prior political experience in panchayat governance and very few had previous personal experience. Viewed in light of the rotation of reserved seats, especially in Gujarat where seats rotate with every panchayat term, the implications are to limit rather than encourage active political participation; that is, Dalit women often were offered little chance to develop their political skills over a longer period in office. As little as 44.6 per cent of the women had never attended government organised trainings, while 75.3 per cent have never attended trainings organised by NGOs. Hence, only between 10 per cent and 20 per cent of the elected representatives had solid knowledge of their own responsibilities, development programmes, officials responsible, funding issues and redress mechanisms.

Further, 37 per cent of women presidents reported direct obstructions while undertaking their panchayat responsibilities, driven primarily from dominant caste men within or outside the panchayat. Note that the above percentage excludes the significant number of proxy presidents whose role was entirely appropriated by others. The obstructions referred to by the women included: being silenced or ignored; caste and sexually-based abuse; having bribes demanded of her; no confidence motions; denial of information on panchayat activities; harassment, threats and assaults on the women or their family members; etc. Village panchayat President Leela in Madurai district in Tamil Nadu was pushed to contest the 2006 elections as a proxy for the dominant castes. After the elections, they demanded that she submit title deeds to her house and land to them, to ensure that she would remain under their control during her term in office. Further, her panchayat powers were auctioned off to the highest dominant caste bidder. While eventually government officials intervened to arrest those participating in the auction, no further action ensued and Leela continues to be a proxy President for the dominant castes.

DISCRIMINATORY PRACTICES

The fundamental right to equality and non-discrimination enshrined in Article 15 of the Indian Constitution notwithstanding, 89.8 per cent of Dalit women elected representatives felt they were treated differently from other elected representatives in their panchayats. These 149 women attributed this primarily to their status as women and Dalits. Additional identities with negative connotations, such as widows or separated women, exacerbated discriminatory practices. A TDO's statement in Gujarat substantiates this data: "Dalit women elected representatives confront problems of traditional gender and caste practices. They have to face all these challenges at the time of election and even after election as well. The caste system is an obstacle which exists at all the panchayat levels in many different forms."

Even the Assistant Development Commissioner in Gujarat openly stated that Dalit women faced a number of problems because "no elected representative supports Dalit women directly." This was confirmed by a dominant caste village panchayat Vice President from Kheda district in Gujarat, in whose opinion "it is impossible for Dalit women to become capable elected representatives. If I make her capable, then she will go against me, so better not to make her capable." Contrast all this with the statement of the Assistant Director of Panchayats in Tamil Nadu that "Dalit women do not face any problems at all."

Aside from the caste or sexually-based abuse which over one-third of the women faced in carrying out their panchayat responsibilities, complex segregation methods surrounding seating arrangements as well as discriminatory practices related to water, tea and food were prevalent in the panchayat offices. These to a large part mirrored socio-cultural practices of untouchability prevailing outside the offices. Thus 38 per cent of women stated that they were not allowed to sit on chairs alongside other elected representatives in the office. The extent of enforced segregation in seating is evident from the case of village panchayat member Rajniben from Ahmedabad district; in her panchayat there were two chairs for the President and Vice President, two mattresses for other panchayat members and a sack on the floor reserved for her.

Over two-thirds of women still stood up when dominant castes entered into the panchayat office in deference to the latter's 'higher' caste status. Discriminatory practices related to water, tea and food in the panchayats were also manifested in a number of ways: 64.5 per cent of Dalit women reported that they were not able to drink water from the same container used by other elected representatives; 53.6 per cent mentioned that they could not drink tea from the same cups used by other representatives; and 38.0 per cent said that they could not eat food/snacks with the same plates/utensils used by the others while others indicated that food/snacks were not served in their panchayat offices.

DEVELOPMENT AND SOCIAL IMPACT

Few Dalit women elected representatives were able to exert any substantial influence in the panchayats to ensure development benefits for their communities, though many did put forward Dalit interests. Only 18.5 per cent of Dalit women presidents felt that they had a significant say in the distribution of development schemes. At one level, the positive development outcomes for Dalits and women that some Dalit women elected representatives achieved took the form of primarily small projects for basic amenities – roads, housing, drinking water, etc. rather than projects that would challenge existing gender-caste inequalities such as land distribution or alternative employment opportunities for Dalits.

According to a dominant caste union panchayat President from Coimbatore district, Tamil Nadu: "To be able to function in a way that ensured distribution of resources/funds to all sections of the panchayat community, as President I saw to it that development projects were distributed to each section. However, to prevent disaffection from the dominant caste communities, prior allotment went to them, and then only to the Dalits. It also happened sometimes that one section of the dominant caste community returned for another allotment or wanted to enjoy the allotment meant for the Dalit community, thereby making the latter forego its due share..."

IMPACT ON PROCESS OF RESOURCE ALLOCATION

The second level of outcomes relates more to changing institutional rules and resource allocations in favour of Dalits and women. On this front, there was little success. The women's ability to generate development outcomes remains significantly limited by government resistance in practice to the implementation of the Panchayati Raj system, including the full devolution of functions, powers and resources. Within this context, there was little evidence to suggest that the Dalit women panchayat representatives were able to significantly increase attention and resources to address the critical livelihood needs of Dalits or women. This was made apparent by their low participation in decision-making on the use of panchayat revenue, development and welfare funds, as well as in dominant caste male monopolisation of panchayat resources and benefits.

ACCOUNTABILITY IN GRAM SABHAS AND FINANCIAL REPORTING

Lines of accountability to one's panchayat constituency through the gram sabhas were disrupted most clearly in the case of proxies, where Dalit women elected representatives played no major role in convening these meetings and directing discussions on panchayat development works for the people. At the other end of the spectrum, a small number of active elected representatives stated that they were able to convene and preside over gram sabhas. In terms of financial accountability for funds received and disbursed for panchayat schemes, a large 59.6 per cent of women could not review how funds were spent, either by monitoring accounts or the implementation of development works. The remaining roughly one-third of women elected representatives personally monitored development works, or checked the accounts to ensure that receipts reflected the funds paid out for actual work done, or took concrete action when they saw people misusing panchayat funds.

OBSTRUCTIONS TO DALIT DEVELOPMENT

Many Dalit women presidents/members indicated the following factors behind low development outcomes for Dalits: others' influence over their decisions regarding development schemes to the detriment of the Dalit community; the panchayat did not prioritise Dalit development needs; their lack of knowledge of development issues and panchayat schemes; active obstructions by others affecting development outcomes. Obstructions included blocking approval of development projects; delaying the release of or misappropriating development funds; obstructing or not allowing approved development projects to be implemented; offering or demanding bribes, commissions or panchayat contracts; damaging or destroying panchayat property the women had seen built; caste and sexually-based verbal attacks on the women's personal character and performance, etc. Consequently, dominant caste economic control was maintained through the panchayats by channelling development benefits towards their communities as well as securing development contracts.

As Dalit woman elected representatives shared in a group interview in Kheda district in Gujarat, "At least we [Dalit women] get our seat due to reservation. But still we don't have any say in the panchayat because the dominant caste panchayat members, including the Talati, take away most of the ongoing work in the village as well as schemes available at the taluka level." Dalit women elected representatives who accomplished development gains for their communities, therefore, did so either individually amidst frequent opposition, or in several cases with the help of others. This included support from Dalit panchayat members, use of political party connections and support base in the panchayat, or negotiation with other caste panchayat members.

SOCIAL IMPACT ON STRUCTURAL INTERESTS

Research data showed little evidence of the third level of change envisaged by Dalit women's active political participation, that is, the restructuring of gender and caste social relations towards social equality and justice. What changes occurred were mostly at the personal and family levels. Examples of personal changes were: greater self-confidence; greater social contacts; greater freedom of movement; increased leadership skills; and heightened awareness of socio-political problems in society. The most common changes at the family level for 66 women were that families shared responsibilities in looking after the children while the elected women were fulfilling their official duties, consulted these women more on important family matters, and allowed them greater decision-making power in family affairs. Overall, greater freedom of speech in both the family as well as public spaces emerged as one of the most significant influences of active Dalit women's political participation. Further benefits included greater public participation and freedom of movement.

Changes to Dalit women's 'low' social status, however, were rare, reflecting entrenched caste and gender interests linked to dominant caste exercise of socio-political power and control over resources. Hence, while over half the Dalit women elected representatives felt they were more respected as a result of their position in the panchayat, few could exercise actual socio-political power and effect longer-term changes in social status. Village panchayat President Jasodaben from Surendranagar district in Gujarat was forthright in stating: "because I was President and useful to them, both Dalits and non-Dalits respected me, but they never supported me as an individual. That was also because of reservations; otherwise who really respects Dalits?" According to 34.3 per cent of Dalit women elected representatives, their political participation had generated some change among women, mainly that some women were able to speak up in their households and gram sabhas more freely.

Other Dalit women also increasingly recognised their own capacities for leadership and expressed greater willingness to contest panchayat elections. By comparison, only 28.9 per cent of Dalit women elected representatives indicated change in attitudes towards them from the Dalit community, mainly in terms of Dalits now approaching these women to represent their developmental problems to government officials; Dalits now settling disputes among themselves under the women's leadership; and other Dalits now feeling that they too had the capacity to play leadership roles in village administration. Some also noted greater confidence exhibited by Dalits as well as increased unity among them. The majority of the women witnessed little transformation of caste prejudices or reduced discriminatory practices either towards themselves or their community. Only 21.1 per cent of Dalit women elected representatives mentioned some change, mainly in terms of greater ability to interact with dominant castes as a result of their public office, greater freedom to walk along dominant caste streets in the villages, and being able to wear shoes while on official panchayat duties. To be noted, though, is that changes in support patterns, respect and attitudes of dominant castes towards Dalit women panchayat representatives that did occur did not include recognition of Dalit women's power and authority, especially as panchayat heads. This was most clearly highlighted through dominant caste support that was withdrawn following the women's support for Dalit development needs or assertions of independence. In the case of Kamachi, twice-elected village panchayat President from Coimbatore district in Tamil Nadu, she faced constant opposition from dominant castes during her tenure as President. Then, after her defeat in the 2006 election, her chair was removed from the office and the dominant castes performed a pooja to 'purify' the office. Only after this did the next dominant caste President come and sit on the president's chair in the office.

By contrast, negative consequences included the reinforcement of gender and caste hierarchies and dominance, thereby helping to preserve the inequitable political status quo and deter Dalit women from active political participation in future. These included fear and insecurity of life caused by harassment, threats and violence, and decreased self-confidence among the Dalit women. In the case of Reshmaben, in addition to an attack on her and other Dalits after she won the election to the village panchayat member's seat in Ahmedabad district in Gujarat, her sub-caste was socially boycotted by the main dominant castes. The instigation of Dalit sub-caste divisions by dominant castes in order to control the exercise of Dalits' political power also raises serious concern, as mentioned by 22.5 per cent of the women. This reality contrasts sharply with the recent statement of Prime Minister Manmohan Singh on the impact of reservations for women in local governance, which he asserted "constitutes a historic measure for gender equality. It has brought about a significant shift in public policy and in social attitudes towards women."

RESPONSIVENESS OF THE STATE

Overall, the Indian law enforcement machinery and district administration repeatedly failed in their national and international obligations to both prevent and respond to obstructions that Dalit women experienced while asserting their right to political participation. This denied the women their right to an effective remedy. These officials repeatedly failed to ensure the implementation of laws and to ensure access to justice for legal violations in relation to Dalit women's political participation. This demonstrated disturbing signs of impunity – impunity exercised in the name of caste power, leaving dominant caste and male perpetrators free from accountability. Dominant caste power therefore remained entrenched both within the state governance and law enforcement systems as well as the local social system.

WOMEN WHO DID NOT SEEK REDRESS FOR OBSTRUCTIONS

Given their socio-political situation, the majority of Dalit women kept silent in 71.3 per cent of instances of obstructions: most felt unable to oppose caste-class-gender norms and discrimination or feared dominant caste reaction, or felt it futile to raise protest or ignored or tried to resolve the problem with the support of their families. For example, Sareekaben, a village panchayat President in Surendranagar district in Gujarat, while taking strong action in response to violations at various times, also let many go by without action. This was because: "they [dominant castes] have money and contacts with the police station, bank, taluka and district panchayat, right up to the State Assembly. In such a situation, any person – no matter how courageous or determined – becomes tired of fighting and loses hope. ....the [dominant castes'] influence is everywhere."

WOMEN WHO DID SEEK REDRESS FOR OBSTRUCTIONS

Dalit women who did seek redress found more often than not that justice was not accessible for them. The women rarely approached non-state actors, especially from their community, with their complaints. This may be explained by various reasons, including the women's understanding that it was the government officials and other formal actors that were actually responsible for taking action to remedy violations faced by them, or the pressure on Dalit village elders to conform to dominant caste interests out of fear, or simply because of the women's lack of faith in the elders' responsiveness. Overall, therefore, just over two-thirds of non-state actors – mainly Dalit elders, traditional panchayat elders, political parties, NGOs, and family members – approached by the women regarding obstructions did not support Dalit women to achieve effective redress.

The most common recourse for those women who did take action regarding 28.7 per cent of obstructions, was to approach mainly government officials linked to the panchayats or the police. Just over half of responses from state actors – the police, administrative and judicial courts, government officials and government related bodies – also suggest a breach in duties. A total of 24.7 per cent of responses from state actors involved further obstructions to the women's efforts, such as chasing the women away, taking no action, demanding a bribe, and refusing to provide any assistance. Pressure or advice not to file any complaint, or pressure to enter into a compromise comprised another 17.9 per cent of state actor responses. Finally, 13.7 per cent of complaints led to registration, but state actors refused to investigate the matter or file a charge sheet, and 1.4 per cent of FIR cases went no further than investigation. This may be due to both compromises outside of police engagement or police refusal to take the matter further.

Far from the norm were the experiences of state officials being responsive to Dalit women – 5.5 per cent of state actors advised the women on how to approach the problem; 16.4 per cent investigated and resolved their problems; and 11.0 per cent filed the women's complaints, investigated the matter and helped the women to reach a compromise or solution. For instance, the District Collector helped Janaki, a village panchayat President in Cuddalore district in Tamil Nadu, by pacifying the Vice President who opposed her, and ensuring the construction of the road she had planned. Finally, a small number of cases went to the stage of judicial proceedings, with 8.9 per cent of state responses leading to court proceedings. Breaking down these cases, 4.8 per cent are still pending, 3.4 per cent had verdicts in favour of the Dalit woman and finally, in one case Shiviben, village panchayat President in Kheda district in Gujarat, lost against a no confidence motion brought against her when a witness turned hostile during the judicial proceedings.

INTERACTIONS WITH GOVERNMENT OFFICIALS

Government officials were often complicit in reinforcing dominant caste male power by adopting the role of neutral facilitator regarding Dalit women's political participation: that is, they failed to intervene when witnessing proxy representation and discrimination, or pleaded lack of power to take action. A BDO in Tamil Nadu stated, "During my tenure [as BDO], many Dalit women members and presidents sought my help. When they come to speak about their problems, their husbands accompany them and they only speak." In fact, some government officials suggested that their sole jurisdiction over issues Dalit women elected representatives brought to them concerned only development schemes and funds.

As an Assistant Director for Panchayats in Tamil Nadu emphasised, "There could have been caste discrimination or violence [in the panchayat]. But the panchayat representatives give more importance to administrative problems and not to any discriminatory practices. We cannot go and force them to talk about such problems... And it is not our duty or responsibility at all to respond to caste problems. We monitor only Dalit women's administration." The afore-mentioned BDO similarly pointed out that officials had no duty to take action on complaints of caste or gender based discrimination. This was confirmed by a TDO from Gujarat, who while noting the problems Dalit women elected representatives faced due to caste and gender discrimination, insisted that government officials cannot intervene in these practices as these are 'very sensitive and emotional issues for the community'. Thus, while constitutional provisions render illegal discrimination on grounds of caste or gender, and reservations in the panchayats aim to correct structural discrimination against Dalits and women, government officials expect those affected by discrimination to deal with such problems. The only conclusion to be drawn is negligence by these officials in the execution of their legally mandated supervisory roles over the panchayats.

For the 117 Dalit women elected representatives who visited government and other officials in connection with their panchayat responsibilities, positive indications are that 39.3 per cent of women had their invitations accepted by officials to visit their panchayats; 36.8 per cent mentioned how officials implemented schemes requested by them or otherwise supported them in implementing schemes; and 34.2 per cent stated that officials took prompt action on the women's requests or complaints. On the other hand, officials also harassed Dalit women elected representatives by making them frequent visit government offices to deal with the same matter, or delayed in implementing schemes despite repeated requests from the women, as mentioned by 23.1 per cent of women. Linked to this, 17.9 per cent of women had to wait for a long time to meet these officials to discuss official panchayat matters. A further 2.6 per cent of women also mentioned how government officials expected bribes in order to render any service to the women. Further, as noted by Jasodaben from Surendranagar district in Gujarat,: "Whenever I approached government officials, they never responded immediately and they didn't do work fast.

Only if they [dominant castes] approach do government officials respond quickly." Another 6.0 per cent of women experienced government officials taking little or no action on their requests. Finally, in the case of four women, they experienced overt forms of discrimination from government officials based on their caste and gender. Government officials also generally failed to adequately monitor the reserved panchayats, displaying a lack of accountability including turning a blind eye to corrupt practices such as the diversion of funds meant for Dalit development. The Indian state, therefore, appeared to limit its obligation to providing free access to panchayats, vis-à-vis specially protected groups such as Dalit women, via the reservation of panchayat seats.

This stops far short of ensuring that the women enjoy the benefits of this policy in its implementation – that they enjoy free and independent political participation. In a complex society structured along highly unequal caste-class-gender lines, to place the entire burden of safety and security in accessing political participation on the shoulders of Dalit women who are traditionally excluded from enjoying this right, and to expect them to act with freedom and independence in the electoral process, suggests abdication of state duty.

KEY RECOMMENDATIONS

The institutionalisation of the Panchayati Raj system – with all its aims and ambitions – must be further revisited on the basis of the core issues elaborated in this research. There are major weaknesses in the current interpretation and implementation of reservations in Panchayati Raj, as well as in broader strategies to transform a society pervaded by caste-class-gender discrimination. At present, these dramatically limit the ability of the panchayats to fulfil their core objectives of equitable development and social justice. Specifically, they impact negatively on the space for Dalit women to create development and social outcomes in line with these objectives.

Essentially, required reforms must recognise that political participation cannot be viewed in isolation: efforts to realise other enabling rights – especially the rights to education and information, to free employment, alongside the right to equality within the family and in society – must be integrated with efforts to ensure Dalit women's enjoyment of their right to political participation. Sustained systemic change requires multiple state and non-state actors at the state and national levels working together to influence formal and non-formal local institutions of power and to strengthen Dalit women's sense of confidence, skills, power and support networks. Creative ways must be explored, with Dalit women as well as Dalit men and non-Dalits, to capitalise on the success stories of Dalit women's political leadership, and cultivate their growth. Inspiring examples of Dalit women elected representatives speak of the great potential for further political and social reform through active participation in panchayat governance. Ultimately efforts must lead to a supportive environment for these women's political participation in order to transform access to and control over resources and benefits in society, as well as promote a human rights culture that itself demands accountable governance and equality for all.

TO THE GOVERNMENT OF INDIA, GOVERNMENTS OF GUJARAT AND TAMIL NADU

Panchayat Structure and Special Support Mechanisms:

- Effectively enforce the reservation policy by ensuring the rights of Dalits to freely and safely vote and stand for election and to exercise their full mandate if elected to their reserved seats. This includes adequate police and government official monitoring and protection of Dalit candidates as well as elected representatives.
- Devolve greater functions, funds and functionaries to the panchayats so that they have effective political authority and discharge their duties and functions as local institutions of self-government within the meaning contemplated by the Indian Constitution. This includes lessening bureaucratic control over panchayat programmes and making bureaucrats more accountable to the panchayats, especially as regards abiding by panchayat decisions.
- Institute quotas in the lower level bureaucracy for SC women and men, ST women and men, and women in general as per panchayat quotas, to ensure that government officials, especially BDOs/TDOs, are representative of these sections of the population. Moreover, the reserved panchayats should come under the direction of these government officials. Similar quotas should be established in the local and district police forces.
- Establish a specific office in each district to act as a support mechanism for Dalit, Adivasi and women panchayat presidents, including providing advice, training and information as well as monitoring their implementation of duties and interventions by others such as panchayat members and government officials. These offices should mediate and resolve problems encountered by the above panchayat representatives and ensure the efficient and effective running of the panchayats. Dalit and Adivasi women and men, as well as other women, should be all represented as much as possible in each office.

Planning and Budgets:

- Facilitate a mandatory process of village, taluka/union and district panchayats preparing a scheduled caste development plan with a clear gender component, which should become a charter to work towards the economic development of Dalit women and men in the panchayats.
- In Gujarat: Allocate separate funds to the Social Justice Committees, which can independently decide on utilisation of these funds. These funds could be used to organise gender awareness camps and camps on the SC/ST (PA) Act.

Gram Sabhas:

- Give the gram sabhas greater powers to monitor the functioning of the panchayats and decide on budgets and the allocation of funds and other resources, as well as the identification of beneficiaries for panchayat schemes. Village development plans should be formulated by the gram sabhas, which would then feed into development plans at the taluka/union and district levels. Information on gram sabha meeting agendas must be publicly shared in advance.
- Establish separate quorums for participation by SC women, SC men, ST women, ST men and women in general in gram sabhas and sub-gram sabhas.

Panchayat Administration:

- Make it mandatory for all panchayat cheques to be signed in the presence of members, for funds to be sanctioned with the signature of the panchayat president alone, and for all accounts to be compulsorily shared with members in all meetings.
- Mandate that in all government contracts related to common properties, these contracts benefit Dalits in proportion to their population.
- Announce incentives before the period for filing nominations to panchayat seats to encourage Dalit women to file nominations for general panchayat seats, and award these to Dalit women who win these seats .

Economic Development:

- In order to improve the economic conditions of Dalits in rural areas, necessary to facilitate their political participation, develop a national perspective plan with explicit short- and long-term goals for overall development of Dalit women within fixed time-bound targets and allocate separate funding for this plan.
- Enforce land reforms and land distribution to the landless on a priority basis and initiate a drive to remove encroachments on government lands and other common lands.
- To the State Election Commissions: Establish a small fund to provide limited basic financial support for election costs for Dalits, Adivasis and women in general falling within stipulated low household income brackets.

- Establish a minimum salary system for all panchayat president posts and members' posts at the higher tiers, with increased travel allowance, dearness allowance and sitting fees considering their powers and duties, to encourage less corruption and more transparency in the panchayat administration.

Monitoring and Accountability Mechanisms:

- Establish an autonomous statutory Directorate for all reserved panchayats at the state level to be headed by a Dalit/Adivasi woman IAS officer, and Assistant Directorates at the district level to function under the Directorate and to be headed by a Dalit/Adivasi woman officer below the rank of IAS. These two institutions should fall under the jurisdiction of the Legislative Assembly through the Governor, to perform such responsibilities as monitoring and reviewing the pre- and post-election performance of the reserved panchayats, and prepare annual reports to the Legislative Assembly. Gram sabhas as well as local non-governmental organisations focusing on Panchayati Raj should be made part of the monitoring mechanisms appointed by the Directorate in consultation with the Assistant Directorates, and the monitoring reports should be made publicly available to villagers in the gram sabhas.
- Make it mandatory for government officials in charge of Panchayati Raj to pay monthly visits to the panchayats and monitor development works in progress as well as, explicitly, issues of discrimination and other obstacles prevailing in panchayats. They should also check the panchayat accounts during their monthly visits.
- The District Collector should convene monthly meetings with all village panchayat presidents, and a separate meeting with presidents in the different categories of reserved posts – Dalit women, Dalit men, Adivasi men, Adivasi women and general women – on a monthly or bi-monthly basis, in order to understand the different needs and obstacles faced by these different groups, and to resolve their specific difficulties and problems. BDOs/TDOs attached to the respective reserved panchayats should also attend these meetings.
- Monitor regularly government training programmes to ensure women are attending and not sending their husbands in their stead, with sanctions applicable to government officials who allow this practice.
- Evolve strict government rules and programmes to eradicate the presence of proxy candidates, by ensuring that: at all panchayat tiers only elected representatives attend panchayat meetings and meetings with government officials; panchayat funds are sanctioned with the signature of the president alone; mechanisms for closer monitoring of panchayats with Dalit, women and Adivasi presidents; educational programmes for all
- Dalit, Adivasi and women presidents and members with little or no literacy skills; comprehensive mandatory training at the commencement of the term for Dalit women, Adivasi women and

other women on panchayat governance; establishing a rule that no two family members should contest elections for posts in the same panchayat.

- Implement strict legal sanctions against government and police officials who neglect to respond to complaints by persons who have filed nominations for panchayat posts or by elected panchayat representatives in reserved panchayats.
- Every five years, evaluate the performance of the panchayat institutions, with specific evaluation of all reserved panchayat posts, both presidents and members, and provide gender-and-sex data on the numbers and functioning of elected representatives, numbers of no confidence motions initiated and ending with dismissal, etc.

Policy and Legal Amendments:

- In Gujarat: Immediately withdraw the government Samras Gram Yojna policy and ensure that all panchayat posts are established through regular, democratic elections.
- In Gujarat: Promulgate a Government Order with a new rule to the Gujarat Panchayats Act 1993, to stipulate that reserved panchayats rotate after every two terms – *i.e.*, ten years.
- Amend both the Gujarat and Tamil Nadu Panchayat Acts to ensure that where it is a SC women or ST or general women reserved panchayat, the Vice President and Talati/Clerk are from the same reserved category.
- Amend both the Gujarat and Tamil Nadu Panchayat Acts to impose an additional burden of proof on panchayats which dismiss presidents from office using no confidence motions. In addition, the use of no confidence motions against Dalit, Adivasi and women presidents should be strictly monitored by government officials, and timely investigations carried out in all cases to ensure that these presidents are given an equal opportunity to serve out their entire term. In this regard, in Tamil Nadu sec. 205 Tamil Nadu Panchayats Act should be repealed so as to remove the discretionary powers of the District Collectors to remove panchayat presidents.
- Amend the SC/ST Act 1989 to include offences related to interference with Dalits' political participation: that is, any person not being a member of a scheduled caste or scheduled tribe forcing, intimidating or bribing a member of a scheduled caste or scheduled tribe to function as a benami for them; and any person not being a member of a scheduled caste or scheduled tribe instigating false or malicious no confidence motions or complaints against panchayat presidents with the intention to remove them from office. The latter offence could be created through a suitable amendment to sec. 3(1)(viii) SC/ST (PA) Act – instituting false, malicious or vexatious suit or criminal or other legal proceedings against a member of a scheduled caste or scheduled tribe – to include no confidence motions in the panchayats.
- Mandate the National and State Scheduled Caste, Scheduled Tribe

and Women's Commissions with sufficient powers, funds and staff to specifically enquire into acts of political obstruction or violence committed against Dalit women, Dalit men, Adivasi women, Adivasi men and other women elected representatives.

- Provide free legal aid for Dalit women panchayat representatives who seek access to judicial redress for obstructions in the performance of their official duties, and review the reasons why Dalit women are unable to access legal aid in many cases.

Capacitation and Support Measures:

- Conduct open information sessions in all panchayat union/taluka headquarters immediately after the announcement of panchayat elections on election procedures, the importance of reservations and Dalit, Adivasi and women's political participation.
- In addition to regular panchayat trainings for all panchayat representatives, devise and conduct special trainings for Dalits, Adivasis and women elected representatives, as closely as possible to the start of their term of office, in order to specifically capacitate them for their panchayat duties. All trainings should include a gender and caste perspective, as well as legal sanctions which apply to those who block Dalit women's political participation.
- Integrate gender and caste awareness training into all trainings for panchayat representatives, including methods of recourse in cases of discrimination and other rights violations towards Dalits, Adivasis and women. These trainings should further specifically focus on promoting a culture of inclusive development, accountability and transparency in the panchayat administration.
- Form associations/networks, or strengthen existing associations/networks of women panchayat representatives at the village, taluka/union and district levels with specific focus on the different experiences of Dalit and Adivasi women representatives. These should operate as both support networks to women elected representatives as well as an effective lobbying block to, among other things, restructure the allocation of resources for Dalit, Adivasi and women's development.
- Capacitate all officials concerned with Panchayati Raj, including election officers, rural extension officers and particularly lower government officials dealing with the panchayats, to understand and respond to issues of caste and gender discrimination, encourage greater information sharing and less bureaucratic control over panchayat development schemes, so that these officials are able to better monitor and support Dalit women elected representatives in the panchayats to ensure others do not coerce the women into relinquishing their powers.
- Conduct training programmes to increase the awareness and capacity of local police and the local and district courts to understand and respond to issues of caste and gender discrimination and violence, including in the panchayats. This should include awareness on

national and international human rights laws, in particular legislation concerning Dalits, and implications for these officials' duties.
- Ensure the universalisation of primary education among Dalit women, and promote their further education. Current strategies for increasing the female literacy rate, especially among Dalit girls and women, must be strengthened.
- Conduct a widespread social education campaign through the media and local fora on gender and caste equality and non-discrimination in order to support broad change in social attitudes towards Dalits, Adivasis and women in particular. One specific component of this campaign should focus on promoting inclusive democracy through the free and independent participation of Dalits, Adivasis and women in the panchayats.

TO CIVIL SOCIETY GROUPS

- Build up a widespread campaign and lobby the respective Gujarat and Tamil Nadu governments as well as the national government in order to strengthen political will to implement the political reforms suggested above. This includes applying pressure through monitoring and further exposing the failure of government monitoring mechanisms for panchayat governance.
- Conduct regular trainings on public speaking, leadership and managerial skills, problem solving and how to interact with government officials separately for elected panchayat representatives as well as those aspiring to become elected representatives.
- Address the female burden of dual responsibility between panchayats and households through greater education and economic programmes targeting Dalit women, as well as lobbying the government to implement or directly providing support mechanisms such as child care facilities.
- Initiate gender sensitisation programmes specifically aimed at Dalit men, to encourage them to extend greater freedom to women in their families and to support Dalit women elected representatives both within and outside the panchayats. Gender and caste sensitisation programmes should also be conduced separately for all male elected representatives as well as government officials dealing with Panchayati Raj.
- Initiate a political awareness campaign on the right to political participation by Dalit women and men, in order to highlight the importance of political unity across Dalit sub-castes and their participation for community development. As part of this campaign, facilitate and support discussions among Dalit elders, men, panchayat members, husbands and male family members about the importance of Dalit women's free and independent political participation.
- Initiate district-level sanghams for women elected representatives,

with a sub-group specifically meant for Dalit women, as a supportive network for all women and specifically Dalit women elected representatives. These sanghams should be strengthened through regular information inputs and capacitation trainings, and should then form a state-level federation. Support must be extended to the collective actions initiated by these groups, including their monitoring and taking action against government and police officials who fail to protect these women's right to political participation.

- Increasingly liaise with the media to expose discrimination faced by women elected panchayat representatives as well as highlight successful efforts and strategies employed by elected representatives.
- Independently monitor the situation of local reserved panchayats in order to ensure discriminatory and obstructive practices against Dalit, Adivasi and other women elected representatives do not take place, and if they do, are exposed and appropriate legal action taken against the perpetrators.
- Monitor the next panchayat elections, especially in reserved panchayats, in order to expose violations of the rights of Dalit and Adivasi women to access the panchayats and bring cases to the attention of the State Election Commissions.
- Political parties: Establish quotas on the numbers of SC women and men, ST women and men, and women in general, in their party structures, especially at higher levels of leadership.
- Political parties: Initiate specific trainings for all party cadre on gender and caste social norms and practices, legal rights and political participation for development, in order to foster a culture of accountability and transparency, as well as drive for local participation in development.

SEXUAL ASSAULT AND DALIT WOMEN RIGHTS

Vulnerably positioned at the bottom of India's caste, class and gender hierarchies, Dalit women experience endemic gender-and-caste discrimination and violence as the outcome of severely imbalanced social, economic and political power equations. Their socio-economic vulnerability and lack of political voice, when combined with the dominant risk factors of being Dalit and female, increase their exposure to potentially violent situations while simultaneously reducing their ability to escape. Violence against Dalit women presents clear evidence of widespread exploitation and discrimination against these women subordinated in terms of power relations to men in a patriarchal society, as also against their communities based on caste.

As the National Commission for Women has commented, "in the commission of offences against... scheduled caste [Dalit] women the offenders try to establish their authority and humiliate the community by subjecting their women to indecent and inhuman treatment, including sexual assault, parading naked, using filthy language, etc." Hence, violence, which serves as a crucial social mechanism to maintain Dalit women's subordinate position in society, is the core outcome of gender-based inequalities shaped and intensified by the caste system. This situation exists in India today despite constitutional guarantees of non-discrimination on the basis of caste and gender *(Article 15(1))*, the right to life and security of life *(Article 21)* and the constitutional directive to specifically protect Dalits from social injustice and all forms of exploitation *(Article 46)*.

Moreover, the Indian State has enacted a series of laws protecting the rights of Dalits and women, acknowledging the prevalence of discrimination and violence against these sections of society. A key law in this regard is the *Scheduled Castes/ Scheduled Tribes (Prevention of Atrocities) Act 1989*. The presence of laws, however, without concomitant implementation to ensure personal security to Dalit women, and without concerted efforts to emancipate the Dalit community and eradiate entrenched gender-and-caste biased notions of (in)equality and (in)justice, is not enough.

The Indian government has itself acknowledged that the institutional forces – caste, class, community and family – arraigned against women's equal rights are powerful and shape people's mindsets to accept pervasive gender inequality. If human rights are the legitimation of human needs, then the needs of Dalit women for personal security, socio-economic development and social justice are priority areas for intervention.

In order to understand, therefore, the reality of Indian society in general, and the Dalit community and Dalit women in particular, an analysis of caste-class-gender dynamics is imperative. It is only by adopting this three-fold lens focusing on the cultural and material dimensions of the intersection of gender and caste discrimination that a true comprehension of key social relations and social inequalities in India emerges. This analytical lens, grounded in Dalit women's subjective experiences, highlights how these women become instruments through which the social system replicates itself and systemic inequality is maintained: violence against Dalit women is systematically utilised to deny them opportunities, choices and freedoms at multiple levels, undermining not only Dalit women's dignity and self-respect, but also their right to development.

An intersectional casteclass- gender analysis also fulfils the need to make Dalit women visible to the public eye through exposing their reality of violence and disempowerment intrinsically related to their social position, in recognition of their selfhood and human dignity. Moreover, analysing these social relations which convert "difference" into systemic oppression and violence enables not only policy makers, but also women's movements and Dalit movements, to better strategise and implement policies and programmes towards the protection of Dalit women's rights: that is, programmes that facilitate wider processes of change, that ensure the comprehensive eradication of caste and gender discrimination and violence, and enable Dalit women to be mainstreamed into the planned development process in India. At the international level, examining patterns of violence against Dalit women can contribute towards an enhanced human rights understanding of racial and gender discrimination, as interacting factors perpetuating violence against racialised and often marginalised women.

And yet, very little information or government data exists today as regards the specific situation of Dalit women in the country. A study was initiated in 2004, therefore, to examine the forms and manifestations, frequency, caste and social status of perpetrators, causes, effects and responses to violence against Dalit women over the period 1999 to 2004. A total of 500 Dalit women were selected, based on information supplied by knowledgeable persons or organisations working with the Dalit community, from a sample of 32 panchayat unions/mandals/blocks falling within 17 districts of the states of Andhra Pradesh, Bihar, Tamil Nadu/Pondicherry and Uttar Pradesh.

These were women who were willing to speak out about their experiences of violence in either or both the general community and in the family, without serious repercussions for their personal security such as threats and further violence from the perpetrators, or renewed caste tensions in the village. The wide-ranging experiences shared by the Dalit women in this study, when analysed, reveal the multiple layers of violence that pervade their lives. Dalit women endure violence in both the general community and in the family, from state and non-state actors of different genders, castes and socio-economic groupings. An overview of the forms, frequency and locations of violence, perpetrators and causal factors for violence highlights the incongruence between Dalit women's reality and the universal right of women to freedom from any gender-based violence that results in physical, sexual or psychological harm. This data, therefore, serves as an indictment of both the Indian state and Indian society for failing to respect, protect and fulfil Dalit women's rights.

As an initial comment, it must be noted that the overwhelming majority of the 500 Dalit women's case narratives were never reported in the media. Given that these cases were selected, in collaboration with those working with the Dalit community, from a small sample, it is likely that many more unrecorded instances of violence exist.

The reasons for this "silence" when it comes to violence against Dalit women are that cases are not spoken out in public by the women themselves, or not reported in the media, or not registered by law enforcement authorities, or hidden by the Dalit women's families, relatives and community, or suppressed by the diktat of the perpetrators and/or the perpetrators' caste community. The effect is the creation and maintenance of a *culture of violence, silence and impunity* when it comes to violence against Dalit women. This further exacerbates the denial of their rights to security of life and basic human dignity.

FORMS AND FREQUENCY OF VIOLENCE

Twelve major forms of violence constitute the basis of this study, nine being violence in the general community – physical assault, verbal abuse, sexual harassment and assault, rape, sexual exploitation, forced prostitution, kidnapping and abduction, forced incarceration and medical negligence – and three being violence in the family – female foeticide and infanticide, child sexual abuse and domestic violence from natal and marital family members. The majority of the 500 Dalit women have faced several forms of violence over the past five years, either in one incident, or in a series of incidents of violence, in either or both the general community and the family.

The more frequent forms of violence that are perpetrated against the majority of Dalit women are verbal abuse (62.4 per cent of total women), physical assault (54.8 per cent), sexual harassment and assault (46.8 per cent), domestic violence (43.0 per cent) and rape (23.2 per cent), in descending order. Although the remaining forms of violence are faced by relatively fewer Dalit women (less than 10 per cent of total women per form of violence), this does not discount their gravity, precisely because of the qualitative factor of force present in these forms of violence.

Violence in the General Community

Verbal abuse from members of the general community, experienced by 312 women in this study, includes derogatory usage of caste names and caste epithets arguably amounting to "hate speech", as well as sexually explicit insults, gendered epithets and threats. One-third of these women have faced violence regularly, indicating the habitual nature of this form of violence. This verbal abuse also highlights the perpetrators' worldview wherein Dalit women are seen as without any rights in the "natural" caste hierarchy, as devoid of any entitlement to resources or respect, and as always sexually available without any requirement for the women's consent.

Verbal abuse often accompanied *physical assault*, perpetrated against 274 women in the study. Over 500 incidents of physical assault on these women were recorded, with 30 women facing regular physical assaults. This combination of violence further links in many cases to a spectrum of sexual violence, from *sexual harassment and/or sexual assault* (234 women), to *rape or gang rape* (116 women).

While many women had been raped in one or more incidents, when it came to sexual harassment and/or sexual assault, often the violence occurred several times or was regular, as was the case for 72 women. Where the male perpetrator has some social or economic hold over the woman, such as her employer, or simply belongs to a dominant caste, then this violence sometimes developed into regular, coerced or induced sexual encounters or *sexual exploitation*. In the case of the 44 women who had been sexually exploited, this violence was most commonly perpetrated through false promises of marriage or lifelong economic maintenance, made to Dalit women in order to sexually exploit them for a period of time.

Kidnapping or abduction of Dalit women, as experienced by 24 women, often led to their forced incarceration and even rape or sexual exploitation. The targets are Dalit women from the time they attain puberty. Hence, parents' fear of their daughters being sexually assaulted and thereby becoming "unmarriageable" explains why, especially in northern states such as Bihar and Uttar Pradesh, Dalit women are getting married at ages as young as five years. At the extreme end of the sexual violence spectrum also lies *forced prostitution,* experienced by 24 women across the four study states. Half of these women are Joginis, dedicated to temple goddesses from early ages in Andhra Pradesh and thereafter considered as religiously-sanctioned village prostitutes. Other women had been forced into prostitution after being sexually exploited by their dominant caste landlord-employers, or by their husbands, or in one case by the police.

Incidents of *forced incarceration* have been endured by 23 Dalit women, involving for some women false cases leading to their detention, or arrest and imprisonment. The failure of the police to fulfil their duty to uphold law and order in these cases stemmed from police negligence or bias in initiating these cases against the women. Otherwise, half of these women had experienced being incarcerated in the perpetrator's home, or workplace, or in some isolated or rented building, bringing in the element of kidnapping and sexual violence from various non-state actors. When it comes to *medical negligence,* doctors and nurses have also demonstrated failure in their professional duty of care towards 17 Dalit women, through careless or pressurised operations especially as regards family planning, or discrimination in turning away Dalit women in need of serious medical attention.

Violence in the Family

Within the family, *domestic violence* is prevalent. A total of 215 Dalit women have recorded regular incidents of domestic violence that span several years of married life. This violence often manifests itself in verbal abuse of the woman, accompanied by physical assault, but also entails sexual abuse including marital rape. Several cases of inter-caste marriages ending in domestic violence reveal caste and gender discrimination against the Dalit wife leading to violence.

In most cases where a Dalit husband is concerned, the violence takes on a strong patriarchal dimension: women are tortured within the home for not bringing enough dowry, for not bearing male children, for being supposedly ugly, or too beautiful, or allegedly unfaithful, for talking back to her husband, etc. Alcoholism among Dalit husbands is also a strong contributing factor to this domestic violence. Domestic violence resulted in some women being deserted by their husbands, or being forced to leave their marital home. For the majority of women, however, the social norms and pressures of married life and "duties" of wives to their husbands ensure that they continue to endure this violence. Moreover, as this violence often commences when they are but children given in marriage, their ability to question and stand up to this violence is often severely diminished.

Female foeticide and infanticide were not recorded as widespread among the Dalit women in this study, with only two women revealing the occurrence of this violence. By comparison, *child sexual abuse* in terms of particularly early child marriages and sexual relations with minor Dalit girls below the age of 16 years is more common. Otherwise, four cases of sexual violence from a brother, father-in-law, brother-in-law and fathers also emerged.

While only 23 girls had experienced child sexual abuse within the past five years, this must be viewed in the light of the fact that 282 women, or 72.2 per cent of the total women in this study, were married below the legal age of marriage of 18 years, of which 39.7 per cent were married below the age of 15 years. These early marriages indicate that the majority of women participating in the study would probably have been legally minors at the age of their first sexual encounter with their husband.

LOCATION OF VIOLENCE

The sites where violence occurs reveal another aspect of Dalit women's vulnerability, in that Dalit women are seen to be accessible in both public and private spaces for any acts of violence. The result is that they are denied spaces in which they can enjoy their rights to privacy and security of life. The majority of Dalit women have faced violence in *public spaces* – streets, women's toilet areas, bus stands, fields, etc. – in and around their villages and towns. The open or public nature of violence committed against them indicates both their specific vulnerability outside of the home, as well as the element of combined individual and collective community punishment meted out through particularly public physical assaults and verbal abuse. Many Dalit women in the study pointed out the perceived additional humiliation of public violence they face from dominant castes, as compared to the generally more private nature of violence committed against dominant caste women.

The next most common place for violence is *within the home.* Aside from domestic violence, a number of women have faced physical assaults, verbal abuse, sexual harassment and sexual assaults in their very home from non-family members. This reveals a common pattern of infringements of their right to privacy where perpetrators of violence invade the women's homes in order to attack and abuse them.

Violence in the *workplace* ranks third in terms of common locations for violence. This relates to Dalit women's greater work participation rates as compared with other women. Their mostly informal sector, daily wage labour occupations, bereft of employment security and many other rights, provide fertile ground for violence. Moreover, given their economic dependence, Dalit women often do not report violence from employers in the workplace, instead keeping silent in order to retain their means of livelihood. In addition, as many Dalit women either work in the perpetrators' home, or have to go there to receive their wages or ask for loans, etc., the *perpetrator's home* also becomes another site for violence perpetrated by general community members.

Finally, *government spaces* become grounds for violence particularly where medical negligence occurs in government hospitals, or where women are forcibly incarcerated, verbally abused, sexually harassed or raped in police stations. Otherwise, verbal abuse is the most common form of violence meted out in government spaces from a range of government actors including the police, district administration officials and doctors.

The multiple sites for violence against Dalit women indicate that while in the brahminical patriarchal system they have greater "space" in which to function as compared with dominant caste women, this space does not translate into greater "freedom"; in other words, while Dalit women are said to enjoy greater freedom of movement, interactions and work opportunities in the "public sphere" than dominant caste women, they do not necessarily enjoy freedom that is safe, secure, productive and progressive, and that ensures their right to choose and decide for themselves.

This is due to limits imposed, restrictions mandated and obstructions placed on Dalit women's movement in the gendered space of the "public sphere" which is mediated by caste; that is, public spaces where men, and particularly dominant caste men, predominantly operate. These public spaces are seized upon as opportune places for exercising power and authority over Dalit women as individuals and as a collective through violence.

SOCIAL STATUS OF PERPETRATORS OF VIOLENCE IN THE GENERAL COMMUNITY

Within the wide range of identified perpetrators of violence against Dalit women in the general community, *dominant caste landlords* emerged as the most prominent group. Landlords are the feudal landed class owning over 10 acres of land, and it is their continuing socio-economic and political power and authority in rural agricultural regions, as well as their connection as employers of many Dalit women agricultural labourers, that provide them disproportionate scope for perpetrating caste violence against these women with impunity. The violence they mete out is physical, verbal and sexual, often in response to Dalit women asserting their economic rights, that is, challenging casteclass relations by demanding their right to wages or land, or their right to sexual integrity, that is, the right to choice in sexual relations.

Police and forest officials, as well as *business people*, also emerge as key perpetrators of violence against Dalit women. Where police are not active perpetrators, they also act in a significant number of cases in collusion with the perpetrators by failing to enforce the law when violence against Dalit women takes place. *Goondas and thugs* also play a role in supporting other perpetrator categories in their acts of terrorising Dalit women with actual or threats of violence. Two other groups of perpetrators whose numbers are significant belong to the *professional category*, namely hospital nurses and doctors and teachers, and the *political category*, namely local political party leaders and elected panchayat members. In all these cases, except for *goondas* and thugs, these perpetrators hold positions of authority or positions entailing a duty of care and responsibility towards other people. Hence, their presence as perpetrators indicates their gross misuse of the power and authority conferred on them by virtue of their professions.

In addition, there are a large number of *"other dominant caste persons"* as perpetrators, for whom only their caste, and not other social status, has been identified by the woman victim-survivors. In other words, these are dominant caste men and women in the village whom the Dalit women have been unable to identify as having any specific social, occupational or political status in the village such as a landlord or teacher. Their significance lies in the fact that they are often ordinary community members who, by virtue of their "higher" caste status vis-à-vis the Dalit women, engage in violence against these women. Moreover, often this violence is committed by these perpetrators not only as individuals, but also as group violence involving people of the same status (for example, where landlords get together to attack a Dalit woman), or different status (for example, where dominant caste villagers join with panchayat or political party leaders to commit violence against a Dalit woman). The group nature of violence (particularly physical assaults, verbal abuse, sexual harassment and gang rapes) often against an individual Dalit woman highlights the particular vulnerability of these women where they are outnumbered by the perpetrators.

Finally, a number of *"other Dalit persons"* have been identified as either active perpetrators of violence against Dalit women, or colluders in the violence. While family members become perpetrators when it comes to dedication of their daughters as Joginis, Dalits often collude in violence when it comes to specific allegations against women of being "witches", or "loose women", or where Dalit women protest against the production and sale of liquor in the villages. Otherwise, their presence indicates both the inter-(sub) caste as well as intra-caste violence that exists within the Dalit community, albeit on a smaller scale to violence against Dalits by the dominant caste groups.

CASTE BACKGROUND OF PERPETRATORS OF VIOLENCE IN THE GENERAL COMMUNITY

Caste-wise, both forward castes (FCs) and backward castes (BCs) are seen to engage in violence against Dalit women, either as individuals or as a group.

Roughly equal numbers of women across the different forms of violence have faced violence at the hands of these two major caste categories. Dalit perpetrators are also present in significant numbers, as mentioned above. Their concentration lies in four forms of violence, namely physical assaults, verbal abuse, sexual harassment and sexual assaults, and rapes. Together, however, they account for around 10 per cent of all perpetrators of violence against Dalit women in the study.

While in some instances the perpetrators of violence belong to one homogenous dominant caste, there are instances where they cut across all dominant caste lines, that is, backward caste and forward caste. This is particularly so where the Dalit woman is seen to transgress established caste norms, for example, by asserting her rights in defiance of "untouchability" practices. The punishment meted out, therefore, takes on the form of collective punishment that is both expressive of caste outrage as well as instrumental in terms of teaching the woman and her community a lesson of "obedience" to caste norms. Otherwise, sexual violence against Dalit women often takes a collective caste aspect, in terms of gang rapes or forced prostitution.

There are also instances of violence wherein the dominant castes – whether forward caste or backward caste – draw in the Scheduled Castes (Dalits) to engage in violence. To be noted is that this tactic is increasingly utilised by dominant castes to thwart the applicability of the *SC/ST (Prevention of Atrocities) Act 1989*, which only applies to atrocities committed by persons not belonging to the Scheduled Caste or Scheduled Tribe community. Dominant caste and Dalit collaboration in violence is also often present in witchcraft cases, with the accusation of witchcraft targeted at the Dalit woman by her family, her community or the dominant caste community. Other traditions such as the Jogini system also yield multiple caste perpetrators of sexual exploitation against Jogini women, as do some gang rapes and some physical assaults where Dalits and dominant castes are engaged together in illegal activities such as logging or illicit liquor production and sales.

PERPETRATORS OF VIOLENCE IN THE FAMILY

As far as violence in the family is concerned, husbands, the Dalit women's in-laws, her relatives and husbands' relatives are perpetrators of violence, in descending order. Pressures exerted from both natal and marital families lead to female foeticide and infanticide, while child sexual abuse takes the predominant form of child marriages (as per the law rape of a minor refers to girls below 16 years of age, though a legal anomaly reduces this age to below 15 years in the case of a husband raping his wife).

Less commonly recorded forms of child abuse are incest (where fathers and brothers are perpetrators) and sexual abuse by other male relatives (by brother-in-laws and father-in-laws). Husbands are also the key perpetrators of domestic violence, followed by mothers-in-law, the women's other relatives, fathers-in-law and their husband's other relatives. Given that most of the Dalit women's natal and marital families are very poor, the day-to-day struggles for survival, caste oppression and gender oppression often translate into frequent violence against Dalit women within the home. In other words, the subjugation, and lack of power and authority in the general community for the women's husbands, marital and natal families, is often replicated in violence in the family, a phenomenon noted in many socially marginalised communities. This domestic violence is further bolstered by the internalised dominant caste ideology of wife fidelity (*pativrata*) and duty of chastity, placing premium on notions of women's "honour", "purity" and "obedience".

CAUSAL FACTORS FOR VIOLENCE

Violence in the General Community

In most cases of violence in the general community where the perpetrator belongs to a dominant caste, the Dalit women clearly identified their gender-caste-class status as the overall or key cause for the violence. Clear examples were given not only in terms of the *jogini* system or violence related to untouchability norms, but also more generally in terms of the petty reasons that often triggered violence against the Dalit women by dominant caste men, women and children (for example, trying to cross a dominant caste's fields, asserting equal rights to access water from common taps, or asserting the right to own economic resources). These reasons fall broadly into two categories: reasons related to coercive violence utilised to maintain caste norms or caste-based gender norms, and reasons related Dalit women's assertions of their rights by defying untouchability norms or asserting their rights to cultural, economic and political resources.

The verbal abuse that is integral to many women's experiences of violence also indicates the dominant caste perpetrators' worldview as regards Dalit women's 'inferior' caste, class and gender status, and consequent powerlessness and vulnerability. Built into the patriarchal caste system is the assumption that Dalit women are available for any form of exploitation and violence, as a consequence of their "low" and "impure" character, and hence the low character of their caste that does not deserve honour and respect. The impunity with which much of this violence is carried out reinforces the normality of this culture of violence. The gender-caste-class axis, therefore, provides the systemic base for violence against Dalit women; that is, this violence is an in-built component of the caste system.

As far as Dalit perpetrators are concerned, the majority being male, many assimilate and reproduce the gender inequality structured into the caste system by using patriarchal norms to commit violence against women of their own community. This is particularly manifested in terms of physical and sexual violence, where patriarchal norms of female subordinate status and submissiveness influence Dalit women's abilities to enjoy their sexual integrity, equality and dignity, freedom, life and physical security in particular.

Flowing from and interlinked with this systemic causal factor for violence (that is, being a Dalit and a woman), Dalit women identified four main discrete and overlapping categories of causal factors for violence against them in their recorded narratives. The primary identified factor for violence in the general community related to the issue of Dalit women's *sexual or bodily integrity*. Accompanying Dalit women's low caste status and the socio-economic and political power of the dominant castes is the latter's view of their superior caste and gender status and accordingly a perceived right over Dalit women's bodies. Dalit women are seen as sexually available as they move in gendered public spaces and engage in productive labour.

Sexual violence is understood in caste ideology as ennobling 'lower' caste women; that is, dominant caste perpetrators of sexual violence against Dalit women expect their "victims" to be grateful for the sexual attention they are receiving from 'higher' caste men. Sexual violence is also a tool utilised by dominant caste men to reinforce the caste 'impurity' of both the Dalit woman and her community, given the hegemonic discourse of women symbolising the group identity and bearing the honour of their community. Hence, socially legitimised reasons for sexual violence and its accompanying physical and verbal assaults against Dalit women include: the women's perceived sexual availability; retaliation against women who rejected men's sexual advances; reaction against women who expressed a desire to leave prostitution work.

A second frequent causal factor for violence in the general community directly links to *gender inequality and the 'natural' caste hierarchy* as often manifested in untouchability practices, and Dalit women's counter discourse of equality, rights, dignity and self-respect. As the caste system hinges on the power of the dominant castes to enforce caste-based rules, including those rules governing what Dalit women should and should not do as impure, low caste women, violence also serves a functional aspect. Thus another set of causes for violence – mostly physical assaults, verbal abuse and sexual harassment or assault – include:

- When women broke "customary" laws by trying to access places of worship, hotels or other public places on equal par with the dominant castes;
- When women allegedly disrespected the caste status of a dominant caste or the gender status of a Dalit male by speaking up, questioning, or raising their voices in protest or to assert their rights;
- When women tried to participate in religious or cultural life;
- When women tried to access water rights or the public distribution system (PDS) ration shop on equal par with dominant castes.

Almost as frequently identified a causal factor for violence in the general community lies in the area of Dalit women's *civil rights*. The violence is either a response to the Dalit women's alleged breach of caste norms by exercising their freedom of expression in speaking out on an issue, or seeking to protect her family or community, or as a means used to reinforce their submissiveness and voicelessness as demanded under the caste system.

These issues include: revenge or retaliation to settle scores with either the woman, her family or her community; response to the women when they questioned the perpetrator/s for violent acts done to them, their children, their family members or other Dalit community members; response to the women when they questioned illicit arrack sales or corruption in government schemes meant for Dalit welfare; where a male member of the woman's household was wanted for questioning by the police; where a woman scolded dominant caste children for destroying the *anganwadi* garden; where women were involved in a road blockade protest; resort to supernatural beliefs to explain sudden illnesses, or family pressures, that led to girl's dedication as a Jogini; doctors' carelessness or negligence in treating or operating on women; insecurity faced as a widow, or a Jogini.

A fourth causal factor for violence in the general community, given the aspect of economic exploitation built into the caste system, related to *economic resources* – land, or other economic resources/capital such as wages, payment for services, etc. – and particularly Dalits asserting their rights to own or utilise resources. Violence also related to Dalit women's poverty levels or economic status, in terms of their landlessness combined with their dependence on dominant castes for their livelihood; that is, with regard to work, wages and loans. Causes for violence related specifically to land and common property resources, being key economic resources in the villages, include: women and their families asserted their rights to own land; women tried to access forests or other common property resources; women questioned dominant castes for destroying, or for their cattle destroying crops; in order to appropriate the land belonging to the Dalit women or their families; reaction against Dalit women and their families owning or leasing land; retaliation for women allowing water to flow onto the dominant caste perpetrator's land, or allegedly wrecking the dividing line between their two fields.

Economic development factors triggering violence against the Dalit women include: where women failed to repay debts; women asked for loans; women asserted their economic rights by asking for monetary payment for services performed or goods sold, or loans given out, or their pensions; women asserted their rights to access government relief schemes or housing schemes; woman asked for the return of her ration card given as surety for a loan she had repaid; women attained or tried to attain a higher economic status than allegedly befitted a Dalit, such as by trying to become quarry owners; women won a contract to cook school midday meals; poverty that led the women's family to dedicate their daughters as Joginis, or that led doctors to discriminate against the women in providing medical care or be negligent in their provision of medical care.

Similarly, causal factors related to Dalit women's labour and work include: women protested against forced or bonded labour; women challenged working conditions; women questioned the delay or part-payment or under-payment or non-payment of wages; women asked for workers' compensation following their husbands' deaths; women allegedly arrived late for work, or allegedly did not work properly, or slept during work, or did not come to work due to illness; woman refused to clean her dominant caste employer's muddy shoes; woman did 'polluted' work of burying unwanted corpses; where a Dalit man wanted to wrest a woman's job away from her; where a dominant caste man did not want a Dalit woman working with him.

Seen together, these four afore-mentioned broad categories of causal factors indicate the crucial areas of sustaining Dalit women's lives, their integrity and their identity. Hence, Dalit women are often attacked in these vulnerable areas in order to deprive them of an economic base and economic independence from the dominant castes, to deny them civil freedoms to express their rights, to damage their bodily and sexual integrity as means of attacking their dignity and identity, all of which are necessary to maintaining their gender-caste-class subordination.

Otherwise, other causal factors that provoked violence include those related to Dalit women's *basic livelihood* outside of economic issues: women asserted their rights to access or enjoy housing, or water, or the public distribution system (PDS), or education, or open spaces for defecation; women questioned the perpetrator for polluting their housing premises with rubbish or sewage water; women asked for immediate medical treatment due to being in intense pain; women did not come to hospital early enough, or were not able to pay for medical treatment due to poverty.

In the realm of *political rights*, several Dalit women spoke of their assertions of basic political rights as provoking violent dominant caste backlashes. The issues that led to violence included: woman canvassed for votes in the dominant caste section of the village; women exercised or attempted to exercise their right to an independent vote in elections; women contested panchayat elections; women exercised or attempted to exercise political authority as elected panchayat representatives.

Another category of causes for violence relates to *relationship issues*, including: women asserted their rights to equality and dignity in relationships, by protesting against violence, or demanding fidelity from man in the relationship, or questioning man for deserting her; women allegedly had illicit relationships with other men, or allegedly were prostitutes, or allegedly encouraged others to have illicit relationships; women asked the perpetrators of rape or sexual exploitation to marry them; women accused perpetrator's son of having raped them; reaction against Dalit woman whose son married a dominant caste woman; women questioned perpetrators for abandoning them after having sexual relationships with them.

This category is very much related to that of sexual integrity, in that the causes for violence expose the underlying ideology of Dalit women's availability for illicit relationships, though not marriage, and the stringent punishments proscribed for inter-caste marriages. Moreover, the Dalit men's and Dalit community's control over Dalit women's sexuality is seen in their violent responses to Dalit women asserting their rights in relationships, or in punishing women whose so-called immoral behaviour allegedly influences other women to have illicit relationships. Two categories of causal factors are related, in dealing with the dominant caste discourse of *criminality* that claims Dalit women as inherently criminal, a consequence of, as well as reinforcement of, their alleged impurity and low caste status.

This discourse pervades conflicts and consequent violence arising out of accusations of trespass, or criminal activity. Examples of accusations of criminal activity against Dalit women include: alleged to be witches or accomplices to witches; allegedly helped bomb a police station; allegedly gave false evidence to the police; allegedly took firewood, or mud, or grass from the perpetrators' fields alleged theft from perpetrator's house or fields; alleged misappropriation of money from Old Age Assistance Fund.

Similarly, examples of accusations of *trespass* include: women's animals strayed into the dominant castes' fields and sometimes ate or destroyed some of the crops; woman bathed in the perpetrator's pond; women simply passed by or crossed the dominant castes' fields; women's animals or children went to the toilet in the perpetrators' fields.

The issue of trespass in particular is worth considering in the context of the systemic denial of economic resources to Dalits under the caste system. Where Dalit women are so often excluded from ownership or enjoyment of land or common property resources, and lack basic livelihood amenities such as toilets in their homes, then it would seem unrealistic to draw a line between public and private resources in villages. Unless issues of land reforms and basic public amenity provisioning, for example, are implemented by the state on a priority basis, can one speak of trespass by persons who are kept systematically excluded from such resources or amenities?

Finally, violence also took place when Dalit women sought *justice and the protection of the law* for violence done to them, or to forestall such action, by any of the following acts: women filed or tried to file a police complaint; women brought or tried to bring incidents of violence to the traditional village panchayat for arbitration; women refused to accept compromises following acts of violence; to prevent women from telling anyone of the violence or filing a police complaint; to prevent women from being witnesses against the perpetrators in a court case. This revisiting of violence upon Dalit women in order to forestall any efforts by them to seek justice, or to punish them further for daring to seek justice, functions to build, maintain and reproduce a culture of impunity for perpetrators and their colluders in violence.

Violence in the Family

Similarly, Dalit women faced violence in the family over a range of issues, suggesting the assimilation of the larger patriarchal caste system's norms by particularly Dalit men, with negative implications for Dalit women's personal lives and interactions in their community.. As previously mentioned, the internalised ideology of brahmanical patriarchy, with its notions of women's "honour", "purity" and "obedience", produces and influences the causal factors for violence in the family. Female foeticide and infanticide stemmed from gender discrimination, combined with poverty or a response to the child being born of an illicit relationship. By comparison, child sexual abuse was primarily seen as the result of husbands asserting their perceived right to sexual relations with their child brides.

When it comes to domestic violence, however, the causes for this violence are much more nuanced and varied. *Gender inequality and norms of female subordination* formed a major category of causal factors for violence meted out by natal and marital family members to Dalit women. Examples of causal factors falling within this category include: women allegedly failed to be dutiful wives; women asserted their rights; women were unable to bear children, or unable to bear sons; caste discrimination from dominant caste husbands and in-laws in inter-caste marriages, or reaction from dominant caste husbands on being ostracised from their dominant caste communities as a result of marrying Dalit women; dominant caste husbands did not want children from their Dalit wives, or did not want their children to visit their Dalit grandparents' house, or not wanting their children to marry a Dalit.

A second major category was *economic* causal factors for domestic violence, including: poverty; insufficient dowry; women earned more income than their husbands, or their natal families had a higher economic status than their marital families; women asked their husbands to account for money given from their earnings to the husbands, or refused to give their earnings to fund their husbands' drinking habits, or refused to mortgage jewellery to satisfy their husbands' spendthrift habits; to deny women their share of their deceased husbands' property, or to appropriate their dead father's pension. A third prominent category of causal factors related to Dalit women's *civil rights*, which include: women's insecurity due to their husband's unemployment or alcoholism; women's insecurity as widows, or orphans, or differently abled, or stepchildren.

Finally, two related categories of causal factors related to rights in *family relationships* and to *sexual integrity*. Internalised brahmanical patriarchal norms entail strict control over Dalit women's sexuality. Hence, reasons for violence surrounding marital relations include: women allegedly having illicit relationships; women's alleged breaches of family honour, particularly in response to women surviving sexual or physical violence in the general community; women caught up in internal family power dynamics.

Evidence of the lack of similar norms applicable to male household members was seen in violence against Dalit wives arising from their husbands having illicit relationships with other women, or marrying again, or wanting to marry again. In a similar manner Dalit women faced violence arising out of *disregard for their sexual integrity*, including: when women did not want to have sexual relations with their husbands, or in one case with her husband's friends; either in furtherance of sexual relations, or retaliation for women having refused to have sexual relations with male relatives; negative or blaming responses from women's natal or marital family members after women were sexually assaulted or exploited.

Overall, much of the domestic violence arose out of a combination of factors such as internalised gender discrimination, poverty, dominant discourses of dowry, wifely fidelity and duties, and distrust of women to guard their own sexuality all leading to husbands' perceived rights over their wives, or their husbands' alcoholism. The message effectively sent home to Dalit women is that they must keep "in their place"; that is, they must remain submissive daughters or wives, and should not assert their rights against Dalit men and other dominant family members.

REMEDIAL ACTION FOR JUSTICE

The Indian Government has an obligation under international human rights law to act with due diligence to prevent, investigate and punish acts of violence against Dalit women in both the general community and in the family, at the hands of state or non-state actors. Any case of violence against a Dalit woman has to pass through the hands of the local police and the judiciary in order for the woman to receive justice under the law. Safeguarding the impartiality of this process, the Indian Constitution stipulates in *Article 14* that all Indian citizens have the right to equality before the law.

However, deeply ingrained normative values of appropriate gender and caste roles and behaviour patterns influence government officials, police and even judges who have the power to interpret and actualise rights. These socio-culturally-religiously rooted biases enforce the discriminatory status quo to the detriment of Dalit women's right to justice where violence takes place. As the United Nations Special Rapporteur on Violence against Women has noted with regard to the situation in India, "constitutional and legislative provisions that have been enacted to protect women from discrimination have not proved to be an effective deterrent."

Moreover, the Indian government's consistent inaction in protecting, promoting and fulfilling rights for its Dalit women citizens – evidenced in official data indicating the increasing rates of crimes against women and Scheduled Castes, its failure to resister many cases of violence against Dalit women, and low disposal rates of Scheduled Caste atrocity cases combined with low conviction rates – all points to structural injustice being perpetuated and the Indian state's failure to comply with its international human rights obligations. These conclusions are substantiated by the justice-seeking efforts of the Dalit women in this study. Considering all 500 Dalit women in the study, in 40.2 per cent of instances of violence the *women have been unable to obtain legal or community remedies for the violence*.

A culture of silence exists when it comes to especially sexual violence, due to the dominant discourse emphasising women's "honour" and the stigma attaching to sex outside of marriage, whether forced or by consent. Other reasons for not attempting to obtain justice include: fear of the perpetrators, arising from the perpetrator's threats of further violence to the women or their family members should they file police complaints, or to deny them work; fear of dishonour or further shame by publicising the violence; ignorance that the violence was an illegal act for which there are legal remedies; lack of money to approach the police, or pay the often requisite bribe in order for the police to take action, or to follow a police case through to the courts; lack of family or community support for the justice-seeking attempt.

The overall effect is to reinforce a culture of impunity for violence by the perpetrators and their colluders, further exacerbating the denial of Dalit women's rights to security of life and basic human dignity. In 26.5 per cent of instances of violence, the women attempt to obtain legal or community redress for the violence, but are *prevented from obtaining justice by the perpetrators and their supporters, and the community at large*. The existence of traditional village panchayats of caste elders/leaders that exists parallel to the formal panchayat system in most Indian villages, in particular, often systematically suppresses women's and Dalits' voices using patriarchal and dominant caste notions of social and moral justice.

Reasons for these thwarted justice-seeking attempts include: perpetrators, or their families, or their caste community threatening or intimidating the victimsurvivor into silence; perpetrators foisting false police cases against the victim-survivors to pressurise them to drop their legitimate cases; traditional village or caste panchayats, and in some cases formal elected panchayats, refusing to take up Dalit women's cases, or refusing to accuse dominant caste perpetrators, or portraying the affected woman as the wrongdoer instead of the perpetrator, or pressurising the affected woman to accept an informal "compromise"; victim-survivor's family pressurising her to drop the case out of fear of family dishonour or dominant caste reprisals; dominant caste community pressurising the victim-survivor to accept informal "compromises" that involve no proper and adequate remedial or justice action.

In cases of panchayat rulings, justice may appear to be done to the Dalit women. Often, however, the perpetrators and supporting dominant caste members/groups contrive "compromises" by taking advantage of their socio-political power and status, instead of dispensing true justice. Of all the instances of violence, only in 1.6 per cent are the Dalit women able to *obtain informal justice rulings in her favour*. In most of these 33 instances, traditional village panchayats or elected panchayats or local NGOs manage to broker informal justice rulings rewarding the victim-survivor with financial compensation and a public apology, while extracting from the perpetrator a fine and/or apology and promise for improved behaviour in the future.

A further 17.4 per cent of all instances of violence reach the notice of the police, but the *justice attempts are blocked by the police* themselves. These include cases in which: police pressurise the woman victim-survivor to drop the case or to accept a "compromise"; police foist false cases against the victim-survivor or her supporters in order to force them to drop their legitimate case; police file victim-survivor's complaints but neglect to take action; police accept bribes from the perpetrators to drop or scuttle the case; police simply refuse to file FIRs. By rendering futile the women's attempt to seek justice through the criminal justice system, the police collude to reinforce the culture of impunity for violence against Dalit women.

Finally, in only 13.8 per cent of instances of violence in this study is *appropriate police or judicial action underway*. The majority of these cases are all pending: investigations are being carried out, charge sheets are yet to be prepared, cases are currently before the courts, etc. Hence, leeway still exists for the cases to be scuttled by the police and/or perpetrators and their community. Notably, only 3.6 per cent of all instances of violence have actually reached the court, and of those, only three cases (that is, less than 1 per cent of total instances of violence) have ended in convictions. Eight other cases have been dismissed by the courts or ended in acquittals of the accused, due to either a forced "compromise" dictated by the accused while the case was under trial, or the perpetrator pressurising the woman victim-survivor or witnesses into turning hostile, or the victim-survivor being unable to obtain the requisite evidence for her case, or the perpetrator dying before the end of the trial.

Hence, the long process to obtain justice for Dalit women victim-survivors of violence is too often effectively stymied by different actors – the perpetrators, their caste community, police, the traditional village panchayats or formal elected panchayats. The brahminical patriarchal discourse of "honour" and fear of further dominant caste reprisals, moreover, influences Dalit women, their families and their communities, not to seek justice where violence takes place. Impunity for violence, therefore, is an intrinsic factor in the maintenance of the caste system and caste-and-gender based norms circumscribing Dalit women's fundamental rights and freedoms. The overall performance of the Indian State, therefore, comes into serious question when measured against the standard of due diligence to prevent violence against Dalit women. This is true for violence at the hands of both non-state actors, as well as state actors themselves. Giving effect to Dalit women's rights requires not only building structures of protection - including investigation, prosecution, fair punishment and compensation for violence – but also rigourously implementing laws and policies designed to facilitate the enjoyment of equal citizenship rights for the 80 million Dalit women in the country today. Taking into account the situation of rising rates of crimes against Dalits, combined with failure of the state machinery to check this rise with stringent action, the Parliamentary Committee on the Welfare of Scheduled Castes and Scheduled Tribes has stated that atrocities on Scheduled Castes and Scheduled Tribes constitute an internal disturbance under *Article 355* of the *Indian Constitution*, and has called for Central Government intervention under various provisions to take strict action against offending states.

The Committee has also castigated the Home Ministry for using "police and public order" being "state subjects" as an excuse for absolving themselves of the responsibility implied under *Article 355*. Finally, the Committee recommended taking "extreme steps" wherever warranted to protect the Dalit community and punish perpetrators of violence against them.viii

EFFECTS OF VIOLENCE

Violence against Dalit women causes social, physical and mental trauma to women, much of which is long-term suffering. Where violence is committed with impunity, aided by the failure of the police to effect arrests and prosecutions, the fact of the perpetrators and their colluders in the violence freely moving about the village and often intimidating the woman and her family has a deep *psychological impact*. Significant are feelings of the futility of legal justice and fatalism about positive changes to address such violence. In total, 71.2 per cent of Dalit women in the study expressed their feelings of helplessness to stop the violence, while 60.4 per cent indicated the atmosphere of constant fear in which they carry on their daily lives. Feelings of depression or low-self esteem and shame also marked out the lives of around 60 per cent of women, while 24 women had tried to commit suicide because of the violence they endured.

At the level of *physical effects*, among other effects of violence, 92 Dalit women experienced long-term physical health complications arising out of the violence, and a further nine women now live with a permanent physical disfigurement or disability. Twenty-three women endured long-term sexual health complications, while seven women miscarried as a result of violence meted out to them. Sexual violence resulted in 40 women becoming pregnant, though 18 women either opted for or were forced to undertake abortions, and one woman's family killed her child at birth.

Social effects of violence include economic punishment in terms of the destruction of Dalit women's livelihood or loss of employment (11 women), or social boycotts (four women). Around 8 per cent of Dalit women (39 women) expressed their inability to get married or to get their child married where especially sexual violence had occurred. Violence also restricted many Dalit women's freedom of movement, while eight girls quit their education due to violence. Otherwise, Dalit women were ostracised from their families (57 women), or their community (16 women), or deserted by their husbands (17 women), or forced to leave their homes (80 women) because of violence in either or both the general community and the family. Finally, 9.6 per cent of women (48 women) experienced contempt or ridicule in the villages following the violence perpetrated against them, often reinforcing the idea that somehow the women were to be blamed for the violence meted out to them.

Thus, the harm caused to Dalit women by violence does not stop at the act itself; it has long-term and multiplying social, psychological and physical effects that are not being addressed. Outside of the social movements and organisations working with the community, little supportive or counselling mechanisms exist in India today to deal with caste-and-gender based violence meted out to Dalit women. The result is that the lives of many Dalit women are underwritten by layers of trauma, hindering their rights to live with dignity and reach their full potential.

COURAGE, STRENGTH AND RESILIENCE OF DALIT WOMEN

Despite all these experiences of violence that leave grave marks on Dalit women's lives and dominant caste perpetrators constantly reiterating gender-based caste norms and Dalit gender subordination, the narratives of the Dalit women also evidence their courage, strength and resilience to assert their right to live a life with dignity. Apart from the courage that Dalit women have shown during violence, their resilience in the post-violence phase is manifested in two respects: first, their determination to pursue a course of action, whatever may be the expected or unexpected outcome, to set right the harm done by the violence; secondly, the tenacity they have shown in their various attempts to sustain their lives against all odds, refusing to let their lives disintegrate further as a result of the violence they have experienced. Whether this was done with success or otherwise in terms of achieving a legal remedy for the injustice they had faced or improving their living conditions, what is significant are their efforts to survive and sustain their lives in some form or another.

It is ironic that instead of the Indian State being the custodian of constitutional rights, it is Dalit women themselves who often dare to uphold the rule of law in the face of the "rule of caste". This is evident from cases where Dalit women assert their rights to equality and fundamental freedoms of life, and also where they approach established legal justice mechanisms instead of taking the law into their own hands as the perpetrators have done.

And yet, in only a few cases does the state rise up to meet Dalit women's expectations of justice. Therefore, what Dalit women look to is not a paternal way of providing them remedial justice, but support mechanisms that clearly establish and uphold their rights, and bring them into mainstream society with dignity. Failure by the Indian state and civil society to respond to Dalit women's legitimate expectations results in these women experiencing greater marginalisation, to the detriment of a healthy and vibrant democratic polity. There also lies a possibility of increased questioning of the rule of law as the appropriate means to securing justice. What Dr B.R. Ambedkar said in 1949 on the occasion of the Third Reading of the Indian Constitution is well worth noting in this regard:

"On [enacting the Constitution], we are going to enter into a life of contradictions. In politics we will have equality and in social and economic life we will have inequality. In politics we will be recognising the principle of one [wo]man one vote and one vote one value. In our social and economic life, we shall, by reason of our social and economic structure, continue to deny the principle of one man one value. How long shall we continue to live this life of contradictions? How long shall we continue to deny equality in our social and economic life? If we continue to deny it for long, we will do so only by putting our political democracy in peril. We must remove this contradiction at the earliest possible moment or else those who suffer from inequality will blow up the structure of political democracy which this Assembly has so laboriously built up."

CONCLUDING REFLECTIONS

In contravention of both national laws and international human rights standards that prohibit any physical, sexual or psychological violence against women, varying forms of violent acts specifically targeting Dalit women are occurring on a large scale across India today. That physical (affecting bodily integrity), verbal (affecting the psyche), and sexual (affecting bodily/sexual integrity) violence are the most common, and often combined, forms of violence suggests that at every level Dalit women's personae is being attacked. Moreover, given that most of this violence is occurring in public spaces, the additional humiliation of being violated in public drives home a message not only to each Dalit woman, but also to her family and community, that she is not considered worthy of being treated with honour, respect or human dignity. As Dalit women also experience violence in the family, they are effectively left with no safe spaces in which to freely express themselves and reach their full potential.

Dalit women would appear to be extremely vulnerable to aggression primarily by dominant caste persons in their villages and towns. Dominant caste status, often combined with patriarchal status and reinforced by a dominant class position (for example, being a landlord), effectively legitimises many dominant caste men's exercise of power, authority and force over Dalit women. Moreover, reading through the 500 Dalit women's narratives reveals the pan-religious element in that perpetrators of violence come from all major Indian religions – Hindus, Muslims, Christians and Sikhs, indicating that even in non-Hindu traditions the caste hierarchy trumps religious ideals of equality and respect for all human beings.

The range of causal factors for violence in the general community is directly attributable to systemic caste-class-gender factors that ascribe Dalit women's low status in society and consequent disempowerment and exploitation. At the core is patriarchy, which is gender-based and gender-biased against women. Male exercise of patriarchal power to subjugate women is overtly manifested in their attacks on Dalit women's sexual and bodily integrity, as well as their rights in inter-personal relationships with men. At the same time, patriarchy in India is influenced by the caste system and its inherent inequalities arising from hierarchal structuring of the system. Dalit women become specifically targeted for violence as an outcome of their positioning at the bottom of both gender and caste hierarchies, which condone violence against those Dalit women who contravene caste and untouchability norms by asserting their right to equality, or criminalises Dalit women's actions, or deems it socio-culturally acceptable to perpetrate sexual violence on Dalit women.

Moreover, reinforcement of Dalit women's lack of or denial of access to land and other economic resources through violence points to their effective class subordination in order to retain them as an exploitable labour force for their mainly dominant caste employers. There are also interconnections between denial of Dalit women's socio-economic rights or right to livelihood, and the denial of their civil rights; that is, their ability to protest and protect themselves depends to a great extent on their having a sound economic base. Finally, the lack of civil and political freedoms, including the right to justice and protection of the law in the event of violence taking place, reinforce the disempowerment of Dalit women at all levels. Such violence is crucial to the maintenance of caste structures and unequal power relations in society, which serves to highlight key areas requiring urgent intervention to safeguard Dalit women's fundamental rights. Similarly, the multiplicity of causal factors for violence in the family suggests the reproduction of the larger patriarchal caste system's norms in Dalit women's personal lives and interactions in their community.

Finally, the culture of impunity built into the caste system has wide-ranging implications as far as violence against Dalit women is concerned. Impunity for violence reinforces that caste-based notions of (in)justice prevail over democratic rights and the rule of law in the country. Justice itself becomes defined in terms of caste-and-gender privileges, with violence serving to reinforce caste law and order at the heavy expense of Dalit women's rights. Violence against Dalit women thus presents one of the greatest challenges to the social justice system in the country, calling for immediate and holistic remedial action at all levels of the government, law and order agents, the judiciary and civil society.

VIOLENCE AGAINST DALIT WOMEN

Vulnerably positioned at the bottom of caste, class and gender hierarchies, Dalit women experience endemic gender-and-caste discrimination and violence as the outcome of severely imbalanced social, economic and political power equations. Their socio-economic vulnerability and lack of political voice, when combined with the dominant risk factors of being Dalit and female, increase their exposure to potentially violent situations while simultaneously reducing their ability to escape. Studies on violence against Dalit women in India presents clear evidence of widespread exploitation and discrimination against these women subordinated in terms of power relations to men in a patriarchal society, as also against their communities based on caste.

This is a widespread phenomenon found in India, Nepal, Pakistan, Bangladesh and Sri Lanka where caste-based discrimination subjects millions of Dalit women to inhumane living conditions and systematic human rights violations. In India the Dalits constitute about 16.20 percent of Indias population in 2001 with little less than half being women, which means that 80 million Dalit women face multiple forms of discrimination in this country alone. Violence against Dalit women reinforces caste norms wherein they are seen as available for all forms of violence, especially sexual violence. According to Indias National Commission for Women, "In the commission of offences against... [Dalit] women the [dominant caste] offenders try to establish their authority and humiliate the community by subjecting their women to indecent and inhuman treatment." Further, when they transgress caste norms such as those prescribing caste endogamy or untouchability practices, or assert their rights over resources or public spaces, violence is unleashed on them. The UN Special Rapporteur on Violence against Women has noted that Dalit women "face targeted violence, even rape and death from state actors and powerful members of dominant castes, used to inflict political lessons and crush dissent within the community..." Similarly, in its 2007 Concluding Comments the CERD Committee noted its concern about the alarming number of allegations of acts of sexual violence against Dalit women primarily by dominant caste men.

FORMS AND FREQUENCY OF VIOLENCE AGAINST DALIT WOMEN

There are nine major forms of violence against Dalit women; six being violence in the general community – physical assault, verbal abuse, sexual harassment and assault, rape, sexual exploitation, forced prostitution, kidnapping and abduction; and three being violence in the family – female foeticide and infanticide, child sexual abuse and domestic violence from natal and marital family members. The more frequent forms of violence that are perpetrated against the majority of Dalit women are verbal abuse, physical assault, sexual harassment and assault, domestic violence and rape, in descending order.

Child sexual abuse in terms of particularly early child marriages and sexual relations with minor Dalit girls below the age of 16 years is also prominent. A recent three-year study of 500 Dalit womens experiences of violence across four Indian states revealed that the majority of Dalit women faced one or more incidents of verbal abuse (62.4 per cent), physical assault (54.8 per cent), sexual harassment and assault (46.8 per cent), domestic violence (43.0 per cent) and rape (23.2 per cent).

LOCATION OF VIOLENCE

The majority of Dalit women face violence in public spaces – streets, womens toilet areas, fields, etc. – in and around their villages and towns. The next most common place for violence is within the home. Aside from domestic violence, a number of women face physical assaults, verbal abuse, sexual harassment and sexual assaults in their very home from non-family members. Violence in the workplace ranks third in terms of common locations for violence.

Finally, government spaces become grounds for violence where women are forcibly incarcerated, verbally abused, sexually harassed or raped in police stations. Otherwise, verbal abuse is the most common form of violence meted out in government spaces from a range of government actors including the police, district administration officials and doctors. Social Status of

PERPETRATORS OF VIOLENCE IN THE GENERAL COMMUNITY

Within the wide range of identified perpetrators of violence against Dalit women in the general community, dominant caste landlords emerge as the most prominent group. Police also emerge as key perpetrators of violence against Dalit women. They are not active perpetrators; they also act in a significant number of cases in collusion with the perpetrators by failing to enforce the law when violence against Dalit women takes place.

Two other groups of perpetrators whose numbers are significant belong to the professional category, namely doctors and teachers. In addition, there are a large number of "other dominant caste persons" as perpetrators. Moreover, often this violence is committed by these perpetrators not only as individuals, but also as group violence involving people of the same status (or different status Finally, a number of "other Dalit persons" are either active perpetrators of violence against Dalit women, or colluders in the violence.

CASTE BACKGROUND OF PERPETRATORS OF VIOLENCE IN THE GENERAL COMMUNITY

While in some instances the perpetrators of violence belong to one homogenous dominant castes, there are instances where they cut across all dominant caste lines, that is, backward castes and forward castes. This is particularly so where the Dalit woman is seen to transgress established caste norms, for example, by asserting her rights in defiance of „untouchability practices. The punishment meted out, therefore, takes on the form of collective punishment that is both expressive of caste outrage as well as instrumental in terms of teaching the woman and her community a lesson of „obedience to caste norms. Otherwise, sexual violence against Dalit women often takes a collective caste aspect, in terms of gang rapes or forced prostitution.

CAUSAL FACTORS FOR VIOLENCE

Violence in the General Community

- The primary identified factor for violence in the general community relates to the issue of Dalit womens sexual or bodily integrity. Accompanying Dalit womens low caste status and the socio-economic and political power of the dominant castes is the latters view of their superior caste and gender status and accordingly a perceived right over Dalit womens bodies. Sexual violence is a tool utilised by dominant caste men to reinforce the caste „impurity of both the Dalit woman and her community, given the hegemonic discourse of women symbolising the group identity and bearing the honour of their community.
- A second frequent causal factor for violence in the general community directly links to gender inequality and the „natural caste hierarchy as often manifested in untouchability practices, and Dalit womens counter discourse of equality, rights, dignity and self-respect.
- Almost as frequently identified a causal factor for violence in the general community lies in the area of Dalit womens civil rights.
- A fourth causal factor for violence in the general community, given the aspect of economic exploitation built into the caste system, related to economic resources – land, or other economic resources/capital such as wages, payment for services, etc. – and particularly Dalits asserting their rights to own or utilise resources.
- In the realm of political rights, several Dalit womens assertions of their basic political rights provoke violent dominant castes backlashes. The issues that led to violence are Dalit women contesting panchayat elections; Dalit women exercising or attempting to exercise political authority as elected panchayat representatives.
- Finally, violence also takes place when Dalit women sought justice and the protection of the law for violence done to them, or to forestall such action

Violence in the Family

Similarly, Dalit women face violence in the family over a range of issues, suggesting the assimilation of the larger patriarchal caste systems norms by particularly Dalit men, with negative implications for Dalit womens personal lives and interactions in their community. When it comes to domestic violence, however, the causes for this violence are much more nuanced and varied. Gender inequality and norms of female subordination formed a major category of causal factors for violence meted out by natal and marital family members to Dalit women.

Impunity for Violence against Dalit Women

The systemic nature of violence against Dalit women is accompanied by equally systemic patterns of impunity. In 2006, the official conviction rate for Dalit atrocity cases was just 5.3 percent. The study of 500 Dalit womens cases of violence revealed:

- In less than 1 per cent of cases were the perpetrators convicted by the courts
- In 17.4 per cent of instances of violence, police obstructed the women from attaining justice.
- In 26.5 per cent of instances of violence, the perpetrators and their supporters, and/or the community at large, prevented the women from obtaining justice.
- In 40.2 per cent of instances of violence, the women did not attempt to obtain legal or community remedies for the violence primarily out of fear of the perpetrators or social dishonour if (sexual) violence was revealed, or ignorance of the law, or the belief that they would not get justice.

One negative implication is that violence against Dalit women is legitimised, spurring further violence.

RECOMMENDATIONS

Affected governments are encouraged to:

- Follow-up on recommendations relevant to the promotion and protection of Dalit womens rights of UN Special Procedures, particularly the Special Rapporteur on violence against women, UN Treaty Bodies, the Universal Periodic Review, etc;
- Enact and implement national legislation to eliminate practices such as dowry, devadasi/jogini, manual scavenging, caste-based discrimination and "untouchability" in accordance with recommendations by the UN Committee on the Elimination of all forms of Discrimination against Women (CEDAW);
- Cooperate fully with the UN Special Rapporteurs by responding to their questions and accepting invitations to country visits;
- Provide disaggregated data on the incidence of crimes against Dalit

women, as well as police and judicial handling of such cases (as per CERD General Recommendation XXIX, 2002) and include the following sections in periodic reports to UN treaty bodies:

- The extent of domestic violence against Dalit women, and on the legislative and other measures taken to address this phenomenon, including facilities and remedies provided for victims;
- The situation of women and the extent to which they enjoy the right to own land and property independent of their male relatives;
- annual data, disaggregated by age, sex, caste, ethnicity and religion, as well as specific benchmarks, to enable adequate monitoring and evaluation of the progress achieved.

NATIONAL DEMANDS

Affected governments should:

- Recognize Dalit women as a distinct social group rather than subsuming them under the general women or Dalit category, and accordingly evolve and implement a specific focus and activities on Dalit women s rights within the broader framework of the Dalit and womens empowerment agenda.
- Ensure full and strict implementation of laws in place to protect Dalit womens rights and implement measures to ensure the abolition of „untouchability practices, and implement strict sanctions against anyone preventing or discouraging victims from reporting incidents of violence or accessing the criminal justice system, including police and other law enforcement officers.
- Ensure the implementation of national penal codes in its jurisdiction, and that law enforcement officials, judges, lawyers, social workers and medical professionals are duly trained on the serious and criminal nature of domestic violence;
- Evolve a national perspective plan aimed at specifically accelerating efforts to reduce the development gap between Dalit women and the rest of the population within fixed time-bound targets.
- Introduce affirmative action policies to increase Dalit womens participation in the police, judiciary, legal professions and education.
- Produce and disseminate disaggregated data on the status of Dalit women, particularly in government plans and development programmes.

AMBEDKAR AND DALIT WOMEN

Ambedkar came to forefront in Indian academics from the decade of nineties with the intensified struggles of Dalits. The struggles of the ordinary people forced the centers of power and knowledge to consider the importance of Ambedkar and his ideas in social reconstruction of the nation. With Ambedkar as the source of inspiration, Dalits are struggling to write their own history by interrogating the dominant Brahminical traditions. The project of De- Brahiminisation of Indian history has appeal among the Dalit scholars in writing Indian history, culture and philosophy. The relevance of Ambedkar has to be read with the fifty years developments of post Ambedkar of post independent India. His approach to Indian society and its history are crucial in understanding contemporary India and the struggles of the oppressed.

The paper will focus on the importance of historical method of Ambedkar in relation to the theories of contemporary historiography of India. Ambedkar's notion of history is identified with 'moral community' imbibed with the principles of equality, liberty and fraternity. His historical method borrows tools from Marxism in understanding the ancient history. Rather than mechanically applying Marxism, he had creatively used it in keeping the specific context of Indian society. He approached Indian society from the point of religion and finds the religion as source for the different ideological position. For instance, Buddhism is considered as revolutionary and Hinduism as counter revolutionary. 'Rationality' is the guiding principle in evaluating the principles and practices of religion. For the claims of religion he applied rationalistic principle. He brings the religion as a focal point in reference to caste system. To construct the Indian history in proper, he avail all the convincing ideas of his times, from liberal to Marxist. This may go in tune of pragmatism. The pragmatism of Ambedkar differs from the context of western societies.

The pragmatic method of Ambedkar came out of his social responsibility and in presenting the history from the victim's point of view. In essence he made a serious attempt in constructing the Indian history in which one finds dignified place for 'sudras' and 'untouchable communities'. Ambedkar is a source of inspiration for contemporary dalit movement and so for constructing history from dalit point of view. Dalit historiography establishes its own method by challenging the colonial, nationalist, marxists and subaltern approaches of Indian historiography.

PHILOSOPHY OF HISTORY

Historians have always tried to provide rationally justified knowledge about past, cause and effects of events. Philosophy of history can function as a conceptual enhancement for working historians and also it can function as a source of rational criticism of specific methods or approaches within contemporary historiography. Historically, there are various attempts to read history from diverse ideological and methodological positions.

Many thinkers contributed to the philosophy of historical ideas. Many who have concerned themselves with questions about the nature of historical knowledge and interpretation of the past have spent a good deal of time studying the history of various historical concepts and ideas; and in doing so some have concluded that there are no absolute ideals of historical method or truth which can be isolated from their own peculiar historical and social contexts. Broadly there are two streams identified in approaching the historical knowledge- idealistic and materialistic. In the realm of epistemological understanding of truth value of historical knowledge- rationalistic and empiricist methods were followed. The empiricist views past as an ordinary object of empirical investigation. The rationalist views past as an object of rational reconstruction and understanding. There raised a basic questions what is history about? Kant, Hegel and Marx have common strand and answered this question differently. For Hegel, history is unfolding of human freedom. Hegel's conception of history presupposes an abstract or absolute spirit. History of humanity becomes history of abstract spirit of humanity, a spirit above and beyond the real man. The clue to history, in Hegel's view, is to be found in the idea of freedom. 'World history', in his words, 'exhibits the development of the consciousness of freedom on the part of spirit, and of the consequent realization of that freedom.' Marx answered in another way – that the underlying driver in historical change is the tension between the forces and relations of production or class struggle. For Marx, the first premise of all human history is, of course the existence of living human beings.

All historiography must begin with these natural bases and their modification in the course of history by men's activity. Unlike the idealist view of history, it does not have to look for category in each period, but remains constantly on the real ground of history, it does not explain the practice from the idea but explains the formation of ideas from material practice. The whole previous conception of history has either completely neglected this real basis of history. Consequently, history has always to be written in accordance with external standard, the real production of life appears to be ahistorical. During the Nineteenth century the central concern is changed from metaphysical issues about 'direction of history' to epistemological issues about 'historical truth'. In twentieth century these concerns about truths in history focus on dispute between two views on question into what is history. A good part of the twentieth century was devoted to a debate sparked by the philosopher of science Carl Hempels claiming that historical explanations — to be legitimately scientific ones have to be developed from the physical sciences. In contrast with Hempel's thesis, some, such as R. G. Collingwood and William Dray' have insisted that the historian is more concerned with understanding the motives of historical agents than with predicting events. Collingwood, author of 'The Idea of History' argues that all history is the history of thought. He replaced the 'positivistic' notion of history with one which treats thought as the fundamental concept of historical enquiry. Philosophy of history-as-discipline has also addressed concerns about the justification and limitations of historical objectivity, the truth of historical claims, and the nature of historical explanations.

Are there any proper methods in understanding history? Is it possible to find the historical method without any ideological and political positions? The discussion further continued that historians' ideological and political positions play a role either approaching the knowledge of past or constructing the ideas of past. The historians are selective in interpreting the knowledge of past. In other words, the contemporary demands force them to probe into the past. As the historian Croce said 'all history is contemporary'. As Carl Becker declares, 'the facts of history do not exist for any historian till he creates them.' As E H Carr explains, 'history is a continuous process of interaction between the historian and his facts and unending dialogue between the past and the present.' 'All history depends ultimately upon its social purpose.'

HISTORIOGRAPHIES IN WRITING INDIAN HISTORY

Keeping the above discussion as a background, this paper, gives emphasis on the historical method of Ambedkar in countering the dominant social groups' construction of the Indian history. Both in construction of history of India and in having its historical method- Colonial, Orientalist, Nationalist, Marxists, Cambridge historians and Subaltern historians who played a vital role. History writing in India as a conscious exercise began with scholars of Colonial and Orientalist persuasion and followed by nationalist elite and others. At present four dominant streams in Indian historiography are important - Colonial, Nationalist, Marxist and Subaltern schools. Each school has its historical social context in emphasizing its method in writing Indian history. Each school argued its case in relation to other.

The decade of eighties is turning point in Indian history in bringing new epistemological positions corresponding to the struggles of Dalits, Women, Adivasis. In writing history, categories wise, caste, gender, region became reference points. On the other hand, struggles rallying religious nationalism are trying to invoke the 'glorious past'. With the many contesting positions, to reach out historical objectivity is not an easy task. When researches into India's past began in the late 18th century and early 19th centuries, Orientalist ideas structured historical representations. Inspired by the romanticism and classicism of the time, Orientalists like William Jones and H.T. Colebrooke returned to the ancient past, discovered its greatness and defined a specific notion of a glorious classical age. It was in this age, so the Orientalists told us, that the essence of Indian civilization – embodied in its language, laws, institutions and religious texts – came into being. Subsequent to this golden age there was a continuous or cyclical decline to a degenerate present before the British rule.

If India had to develop, its lost past had to be rediscovered, its essence had to be properly understood, its juridical and religious texts had to be translated and canonized, its poetry had to be recaptured. The Orientalists saw themselves as the mediators who would define this relationship between the past and the present. As codifiers and translators they would be the ones to discover the ancient texts and ascribe to them their true meanings. By the early 19th century, with liberalism gaining ground, Orientalist histories were questioned from within the fold of imperial thought. If Orientalists had glorified India's past, the liberals condemned it. From a veneration of classicality we moved to a phase of arrogant deification of modernity. Liberal histories idealized the modern West and the assumed principles of its order – individualism, freedom and democracy. Other societies – of the past and present – were understood and characterized only in terms of the presence and non-presence of liberal values. While Orientalists had discovered in India's past a succession of golden ages, liberals like James Mill and Thomas Macaulay could see only shades of darkness. In the West liberal histories traced a series of great transitions – from darkness to light, irrationality to rationality, magic to science, superstition to reason. Modernity had emerged from the age of darkness, through the Renaissance and Enlightenment into the modern age. In India and other 'dark continents', as the liberals saw it, this transition never took place. India had remained unchanged, constrained by the social institutions that defined it – caste, village community and Oriental despotism. The colonial historians were tried to construct the Indian history that suits their political interests.

The colonial historians tried to show that Indian nationalism was nothing more than an unprincipled, selfish, amoral bid for power by a few Indian elites. They had used the traditional bonds of caste and communal ties to mobilize masses for their own ends. The colonial assumptions of historical thought was enshrined by Hegel and expounded by Macaulay, Mill, Seeley, and many others. In the historical literature, colonial powers escaped serious interrogation outside of the specific contestations of the nationalist struggle until new critical enquiries were initiated by figures as various as Bernard Cohn, Edward Said, and Ranjit Guha. Nicholas Dirks argues that British colonialism played a critical role in both the identification and production of Indian 'tradition'. Essentially colonial history of India is Eurocentric and imperialistic.

The tendency to read Indian history in terms of a lack, an absence, or incompleteness that translates into 'inadequacy' is obvious in these excerpts. The British conquered and represented the diversity of 'Indian' pasts through a homogenizing narrative of transition from a 'medieval' period to 'modernity'. The terms have changed with time. The 'medieval' was once called 'despotic' and the 'modern', the 'rule of law'. 'Feudal/capitalist' has been a later variant. While the nationalists mounted a critique of colonial ideas, they continued to accept many of the key categories through which imperial representations of Indian society were fashioned. But in their critiques, nationalists still borrowed from the Orientalists, transforming the founding Orientalist notions of India's past – the idea of classical golden ages and the corollary myth of a subsequent civilizational decline – into accepted orthodoxies of Indian history. But most nationalist histories continued to periodize pre-colonial history through religious categories. They referred to ancient India as Hindu and medieval India as Muslim – as if a unitary religious essence permeated the entire age and the whole society.

By the 1980s history writing in India saw a new phase of dramatic change. Influenced by the new social history in England and the cultural turn in social sciences, Subaltern Studies challenged the elitism of earlier histories that attributed historical agency to the elites and looked at the world from above. Subaltern histories emphasized the need to understand the experiences and lives of the dominated – peasants and workers, tribals and lower castes, women and dalits – people who leave few written records, whose voices are difficult to hear, whose actions appear inconsequential. The cultural turn in history writing all over the world shifted the focus away from economist and reductive reading of historical processes. Power and domination, economy and society, experience of work and leisure, identities and interests, were all seen as culturally constituted.

The real break came with the rise of a much more sophisticated historiography from the 1950s and '60s pioneered by scholars, to name few of the most important, like D.D. Kosambi, R.S. Sharma and Irfan Habib. There was a veritable paradigm shift, particularly in ancient and medieval Indian history. The historiography of the Hindu Right necessarily sticks to periodization by religion: in effect, the religion of rulers, for that is the only way through which the premise of medieval 'Muslim domination' or 'tyranny' can be made credible. The only real evil for it is religious, cultural or political domination coming from sources it considers external and alien, because non-Hindu. The failure to go beyond the single evaluative standard set by the colonial/anti-colonial binary produces similar problems for histories of subordinate caste and Dalit protest. Arun Shourie's onslaught on Ambedkar typifies this tendency at its worst, but an indication of the difficulties is revealed by the interesting recent attempt by G. Aloysius to write an alternative history of modern India from a 'Dalit-Bahujan' perspective. Its many virtues include a valid stress on the complicities between colonialism and continued or refurbished high caste domination, as well as on the numerous overlaps between 'mainstream' nationalism and Hindutva.

Even Nehru's Discovery of India is revealed as being not entirely immune from such contamination. In the decade of eighties, a group of scholars identifying with subaltern historiography got prominence by differing with earlier nationalist and Marxist historiography. This rise coincided with that of the Dalit movement which was taking aspiration from the philosophy of Ambedkar. Dalit movement, on the one hand, questions Brahminism and its basic assumptions and on the other hand finds 'faults' with Marxism in practice as an alternative to dominant classes. The scholars influenced by the

Dalit movement are even critical about the subaltern studies especially their treatment of the issue of caste. Subaltern studies came into prominence from the decade of eighties in projecting a new method of historiography by countering the earlier ones.

This approach came along the line of 'history from below' approach of European history writing in 1970 and 1980s. It came in opposition to both colonialist and nationalist historiography. It is skeptical about the established orthodoxies of both liberal nationalist and Marxist historiographies. Writing history from subaltern point of view was to show that neither nationalist nor left progressive historiography had a place for autonomous historical actions of the subaltern classes. As mentioned by Rajit Guha in an introductory note to Subaltern studies Vol.1: 'The historiography of Indian nationalism has for a long time been dominated by elitism- colonialist elitism and bourgeois-nationalist elitism.' The thrust of the argument is subaltern consciousness is distinct and autonomous.

The histories of class divided societies have been written and preserved in accordance with interests of dominant classes. Only rarely does subaltern consciousness appear in its autonomous form in these accounts. Subaltern consciousness evolved out of the experience of subordination, out of struggle, despite the daily routine of servitude, exploitation and deprivation. The subaltern consciousness can not be found in archival material conventionally used by historians, since it is prepared and preserved by dominant groups. For the most part, those materials only show the subaltern as subservient. It is only the moment of rebellion that subaltern appears as the bearer of independent personality. The subaltern studies are criticized by scholars on different grounds.

The criticism is on the agency involved in this project and on the method. Many complained that subaltern history was becoming bhadralok history, the history of elites. Sumit Sarkar in an article, 'The decline of the subaltern in subaltern studies' argued that in the name of theory, a tendency emerged towards essentializing the categories of 'subaltern' and 'autonomy', in the sense of assigning to them more or less absolute, fixed, de-contextualized meanings and qualities. They were not advanced further by pointing out the economic reductionism of Marxism. What is conveniently forgotten is that the problems do not disappear through a simple substitution of 'class' by 'subaltern' or 'community'. Reifying tendencies can be actually strengthened by the associated detachment from socio-economic contexts and determinants out of a mortal fear of economic reductionism.

The handling of the new concepts, further, may remain equally naïve. The subaltern studies, symptomatically has ignored histories of the left and of organized anti-caste movements throughout, and the line between past and present-day neglect can be fairly porous. He further argues that subaltern studies don't have ideological strength to counter the communal violence.

There is another criticism by branding the subaltern school as idealistic. 'Guha masks his idealism by formulating a critique of official, liberal and left historiography. Guha's idealism can be seen most clearly in his attempt to criticize the analysis of the social and economic conditions which generate rebellion. By accepting the basic premises of idealism, peasant consciousness is rendered supra-historical as it is not determined by any objective historical forces. It is at a par with the Hegelian 'geist' which is not determined by history, while the development of history is march towards the self realization of this spirit. Guha's idealism consists not in emphasizing the importance of consciousness, but in placing consciousness beyond the pale of historical determination or mediation.

Definitely there is a breakthrough in methodology in constructing the history with much authenticity. Subaltern Studies becomes a blanket term for all subaltern communities like dalits, women, peasants, adivasis etc. in countering the hegemony of the dominance. Within the subaltern studies, if each community had its own logic and approach to history, then the project of subaltern studies is in trouble. For instance, the issue of caste is important in writing the history so as the historians/scholars from the dalit communities had altogether different approach in constructing/imagining Indian history. Immediately, it even dismisses the so called subaltern by dismissing them as elite/ or non dalits.

Dalit historiography throws a challenge to colonial, nationalist, Marxist and right wing and even to the so called historians of subaltern studies. In this context, Ambedkar's method of constructing the history from dalit perspective is path breaking, and provides insights for contemporary historians of all shades. Infact, very few historians worked out in the field of ancient history with sound ideological commitment and with a purpose of liberating the oppressed masses from dominant social and philosophical systems.

AMBEDKAR: IN PURSUIT OF HISTORICAL TRUTH

One may derive Ambedkar's 'historical method' in all his major writings on Indian history, culture and philosophy. The writings on this kind of issues not only provoked the scholars, political leaders of nationalist movement and orthodox Hindus of his times but helped deconstruct the dominant construction of ideas of Indian society. He made a systematic attempt to construct the histories and genealogies of the submerged social groups of Indian society by questioning the elite and dominant established Brahminical positions. He seems confident of his position by declaring it as 'fresh insights and new visions' in looking at Indian history and philosophy. In the year 1946, Ambedkar identified five streams of thoughts among the Hindus of Indian society in his writing on 'who are Shudras'- Orthodox, Aryasamajists, respecters of law (Hindu social system is all wrong, but who holds that there is no necessity to attack it. Since law does not recognize it, it is dying, if not dead system) Political minded (Swaraj is important than social reform) and

Rationalists (regard social reform as primary and even more important than Swaraj).Among these five classes of Hindus, Ambedkar would like to identify his position with rationalist Hindus who were arguing for social reform as immediate agenda rather than any other. In the words of Ambedkar; "I claim that in my research I have been guided by the best tradition of the historian who treats all literature as vulgar- I am using the word in its original sense of belonging to the people –to be examined and tested by accepted rules of evidence without recognizing any distinction between the sacred and profane and with the sole object of finding the truth."

As has been well said, an historian ought to be exact, sincere, and impartial; free from passion, unbiased by interest, fear, resentment or affection; and faithful to the truth, which is the mother of history, the preserver of great actions, the enemy of oblivion, the witness of the past, the director of the future. In short he must have an open mind, though it may not be an empty mind, and readiness to examine all evidence even though it be spurious. The non-brahmin scholar may find it difficult to remain true to this spirit of historian. He is likely to import the spirit of non-brahmin politics in the examination of the truth or falsity of ancient literature which is not justifiable. I feel certain that in my research I have kept myself free from such prejudice. In writing about sudras I have had present in my mind no other consideration except that of pure history. Respect and reverence for the sacred literature cannot be made to order.

They are results of social factors which make such sentiments natural in one case and quite unnatural in another. Respect and reverence for sacred literature of the hindus is natural to a Brahmin scholar. But it is quite unnatural in a non-Brahmin scholar. In the historical method of Ambedkar; man is the maker of history: Ambedkar evaluates the three different views on the causes of historical changes, Augustine, Buckle and Marx.

According to Augustinian, history is only an unfolding of divine plan in which mankind is to continue through war and suffering until that divine plan is completed at the day of judgment. Ambedkar pointed out that this is not acceptable to many except theologians. For Buckle, history was made by geography and physics. As per Marx, history was the result of economic forces. Ambedkar finds the limitations of these three arguments by holding the opinion that none of these would admit that history is the biography of great men. Indeed they deny man any place in making of history. He considers there is a truth in Buckle and Marx, but their views do not represent the whole truth.

They are quite wrong in holding that impersonal forces are everything and that man is no factor in the making of history. That these impersonal forces are a determining factor can not be denied, however, the effect of impersonal forces depends on man must also be admitted.' The methods employed by Ambedkar in reconstructing the history are unique and convincing. In developing an historical method he followed Goethe, as he said 'the historian's duty is to separate the truth from false, the certain from the uncertain...' Ambedkar agrees with Goethe in bringing out the relevant and necessary facts to forefront. Ambedkar proceeds further and points out into what the duty of historian in reconstructing the authentic history in situations, where he confronts with many missing links, *i.e.* when no direct evidence of connected relations between important events is available. He himself faced this kind of situation in explaining the origin of sudras and untouchables as in both cases no documentary evidences were available or its antiquity.

"In case of reconstructing history where there are no texts, and if there are, they have no direct bearing on the question. In such circumstances what one has to do is to strive to divine what the texts conceal or suggest without being even quite certain of having found the truth. The task is one of gathering survivals of the past, placing hem together and making them tell the story of their birth. The task is analogous to that of the archaeologist who constructs a city from broken stones or of the paleontologist who conceives an extinct animal from scattered bones and teeth or of a painter who reads the lines of the horizon and the smallest vestiges on the slopes of the hill to make up a scene."

Ambedkar appears very much aware of the role of historian's social affinity in dealing the material in relation to the problems of social history. In an introduction to 'who are the Shudras', he made this point more clear. He finds the difference between the non-Brahmin scholar and Brahmin scholar in treating the same source material of sacred literature of Hindus. The Brahmin scholar's attitude is identified as uncritical commendation, and where as the Non-Brahmins attitude in dealing this is unsparing condemnation. Ambedkar finds both the attitudes are harmful to historical research. It is often argued by many Brahmins that sacred literature has to be treated with reverence and respect.

Ambedkar staunchly believes that in pursuit of historical truth, there is nothing wrong in exposure of these very sacred texts which are responsible for the decline and fall of nation and society. It is the duty of a scholar to treat the literature without having any distinction of sacred or profane in pursuing truth. It is quite natural for Brahmin scholar to treat it as sacred with lot of respect and reverence. More over its object is to sustain the superiority and privileges of Brahmins as against the non-brahmins. Since he finds the comfort and privilege, it is not possible for the Brahmin scholar to be critical about sacred literature. In fact, it is his whole production and finds livelihood on it. 'Knowing that what is called the sacred literature contains an abominable social philosophy which is responsible for their social degradation, the non-brahmin reacts to it in a manner quite opposite to that of the brahmin..... I am a non-brahmin, not even a non-brahmin, but an untouchable.' Ambedkar had more focus on philosophy of religion in understanding the socio-historical phenomenon and the moral basis of Indian society, than exclusively depending on either religion or philosophy. He developed it as a method. It seems in evolving this method, he got influenced by John Dewey. Dewey is one of those pragmatic philosophers who wrote extensively on philosophy of religion from this perspective. In the west, religion is identified with faith, and philosophy is with reason/science/ rationality, in the age of enlightenment. It is also understood as tradition and modernity dichotomy.

Religion and science started considering adverse to each other. In this backdrop pragmatism of Dewey got importance by considering religion on practical utility. Religion is an institution or an influence and like all social influences and institutions, it may help or harm a society which is in its grip. Religion not only crossed everywhere the wrap of Indian history it forms the wrap and woof of Hindu mind. The life of the Hindu is regulated by religion at every moment of his life. Besides religion acts as a social force, and it stands for a scheme of divine governance.

The scheme becomes an ideal for society to follow. 'The power of religious ideal depends upon its power to confer material benefit'. Ambedkar favours for religion that stand for reason rather negating religion. He felt that Hindu religion need to undergo a reform. Caste is a natural outcome of certain religious beliefs which have the sanction of shastras. To abolish the sanctity and sacredness of caste, one has to destroy the authority of the shastras and Vedas. One has to destroy the religion of sruti and smriti. Ambedkar not only proposed the religion that should stand for reason, but also tries to link it up with the governing principle of politics. In simple terms, he thought reason and critical analysis as a method used for the study of religion.

9

The Human Rights Council

INTRODUCTION

The Human Rights Council is an inter-governmental body within the UN system made up of 47 States responsible for strengthening the promotion and protection of human rights around the globe. The Council was created by the UN General Assembly (The General Assembly is the main deliberative, policymaking and representative organ of the United Nations. Comprising all 192 Members of the United Nations, it provides a unique forum for multilateral discussion of the full spectrum of international issues covered by the Charter.

The Assembly meets in regular session intensively from September to December each year, and thereafter as required.) on 15 March 2006 with the main purpose of addressing situations of human rights violations and make recommendations on them. One year after holding its first meeting, on 18 June 2007, the Council adopted its "Institution-building package" providing elements to guide it in its future work. Among the elements is the new Universal Periodic Review mechanism which will assess the human rights situations in all 192 UN Member States.

Other features include a new Advisory Committee (Pursuant to Human Rights Council resolution 5/1, the Human Rights Council Advisory Committee (hereinafter "the Advisory Committee"), composed of 18 experts, has been established to function as a think-tank for the Council and work at its direction. The Advisory Committee replaces the former Sub-Commission on the Promotion and Protection of Human Rights. The aim of the nomination procedure of the Committee members, including the technical and objective requirements contained in Council decision 6/102, is to ensure that the best possible expertise is made available to the Council. The function of the Advisory Committee is to provide expertise in the manner and form requested by the Council, focusing mainly on studies and research-based advice. Such expertise shall be rendered only upon the latter's request, in compliance with its resolutions and under its guidance.

The Advisory Committee should be implementation-oriented. The scope of its advice should be limited to thematic issues pertaining to the mandate of the Council; namely promotion and protection of all human rights. The Committee shall not adopt resolutions or decisions, but may propose to the Council, within the scope of its work as set out by the Council, suggestions for further enhancing its procedural efficiency, as well as further research proposals within the scope of the work set out by the Council.

In the performance of its mandate, the Advisory Committee is urged to establish interaction with States, national human rights institutions, non-governmental organizations and other civil society entities in accordance with the modalities of the Council. Member States and observers, including States that are not members of the Council, the specialized agencies, other intergovernmental organizations and national human rights institutions, as well as non-governmental organizations shall be entitled to participate in the work of the Advisory Committee based on arrangements, including Economic and Social Council resolution 1996/31 and practices observed by the Commission on Human Rights and the Council, while ensuring the most effective contribution of these entities.

The Advisory Committee shall convene up to two sessions for a maximum of 10 working days per year. Its inaugural session was held from 4 to 15 August 2008 at the Palais des Nations, United Nations Office at Geneva.The Advisory Committee has been meeting for 5 days during the first week of August and for 5 days during the last week of January.) which serves as the Council's "think tank" providing it with expertise and advice on thematic human rights issues and the revised

COMPLAINTS PROCEDURE

(On 18 June 2007, the Human Rights Council adopted the President text entitled "UN Human Rights Council: Institution Building" by which a new Complaint Procedure is being established to address consistent patterns of gross and reliably attested violations of all human rights and all fundamental freedoms occurring in any part of the world and under any circumstances. The new Complaint Procedure is established in compliance with the mandate entrusted to the Human Rights Council by General Assembly resolution 60/251 of 15 March 2006, in which the Council was requested to review and, where necessary, improve and rationalize, within one year after the holding of its first session, all mandates, mechanisms, functions and responsibilities of the former Commission on Human Rights, including the 1503 procedure, in order to maintain a system of special procedures, expert advice and a complaint procedure.

ECOSOC resolution 1503 (XLVIII) of 27 May 1970 as revised by resolution 2000/3 of 19 June 2000, served as a working basis for the establishment of a new Complaint Procedure and was improved where necessary to ensure that the complaint procedure be impartial, objective, efficient, victims-oriented and conducted in a timely manner.

How does the Complaint Procedure Work?

Pursuant to Council resolution 5/1, the Complaint Procedure is being established to address consistent patterns of gross and reliably attested violations of all human rights and all fundamental freedoms occurring in any part of the world and under any circumstances. It retains its confidential nature, with a view to enhancing cooperation with the State concerned. The procedure, inter alia, is to be victims-oriented and conducted in a timely manner. Two distinct working groups - the Working Group on Communications and the Working Group on Situations - are established with the mandate to examine the communications and to bring to the attention of the Council consistent patterns of gross and reliably attested violations of human rights and fundamental freedoms.

Manifestly ill-founded and anonymous communications are screened out by the Chairperson of the Working Group on Communications, together with the Secretariat, based on the admissibility criteria. Communications not rejected in the initial screening are transmitted to the State concerned to obtain its views on the allegations of violations.

The Working Group on Communications (WGC) is designated by the Human Rights Council Advisory Committee from among its members for a period of three years (mandate renewable once). It consists of five independent and highly qualified experts and is geographically representative of the five regional groups. The Working Group meets twice a year for a period of five working days to assess the admissibility and the merits of a communication, including whether the communication alone or in combination with other communications, appears to reveal a consistent pattern of gross and reliably attested violations of human rights and fundamental freedoms. All admissible communications and recommendations thereon are transmitted to the Working Group on Situations.

The Working Group on Situations (WGS) comprises five members appointed by the regional groups from among the States member of the Council for the period of one year (mandate renewable once). It meets twice a year for a period of five working days in order to examine the communications transferred to it by the Working Group on Communications, including the replies of States thereon, as well as the situations which the Council is already seized of under the complaint procedure.

The Working Group on Situations, on the basis of the information and recommendations provided by the Working Group on Communications, presents the Council with a report on consistent patterns of gross and reliably attested violations of human rights and fundamental freedoms and makes recommendations to the Council on the course of action to take. Subsequently, it is the turn of the Council to take a decision concerning each situation thus brought to its attention.

Criteria of Communication for Examination

A communication related to a violation of human rights and fundamental freedoms is admissible, unless:

- It has manifestly political motivations and its object is not consistent with the UN Charter, the Universal Declaration of Human Rights and other applicable instruments in the field of human rights law; or
- It does not contain a factual description of the alleged violations, including the rights which are alleged to be violated; or
- Its language is abusive. However, such communication may be considered if it meets the other criteria for admissibility after deletion of the abusive language; or
- It is not submitted by a person or a group of persons claiming to be the victim of violations of human rights and fundamental freedoms or by any person or group of persons, including NGOs acting in good faith in accordance with the principles of human rights, not resorting to politically motivated stands contrary to the provisions of the UN Charter and claiming to have direct and reliable knowledge of those violations. Nonetheless, reliably attested communications shall not be inadmissible solely because the knowledge of the individual author is second hand, provided they are accompanied by clear evidence; or
- It is exclusively based on reports disseminated by mass media; or
- It refers to a case that appears to reveal a consistent pattern of gross and reliably attested violations of human rights already being dealt with by a special procedure, a treaty body or other United Nations or similar regional complaints procedure in the field of human rights;
- The domestic remedies have not been exhausted, unless it appears that such remedies would be ineffective or unreasonably prolonged.

The National Human Rights Institutions (NHRIs), when they are established and work under the guidelines of the Principles Relating to Status of National Institutions (the Paris Principles) including in regard to quasi-judicial competence, can serve as effective means in addressing individual human rights violations.)

SPECIAL PROCEDURES

(Special procedures" is the general name given to the mechanisms established by the Human Rights Council to address either specific country situations or thematic issues in all parts of the world. Currently, there are 33 thematic and 8 country mandates. The Office of the High Commissioner for Human Rights provides these mechanisms with personnel, policy, research and logistical support for the discharge of their mandates. Special procedures' mandates usually call on mandate holders to examine, monitor, advise and publicly report on human rights situations in specific countries or territories, known as country mandates, or on major phenomena of human rights violations worldwide, known as thematic mandates. Various activities are undertaken by special procedures, including responding to individual complaints, conducting studies, providing advice on technical cooperation at the country level, and engaging in general promotional activities.

Special procedures are either an individual (called "Special Rapporteur", "Special Representative of the Secretary-General" or "Independent Expert") or a working group usually composed of five members (one from each region). The mandates of the special procedures are established and defined by the resolution creating them. Mandate-holders of the special procedures serve in their personal capacity, and do not receive salaries or any other financial compensation for their work. The independent status of the mandate-holders is crucial in order to be able to fulfill their functions in all impartiality.

Most Special Procedures receive information on specific allegations of human rights violations and send urgent appeals or letters of allegation to governments asking for clarification. In 2010, a total of 604 communications were sent to Governments in 110 countries. 66 per cent of these were joint communications of two or more mandate holders. Mandate holders also carry out country visits to investigate the situation of human rights at the national level. They typically send a letter to the Government requesting to visit the country, and, if the Government agrees, an invitation to visit is extended. Some countries have issued "standing invitations", which means that they are, in principle, prepared to receive a visit from any special procedures mandate holder.

As of 31 December 2010, 73 States had extended standing invitations to the special procedures. After their visits, special procedures' mandate-holders issue a mission report containing their findings and recommendations. Starting June 2006, the Human Rights Council engaged in an institution building process, which included a review of the special procedures system. On 18 June 2007, at the conclusion of its fifth session, the Human Rights Council adopted a Resolution 5/1 entitled "Institution-building of the United Nations Human Rights Council," which included provisions on the selection of mandate holders and the review of all special procedures mandates. The review was conducted throughout 2007 and 2008.

All thematic mandates were extended. New thematic mandates have also been established, namely on contemporary forms of slavery (2007), on access to safe drinking water and sanitation (2008), on cultural rights (2009), on the rights to freedom of peaceful assembly and of association (2010) and a Working Group on the issue of discrimination against women in law and in practice (2010). Country mandates have been extended with the exception of Belarus,

Cuba, the Democratic Republic of the Congo and Liberia. At its 11th session, the Human Right Council created the mandate of independent expert on the situation of human rights in the Sudan which replaced a previous country mandate, for a period of one year. The independent expert was appointed at the 12th session of the Human Rights Council. A mandate-holder's tenure in a given function, whether it is a thematic or country mandate, will be no longer than six years (two terms of three years for thematic mandate-holders).

In June 2007, the Council also adopted Resolution 5/2, containing a Code of Conduct for special procedures mandate holders. At the Annual Meeting of special procedures in June 2008, special procedures mandate holders adopted their Manual, which provides guidelines on the working methods of special procedures. At the same meeting, they also adopted an Internal Advisory Procedure to review practices and working methods, which allows any stakeholder to bring issues relating to working methods and conduct to the attention of the Coordination Committee. The procedure was devised to enhance the independence and effectiveness of special procedures and cooperation by States, and to contribute to the self-regulation of the special procedures system and of individual mandate-holders. At its 8th session, the Human Rights Council adopted a Presidential statement concerning the terms of special procedures mandate holders and their compliance with the Code of Conduct.

10

Human Rights: Social Policy as Social Risk Management

INTRODUCTION

Social welfare in an economy depends on its ability to satisfy the needs of its members and to manage the risks threatening the well being of the same people. Outside paradise, the satisfaction of needs require some individual- and social actions. But both the ability to act and the possibility to realise positive results are subject to uncertainty and may be threatened by risks. Societies have developed various ways to deal with these basic problems and elsewhere we attempt to analyse and compare the variety in, what we call, the social management of risks. Traditionally a large part of social risk management has been defined as either social policy or more narrowly welfare state policy. However, social risks and needs have always been taken care of even in the absence of deliberate social policy or welfare state arrangements. Three major institutions are used to satisfy needs and to take care of risks: the market, the family and the state.

Each of them has different historical and geographical appearances, but basically they are found in all societies across time and locations. Economies and societies have blended the three basic elements in different portions and different formats, but the three elements are always present. Is we disregard the role of the three institutions and the links between them, as suggested, not be able to assess and compare the impact, effectiveness and efficiency of social risk management arrangements across societies. This also implies that the analysis of public interventions cannot be limited to social policy in the narrow sense, but should take into consideration public interference with families and markets as well. It is important to note that very concepts of markets, families and the state should be interpreted in their broadest meaning. Markets not only refer to monetarised transactions but also to barter trade; families not only refer to biological ties, but also to extended families and social network-based solidarity; the state not only refer to nation-states and national governments but also to public authorities of different natures.

INDIVIDUAL PROBLEMS–INDIVIDUAL SOLUTIONS

Individuals who are confronted with a problem will react. Their reaction consists of two basic elements: solve the problem at hand and take action to prevent the problem from arising again. Let's take a simple problem and one that is hard to imagine that it would not shared by everybody: every individual needs means to survive. In a monetarised economy, this is an economy where transactions are made by using money, this implies that an individual needs money to buy the goods that are necessary to survive (or, in other words, to satisfy his/her basic needs). Solving the problem in this case means: make sure you get money to buy basically food and protection against the elements (cloths, a shelter). In modern economies the option that most people will opt for, is to look for a job that provides the money that is needed.

This is, however, not the only option an individual has. One could also try to produce the goods that you need yourselves. Another option would be to ask your family (your parents, grandparents, children, grandchildren, brothers, sisters, ...) to provide the money. Or, even in a monetarised economy, to ask them for the direct provision of the goods that you need. You even may fall back on begging and charity, but that can be regarded as a peculiar way of employment (you will need to undertake some activity in order to have access to the goods) or as a special case of social network based solidarity (resembling the family). Finally, there is the option to steal either the money or the goods. The latter option, though clearly chosen by some, will be largely disregard in this context. This means that as suggested, exclude actions implying the use of violence or force by individuals.

Summarising; in absence of a benevolent public authority individuals wanting to satisfy their basic needs can rely on some form of activity on the market (either the labour market or a product market) or rely on their family or a wider form of socially available networks. Although we now outlined the options for the simplest form of our problem, we still are left with the task to lay out the options for preventing the problem to arise again in the future. Persons wanting to secure the fulfilment of their basic needs in the future should save which means, postponing consumption or, more technically substitute immediate consumption for consumption in the future.

They may either do that by just putting the money (or in some cases the goods) aside or using the capital market to make sure the level of their future income is satisfactory to meet their basic needs. It is important to note that using the capital market has at least two sides: it can imply putting money in saving accounts or insurance accounts and it can imply borrowing money. But there are other options as well.

Individuals have also in this case the same choice as before: they either rely on some market activity or they rely on their social network, say the family. That is to say, they make sure that either income from (self-) employment will be generated in the future or that they will be able to rely on their family. The family option is easy to understand, but the labour or product market options require some explanation. Making sure that you will be able to sell products in the future or that you will be employed against a certain wage is only possible if some form of contract is used.

On a product market it means to sign a contract that guarantees that someone will buy your goods in the future. On the market for labour it implies a contract that guarantees effort against wage in the future as well. The individual makes a contract with an employer to make sure that the latter will keep him/her employed whatever happens to him/her (for example when he/she gets ill). This simple example illustrate why its is important to pay considerable attention to labour market policy including employment protection; it lies in the heart of social risk management and social policy and forms an integral part of the protection that societies offer to their members.

Remark that signing a contract is by no means ruling out uncertainty completely: the buyer of your goods may die, your employer may suspend operations or your insurance company may go bankrupt. We may rephrase the problem of satisfying basic needs in the future in an interesting way. If we consider needs to be satisfied by an income stream (again "income" referring to much more than money) over the life of individuals, the problem of guaranteeing satisfaction of needs in the future can be reformulated as the problem of synchronising the income stream of individuals with their consumption stream.

My income stream may be enough to satisfy my basic needs now, but will it also by satisfactory in the future, which is inherently uncertain in many different ways. The basic welfare problem when the future enters the analysis then becomes a storage problem: how can we store income (or goods and services) in order to be sure that as suggested, be able to satisfy my needs in the future? Of course my possibilities for storage depends on how much we can store after having satisfied my basic needs in the present. My needs for "storage" will depend on my assessment of the likelihood that as suggested, not have enough income, goods or services to satisfy my needs in the future. For the argument in this part it is enough to understand that this "storage" problem can be solved in many different ways including the simple storage of goods or money (saving), making (implicit) contracts with parties in the product-or labour-markets or within my family or by using instruments of the capital market including insurances and investment.

Basically we now have the major elements that we need in order to proceed with our analysis: individuals faced with the problem of securing the satisfaction of their basic needs of food and shelter now and in the future, can cover their needs by activities on markets (the product market, the labour market and the capital market) or by relying on their families (or other social networks). Remark that we phrased the context and the problem deliberately in very broad terms and also allow individuals for example to produce and stock their own food and shelter. This may sound somewhat outlandish to readers in, say OECD economies, it is relevant if we want to use the framework to analyse for example coping strategies of people in countries in other stages of economic development or in along other paths of development in Africa or Asia. Moreover, a lot of the welfare production and welfare distribution in advanced capitalist economies take place in families outside the market place and without monetary intermediary. Even in the later case as suggested, need the broad definition of the production and distribution of welfare in order to be able to understand the full implication of the interaction between markets, families and the state.

Understanding to role of public authorities in designing and implementing social policy is framed in all cases by the same basic options that individuals have. This means that, whatever social policy mix is chosen, it is bound to interfere and interact with these basic options for individuals. When the future enters the analysis, individuals have in principle the same options as before when dealing with the problem of making sure that their basic needs are covered in the future: they take some action on a market or they rely on their family (or social network).

However, there are a few new elements that we have to consider when trying to analyse the new situation. First of all and obviously, individuals need to make decisions and choices that stretch out over a longer period, or easier to deal with conceptually, that stretch out of at least two periods. Secondly, individuals have to regard the satisfaction of their needs in the future as a problem they have to deal with: this introduces the standard and plausible assumption of risk-aversion among individuals (individuals would like to avoid the risk of not having their needs satisfied). Thirdly, individuals have to have idea of the likeness (the probability) that a certain unfortunate event (contingency) may happen and fourthly they will need a counterpart either on a market or within the family who is willing to share his/her views on the need to make decisions over at least two periods and on the definition of the probabilities of the contingency (no agreement on the probabilities themselves is needed).

We enter now a much more complicated world that requires that we are able to analyse behaviour under uncertainty, *i.e.* choices and transactions are made without knowing for sure what will be the exact outcome. Even in the simpler case before, adopting a market solution or a family solution requires that there is another party, another individual on the market or in the family. If an individual decides to offer his/her labour in exchange for payment, it is implied that on the labour market there is another individual who is prepared to hire the first person and pay out the agreed wage. If an individual decides to grow vegetables and sell them on a market it is implied that there is another individual willing and able to buy these vegetables (or exchange them for something else).

If an individual decides to ask a family member to provide food and shelter it is necessary for the option to be viable, that there is at least one other family member who is prepared and able to provide the goods. Inherently market solutions and family solutions are "social" and require reciprocity between individuals. The reciprocity on a market is direct (something is exchanged immediately for something else); the reciprocity within a family is indirect (in the simplest case, something is received under the implicit promise to return a similar service to other members of the family). All in all it seems that the "individual solutions" in the title of this part are less individual than they first appeared.

Yet when considering risks over more than one period, market-and family-solutions require not only other individuals willing to trade or to provide, but also common views on the future however vague they may be. So even without the state or any other collectivity in the analysis, we have to conclude that individuals are not able to deal with their risks on their own. They need at least one other person to trade with or to receive from. But of course in the realm of the real world, individuals will use sophisticated forms of markets, institutions and contracts. We gave already the example of a labour market that encompasses more than a direct quid-pro-quo; we can easily add insurance markets as another example of an institution that is needed in the analysis of how social welfare is produced.

It makes clear that already in these simple cases there may be situations where no market-or family-solution is available, simply because there is no counterpart on the market or within the family. That is to say, situations wherein individuals may have opted for a market-or a family-solution for the satisfaction of their basic needs but are unsuccessful in realising the option. These situations are called market failure and family failure respectively. A look on what actually are the needs and the risks that we are analysing is necessary and we also need to relax the assumption that all individuals are equal (this assumption has been made implicitly so far).

BASIC NEEDS OR MAIN NEEDS

The argument so far referred to the satisfaction of basic needs only. This reduced the analysis to something we thought was understood similarly by all of us. In fact, this was an (temporary useful) illusion. Although all agree that some food and some physical protection in the forms of clothing and a shelter are needed to survive, we would start to disagree when we would try to define what exactly this would mean. How much food? Which food? How much clothing and which clothing? And what kind of roof above our head? It is easy to understand that the actual definition of the content or even the level of basic needs that need to be fulfilled highly depend on physical and geographical location. The need for shelter in Alaska is different from that in the Caribbean; the cloths providing adequate protection against the wind and the sun in the Central African deserts are different from what is basically needed in French Polynesia or in Paris. Attempts to retract to the very basics and talking about minimum calorie-intake when talking about food, may give you the illusion of getting near a universal definition of basic needs. It is, however, defective as well. Even if it would be possible to define the absolute minimum to avoid starvation, the composition of the intake in terms of minerals, proteins and other substances would matter. And the issue would start to be complicated further if the question arises "avoid starvation to do what?" To sit down in the shadow of a tree, to work on farm-land, to deliver (healthy) babies, to attend school or to work in the metal industry?

But yet the complication is not complete: needs also differ across time. Certainly the definition of the basic assets and goods that you need to survive in New York City or Brussels in the twenty first century differ from those needed in the same places just after the Second World War. And we could go on. It comes down to the observation that it is nearly impossible and perhaps not very useful to try to define what basic needs exactly are. We better talk about needs that individuals want to be fulfilled. They differ across time and location and they are relative to the prevailing standards of a given society. This does not mean we that we can dismiss the question if minimum standards all together; it comes up again at length when measurement problems and poverty and actual social policy practices are discussed.

It has, however, one important implication at the introduction of this analysis: it de-links the notion of social policy and the idea of securing the fulfilment of basic needs. Social policy is definitely not limited to public interventions aimed at providing means to everybody to fulfil basic needs only. Some parts of social policy are related to that specific aim, but many other parts are not. The link between basic needs and social policy is sometimes brought to the footlight in the political rhetoric surrounding the reform of social policy or the welfare state but it is far from actual reality in all the economies that we consider. However, does this imply that from now on all needs will be considered as the potentially being linked to social policy? Theoretically this would defendable, but this is as far from actual policy practice as the myopic view that links social policy to basic needs only. Some demarcation of the area is useful and inevitable if we do not want to get lost. The criterion to use for deciding what needs shall be envisaged when talking about the social management of risks, can not be found in theoretical decisions; we have not much more than common sense and policy practices in the countries we focus on. Amartya Sen's approach of talking about capabilities is of relevance here though.

The needs that can be considered as mostly prominently to the realm of the social management of risks are:

- Access to housing and utilities
- Access to food

- Access to health and healthy sexual reproduction
- Access to security, civil-and human-rights
- Access to social participation.

The first three are easy to understand ("healthy reproduction" referring to the physical and social circumstances that allows human beings to prorecreation). Access to security reflects the need to be protected from criminal activities and the access to human rights; access to social participation refers to the need for individuals to be truly embedded in the social and economic life of the community they live in; when this access is not secured we can speak of "social exclusion".

Starting from this list it can be seen that a lot of what we would define as social policy, is difficult to assess as directly related to one of these needs except for those policies that would define benefits in kind only, such as health care, food distribution, housing. The reality, however, is that much of what we would regard as the social management of risks or social policy is not directly related with providing goods and services that would satisfy these needs, but is focussed on the means to get access to the fulfilment of these needs. In many situations and in most of the countries we study, this implies in the first place to secure income for all individuals in order to guarantee that they can buy access to all these things.

And besides on income directly, a lot of social policy is related to mechanisms that allow individuals to generate the income themselves now and in the future namely to labour and to education. On the other hand, while very important if absent, the access to security in terms of physical protection and human rights is usually not defined as part of social policy. For advanced capitalist economies we could assume that these rights are secured but that does not mean it can be left out of the analysis completely and certainly not when less developed economies are considered. Individual political-and economic-freedom, equal (legal) treatment regardless of gender, ethnicity or religion and institutions guaranteeing democracy are important pre-requisites for successful social policy.

Access to income has to be understood in its most broad meaning referring not only to income (or stocked wealth) in monetary terms, but also encompassing all means of existence provided in kind.

In advanced capitalist societies social policy cannot be understood if we refer to direct "income" provision only; a big part of social policy is linked to instruments that guarantee or improve the access to income for all members of a society namely labour and education. Therefore we explicitly add these two mechanisms to describe the scope of social policy (and of this book) knowing that the correlation between "income" on the one hand and labour and education on the other, are high:

- Access to labour (as the main income-generating mechanism)
- Access to education (as the main source for future income).

Access to security and civil-and human-rights has a different nature in this respect. These are goods that are difficult to provide on markets or families. Partial physical protection of your person and belongings can be bought on a market (security firms, private security agents, body guards) or provided by a family, but they cannot be fully regarded as normal economic goods (given their public goods elements). Civil-and human-rights are definitely never provided by markets or families. Guaranteed property rights, political rights and enforced equal treatment for example can only be produced by recognised and legitimate public authorities or a state. We regard them here as necessary and important prerequisites for social policy as we study it. This implies that, if civil-and human-rights are not secured, the analysis of the social management of risks has to start with a serious study of the impact of the lack of civil-and human-rights (the exclusion of certain groups from basic rights can not be ignored when studying the impact of social policy; for example a society guaranteeing access to education to its members but excluding women).

If, however, basic civil-and human-rights are secured, it does not mean that the issue can be ignored completely. This is more than a theoretical discussion even in advanced capitalist economies, wherein we may accept that these basic rights are secured. All legislation and certainly social policy legislation use a definition of the covered population in terms of citizenship, residence or contributors.

This regularly leaves members of society not fitting these criteria often without (social) protection. Illegal immigrants and refugees form a problem in this respect and not only because they themselves are deprived of protection, but also because they form an additional management problem for the protected part of the population. If for example illegal immigrants are denied access to the health system, a case of open tuberculosis threatens not only the health of the infected uncovered person but also the health of all the others persons he or she may infect. In spite of what we said, as suggested, focus our attention to the main needs assuming that basic civil-and human-rights are secured in the societies we study.

Although the problem setting seems to have shifted considerably compared with the simple case we started with in the beginning, it is theoretically only a minor change. Talking about main needs and the mechanisms applied to fulfil them does not change the options for the individuals fundamentally: individuals can still use markets and families to satisfy their needs. Markets will often be used, but families stay important as well, even outside the realm of the basic needs. In many more cases than believed at first sight, the production of wealth within families is an important substitute for the production of wealth on markets. Where markets fail, families will provide an obvious substitute in many cases. But even without failing markets, families will produce a significant part of welfare, although its actual amount depends on many variables (history, tradition, economic development, etc.). The state or public policy comes in where actually markets and families fail or where it is understood that the solutions produced by markets are either not efficient or not acceptable (not effective); hence when individuals are not believed, rightly or wrongly, to be able to manage the risks related to these needs and their mechanisms independently and that thus some social management is requested.

RISKS

What type of risks exactly are we considering? Basically only one risk, although it comes in many different forms, namely the risk of not or no longer being able to rely on either markets or the family to secure the satisfaction of the main needs. Under the assumption that different types of risks require different types reactions (by markets, by the family or by the state), it is useful for the analysis to distinguish different types of risks and different types of effects. As suggested, need these distinctions to analyse the efficiency and effectiveness of different welfare solutions provided by markets, families and the state now and in the past.

The first criterion to distinguish risks is by the population that is potentially affected. We then distinguish three basic forms, universal risks, life-cycle risks and categorical risks. Universal risks are in principle shared by all regardless of their age, gender or position in society. An easy example is the risk of getting involved in an accident that limits or prevent further activities on labour-or product-markets. It is tempting to believe that universal risks are randomly distributed among the population, but this is in fact not true and theoretically unnecessary.

Universal risks can strike theoretically everybody in a society, but that does not imply that everybody is exposed to same degree to the risk. In our example, everybody can be involved in an accident, but some groups in society are more "accident-prone" than others. This is an important remark and as suggested, need this as an element to explain insurances and government interventions in insurance markets in.

Life-cycle risks are also in principle shared by all but are specific to a certain age or to specific stages in the course of life for everybody. Old age infirmity caused by Alzheimer disease for example is an obvious example. Categorical risks (sometimes called class-or group-risks) are risks that are peculiar to certain groups in the society for example miners, women or men. The risk to develop mining-related lung diseases or to develop breast-or prostate-cancer is not shared by everybody. Trying to distinguish risks by their effects, three categories stand out: incident effects, lifetime effects and intergenerational effects. Incident effects refer to the effects that are directly related to the event and disappear after a relatively short period of time. Temporary unemployment and short-term illnesses usually have only incident effects. Lifetime effects are related to risks that usually have a long lasting effect on a persons' life. Long-term unemployment and disability usually can be seen as having lifetime effects. Inter-generational effects are seen when the effects of an unfortunate event are passed on to the next generation and reproduced over the generations. Disability leading to welfare benefit dependency may affect the earning capacity of a breadwinner in a way that it jeopardises the chances of his/her children to invest in education and to enter the labour market.

Remark that risks can have various effects simultaneously; an event can first lead to incident effects, but later lifetime and/or inter-generational effects may result. Risks and their effects can be classified according to these criteria and further refining in the classifications can be made. These distinctions will be important in order to analyse how much of the risk management is left to markets and the family and how much is (or could be) taken up by public interventions (the state). The typology and intuitively it can already be understood that markets and families will have more difficulties in coping with the risks.

WHERE ARE WE

Individuals faced with the problem of fulfilling their main needs can cover their needs by actions on (product-and labour) .markets and by relying on the family. We introduced a couple of characteristics of markets and families that are important in understanding their basic functioning (for example that they are essentially social and assume reciprocity). We also discussed briefly a first set of conditions for their functioning and introduced limitations to their potential impact. Nothing was said so far on public interventions and social policy.

Individuals face risks that come in many forms and appearances. That is a complication compared to the previous situation because it introduces the time dimension. The basic risk is that individuals are uncertain on whether they will be able to fulfil their mains needs in the future. This may be due to the fact that either the outcome of their actions on markets or the support provided by families is uncertain or due to external shocks disrupting or disturbing the mechanisms by which markets and families can guarantee the fulfilment of main needs. We had to introduce the capital market as an extra possibility for individuals to cope with risks. A good deal of the social policy literature is devoted to the analysis under which theoretical conditions and historical circumstances public policy is used and/or needed to complement market-and family-solutions to the problem of the fulfilment of main needs under uncertainty/risks.

We assessed the needs that we are studying as main needs to be distinguished from basic needs leaving a broad area as possibly be covered by social policy in conjunction with markets and the family. Again the standard literature analyses which historical and theoretical forms this social policy can take and has taken in various countries. We introduced a typology of risks (related to external shocks). That gave us a first impression about how for various risks and effects different combinations of markets, families and the state are used to cover risks. In order to complete our "tour d' horizon" of the concepts that we need to proceed with the analysis and of the interrelation between the concepts, there are two additional issues that have to be introduced:

1. Unequal individuals and
2. A typology of government interventions that can be regarded as social management of risks.

INDIVIDUALS ARE NOT EQUAL

So far we talked about individuals as if all individuals are alike and all have the same options and possibilities. This is a useful assumption that actually is used extensively in economic and social theory in order to bring the analysis to level of complication that we can handle. But we want to relax the assumption now (temporarily) because its upholding would hide the view on an important set of risks and on crucial aspects of social policy. Moreover, we are not able to understand the standard equity arguments for social policy if we do not explicitly account for inequality among individuals (remark that by distinguishing categorical-and life-cycle risks we already introduced some forms of inequality).

Individuals are not equal in many respects. First people differ in their capabilities and talents they are born with, however we may assume that these capabilities and talents are randomly distributed in the economy. More importantly in this context, however, is that individuals are not living in equal or even similar social environments. We abstract here from geographical differences: of course it matters whether you are born in Japan, South-Africa, The United States or Germany, but these are not the differences we want to focus on. Even within countries there are huge differences.

The major differences that are important is this context are twofold:

1. Individuals are born within a household with a specific place in the income distribution;
2. Individuals are embedded in different social network-settings.

For simplicity's sake we often disregard the first difference in economic theory, but when trying to understand the logic and practice of social policy, it is impossible to ignore it. As a major consequence individual differ sharply in the way then can rely on markets and especially on families when it comes to coping with needs and risks. It is not difficult to understand that inherited wealth and family wealth can make a big difference in the way a family can support its members in order to fulfil basic needs and to cope with the risks surrounding them. It is, however, also important when dealing with market options. Statistically spoken, persons growing up in households that belong to higher income groups usually have better educational opportunities and thus we have more possibilities on the labour market. Also their bargaining power on capital markets may differ seriously from the possibilities of people growing up in lower income brackets households. In general and from a statistical point of view, markets tend to reproduce and reinforce inequalities. The resulting inequality is not a theoretical issue when thinking about social policy, but has played a decisive role in the way social policy has been shaped throughout the centuries.

Trying to unlink wealth levels of parents and children is associated with notions of social justice and is still regarded by many societies as an important aim of social policy. This is not saying that individuals cannot change their place in the income distribution. Many examples can be referred to in order to argue that indeed there is upward-and downward social mobility, but that does not imply that in most of the economies, market outcomes tend to reproduce rather than to change the place of individuals within the income distributions. The issue is that, not only financial and economic possibilities and capabilities of individuals differ according to their place in the income distribution, but also the nature, extent and quality of the social network they belong to differ along the same line. This is usual referred to as the social capital of persons. We prefer to emphasize the embeddedness of individuals in networks in general.

Again, outside the market, it can be understood easily that networks may act as an important extension of the family when it comes to the production and distribution of welfare. Many research results, however, also point to the importance of networks (their extent and quality) when an individual operates on markets. The access and place an individual get into the job market differ significantly across persons with different networks to give only one example. Networks are more dynamic than the income distribution and a person will change networks during his/her life-cycle, but still there is a certain degree of stability and individuals can not change their network voluntary as the change their cloths. Moreover, networks have another interesting and relevant aspect in the context of social policy. Sometimes networks develop into institutions by establishing a certain degree of routine and formality into themselves. We cannot explore the mechanisms of institution building in detail in this context, but it is important to understand that institutions have played and important role in the context of social policy design, formation and implementation. To quote only one institution that definitely has had (and still has) his influence on social policy we would refer to labour unions.

As suggested, argue later that labour unions are not only important to explain historical forms of social policy, but for example are also important institutions in the opposition to changes in the design of social policy, even if the members of the network constituting the institution would favour the changes. The analytically important element is here that when it comes to analyse the practice of social policy, it will not be sufficient to look at individual persons only, but collective actors play a decisive role. We need this as an element to explain changes and international differences in social policy practice. It all goes well beyond the level of analysis were we can limit ourselves to analyse individuals only. We confine ourselves here to concluding that individuals may have a new option related to the fulfilment of main needs and coping with risks. Rather than turning to the market or to the family, individuals may associate themselves with other individuals in the context of a network or an institution. Voluntary informal insurance associations or sickness funds associations for example have played an important role in shaping the social management of the health risk.

POLICY STRATEGIES AND POLICY INSTRUMENTS

The definition of social policy as the social management of risks, allows a new and more interesting view on policy options. The policy strategies and the policy instruments that public authorities can theoretically use in the social policy area become more divers and more in accordance with the policy practices. Traditionally the definitions of social policy, social protection policy, social security policy or welfare state policy have followed the rationale of the grounds for government interventions in an economy: efficiency grounds and equity grounds. This implied that government instruments for interventions are categorised as either correcting the outcome (distribution) of market-and family-processes (usually on equity grounds) or correcting/ substituting the functioning of markets (largely on efficiency grounds). Defining social policy as the social management of risk does not make the catalogue of policy instruments much bigger, but it puts the various instruments in relations to each other.

Moreover, it emphasises the impact of combination of instruments rather than the impact of single instruments and it focuses our attention to the fact that public authorities are only one of the corners of the triangle that deals with welfare production and the management of risks. It also allows us to deal with instruments and strategies that are traditionally not seen as belonging to the core of social policy and to make international comparisons of how societies deal with the impact of contingencies or of market-and family-failure. With the growing sophistication in social policy instruments and the advances made in the analysis of their impact, it became clear that the analytical separation of social policy from other policy areas (such as for example education, business-cycle policy, structural adjustment policy, etc.) and from market-and family-based risk-managing-options is increasingly difficult. The international comparative analyses of the welfare state as made by Esping-Andersen and the OECD (among others), the attempts to conceptualise and international comparative notion of "social quality" (as attempted for example by the UNinspired human development index and others), the attempts to understand social policy under the old Soviet system and its transition into an market-oriented economy and the everyday practice of policy formulation, all made us aware that governments and public authorities may use very different instruments to meet objectives traditionally linked to social policy only.

Addressing the risk of an income loss due to unemployment for example is traditionally linked in Western welfare states to unemployment insurance benefits and contributions only. But of course we know that this problem may be addressed by many different instruments including providing unemployment insurance benefits but also including assisting unemployed with labour exchange services, creating public work jobs, enforcing workfare programmes, stimulating people to leave the labour force by early retirement, disability benefits or prolonged schooling, advocating lower wages, increasing labour market flexibility, reducing inflation, securing private firms' profits, stimulating people to live together (or stay with their parents) so that they are not depending on a single wage or a single income source, stimulating workers to save so that they can smooth their income over time, supporting charity through NGO's, stimulating people to become self-employed, stimulating labour hoarding within private and public enterprises, and many more. The policy objective "reducing the effects of income losses due to unemployment", can be met by all these instruments.

This goes far beyond the traditional social policy instrument of unemployment insurance. All these instruments are found in the policy-practise of various countries, but if we would try to compare countries in the way they deal with the policy objective on the basis of how they deal with unemployment insurance only, the analysis would be seriously hampered and be left incomplete. The concepts introduced with the social management of risks allow us to subdivide public policy strategies in a more interesting way. Following Holzman and Jørgensen we distinguish preventive strategies, mitigation strategies and coping strategies.

Preventive strategies are aimed at avoiding the risk by organising economic and social life in a way the probability of a contingency is reduced. Good governance of the physical environment for example, macroeconomic stabilisation policy, sufficient regulation of markets, effective law enforcement are all examples of instruments that can be used in this respect. Special attention should be given to effective employment protection and regulation of labour contracts, since they protect at least the main income source for many individuals in an economy. Many more policy actions be referred to in this context. All the initiatives have in common that they intend to produce a less risky environment for the members of a society. Mitigation strategies are aimed at reducing the potential impact of a contingency once the risk materialises. Public stimulation of saving accounts and mandated or public pension systems are example of instruments in this respect. Largely mitigation strategies can consist of portfolio diversification strategies and insurance mechanisms. Portfolio diversification strategies aim at reducing the impact of a contingency by spreading the income or social-and economic-resources of an individual. Investment in human capital, investment in social capital (networks), extended family formation and savings in cash and kind belong to this category. Insurance mechanisms pool the risks of many individuals and spread the impact of a contingency over many persons.

Coping strategies relieve the impact of a contingency that is not covered by a mitigation strategy-instrument. Direct social assistance in cash and kind and other direct income transfers are examples of public interventions that belong to this category. This is also the place to stress again that a government may focus solely on finding a solution that is entirely under its own control. It is, however, equally possible that the public authorities take actions that require or even rest entirely on the families or markets taking up their responsibilities. In all these activities public authorities can use the traditional instruments as found in the standard public finance literature and aimed at correcting the functioning of markets and families, at complementing the functioning of markets and families and at substituting markets and families.

The actual tools applied to realise these aims are usually given by the following list:

- Information
- Regulation
- Taxes and subsidies
- Prohibition of production
- Public production
- Income transfers.

CONCLUSION

The thesis introduces a conceptual framework that redefines social policy in a way that facilitates the analysis of actual policy practices and allows a more comprehensive international comparative analysis. The conceptual framework starts with the notion of main needs and defines and subdivides the risks threatening the satisfaction of these main needs. An important feature of the framework is that social policy is not only linked to the satisfaction of the main needs at a certain moment, but to the risk that, at a certain moment in the life-course of an individual, the needs cannot not be satisfied.

Social policy is then no longer solely focussed on the guaranteeing that all individuals in an economy can fulfil their main needs in a static framework. Quite the contrary, social policy is focused on preventing contingencies to materialise, on mitigating the effects before they materialise and on coping with the unfortunate moment bad luck, shocks or unfortunate events strike. The social risk management framework rests on the observation that the satisfaction of main needs and the management of risks, is not the sole responsibility of public authorities. Social welfare is produced by at least three institutions symbolically summarised as the social welfare triangle of which markets, families and public authorities form the corner-points. It may sound as if the Social Risk framework provides us with the ultimate yardstick to judge the efficiency and effectiveness of social policy and to compare its results across countries and time. This is, however, not true. What it does, is providing a framework that widens our scope of policy instruments and strategies when it comes to designing social policy. It also enhances our understanding of the interdependencies between what public authorities do and what markets and family contribute to the optimisation of social welfare and it even provides a unified scheme for mapping policy initiatives and their impact. It is a major progress compared to the practice where social policy or welfare states were compared on the basis of usually Continental European or Anglo-Saxon social security institutions, but it does not solve the problem that judgments have to be made. Societies and governments make choices and these choices are not pure technical.

They encompass visions on what is desirable in terms of outcomes and on what is acceptable in terms of costs. It still makes a lot of difference whether a society aims at relieving extreme poverty or whether a society wants the welfare of persons to become independent from the welfare of their parents. Trying to judge the first policy objective with the yardstick of the latter, or vice versa, is uninteresting and misleading. The introduction of the social risk management framework does not change that. It does change, however, our view on the toolkits we may use in order to reach the policy objectives set and it provides us with a comprehensive and powerful conceptual instrument to understand the outcomes and impact of social policy as well as its costs.

11

Social Cognitive Theory of Gender Development

The present object addresses the psychosocial determinants and mechanisms by which society socializes male and female infants into masculine and feminine adults. Gender development is a fundamental issue because some of the most important aspects of people's lives, such as the talents they cultivate, the conceptions they hold of themselves and others, the sociostructural opportunities and constraints they encounter, and the social life and occupational paths they pursue are heavily prescribed by societal gender-typing. It is the primary basis on which people get differentiated with pervasive effects on their daily lives.

Gender differentiation takes on added importance because many of the attributes and roles selectively promoted in males and females tend to be differentially valued with those ascribed to males generally being regarded as more desirable, effectual and of higher status. Although some gender differences are biologically founded, most of the stereotypic attributes and roles linked to gender arise more from cultural design than from biological endowment. This object provides an analysis of gender role development and functioning within the framework of social cognitive theory and distinguishes it from other theoretical formulations.

THEORETICAL PERSPECTIVES

Over the years several major theories have been proposed to explain gender development. The theories differ on several important dimensions. One dimension concerns the relative emphasis placed on psychological, biological, and sociostructural determinants. Psychologically-oriented theories tend to emphasize intrapsychic processes governing gender development. In contrast, sociological theories focus on sociostructural determinants of gender-role development and functioning. The biologically-oriented theories, gender differences arising from the differential biological roles played by males and females in reproduction underlie gender-role development and differentiation. A second dimension concerns the nature of the transmission models.

Psychological theories typically emphasize the cognitive construction of gender conceptions and styles of behaviour within the familial transmission model. This model was accorded special prominence mainly as a legacy of Freud's emphasis on adoption of gender roles within the family through the process of identification. Behaviouristic theories also have accorded prominence to parents in shaping and regulating gender-linked conduct. In theories favouring biological determinants, familial genes are posited as the transmission agent of gender differentiation across generations.

Sociologically-oriented theories emphasize the social construction of gender roles mainly at the institutional level. Social cognitive theory of gender-role development and functioning integrates psychological and sociostructural determinants within a unified conceptual framework. In this perspective, gender conceptions and role behaviour are the products of a broad network of social influences operating both familially and in the many societal systems encountered in everyday life. Thus, it favours a multifaceted social transmission model rather than mainly a familial transmission model.

The third dimension concerns the temporal scope of the theoretical analyses. Most psychological theories treat gender development as primarily a phenomenon of early childhood rather than one that operates throughout the life course. However, rules of gender-role conduct vary to some degree across social contexts and at different periods in life. Moreover, sociocultural and technological changes necessitate revision of pre-existing conceptions of what constitutes appropriate gender conduct. Gender role development and functioning are not confined to childhood but are negotiated throughout the life course. While most theories of gender development have been concerned with the early years of development or have focused on adults, sociocognitive theory takes a life-course perspective.

Therefore, the analysis of the sociocognitive determinants of gender orientations will span the entire age range. Nor is the theory restricted predominantly to cognitive or social factors. Rather cognitive, social, affective and motivational processes are all accorded prominence. Before presenting the sociocognitive perspective on gender development, the main psychological, biological and sociological perspectives on gender differentiation are briefly reviewed.

PSYCHOANALYTIC THEORY

Psychoanalytic theory posited different processes to explain gender development in boys and girls. Initially, both boys and girls are believed to identify with their mothers. However, between 3 to 5 years of age this changes and children identify with the same-sex parent. Identification with the same-sex parent is presumed to resolve the conflict children experience as a result of erotic attachment to the opposite-sex parent and jealousy towards the same-sex parent. This attachment causes children much anxiety as they fear retaliation from the same-sex parent. The lack of a visible genitalia in girls fuels boys' castration anxieties. Girls face a more complex situation. They feel resentment over being deprived of a penis, inferior, and fear retaliation from the mother for their designs on their father. The conflicting relationship is resolved through identification with the same-sex parent.

The process of identification is depicted as one in which children undertake wholesale adoption of the characteristics and qualities of the same-sex parent. Through this process of identification, children become sex-typed. Because identification with the same-sex parent is stronger for boys than girls, boys are expected to be more strongly sex-typed. Although psychoanalytic theory has had a pervasive early influence in developmental psychology, there is little empirical evidence to support it. A clear relationship between identification with the same-sex parent and gender-role adoption has never been empirically verified. Children are more likely to model their behaviour after nurturant models or socially powerful ones than after threatening models with whom they have a rivalrous relationship.

Lack of empirical support for classic psychoanalytic theory has led to a variety of reformulations of it. In the gender domain, a notable recasting is offered by Chodorow. In this view, gender identification begins in infancy rather than during the later phallic stage as proposed by Freud. Both male and female infants initially identify with their mother. However, because the mother is of the same sex as her daughter, identification is expected to be stronger between mothers and their daughters than between mothers and their sons. During the course of development, girls continue to identify with their mothers and they also psychologically merge with her. As a consequence, the daughter's self-concept is characterized by mutuality and a sense of relatedness that orients her towards interpersonal relationships. This interpersonal orientation is the main reason why women engage in mothering. They seek to re-establish a sense of interpersonal connectedness reminiscent of their relationship with their mother but absent in their adult relationships with men. This pattern of development contrasts with that of boys who increasingly separate themselves from their mothers and define themselves in terms of difference from females. They begin to denigrate femininity in an attempt to establish their own separateness and individuation.

The empirical findings, however, are no more supportive of Chodorow's theory than of classic psychoanalytic theory. There is no evidence that the attachment bond is any stronger between mothers and daughters than mothers and sons. Nor is there any evidence that women's relational needs and sense of well-being are fulfilled only by being mothers. Bernard notes that women whose sole role is one of mother and wife have higher rates of mental dysfunction than childless married and single women and working mothers. Finally, this theory is at odds with women's striving for greater independence and equality between the sexes.

COGNITIVE DEVELOPMENTAL THEORY

Cognitive developmental theory, gender identity is postulated as the basic organizer and regulator of children's gender learning. Children develop the stereotypic conceptions of gender from what they see and hear around them. Once they achieve gender constancy—the belief that their own gender is fixed and irreversible—they positively value their gender identity and seek to behave only in ways that are congruent with that conception. Cognitive consistency is gratifying, so individuals attempt to behave in ways that are consistent with their self-conception. Kohlberg posited the following cognitive processes that create and maintain such consistency: "I am a boy, therefore I want to do boy things, therefore the opportunity to do boy things is rewarding". In this view, much of children's conduct is designed to confirm their gender identity. Once children establish knowledge of their own gender, the reciprocal interplay between one's behaviour and thoughts leads to a stable gender identity, or in cognitive-developmental theory terms, the child achieves gender constancy.

Kohlberg defined gender constancy as the realization that one's sex is a permanent attribute tied to underlying biological properties and does not depend on superficial characteristics such as hair length, style of clothing, or choice of play activities. Development of gender constancy is not an all or none phenomenon. Three discrete levels of gender understanding comprise gender constancy. From least to most mature forms of gender understanding, these are designated as the gender identity, stability, and consistency components of gender constancy. "Gender identity" requires the simple ability to label oneself as a boy or girl and others as a boy, girl, man, or woman. "Gender stability" is the recognition that gender remains constant over time—that is, one's sex is the same now as it was when one was a baby and will remain the same in adulthood.

The final component of gender constancy, "gender consistency", is mastered at about age six or seven years. The child now possesses the added knowledge that gender is invariant despite changes in appearance, dress or activity. Children are not expected to adopt gender-typed behaviours consistently until after they regard themselves unalterably as a boy or a girl, which usually is not achieved until about six years of age.

Although Kohlberg's theory attracted much attention over the decades, its main tenets have not fared well empirically. Studies generally have failed to corroborate the link between children's attainment of gender constancy and their gender-linked conduct. Long before children have attained gender constancy, they prefer to play with toys traditionally associated with their gender, to model their behaviour after same-sex models and to reward peers for gender- appropriate behaviour. Moreover, growing awareness of gender constancy does not increase children's preferences for same-gender roles and activities.

The findings of other lines of research similarly fail to support the major tenets of this theory. Although stable gender constancy is not attained until about six years of age, 2-year olds perform remarkably well in sorting pictures of feminine and masculine toys, objects of clothing, tools and appliances in terms of their typical gender relatedness. Children's ability to classify their own and others' sex and some knowledge of gender-role stereotypes is all that is necessary for much early gender typing to occur. These categorization skills are evident in most three- and four-year olds. Clearly, gender constancy is not a prerequisite for gender development. Factors other than gender constancy govern children's gender-linked conduct.

In response to the negative findings, the gender constancy measure was modified to demonstrate that the assessment procedure rather than the theory is at fault for the lack of linkage of gender constancy to gender conduct. The modifications included altering the inquiry format, the use of more realistic stimuli, and less reliance on verbal responses. Although some of these modifications showed that children understand gender constancy earlier than Kohlberg had suggested, most children under 4 years do not fully understand the concept of constancy regardless of the form of its assessment. More importantly, there is no relationship between children's understanding of gender constancy and their preference for gender-linked activities, preference for same-gender peers, or emulation of same-gender models, regardless of how gender constancy is assessed.

GENDER SCHEMA THEORY

Several gender schema theories have been proposed to explain gender development and differentiation. The social psychological approaches advanced by Bem and Markus and her associates have centered mainly on individual differences in gender schematic processing of information. Martin and Halverson's approach emphasizes the developmental aspects of schema development and functioning. This theory has many similarities to cognitive-developmental theory, but departs from it in several ways.

Rather than requiring the attainment of gender constancy for development of gender orientations, only the mastery of gender identity, the ability of children to label themselves and others as males or females, is considered necessary for gender schema development to begin. Once formed, it is posited that the schema expands to include knowledge of activities and interests, personality and social attributes, and scripts about gender-linked activities. The schema is presumably formed from interactions with the environment, but the process by which gender features that constitute the knowledge structure of the schema are abstracted remain unspecified. Once the schema is developed, children are expected to behave in ways consistent with traditional gender roles. The motivating force guiding children's gender-linked conduct, as in cognitive developmental theory, relies on gender-label matching in which children want to be like others of their own sex. For example, dolls are labeled "'for girls' and 'I am a girl' which means 'dolls are for me'". However, in addition to the lack of specification of the gender-abstraction process, empirical efforts to link gender schema to gender-linked conduct in young children have not fared well.

Results of empirical tests call into question the determinative role of gender schema. The evidence linking gender labeling to activity and peer preferences is mixed at best. A few studies have found a link, others report conflicting results across different measures of gender-linked conduct and still others have failed to find any link at all. Even in the studies that report a relationship, it remains to be determined whether gender labeling and gender-linked preferences are causally linked or are merely coeffects of social influences and cognitive abilities. Parents who react evaluatively to gender-linked conduct have children who are early gender labelers. Hence, gender labeling and preference may both be products of parental influence.

Knowledge of gender stereotypes, which are generalized preconceptions about the attributes of males and females, is similarly unrelated to gender-linked conduct. Children's preferences for gendered activities emerge before they know the gender linkage of such activities. A gender schema represents a more generic knowledge structure about maleness and femaleness.

Gender schema theory would predict that the more elaborated the gender knowledge children possess, the more strongly they should show gender-linked preferences. However, this hypothesized relationship receives no empirical support. Adults, for example, may be fully aware of gender stereotypes but this does not produce incremental prediction of gender-linked conduct as such knowledge increases. These various results fail to confirm gender knowledge as the determinant of gender-linked conduct.

Gender schema theory has provided a useful framework for examining the cognitive processing of gender information once gender schemas are developed. In particular, it has shed light on how gender-schematic processing affects attention, organization, and memory of gender-related information. Other models of gender schema that focus on adults have similarly demonstrated gender biases in information processing. The more salient or available the schema, the more individuals are expected to attend to, encode, represent, and retrieve information relevant to gender. However, gender-schematic processing is unrelated to either children's or adult's gender conduct or the findings are inconsistent across different measures of gender schematization.

A gender schema is not a monolithic entity. Children do not categorize themselves as "I am girl" or "I am a boy" and act in accordance with that schema invariantly across situations and activity domains. Rather they vary in their gender conduct depending on a variety of circumstances. Variability is present at the adult level as well. A woman may be a hard-driving manager in the workplace but a traditionalist in the functions performed in the home. Some students of gender differentiation, drawing on Lifton's "protean self", explain contradictory gender-role behaviour in terms of subselves doing their separate things. The problems with a multiple-self theory have been addressed elsewhere and will be mentioned only briefly here. It requires a regress to a superordinate self who has to manage the inharmonious subselves. There is really only one self that can do diverse things, including discordant ones on different occasions and under different circumstances. The selective engagement and disengagement of self-regulatory mechanisms by the same being predict variation in conduct, including contradictory styles of behaviour.

A further limitation of gender schema theory is that it cannot explain the asymmetry in findings between boys and girls. Boys and girls differ in the extent to which they prefer same-gender activities, emulate same-gender models and play with same-gender peers, yet most studies find no differences in girls' and boys' gender stereotypic knowledge. Both cognitive-developmental theory and gender schema theory have focused on gender conceptions, but neither devotes much attention to the mechanisms by which gender-linked conceptions are acquired and translated to gender-linked conduct. Nor do they specify the motivational mechanism for acting in accordance with a conception.

Knowing a stereotype does not necessarily mean that one strives to behave in accordance with it. For example, self-conception as an elderly person does not enhance valuation and eager adoption of the negative stereotypic behaviour of old age. Evidence that gender conception is insufficient to explain variations in gender-linked conduct should not be misconstrued as negation of cognitive determinants.

As will be explained in subsequent sections, social cognitive theory posits a variety of motivational and self-regulatory mechanisms rooted in cognitive activity that regulate gender development and functioning. These include, among other things, cognitions concerning personal efficacy, evaluative standards, aspirations, outcome expectations rooted in a value system, and perception of sociostructural opportunities and constraints.

BIOLOGICAL THEORIES

Biologically-oriented theories have also been proposed to explain gender development and differentiation. Evolutionary psychology is one such theory that views gender differentiation as ancestrally programmed. The ancestral origin of differences in gender roles is anlaysed in terms of mate preferences, reproductive strategies, parental investment in offspring, and the aggressive nature of males.

Viewed from this perspective, contemporary gender differences originated from successful ancestral adaptation to the different reproductive demands faced by men and women. Men contributed less to their offsprings' chances of survival so they sought multiple partners and were less choosy with whom to mate. In addition, uncertainty of paternity raised the risk of investing resources in children who were not their own. In contrast, women have to carry the fetus and care for their offspring years after their birth.

Women adapted to their greater imposed role in reproduction and parenting by preferring fewer sexual partners and favouring those who would be good long-term providers of the basic necessities of life for themselves and their offspring.

Men, in contrast, attempted to maximize the likelihood of paternity by reproducing with numerous young and physically attractive females, suggestive of high fertility. Because of their size and strength advantage, males resolved problems arising from conflicting reproductive interests by exercising aggressive dominance over females.

Coercive force enables males to control female's sexuality and to mate with many females. As a legacy of this evolutionary history, women have come to invest more heavily than men in parenting roles. Males, in turn, evolved into aggressors, social dominators and prolific maters because such behaviour increased their success in propagating their genes.

The evolutionary psychology, many current gender differences, such as the number of sexual partners preferred, criteria for selecting sexual partners, aggression, jealousy and the roles they fulfill originated from the ancestral sex differentiated reproductive strategies. For example, the findings that men prefer women who are young and physically attractive and women prefer men who are financially well resourced as mates are considered supportive of biological selection.

Not all evolutionary theorists speak with one voice, however. Psychological evolutionists often take a more extreme deterministic stance regarding the rule of nature than do many biological evolutionists. Psychological evolutionists are also quick to invoke evolved behavioural traits as cultural universals, whereas biological evolutionists emphasize functional relations between organism and situated environment that underscores the diversifying selection influence of variant ecological contexts. It should also be noted that evolutionary psychology grounds gender differences in ancestral mating strategies, but it does not address at all the developmental changes that occur in gender conceptions and gendered conduct. Nor does it specify the determinants and mechanisms governing developmental changes across the life course.

Natural selection shapes for proximate utility not future purpose. Bodily structures and biological potentialities are shaped by the aimless forces of natural selection acting on random mutations or new gene recombinations. Depiction of ancestral males as seeking to maximize paternity and of ancestral females as looking for good providers suggest that they are acting on deliberate or tacit purpose. Strategies subserve goals.

Such appending of purpose to mating patterns and calling them "strategies," which are designed to bring about some goal, sounds more like a teleological explanation than a Darwinian functional explanation. Disclaimers that the strategies are not always in awareness still leaves them undertaken for some particular end. Moreover, it is conceptually and methodologically problematic to use mindful self-ratings as the indicants of mating preferences to which the individuals supposedly have no conscious access. The claim that evolutionary psychology provides the solution to the origin of gender differences in social behaviour simply raises the regress problem. For example, evolutionary explanations that attribute mating practices to "strategies" rather than to the work of blind selection forces beg the question of why males should seek to maximize paternity.

Evolutionary psychology is proposed as a superior alternative to more socially oriented explanations of gender differentiation. However, this view, which attributes overriding power to biology, is not without serious problems. It is mainly a descriptive and post hoc explanatory device that lacks the scientific rigor required of evolutionary analyses. What were the environmental pressures operating during the ancestral era when the differential reproductive strategies were allegedly developed? Neither molecular evidence from fossilized human remains nor detailed archaeological artifacts are provided to support the evolutionary storytelling about ancestral environmental selection pressures and the accompanying changes in genetic make-up. The genetic variation on which selection forces could have operated in the past of course remains unknown, but is there any evidence of genetic differences between present-day philanderers and monogamists? What empirical evidence is there that males prefer young fertile-looking females and females prefer richly-resourced males because of different genes?

Psychological evolutionism does not provide the mechanisms responsible for social patterns of behaviour nor does it specify the nature of the interactional relationship between genetic and environmental influences for disentangling their impact. Contrary to claims, predictions from psychological evolutionism are not consistently supported in comparative tests of evolutionary and sociostructural theories or by the attributes males and females prefer in their mates even question the evolutionary validity of some of the predictions made from evolutionary biology by psychological evolutionists.

Others challenge universalized predictions that are evolutionally relevant but portray organisms as disembodied from variant ecological conditions under which they live that present quite different selection pressures. Variations in ecological selective forces promote different adaptational patterns of behaviour. To add to the cultural diversity, belief systems about how reproduction works perpetuate distinctive mating patterns. For example, in societies where people believe it requires cumulative insemination by multiple partners to produce a baby, women have sexual intercourse with different men without attendant sexual jealousy. Aggressive skill may have had reproductive advantage in ancient times when males could lay claim to females at will, but cultural evolution of social norms and sanctions has essentially stripped it of reproductive benefit. Some males rule females by physical force, but most do not. Physical and sexual aggressors are more likely to populate prisons than the gene pool. Reproduction rates are governed mainly by sociocultural norms, socioeconomic status, religious beliefs and adoption of contraceptive methods rather than by aggressive proclivities and skill in intermale aggression.

The methods and data used by psychological evolutionists to link ancestral gender differentiation to current gendered preferences, attributes and roles have also come under fire. The research relies mainly on survey studies using rating scales without the type of detailed analysis of genetic make-up and genetic transmission mechanisms conducted in the evolutionary tradition. Surprisingly, mating behaviour is rarely measured.

For example, evidence for gender differences in the types of partners selected is based mainly on self-reported preferences rather than on actual choices. Evolutionary processes are governed by what people do not by what they say. Sprecher has shown that in their self-reports of what attracts them, males are more influenced than females by the partners' physical attractiveness but, in actual choices, both sexes are equally influenced by physical attractiveness. Zohar and Guttman likewise report very similar preferences by males and females in mate selections in their actual choices of mates.

If physically attractive females are the objects of sexual pursuit, what evidence is there that the attractive ones are selectively impregnated at higher rates than those regarded as less attractive just as to the prevailing cultural standards? Preference ratings cannot substitute for impregnation rates. Contrary to the view that parenting is the prime investment of women men in long-term partnerships invest extensively in their offspring and are quite selective in their choice of mates. The conversion of typicality ratings into proclivitive universalities is another major problem. Small gender differences in the statistical average of self-reported preferences for a spread of ratings that overlap markedly across the genders get invoked as universal biological proclivities ascribed to males and females as though they all behaved alike as dichotomously classified. The substantial diversity within gender groups, which an adequate theory must explain, is simply ignored.

Survey reports in which males say that, on average, they would like about 18 sexual partners, whereas women would settle for about 4 or 5 mates, are cited as corroborating evolutionary psychological theory. There is a big difference between verbalized preference and action. The more relevant data regarding male mating are what males do rather than what they say, and the variation in sexual practices among men. Widerman found that lifetime incidence of extramarital affairs was 23 per cent for males and 12 per cent for females, but affairs did not differ by gender for those under 40. The explanatory challenge for psychological evolutionism is why most males mate monogamously, and relatively few roam around impregnating young fertile females to populate the gene pool for subsequent generations. If prolific uncommitted sexuality is a male biological imperative, it must be an infirm one that can be easily overridden by psychosocial forces. Why married women would get sexually involved with multiple men, and thereby risk jealous assaults and loss of resources provided by the long-term mate is also problematic for psychological evolutionism. An explanation in terms of seeking socioemotional satisfaction and nonreproductive sexual pleasure is more plausible than ad hoc explanations that they are seeking better genes, supplemental resources or richer providers.

One can, of course, construct evolutionary scenarios of evolved genetic dispositions for males behaving as uncommitted sexual free lancers but then as committed monogamists, and homebody females as straying into infidelity. But such temporally flexible explanations, in which biological dispositions suddenly reverse direction from promoting philandering to upholding monogamy, are more like ad hoc theorizing than as derivations from an integrated core theory.

Evolutionary psychology fails to specify a mechanism governing the posited dispositional reversal, what triggers it, and when the reversal should occur. Not all males necessarily go through a philandering phase before settling down to a monogamous life. This casts serious doubt on the inherentness of the posited temporal sequencing of reproductive "strategies." How does the genetically-driven disposition know when a heterosexual relationship is a short-term affair or the beginning of what will become an enduring monogamous relationship? Many of the human characteristics that are sexually arousing—corpulence or skinniness; upright breasts or long pendulous ones; shiny white teeth or black pointed ones; distorted ears, noses or lips; light skin colour or dark—not only vary markedly across societies but bear no relevance to "good genes" or reproductive fertility and value. Human sexual arousal is driven more by the mind through cultural construction of attractiveness than by physical universals.

As indicated in the preceding comments, there is often selective inattention to discordant aspects of the very type of evidence marshaled in support of psychological evolutionism. Human aggression provides a further example. In response to meta-analytic studies showing small gender differences in aggression, Archer cites higher homicide rates in males as evidence that an evolved disposition is animating the homicidal behaviour. In fact, only a minute fraction of humans ever commit a homicide. Given the stiff competitiveness for desirable mates, the explanatory challenge for psychological evolutionism is why an intermale assaultive disposition that is considered so central in mate access and control is so rarely manifested. Nor can evolutionary factors explain large fluctuations in homicide rates over short periods, which are largely tied to level of drug activities rather than to reproduction battles. Of the small number of people who happen to kill, they do so for all sorts of reasons, the least of which may be a drive to maximize paternity.

With regard to intergender violence, sexual assaults against women are prevalent in societies where male supremacy reigns, aggressive sexuality is valued as a sign of manliness and women are treated as property. In contrast, sexual assaults are rare in societies that repudiate interpersonal aggression, endorse sexual equality and treat women respectfully. The extensive cross-cultural and intracultural variability in male-female power relations and physical and sexual violence towards women disputes the view that using physical force against women is the rule of nature.

Ancestral origin and the determinants governing contemporary social practices are quite different matters. Because evolved potentialities can serve diverse purposes, ancestral origin dictates neither current function nor singular sociostructural arrangements. Did ancestral mating pressures really create a biological imperative to deny women voting rights until 1926 in the United States, disallow them property rights; give men custody of children even though child caretaking is supposedly not men's inherent nature; curtail women's educational opportunities; bar them from entry into prestigious universities such as Yale until 1969; deny them equal pay for comparable work; impede their efforts to secure occupational advancements at upper organizational ranks; and refuse them membership in clubs where social networking and business transactions spawn occupational successes?

Evidence to be presented later suggests that the inequitable gender differentiation just described reflects, in large part, the constraints of custom and gender power and privilege imbalances in how the societal subsystems that preside over gender development are structured and operate. We shall return to some of these issues shortly when we consider the role of evolutionary factors in a social cognitive theory of gender role development. Other analyses of gender differences from a biological perspective have centered on hormonal influences and estimates of heritability. Hormones affect the organization of the neural substrates of the brain, including lateralization of brain function. It has been reported that females show less lateral brain specialization than do males, but the differences are small and some studies find no such difference. Difference in degree of brain lateralization is assumed to produce gender differences in cognitive processing.

Although girls generally do better on verbal tasks, and boys do better on some types of mathematical tasks, the differences are small. Moreover, the gender differences have been diminishing over the past decade, which is much too short a time to be genetically determined. However, there are clear and reliable differences in spatial skills favouring males. But this difference has also been diminishing in recent years, most likely as a function of social changes. Although hormones may play a part in spatial ability, the evidence suggests that environmental factors play a central role in the observed differences. Compared to girls, boys grow up in more spatially complex environments, receive more encouragement for outdoor play, and engage extensively in activities that foster the development of spatial skills. In accord with a social source, gender differences in spatial ability are not found in cultures where women are granted greater freedom of action.

The search for a hormonal basis for gender differences in social behaviour has produced highly conflicting results. Despite considerable research, the influence of hormones on behavioural development and cognitive functioning remains unclear. Drawing on atypical populations in which the developing fetus is exposed to high levels of prenatal male or female hormones, the findings show that girls increase engagement in traditionally male- and female-related activities, respectively. The causal link between hormones and behaviour, however, has not been established. Because these children often look different from other children of their own sex and parents are very much aware of their atypical condition, hormonal influences cannot be disentangled from social ones. In addition, the lack of relationship between prenatal hormones and gender-linked behaviour for boys raises further questions about whether hormonal factors could be the basis for gender-differentiated conduct.

Because of the empirical inconclusiveness and methodological problems associated with research on atypical populations, researchers have turned to studying conduct as a function of variations in hormonal levels where no abnormality exists prenatally. However, these findings not only fail to support those from atypical populations, but contradict them. For example, girls with naturally high levels of male hormones prenatally show low spatial ability in childhood, but girls wiThelevated male hormones prenatally occurring either artificially or from a genetic defect show high spatial ability. However, boys' spatial ability is unaffected by their prenatal hormonal levels. To add to the conflicting findings, male hormones in late adolescence and adulthood are weakly related to aggressive and antisocial conduct for males but not for females, whereas in childhood and early adolescence male hormones predict aggression for girls but not for boys. If the conditions governing this variability are identified, it would still remain to be determined whether hormonal levels are the cause or the effect of aggressive conduct or whether they operate only indirectly by lowering tolerance of frustration.

Researchers working within the framework of behavioural genetics examine gender differences in terms of the relative contribution of environmental and genetic factors to variation in given attributes. Identical and fraternal twins reared apart in different environments are tested for differences on a variety of cognitive abilities and personality characteristics.

Based on the results of such studies, it is concluded that genetic factors make low to moderate contribution to personality attributes. Most of the remaining variance is ascribed to nonshared environments unique to individual family members with little of it left to shared environments common to all members of the family. Although most of this research has focused on individual differences in general, several studies of children's gender-linked personality characteristics, namely masculinity and femininity, also report heritability estimates ranging from small to moderate. Mitchell and her colleagues report a higher genetic contribution to attributes traditionally sex-typed as masculine than to those sex-typed as feminine.

However, Rowe neither found any significant genetic contribution to femininity, nor could specify any biological processes that would render masculine-typed characteristics more heritable than feminine-type characteristics. The findings reveal a substantial contribution of nonshared environmental influences to these gendered personality characteristics. The results have led to downgrading parental influences on children's development and upgrading the impact of peers as a nonshared environment. However, this conclusion relies for its plausibility on a disputable environmental dualism and highly questionable assumptions on how social subsystems function. As will be shown later, parental and peer subsystems operate interdependently not as disjoined entities. Parents play an active role in structuring peer associations, fostering peer ties that are to their liking and discouraging those they disfavour.

Children who adopt parental values and standards choose friends on the basis of parental values. Consequently, the peer group serves to reinforce and uphold parental values. In discordant families, children may pick peer associates who bring them into conflict with their parents. Even in the latter case, parents also exert influence on peer selection, albeit through a rebuffing rather than adoptive process.

Parents are also linked interdependently to the peer group through their children's communication about their activities with peers outside the home. Parents, in turn, offer social support and guidance on how to manage predicaments that arise in peer relations. Given the complex interplay of personal, familial, peer and other social influences, dichotomous partitioning of social environments into segregated shared and nonshared entities distorts rather than clarifies causal processes. It should also be noted that the estimates of the environment are almost always based on cursory self-reports rather than on actual observation of familial and extrafamilial interactions and social practices and the degree of bidirectionality of influence.

Studies of the heritability of personality attributes rely almost exclusively on questionnaires that construe personality as global, decontextualized entities. In fact, personal proclivities are multifaceted, characterized by domain specificity and manifested contextually and conditionally. These global subdivisions of collections of ecologically-stripped behaviour represent neither the nature nor structure of personal determinants, and say nothing about the self-regulatory mechanisms governing their conditional expression. The heritability of multifaceted dispositions that better capture the dynamic nature of personality remains to be determined.

Some attributes, such as height, are more heritable than others, such as aesthetic preferences. High heritability does not mean unmodifiability by environmental means. For example, although height is highly heritable, it can vary substantially as a function of quality of nutrition. Cooper and Zubek placed genetically bred bright and dull learning rats in enriched or impoverished environments. Dull rats placed in an enriched environment performed as well as the bright ones reared normally, and bright rats placed in an impoverished environment performed as poorly as dull rats reared normally.

Clearly, heritability does not ordain destiny. The partitioning of behavioural variance into per cent biology and per cent environment flies in the face of their interdependence. Heritability refers to degree of genetic contribution to group variance not to individual causation. To explain individual behaviour, which is typically the product of multicausality, one must specify how the relevant constellation of determinants operate in concert within the causal structure rather than try to compute the per cent of the behaviour due to nature and the per cent due to nurture.

SOCIOLOGICAL THEORIES

In sociological theories, gender is a social construction rather than a biological given. The sources of gender differentiation lie more in social and institutional practices than in fixed properties of the individual. Drawing on diverse bodies of research, Geis documents masterfully the social construction and perpetuation of stereotypic gender differentiation. Gender stereotypes shape the perception, evaluation and treatment of males and females in selectively gendered ways that beget the very patterns of behaviour that confirm the initial stereotypes. Many gender differences in social behaviour are viewed as products of division of labour between the sexes that get replicated through sociostructural practices governed by disparate gender status and power.

Many sociologists reject the dichotomous view of gender, in that the similarities between men and women in how they think and behave far exceed the differences between them. With social changes in opportunity structures and constraining institutional arrangements, gender differences have declined over time. Gender is not a unitary monolith. The homogeneous gender typing disregards the vast differences among women and the similarly vast differences among men depending on their socioeconomic class, education, ethnicity, and occupation.

The practice of lumping all men and women into dichotomous gender categories, with men preordained for agentic functions and women for expressive and communion functions similarly comes in for heavy criticism. With regard to the emotionality stereotype, Epstein reminds us that although women are supposedly more emotional than men, in Mid-Eastern cultures, such as Iran, it is men who express emotions most fervently. She maintains that gender theorists who contend that males and females are basically different in their psychological make-up are contributing to gender stereotyping and polarization.

The exaggeration of the nature and extent of gender differences, the theorists argue, promotes the social ordering of gender relations and serves to justify gender inequality, occupational stratification and segregation, and the situating of women in positions of predominately lower status. Viewed from this sociological perspective, the pattern of opportunity structures and formal and informal constraints shape gendered styles of behaviour and channel men and women into different life paths. The coupling of gender roles to biological sex status legitimates social arrangements as accommodations to differences attributed to inherent nature.

Not all people of the same socioeconomic status, and who live under the same opportunity structures, social controls, familial, educational and community resources and normative climate, behave in the same way. The challenge is to explain adaptational diversity within sociostructural commonalty. As will be shown later, social cognitive theory adopts an integrated perspective in which sociostructural influences operate through self-system mechanisms to produce behavioural effects.

However, the self system is not merely a conduit for external influences. People are producers as well as products of social systems. Social structures are created by human activity. The structural practices, in turn, impose constraints and provide resources and opportunity structures for personal development and functioning.

SOCIAL COGNITIVE THEORY

Social cognitive theory acknowledges the influential role of evolutionary factors in human adaptation and change, but rejects one-sided evolutionism in which social behaviour is the product of evolved biology, but social and technological innovations that create new environmental selection pressures for adaptiveness have no effect on biological evolution. In the bidirectional view of evolutionary processes, evolutionary pressures fostered changes in bodily structures and upright posture conducive to the development and use of tools, which enabled an organism to manipulate, alter and construct new environmental conditions. Environmental innovations of increasing complexity, in turn, created new selection pressures for the evolution of specialized biological systems for functional consciousness, thought, language and symbolic communication. Social cognitive theory addresses itself to a number of distinctive human attributes. The remarkable capability for symbolization provides a powerful tool for comprehending the environment and for creating and regulating environmental conditions that touch virtually every aspect of life. Another distinctive attribute is the advanced capability for observational learning that enables people to expand their knowledge and skills rapidly through information conveyed by modeling influences without having to go through the tedious and hazardous process of learning by response consequences.

The self-regulatory capability, rooted in internal standards and self-reactive influence, provides another distinctive attribute for the exercise of self-directedness. The self-reflective capability to evaluate the adequacy of one's thinking and actions, and to judge one's agentic efficacy to produce effects by one's actions also receive prominent attention in social cognitive theory. The evolved information processing systems provide the capacity for the very characteristics that are distinctly human—generative symbolization, forethought, evaluative self-regulation, reflective self-consciousness, and symbolic communication. Evolved morphology and special purpose systems facilitate acquisitional processes. Social cognitive theory does not assume an equipotential mechanism of learning. In addition to biological biases, some things are more easily learnable because the properties of the events can facilitate or impede acquisitional processes through attentional, representational, productional, and motivational means. Human evolution provides bodily structures and biological potentialities not behavioural dictates.

Sociostructural influences operate through these biological resources in the construction and regulation of human behaviour in the service of diverse purposes. Having evolved, the advanced biological capacities can be used to create diverse cultures—aggressive ones, pacific ones, egalitarian ones, or autocratic ones. As Gould notes, biology sets constraints that vary in nature, degree and strength across different spheres of functioning, but in most domains the biology of humans permits a broad range of cultural possibilities. He argues cogently that evidence favours a potentialist view over a determinist view of nature. He makes the further interesting point that biological determinism is often clothed in the language of interactionism: The bidirectional biology-culture coevolution is acknowledged but then the major causation of human behaviour is ascribed to evolved biology.

The cultural side of this two-way causation, in which genetic make-up is shaped by the adaptational pressures of socially constructed environments, receives little notice. Biological determinism is also often clothed in the language of changeability: The malleability of evolved proclivities is acknowledged but determinative potency is then ascribed to them with caution against efforts to change existing sociostructural arrangements and practices allegedly ruled by evolved dispositions because such efforts are doomed to failure. The conception of the operational nature of human nature affects the relative explanatory weight given to genetic mismatch and to the counterforce of entrenched vested interests for resistance to sociostructural changes. Biological determinists favour heavily the rule of nature, whereas biological potentialists see human nature as permitting a range of possibilities that gives greater saliency to the rule of distributed opportunities, privileges and power.

Theories that heavily attribute human social behaviour to the rule of nature are disputed by the remarkable cultural diversity. Consider aggression, which is presumably genetically programmed as a biological universal and more so for males than for females. As explained elsewhere, there are three types of cultural diversity that challenge the view that people are inherently aggressive. The first concerns intercultural diversity. There are fighting cultures that breed aggression by modeling it pervasively, attaching prestige to it, and just as it functional value for gaining social status, material benefits and social control. There are pacific cultures in which interpersonal aggression is a rarity because it is devalued, rarely modeled and has no functional value. Is the genetic make-up of the Germans who perpetrated unprecedented barbarity during the Nazi regime really different from the genetic make-up of peaceable Swiss residing in the German canton of Switzerland? People possess the biological potentiality for aggression, but the answer to the differential aggressiveness in the latter example lies more in ideology than in biology.

The second form of variability concerns intracultural diversity. Ours is a relatively violent society but American Quakers and Hutterites, who adopt pacifism as a way of life, eschew aggressive conduct. The third form of variability involves rapid transformation of warring societies into peaceful ones. For ages the Vikings plundered other nations. After a prolonged war with Russia that exhausted Sweden's resources, the populous rose up and collectively forced a constitutional change that prohibited kings from starting wars. This political act promptly transformed a fighting society into a peaceable one that has served as a mediator for peace among warring nations. Sweden ranks at the very bottom of all forms of violence with virtually no incidence of domestic violence.

A biologically deterministic view has problems not only with cultural diversity, but with the rapid pace of social change. The process of biological selection moves at a snails pace, whereas societies have been undergoing major changes in sexual mores, family structures, social and occupational roles and institutional practices. In the past, a great deal of gender differentiation arose from the biological requirement of women bearing children and caring for them over a good part of their lives. With marked reductions in infant mortality and family size, and technical innovations of household labour-saving devices, women spend only a small portion of their expanded life span in childbearing and rearing. Contraceptive devices provide them with considerable control over their reproductive life. For these and other reasons, educational and occupational pursuits are no longer thwarted by prolonged childbearing demands as they did in the past. Inequitable social constraints and opportunity structures are being changed by social means rather than by reliance on the slow protracted process of biological selection. Dobzhansky reminds us that the human species has been selected for learnability and plasticity of behaviour adaptive to diverse habitats and socially constructed environments, not for behavioural fixedness. The pace of social change gives testimony that biology, indeed, permits a range of possibilities.

The parts, that follow present the basic structure of social cognitive theory, the main determinants it posits and the mechanisms through which they operate. Later parts address the applications of the theory to the various aspects of gender-role development and functioning. In social cognitive theory, gender development is neither totally shaped and regulated by environmental forces or by socially nonsituated intrapsychic processes. Rather, gender development is explained in terms of triadic reciprocal causation.

CAUSAL STRUCTURE

In the model of triadic reciprocal causation, personal factors in the form of cognitive, affective and biological events; behaviour patterns; and environmental events all operate as interacting determinants that influence each other bidirectionally. The personal contribution includes gender-linked conceptions, behavioural and judgmental standards and self-regulatory influences; behaviour refers to activity patterns that tend to be linked to gender; and the environmental factor refers to the broad network of social influences that are encountered in everyday life.

In this model of triadic causation there is no fixed pattern for reciprocal interaction. Rather, the relative contribution of each of the constituent influences depends on the activities, situations, and sociostructural constraints and opportunities. Under low environmental dictates, as in egalitarian social systems, personal factors serve as major influences in the self-regulation of developmental paths. Under social conditions in which social roles, lifestyle patterns and opportunity structures are rigidly prescribed, personal factors have less leeway to operate. Bidirectional causation does not mean that the interacting factors are of equal strength. Their relative impact may fluctuate over time, situational circumstances, and activity domains.

The model of triadic reciprocality differs from those favoured by cognitive developmental theory and gender schema theory in that factors apart from cognitive ones are accorded considerable importance. Motivational, affective, and environmental factors are included as determinants of gender development and functioning as well as a broader array of cognitive factors than gender schematic and stereotypic knowledge. Moreover, which cognitions come into play and the strength of their influence on gender-linked behaviour is dependent on the particular constellation of environmental influences operating in a given situation.

ENVIRONMENTAL STRUCTURES

The environment is not a monolithic entity disembodied from personal agency. Social cognitive theory distinguishes among three types of environmental structures. They include the imposed environment, selected environment, and constructed environment. Gradations of environmental changeability require the exercise of increasing levels of personal agency. In the case of the imposed environment, certain physical and sociostructural conditions are thrust upon people whether they like it or not. Although they have little control over its presence, they have leeway in how they construe it and react to it. Thus, for example, school attendance and academic curricula are mandated for children regardless of their personal preferences. Some of the environmental impositions involve constraints, as when women were disenfranchised and prohibited from certain social, educational, and occupational pursuits or membership in certain social organizations.

There is a major difference between the potential environment and the environment people actually experience. For the most part, the environment is only a potentiality with different rewarding and punishing aspects that do not come into being until the environment is selected and activated by appropriate courses of action. Which part of the potential environment becomes the actual experienced environment thus depends on how people behave. This constitutes the selected environment. The choice of associates, activities, and educational pursuits are examples of environmental selectivity that affect developmental pathways.

The environments that are created do not exist as a potentiality waiting to be selected and activated. Rather, people construct social environments and institutional systems through their generative efforts. For example, much early role learning occurs in children's symbolic play. By their choice of playmates and creative structuring of play activities, children construct their symbolic environment. The selection and construction of environments affect the reciprocal interplay between personal, behavioural, and environmental factors.

SOCIOCOGNITIVE MODES OF INFLUENCE

Gendered roles and conduct involve intricate competencies, interests and value orientations. A comprehensive theory of gender differentiation must, therefore, explain the determinants and mechanisms through which gender-linked roles and conduct are acquired. In social cognitive theory, gender development is promoted by three major modes of influence and the way in which the information they convey is cognitively processed. The first mode is through modeling.

A great deal of gender-linked information is exemplified by models in one's immediate environment such as parents and peers, and significant persons in social, educational and occupational contexts. In addition, the mass media provides pervasive modeling of gendered roles and conduct. The second mode is through enactive experience. It relies on discerning the gender-linkage of conduct from the outcomes resulting from one's actions. Gender-linked behaviour is heavily socially sanctioned in most societies. Therefore, evaluative social reactions are important sources of information for constructing gender conceptions. People have views about what is appropriate conduct for each of the two sexes. The third mode of influence is through direct tuition. It serves as a convenient way of informing people about different styles of conduct and their linkage to gender. Moreover, it is often used to generalize the informativeness of specific modeled exemplars and particular behavioural outcome experiences.

The relative impact of the three modes of influence varies depending on the developmental status of individuals and the social structuring of experiences. Therefore, some modes of influence are more influential at certain periods of development than at others. Modeling is omnipresent from birth. Infants are highly attentive to modeling influences and can learn from them, especially in interactive contexts. As children gain mobility and competencies to act on the environment they begin enacting behaviour that is socially linked to gender and experiencing social reactions. They regulate their behaviour accordingly. As they acquire linguistic skills, people begin to explain to children what is appropriate gendered conduct for them.

The rate of acquisition varies depending on the mode of influence. Learning conceptions through modeling is faster than from enactive experience. In modeling, the gendered attributes are already clustered in a structured form. In enactive learning, response outcomes serve as an unarticulated way of informing performers of what constitutes appropriate patterns of behaviour. This is a much more laborious attribute abstraction process. In the enactive mode, conceptions of gendered conduct must be constructed gradually by observing the differential outcomes of one's actions. When people fail to recognize the effects their actions produce, or inadequately process the outcome information provided by variations in actions over time and social contacts, they do not learn much, although the consequences repeatedly impinge on them.

Tuition also presents the role behaviour in integrated form, but its instructional function is weakened by the abstractness and the complexity of language, especially for young children. Verbal instruction alone, therefore, has less impact on conception acquisition than does modeling. However, as previously noted, tuition can help to generalize the impact of modeling and enactive experiences by adding generic significance to particular exemplars and outcomes.

These different modes of influence operate in complexly interactive ways. For the most part, they are oriented towards promoting the traditional forms of gendered conduct. However, because of the changing views on gender in some quarters, there is increasing diversity in the different sources of influence, which do not always operate in concert. There are differences within and between parents, peers, teachers and the media in the gendered styles of behaviour they promote and between what they preach and practice. Gender development is straightforward under conditions of high social consensus concerning gendered conduct and roles. Disparity of influence complicates the development of personal standards of conduct.

The different forms of social influence affect four major aspects of gender-role development and functioning. They affect the development of gender-linked knowledge and competencies, and the three major sociocognitive regulators of gendered conduct. These include outcome expectations concerning gendered conduct and roles, self-evaluative standards, and self-efficacy beliefs.

MODELING INFLUENCES IN GENDER DEVELOPMENT

Modeling is one of the most pervasive and powerful means of transmitting values, attitudes, and patterns of thought and behaviour. Modeling is not simply a process of response mimicry as commonly believed. Modeled activities convey the rules and structures embodied in the exemplars for generative behaviour. This higher level of learning is achieved through abstract modeling. Rule-governed action patterns differ in specific content and other details but they embody the same underlying rule. Once observers extract the rules and structure underlying the modeled activities they can generate new patterns of behaviour that conform to the structural properties but go beyond what they have seen or heard. Hence, social cognitive theory characterizes learning from exemplars as modeling rather than imitation, which has come to mean just mimicking the particular action exemplified. Modeling serves a variety of functions in gender development. Consider first the vicarious acquisition function.

ACQUISITION OF GENDER CONCEPTIONS AND COMPETENCIES

In the social cognitive analysis of observational learning, modeling influences operate principally through their informative function. Observational learning is governed by four constituent processes. Attentional processes determine what is selectively observed in the profusion of modeled activities and what information is extracted from ongoing modeled events. Numerous factors influence the exploration and construal of what is modeled in the social and symbolic environment. Some of these determinants concern the cognitive skills, preconceptions, and value preferences of observers. Others are related to the salience, attractiveness, and functional value of the modeled activities themselves. Models exemplify activities considered appropriate for the two sexes. Children can learn gender stereotypes from observing the differential performances of male and female models. Given comparable access, both sexes learn male and female stereotypes from observing models. However, the extent to which they learn the details of the styles of behaviour and become proficient at them depend on their perceived efficacy to master the modeled activities, opportunities to put them into practice, and the social reactions they produce.

Perceptions are guided by preconceptions. Observers' cognitive competencies and perceptual sets dispose them to look for some things but not others. The greater cognitive skills and prior knowledge, the more subtleties observers will perceive. Once children can differentiate the sexes, they prefer to attend more to same-gender than to other-gender models. Observers' pay greater attention to, and learn more about, modeled conduct that they regard as personally relevant. Because adherence to gender roles is socially stressed more for boys than for girls across the life-span, boys tend to pay more attention to same-gender models than do girls.

Observers' selective attention to models is partly dependent upon the conditions under which the observation takes place. Under forced exposure to a single model, as is usually the case in laboratory studies, children attend to and learn equally the behaviour of same-gender and other-gender models. However, when children are exposed simultaneously to male and female models and must choose to attend to one or the other, then selective attention to, and learning about, same-gender models is likely to occur. When children can select the models with whom to associate, the selective association produces even greater differences in what is learned observationally. In laboratory tests of factors hypothesized to affect modeling, children often have no choice but to observe the model presented to them. Studies using forced exposure may yield highly misleading results when the factors being examined actually affect what is acquired via modeling through their influence on associational preferences.

Other factors that affect what people attend to and learn pertain to the structural arrangements of human interactions and associational networks. These social arrangements largely determine the types of models to which people have ready access. Societies vary in the extent to which gender is a salient category, whether traditional gender conduct dominates, and the degree of stratification and segregation along gender lines. A social universe stratified and segregated by gender limits the opportunities to learn diverse styles of conduct and roles. In most Western societies organized around gender, there is no shortage of models displaying traditional gender conduct. The extent to which egalitarian roles are modeled varies in different societies and subgroups within them. In most societies, high social differentiation between the sexes makes differences in gender-typed behaviour readily observable. Although the immediate models that observers are exposed to can exert considerable impact, televised modeling has vastly expanded the range of models available to children and adults alike. As will be shown later, not only are the sexes sharply differentiated in the media, but their roles tend to be even more traditional than is actually the case.

The discussion thus far has focused on factors that regulate attentional orientations and processes. People cannot be much influenced by modeled events if they do not remember them. A second major subfunction governing observational learning concerns cognitive representational processes. Retention involves an active process of transforming and restructuring information about events for memory representation in the form of rules and conceptions of styles of behaviour. Retention is greatly enhanced by symbolic transformations of modeled information into memory codes and cognitive rehearsal of the representations. Preconceptions and affective states exert biasing influences on these representational processes as well. Similarly, recall involves a process of reconstruction rather than simply retrieval of registered events. Symbolic representation and rehearsal of modeled activities not only enhance acquisition of competencies, but raise perceived self-efficacy to execute the activities successfully. Such boosts in perceived self-efficacy improve performance by reducing self-impairing thought processes and by enlisting and sustaining the motivation needed to succeed. The third subfunction governing observational learning involves behavioural production processes whereby symbolic conceptions are translated into appropriate courses of action. This is achieved through a conception-matching process in which conceptions guide the construction and execution of styles of behaviour and the adequacy of the behaviour is judged through comparison against the conceptual model. The behaviour is then modified, if necessary, based on the comparative information to achieve close fit of conception to action.

The mechanism for translating conception to appropriate action involves both transformational and generative operations. Execution of a skill must be constantly varied to fit changing circumstances. Adaptive functioning, therefore, requires a generative conception rather than a one-to-one mapping between conception and action. This enables people to produce many variations on the skill. The more extensive the subskills that people possess, the easier it is to integrate them into complex patterns of behaviour.

The fourth subfunction in modeling concerns motivational processes. Social cognitive theory distinguishes between acquisition and performance of given styles of conduct because people do not perform everything they learn. For example, boys learn a lot about the homemaking role through repeated maternal modeling but rarely adopt such activities in their everyday life. When children are exposed to aggressive models, boys adopt that style of behaviour more extensively than do girls. But tests of acquisition reveal few, if any, sex differences in the degree to which they learned the modeled patterns of behaviour. Performance of observationally learned behaviour is regulated by three major types of incentive motivators—direct, vicarious and self-evaluative. People are more likely to adopt modeled styles of behaviour if they produce valued outcomes than if they have unrewarding or punishing effects. The observed cost and benefits accruing to others influence the adoption of modeled patterns vicariously in much the same was as do directly experienced consequences. People are motivated by the success of others who are similar to themselves, but are discouraged from pursuing courses of behaviour that they have seen often result in aversive consequences. The evaluative reactions people generate to their own conduct also regulate which observationally learned activities they are most likely to pursue. They express what they find self-satisfying and reject what they personally disapprove.

The distinction between acquisition and adoption is critical in evaluating whether given factors exert their effects on spontaneous adoption of modeled gender patterns of behaviour or on their acquisition. When exposed to multiple male and female models who command power or not, children model their behaviour after social power and same-sex status of the model. However, when instructed to re-enact the various behaviours displayed by the male and female models, there were no gender differences in acquisition as a function of either sex status of the model or power differential. Developmental research may be misleading rather than informative when propositions about development of gender-typed behaviour are tested with measures of spontaneous performance rather than acquisition, as is usually the case.

MOTIVATIONAL, EMOTIONAL AND VALUATIONAL EFFECTS OF MODELING

In addition to promoting differential styles of behaviour, modeling influences can alter incentive motivation. Seeing others achieve valued outcomes by their efforts can instill motivating outcome expectancies in observers that they can secure similar benefits for comparable performances. Modeled performance outcomes thus create incentives and disincentives for action. By the same token, seeing others punished for engaging in certain activities can instill negative outcome expectations that serve as disincentives. These motivational effects rest on observers' judgments that they have the efficacy to produce the modeled performances and that comparable behaviour will bring them similar outcomes.

People are easily aroused by the emotional expressions of others. What gives significance to vicarious emotional influence is that observers can acquire lasting attitudes, and emotional and behavioural proclivities towards persons and activities that have been associated with modeled emotional experiences. They learn to fear things that frightened the models, to dislike what repulsed them, and to like what gratified them. Fears and behavioural restraints are reduced by modeling influences that convey information about coping strategies for exercising control over threats. The stronger the instilled sense of coping efficacy, the bolder the behaviour. Values can similarly be developed and altered vicariously by repeated exposure to modeled preferences. The actions of models can also serve as social prompts for previously learned behaviour. The influence of models in activating, channeling, and supporting social behaviour is abundantly documented in both laboratory and field studies. Thus, the types of models that prevail in a given social milieu partly determine which personal qualities, from among many alternatives, are selectively expressed.

Most theories of gender development assign a major role to modeling in gender-role learning. However, Maccoby and Jacklin questioned whether modeling is influential in the development of gender-linked roles. They point to findings that, in laboratory situations, children do not consistently pattern their behaviour after same-gender models. In everyday life, of course, children observe multiple exemplars in both their immediate environment and media representations of gender roles. The power of modeling is enhanced by typicality and similarity in role behaviour within sex status. Indeed, in a set of studies varying the degree of modeled consensus the propensity of children to pattern their behaviour after same-gender models increases as the percentage of same-gender models displaying the same conduct increases.

We noted earlier that just as to cognitive developmental theory, it is only after children have achieved gender constancy that they prefer to emulate models of the same gender. Gender constancy is viewed as an antecedent of modeling, rather than as a product of it. In social cognitive theory, repeated modeling of gender-typed behaviour in the home, in schools, in workplaces, and in televised portrayals serves as a major conveyer of gender-role information. Through modeling and the structuring of social activities, children learn the prototypic behaviours associated wiTheach of the sexes. In this view, gender constancy is the product rather than an antecedent of the emulation of same-sex models. Support for this position was found by Bussey and Bandura.

When children observe models of their gender collectively exhibit stylistic behaviours that diverge from those displayed by other-gender models, children pattern their behaviour more after same-gender than other-gender models. This preference for same-gender models occurs irrespective of children's level of gender constancy. After a more abstract conception of gender coupled with conditional outcome dependencies is formed, gender conceptions and gender-typed learning operate as bidirectional influences. Social modeling operates at the collective level as well as individually. Modeling is a major social mechanisms through which behavioural patterns, social roles and sociostructural arrangements get replicated across generations. But modeling contributes to cultural evolution as well as to cultural transfer.

When exposed to models who differ in their styles of thinking and behaviour, observers rarely pattern their behaviour exclusively after a single source, nor do they adopt all the attributes even of preferred models. Rather, observers typically combine various aspects of different models into new amalgams that differ from the individual sources. Because observers vary in what they adopt from the social diversity they observe, different observers create new blends of characteristics.

Boyd and Richerson anlayse the mechanisms of cultural evolution from a population view of social learning. Within their conceptual framework, multiple modeling influences, environmental conditions, and personal experiences operate interactively to change the distribution of cultural behavioural variants over time and to foster convergence towards variants that are especially efficacious in particular milieus. The different ways in which social learning influences favour some behavioural variants over others receive detailed consideration in the social cognitive theory of social diffusion of innovations. Moreover, symbolic modeling is an influential vehicle of rapid social change in contrast to the slower pace of incremental change. Challengers of inequitable social practices are enabled and motivated by the modeled successes of others who, under subordinating conditions, altered institutional practices by concerted collective action that changed their lives for the better.

ENACTIVE EXPERIENCE

People differ in how they respond to the same gender-linked conduct displayed by children. They can develop and refine gendered orientations by observing the positive and negative consequences accompanying different patterns of behaviour. Moreover, some people are more concerned and reactive to gender-linked conduct. Fathers, for example, react more negatively than mothers to their sons' feminine toy play. The wider the array of people and social systems that children are exposed to and interact with, the more diverse the array of outcomes they experience for various types of gender-linked conduct. The same behaviour can meet with different reactions from different people and in different contexts within the child's social milieu. Children extract, weigh and integrate this diverse outcome information in constructing guides for conduct.

DIRECT TUITION

Gender roles and conduct can be affected by direct tutoring as well as through modeling and social evaluative reactions. In this mode of influence gender conceptions are drawn from the tutelage of persons in one's social environment. As in other forms of influence, direct tuition is most effective when it is based on shared values and receives widespread social support. Models, of course, do not often practice what they preach. The impact of tuition is weakened when what is being taught is contradicted by what is modeled.

Discordances between the style of behaviour modeled by adults and peers adds further to the complexity of modeling processes. Children vary in the relative weight they give to the divergent sources of influence. As is evident from the preceding analysis, people do not passively absorb gender role conceptions from whatever influences happen to impinge upon them. Rather they construct generic conceptions from the diversity of styles of conduct that are modeled, evaluatively prescribed and taught by different individuals or by even the same person for different activities in different contexts. The development of gender role conceptions is a construction rather than simply a wholesale incorporation of what is socially transmitted.

REGULATORS OF GENDERED CONDUCT AND ROLE BEHAVIOUR

The discussion thus far has centered on the acquisition of gender conceptions and competencies. This is only part of the theoretical framework. Social cognitive theory also addresses the factors that regulate gender-linked conduct and how their relative influence changes developmentally. These factors include self-regulatory mechanisms rooted in social sanctions and self sanctions. In addition, self-efficacy beliefs play a pivotal role in both the acquisition and regulation of gendered roles and styles of conduct.

GENDER-LINKED SOCIAL SANCTIONS

Children have to gain predictive knowledge about the likely social outcomes of gender-linked conduct in different settings, towards different individuals and for different pursuits. The three basic modes of influence reviewed similarly promote learning about the incentive structures of the social environment. Children acquire predictive outcome knowledge from observing the outcomes experienced by others, from the outcomes they experience first hand, and what they are told about the likely consequences of behaving in different ways for their sex.

In the gender domain, most gender-linked outcomes are socially prescribed rather than intrinsic to the action. They include socially based consequences such as approval, praise and reward for activities traditionally linked to the same gender, and disapproval or even punishment for those linked to the other gender. It is not naturally foreordained that the same behaviour enacted by females should produce different outcomes than when enacted by males.

In sociocognitive theory, evaluative social outcomes influence behaviour mainly through their informational and motivational functions. First, outcomes convey information about the social norms and the system of sanctions governing gender-linked behaviour. The second function that anticipated outcomes serve is as incentives and disincentives for action. Forethought converts foreseeable outcomes into current motivators of behaviour. People pursue courses of action they believe will bring valued outcomes and refrain from those they believe will give rise to aversive outcomes.

The sociocognitive conception of incentive motivation, which combines the informational and motivational functions of social sanctions, differs from gender schema theory, which concerns only information about gender-linked stereotypes and gender identity. As noted earlier, simply knowing the stereotypes, which increase with age, do not necessarily motivate children to act in accord with them. Indeed, a meta-analytic study showed that as children become increasingly knowledgeable about gender-role stereotypes, they believe less strongly, especially girls, that those stereotypes should exist. Therefore, a comprehensive theory of gender development must consider not only knowledge about what is considered acceptable for the two sexes, but the motivation to act on that knowledge. We shall shortly examine the influential role of outcome expectations rooted in social sanctions in the development and regulation of gender-linked conduct.

REGULATORY SELF-SANCTIONS

Social cognitive theory posits that, in the course of development, the regulation of behaviour shifts from predominately external sanctions and mandates to gradual substitution of self sanctions and self direction grounded in personal standards. After self-regulatory functions are developed, children guide their conduct by sanctions they apply to themselves. They do things that give them self-satisfaction and a sense of self-worth. They refrain from behaving in ways that violate their standards to avoid self-censure. The standards provide the guidance; the anticipatory self-sanctions the motivators. Self-sanctions thus keep conduct in line with personal standards.

Self-regulation operates through a set of psychological subfunctions that must be developed and mobilized for self-directed influence. These include self-monitoring of gender-linked conduct, judgment of conduct in relation to personal standards, and environmental circumstances, and self-reactive influence. To exercise self-influence, people have to monitor their behaviour and the situational circumstances in which they find themselves enmeshed. As children become aware of the social significance attached to gender, they increasingly attend to this aspect of their behaviour.

In mixed-sex groups children are more likely to monitor behaviour just as to its gender linkage. Compared to girls, boys monitor their behaviour on the gender dimension more closely because, as already noted, they are more likely to be reproached for conduct that deviates from their gender. Moreover, boys have a strong incentive to oversee male-linked behaviour because it usually carries higher status and power than female-linked behaviour. Social power has strong impact on modeling. Although boys clearly favour male models, when females command power over rewarding resources, boys adopt their behaviour. Power, of course, plays a highly influential role in adult pursuits. For example, in the occupational sphere men earn more than women and male-dominated occupations tend to be more highly paid and valued than female-dominated ones. Even on the athletic field, the media is considerably more attentive to, and broadcasts more widely, men's athletic contests than those of women.

Self-monitoring is the first step towards exercising influence over one's behaviour but, in itself, such information provides little basis for self-evaluative reactions. Actions give rise to self-reactions through a judgmental function in which the appropriateness of the behaviour is evaluated against gender-linked standards and the circumstances under which it occurs. Personal standards are developed from information conveyed by the three principal modes of influence. People form personal standards partly on the basis of how significant persons in their lives have reacted evaluatively to their behaviour. Sociological theories of the self tend to emphasize this particular mode of influence. Standards are also drawn from the tutelage of influential persons in one's social environment or from the standards prescribed by them. Advocating certain standards of behaviour, even if they are widely shared, does not ensure their adoption. Thus if parents preach gender egalitarianism but model traditional roles, the precepts soon lose their force. Effective tuition requires some social validation through supportive behavioural feedback.

People not only teach and evaluatively prescribe standards for others, they also exemplify them in their evaluative reactions to their own conduct. They respond with self-satisfaction and self-approval when they fulfill their personal standards but negatively when they fall short of, or violate, their standards. Children's own self-evaluative standards are affected by modeled ones to which they have been exposed. People construct their standards through reflective processing of these multiple sources of direct and vicarious influences, which may vary across individuals and even within individuals in what they practice for themselves and prescribe for others. From such diverse experiences children learn the evaluative significance of gender in a wide variety of contexts. These include familial roles, peer interactions, occupational and leisure pursuits. Added to this diversity is the need to consider the changing and conflicting messages about the value of traditional gender roles. Therefore, the standards people construct for themselves are not merely facsimiles of what they have been taught, evaluatively prescribed, or have seen modeled.

With increasing cognitive capabilities, children become more aware of the variability and diversity of gender role behaviour. Widespread cultural changes add further to the heterogeneity and changeability of gender conceptions and standards. When long hair and culinary skill became in vogue for men, those who were adorned with flowing locks and cultivated their cooking skills viewed themselves as masculine as did men with cropped hair who eschewed the kitchen. Similarly, with the rebirth of the women's movement in the 1960's, women sought to redefine their role beyond homemaking and childcare. Their struggle for equal rights and opportunities has increased the numbers of women entering a wide variety of occupations including male dominated ones. Although the workforce remains extensively gender segregated and men tend to dominate the higher status positions, it now is more acceptable for women to combine occupational pursuits with family responsibilities through choice rather than need.

Judgments of one's behaviour against personal standards sets the occasion for self-reactive influence. Self-evaluative reactions provide the mechanism through which standards regulate courses of action. Self-approving reactions for behaviour that measures up to personal standards, and self-censure for behaving in ways that violate those standards give direction to behaviour and provide motivators for it. Both gender constancy and gender schema theory emphasize conception matching as the primary regulative process. Social cognitive theory posits both the standard-matching function and the motivating self-reactive function. Research conducted in different domains reveal that both functions are necessary in the motivation and regulation of conduct.

The power of self-reactive regulation has been verified in major domains of functioning including academic development; creativity; health behaviour; organizational functioning; transgressive conduct; and aggressive patterns of behaviour. After self-regulatory capabilities have been developed, behaviour usually produces two sets of outcomes: self-evaluative reactions and social reactions. They may operate as complementary or as opposing influences on behaviour. The way in which gender roles are orchestrated is largely determined by the interplay between personal and social sources of influence.

ROLE OF PERCEIVED SELF-EFFICACY IN THE DEVELOPMENT AND REGULATION OF GENDER-ROLE CONDUCT

In the agentic sociocognitive view, people are self-organizing, proactive, self-reflective, and self-regulating not just reactive organisms shaped and shepherded by external events. The capacity to exercise control over one's thought processes, motivation, affect and action operates through mechanisms of personal agency. Among the mechanisms of agency, none is more central or pervasive than people's beliefs in their capabilities to produce given levels of attainments. Unless people believe they can produce desired effects by their actions they have little incentive to act or to persevere in the face of difficulties. Perceived efficacy is, therefore, the foundation of human agency.

The theoretical analysis and growing body of research on how efficacy beliefs are formed, the processes through which they operate, their diverse effects and their modification have been extensively reviewed elsewhere and will only be summarized briefly here because of space limitations. Meta-analyses conducted across age levels and spheres of functioning attest to the psychosocial impact of beliefs of personal efficacy. Developmental analyses reveal that perceived self-efficacy is a common pathway through which different forms of social influence affect the quality of human functioning throughout the life course.

People's beliefs in their efficacy can be developed in four major ways. The most effective way of instilling a strong sense of efficacy is through graded mastery experiences. Successes build a robust belief in one's personal efficacy. Failures undermine it. A resilient sense of efficacy requires experience in overcoming obstacles through perseverant effort. The second way of creating and strengthening self-efficacy is by social modeling. Models transmit knowledge, skills and strategies for managing environmental demands. Seeing people similar to oneself succeed by sustained effort raises observer's beliefs in their own capabilities. The failures of others instill self-doubts about one's own ability to master similar activities.

Social persuasion is the third mode of influence. Expressing faith in people's capabilities raises their beliefs that they have what it takes to succeed. But effective efficacy builders do more than convey positive appraisals. They structure activities in ways that bring success and do not place people prematurely in situations likely to bring failure. People also rely partly on inferences from their physical and emotional states in judging their capabilities. The fourth way of modifying efficacy beliefs is to reduce people's stress and depression, build their physical strength and change misinterpretations of their physical states.

Efficacy beliefs exert their effects through their impact on cognitive, motivational, and affective processes and on selection of activities and environments. Perceived personal efficacy influences the choices people make, their aspirations, how much effort they mobilize in a given endeavor, how long they persevere in the face of difficulties and setbacks, whether their thought patterns are self-hindering or self-aiding, the amount of anxiety and stress they experience in coping with taxing and threatening environments, their vulnerability to depression, and their resilience to adversity.

Efficacy beliefs play a pivotal role in the exercise of personal agency because they not only operate on behaviour in their own right, but through their impact on other classes of motivators. The effects of goals, outcome expectations, causal attributions, and perceived environmental opportunities and impediments on motivation are partly governed by beliefs of personal efficacy. The outcomes people anticipate depend largely on their beliefs of how well they can perform in given situations. Those of high efficacy expect to gain favourable outcomes; those who expect poor performances of themselves conjure up negative outcomes. It is partly on the basis of efficacy beliefs that people choose what goal challenges to undertake, how much effort to invest in the endeavor, and how long to persevere in the face of difficulties. When faced with obstacles, setbacks, and failures, those who doubt their abilities slacken their efforts, give up, or settle for mediocre solutions.

Those who have a strong belief in their abilities redouble their effort to master the challenges. Efficacy beliefs influence causal attributions. People who regard themselves as highly efficacious ascribe their failures to insufficient effort, inadequate strategies, or unfavourable circumstances. Those of low efficacy attribute their failures to low ability. Efficacy beliefs also play an influential role in how formidable obstacles appear. People of high perceived efficacy view impediments as surmountable; those of low efficacy view them as daunting obstacles over which they can exert little control. In judging their environmental circumstances, people who are assured in their efficacy focus on the opportunities worth pursuing rather than dwell on risks, and take a future time perspective in structuring their lives.

Research in diverse activity domains has furthered understanding of how efficacy beliefs enable children and adults to contribute to their accomplishments and well-being through the exercise of self-regulatory influences. People are partly the product of their environment. Hence, they can also have a hand in what they become by the types of activities they choose to get into. In efficacy guided self-development through choice processes, personal destinies are shaped by selection of environments known to cultivate valued potentialities and lifestyles.

The power of efficacy beliefs to affect the life paths of men and women through selection processes is most clearly revealed in studies of career choice and development. Occupational choices are of considerable importance because they structure a major part of people's everyday reality, provide them with a source of personal identity and determine their satisfaction and the quality of their worklife. Efficacy beliefs set the slate of options for serious consideration. For example, people rapidly eliminate from consideration entire classes of vocations on the basis of perceived efficacy, regardless of the benefits they may hold. Those who have a strong sense of personal efficacy consider a wide range of career options, show greater interest in them, prepare themselves better for different careers and have greater staying power in their chosen pursuits.

Occupational pursuits are extensively gendered. The pervasive stereotypic practices of the various societal subsystems, which we examined earlier, eventually leave their mark on women's beliefs about their occupational efficacy. Male students have a comparable sense of efficacy for both traditionally male-dominated and female-dominated occupations. In contrast, female students judge themselves more efficacious for the types of occupations traditionally held by women, but have a weaker sense of efficacy that they can master the educational requirements and job functions of traditionally male gendered occupations, even though they do not differ in actual verbal and quantitative ability. The disparity in perceived efficacy for male-dominated and female-dominated occupations is greatest for women who view themselves as highly feminine, distrust their quantitative capabilities, and believe there are few successful female models in traditionally male-dominated occupations. Although efficacy beliefs contribute more heavily to occupational preferences than beliefs about the benefits attainable by different pursuits, women base their occupational preferences even more heavily on their perceived efficacy than on the potential benefits the vocations yield.

Gender differences disappear, however, when women judge their efficacy to perform the same activities in everyday situations in stereotypically feminine tasks than in the context of male-dominated occupations. Such findings suggest that gender related efficacy impediments arise from stereotype linkage rather than actual capabilities. Gender stereotyping of pursuits that suggests lesser ability diminishes judgments of personal efficacy. Women's beliefs about their capabilities and their career aspirations are shaped by undermining social practices within the family, the educational system, peer relationships, the mass media, the occupational system, and the culture at large.

Because quantitative abilities are an essential entry skill for scientific and technical occupations, a low sense of mathematical self-efficacy operates as a major barrier to a whole range of occupational pursuits requiring quantitative skills. Research conducted by Hackett provides evidence that perceived efficacy is a central mediator through which socialization practices and past experience affect educational and career choices. Gender affects perceived mathematical efficacy through mathematical preparation in high school, mathematical achievement, and masculine gender-role orientation. Masculine gender-role orientation and level of mathematical achievement foster math-related educational and career choices through their effects on perceived mathematical efficacy rather than directly. Perceived mathematical efficacy promotes selection of mathematically-orientated educational and career pursuits both directly and by lowering vulnerability to anxiety over mathematical activities. Gender and prior mathematical preparation also have a direct effect on choice of academic major.

As in selection of quantitatively-oriented course work, the effect of gender on mathematical performance is mediated through perceived self-efficacy rather than operates directly. Simply invoking the gender stereotype can undermine women's efficacy to make good use of the mathematical competencies they possess. Women's lowered sense of mathematical efficacy is, of course, changeable. Mastery experiences eliminate gender differences. Computer systems are playing an increasing role in educational development and serving as a major information management and decision-making tool in the modern workplace. Through their association with mathematics and electronic technology, computers have become masculinized. As a result, boys receive encouragement from an early age by parents and teachers to develop computer literacy. As a consequence, they regard computer skills as more important to their career development than do girls. Societal practices that breed perceived inefficacy in the use of computer tools is thus creating new occupational impediments for women. Even at an early age, girls express a lower sense of computer efficacy than do boys. Gender differences in perceived computer efficacy extend to the college level as well.

Those of low perceived efficacy show less interest in acquiring computer competencies, are less inclined to pursue computer coursework and see computer literacy as less relevant to their future careers. Thus, men are benefiting much more than women from these technological advancements. In focusing on the influential role of perceived efficacy in gender differences in career aspirations and pursuits one should not lose sight of the earlier discussion that cultural constraints, inequitable incentive systems, and truncated opportunity structures shape women's career development. These social realities form an important part of the triadic model of causation. It should also be noted that the variability within sexes exceeds the differences between them.

Therefore, modal sex characteristics in perceived efficacy should not be imputed to all members within each sex group. Indeed, women who take a more egalitarian view towards the role of women display a higher sense of efficacy for traditionally male occupations and are more oriented towards such careers in high school and pursue them in college. They construct different identities and futures for themselves. Perceived self-efficacy predicts career nontraditionality.

The self-efficacy component of social cognitive theory does more than identify a contributory factor to career development. The theory provides the means for enhancing the personal source of control over the course of one's self-development. For example, at the elementary school level, girls mathematical self-efficacy and skills can be raised to the level of boys by guided mastery experiences. Similarly, at the occupational level, programs combining modeling wiThenabling feedback, build perceived self-efficacy and skill in using financial software for varied business functions in women who harbored strong self-doubts about their efficacy to use computerized systems. The same set of factors posited by social cognitive theory to explain and predict behaviour inform and guide effective interventions as well across diverse spheres of functioning.

Gender differences are also evident in the way in which beliefs of personal efficacy affect emotional well-being. For example, women are generally more prone to depression than men, a difference that emerges in late adolescence. Because of its prevalence and impairment of functioning, children's depression can have an important impact on the course of gender development.

Perceived inefficacy to control things one values contributes to depression in several ways. One route is through unfulfilled aspirations. People who impose on themselves standards of self-worth they judge they cannot attain drive themselves to depression. A second route to depression is through a low sense of social efficacy to develop social relationships that bring satisfaction to one's life and make chronic stressors easier to bear. Social support, in turn, produces beneficial effects only to the extent that it raises perceived coping efficacy. The third route to depression is through thought control efficacy. Much human depression is cognitively generated by dejecting, ruminative thought. A low sense of efficacy to control ruminative thought contributes to the occurrence, duration and recurrence of depressive episodes. Microanalyses reveal that the self-efficacy pathways to childhood depression differ across gender. A low sense of social efficacy contributes more heavily to depression in girls than in boys. Moreover, girls are more likely to get depressed over beliefs about academic inefficacy even though they surpass their male counterparts in their academic work. Gender differences also appear in perceived efficacy for affect regulation.

A strong sense of efficacy to manage positive emotions is accompanied by high prosocialness similarly for males and females. In contrast, a low sense of efficacy to manage negative emotions is highly depressing for females but not for males. The heavier involvement of social and affective facets of perceived self-efficacy for girls may help to explain their greater proneness to depression in late adolescence and adulthood.

Preexisting perceived self-inefficacy in more aspects of their lives make it more difficult to manage heightened transitional stressors and new role demands without experiencing despondency. Indeed, Nolen-Hoeksema and Girgus build a strong case that the interaction of preexisting gender differences in sociocognitive depressogenic factors with more stressors linked to the female role accounts for the emergence of gender differences in late adolescence.

PERCEIVED COLLECTIVE EFFICACY AND SOCIOSTRUCTURAL CHANGE

Social cognitive theory extends the analysis of human agency to collective agency. Personal and collective efficacy differ in the unit of agency but both forms of efficacy beliefs serve similar functions and operate through similar processes. People's shared beliefs in their efficacy influence the type of futures they seek to achieve collectively; how much effort they put into their group endeavors; their staying power when collective efforts fail to produce quick results or meet forcible opposition; their vulnerability to discouragement, and the social changes they are able to realise. Beneficial gender role development is a social matter not just a personal one. Handicapping practices that are built into the social order require social remedies. The collective social efforts must address the expectations, belief systems, and social practices in the home, school, mass media and the workplace that not only diminish personal efficacy and aspirations but erect institutional impediments to making the most of one's talents. The exercise of collective efficacy for social and policy initiatives is aimed at raising public awareness of inequitable practices, educating and influencing policymakers and mobilizing public support for warranted social changes. Women gained voting rights after a prolonged struggle through the forcible collective action of the Women's Suffrage Movement. In contemporary efforts in the political arena, through the organized collective power of its political network, Emily's List is elevating women to positions of legislative power by providing financial support, building winning campaigns, and mobilizing women voters.

SOCIAL COGNITIVE ANALYSIS OF GENDER ROLE DEVELOPMENT AND FUNCTIONING

The earlier analyses of extant conceptions of gender development document the need for an alternative theory of gender development and functioning. To recap briefly the major conceptual and empirical problems, although gender identity and constancy were posited as the factors governing gender development, the mechanisms by which they come into being remain unspecified. They are simply assumed to be products of interaction with the environment. However, this deficiency is the least of the problems because it is conceptually remediable.

The nonpredictiveness of the posited cognitive factors seriously question the viability of the major tenets of the theories themselves. Neither gender identity, gender constancy, nor gender stereotypic knowledge predicts gender-linked conduct. Young children exhibit preferences long before they acquire gender conceptions or understand the gender linkage of their preferences. Nor does knowledge of gender stereotypes predict gender-linked conduct in older children or adults. Virtually all of them know the stereotypes but vary in their behaviour.

Cognitive-developmental and schema theories posited knowledge of gender identity or constancy as the intrapsychic automotivator of gender-linked conduct. That is, attainment of gender self-knowledge leads one to emulate and do "girls things" or "boy things". The behavioural nonpredictiveness of gender self-knowledge alone calls into question the regulatory tenets of the theory as well. Clearly, other motivational and regulatory mechanisms govern gender-linked conduct.

Differentiation of gender roles is a sociostructural phenomenon, rather than merely an intrapsychic one. Human development and functioning operate within a broad network of social influences rather than within a socially insulated cognitivism. If doing "girl things" and "boy things" had no differential social effects gender labeling would lose its significance. Gender typing remains highly salient because it makes a big difference in one's life experiences. The constellation of gender attributes and roles people adopt are socially propagated matter not just an intrapsychic one.

Sociostructural theories and psychological theories are often viewed as rival conceptions of human behaviour or as representing different levels of causation. Human functioning cannot be fully understood solely in terms of sociostructural factors or psychological factors. A full understanding requires an integrated perspective in which social influences operate through psychological mechanisms to produce behavioural effects. When anlaysed within a unified causal structure, sociostructural influences produce behavioural effects largely through self processes rather than directly. The effects of sociostructural influences on the functioning of social systems are also in large part mediated through the collective agency of the operators of the systems.

The preceding parts reviewed the main tenets of social cognitive theory concerning the determinants and mechanisms governing the acquisition, motivation, and regulation of conduct especially relevant to the gender domain. The succeeding parts specifically apply the sociocognitive principles to gender role development and functioning.

PRE-GENDER IDENTITY REGULATION OF GENDER CONDUCT

Even before children can label themselves and others by gender, which does not occur until shortly after the second year of life, they can differentiate the sexes and act in ways consistent with traditional gender-linked practices. During the first year of life infants can distinguish between the two sexes and by the second year they engage in gender-linked conduct and prefer activities associated with their own gender.

Because gender is such a significant category for societal organization, it takes on special importance from birth. Children learn to categorize people on the basis of their gender from a very early age. By 7 months infants can discriminate between male and female faces and between male and female voices. Hair length and voice pitch are distinguishing features for such discriminations. By 9 months, infants begin to show intermodal gender knowledge. When presented with pairs of male and female pictures they attend more to female faces when they hear female voices, and by 12 months they attend more to male than female faces when they hear male voices.

Consider the pervasive social forces that are brought to bear on the development of gender orientation from the very beginning of life. Parents do not suspend influencing gender orientations until children can identify themselves as girls and boys. On the contrary, parents begin the task at the very outset of development. They do so by the way they structure the physical environment and by their social reactions around activities. From the moment of birth, when infants are categorized as either male or female, many of the social influences that impinge on them are determined by their gender. Parents reveal strong gendered beliefs about their newborns even when there are no objective differences in size or activity. Parents of newborn girls rate them as finer featured, weaker, softer, and more delicate than parents of newborn boys. For most children, both their physical and social environments are highly gendered.

Names, clothing, and decoration of infants' rooms are all influenced by their categorization as either female or male. Boys are adorned in blue and girls in pink. Boys are attired in rugged trousers, girls in pastel jeans or skirts. They are given different hair styles as well. Children come to use differential physical attributes, hair styles, and clothing as indicants of gender. Much early role learning occurs in play. The forms play takes are structured and channeled by social influences. Parents stereotypically stock their sons' rooms wiTheducational materials, machines, vehicles, and sports equipment, and their daughters' rooms with baby dolls, doll houses, domestic items, and floral furnishings. Boys are provided with a greater variety of toys than girls. These play materials orient boys' activities and interests to gender roles usually performed outside the home.

By contrast, girls are given toys directed towards domestic roles such as homemaking and child care. Parents are also more likely to purchase gender-traditional than gender-nontraditional toys requested by their children. The amount of time spent playing with toys traditionally linked to one's gender or the other gender is highly related to the types of toys parents provide. Thus, the gender-linked play materials arranged for children channels their spontaneous play into traditionally feminine or masculine roles. The differentiation of the sexes extends beyond the realm of attire, make-believe play, and other playful activities. Whenever appropriate occasions arise, parents and others instruct children in the kinds of behaviour expected of girls and boys and provide evaluative feedback when it is performed. Mothers respond more negatively when their children engage in gender-atypical than gender typical activities.

Although not all parents are inflexible gender stereotypers in all activities, most accept, model, and teach the sex roles traditionally favoured by the culture. Social sanctions bear heavily on gender-linked conduct even in the earliest years. Parents convey to their children positive and negative sanctions through affective reactions and evaluative comments. Affective communication through intonation patterns, smiles and frowns are highly salient events that direct infant's behaviour when their verbal skills are limited. Positive affective reactions promote approach behaviour, whereas negative affective reactions promote avoidant forms of behaviour. For preverbal children, the intonation of maternal comments has more impact on their behaviour than does the semantic content.

Although preverbal children cannot label their own sex or that of others or even the gender linkage of objects, parental affective reactions and communications about the objects are sufficient to sway their children's play. Parents are excited, smile, and comment approvingly when their children engage in activities considered appropriate for their gender, but they are likely to show and voice disapproval when their children take up activities deemed appropriate for the other gender. These affective reactions, depending on their nature, create positive and negative orientations to gender-linked objects and activities.

These findings are in accord with a great deal of evidence from other spheres of functioning on parental affective regulation of children's approach and avoidance reactions to ambiguous and novel objects. Modeled affective reactions not only shape behavioural orientations but alter the valence of the activities themselves. Objects and activities thus get gendered through such reactive, instructive, and modeled social means. Even during the early years, fathers are more stereotypic socializers than are mothers. One father, when he discovered trucks in a box of toys for his daughter in a gender-typing experiment, remarked, "Oh, they must have boys in this study". The father's intonation probably alerted the child to avoid the "masculine" toys as much as what he said. Starting in infancy and continuing through to middle childhood, fathers are more encouraging of physically active play for sons than for daughters.

Apart from parental evaluative reactions and direct tutelage concerning gender-linked conduct, children also notice the various activities modeled by their parents and peers. Modeling influences are important even in children's early gender development. Because gender is a category carrying consequential outcomes, girls attend closely to female models and boys to male models before they can label themselves or others just as to gender. The ability to differentiate the two sexes and to link them to different activities and their associated social sanctions is all that is necessary for children to begin to learn gender-role stereotypes.

The children choose activities consistent with gender-linked stereotypes from having observed certain activities occur correlatively with the two sexes before they have a conception of gender. This level of gender understanding precedes gender self-identity which already involves abstraction of a set of gender attributes integrated into a more general knowledge structure. When exposed to a female model engaging in male- and female-stereotyped activities, boys of 25 months emulated male-stereotyped activities to a greater extent than female-stereotyped ones. In contrast, girls of this age showed no differential emulation of the female- and male-stereotyped sequences. Evidently, the stronger gender-typing pressures for boys leads them to favour male-stereotypical activities, even before they had acquired gender stereotypical knowledge.

SELF-CATEGORIZATION AND ACQUISITION OF GENDER-ROLE KNOWLEDGE

As children become more cognitively adept, their knowledge of gender extends beyond nonverbal categorization of people and objects, to explicit labeling of people, objects, and styles of behaviour just as to gender. As children begin to comprehend speech, they notice that verbal labeling in masculine and feminine terms is used extensively by those around them. It does not take them long to learn that children are characterized as boys and girls, and adults as mothers and fathers, women and men. Gender labeling gives salience not only to sorting people on the basis of gender but also aggregates the features and activities that characterize each gender.

We saw earlier that gender labeling takes on considerable importance because a great deal depends on it. It not only highlights gender as an important category for viewing the world, but as the basis for categorizing oneself. Once such self-categorization occurs the label takes on added significance, especially as children increasingly recognize that the social world around them is heavily structured around this categorical differentiation. One's gender status makes a big difference. It carries enormous significance not only for dress and play, but the skills cultivated, the occupations pursued, the functions performed in family life, and the nature of ones leisure pursuits and social relationships.

Social cognitive theory posits that, through cognitive processing of direct and vicarious experiences, children come to categorize themselves as girls or boys, gain substantial knowledge of gender attributes and roles, and extract rules as to what types of behaviour are considered appropriate for their gender. However, unlike the gender constancy and schema theories, it does not invest gender conceptions with automatic directive and motivating properties. Acquiring a conception of gender and valuing the attributes defining that conception are separable processes governed by different determinants. In the preceding parts, we have seen how self-regulatory mechanisms operate through perceived self-efficacy, anticipated social sanctions, self-sanctions, and perceived impediments rather than gender labeling itself motivating and guiding gender-linked conduct.

Just as having a conception of one's own gender does not drive one to personify the stereotype it embraces, nor does the self-conception of gender necessarily create positive valuation of the attributes and roles traditionally associated with it. Both the valuation of certain attributes and roles and the eagerness to adopt them are influenced by the value society places on them. Societies that subordinate women may lead many of them to devalue their own gender identity. Boys clearly favour male models, but girls, who are fully cognizant of their gender constancy, do not display the exclusive same-gender modeling as the cognitivistic theories would have one believe. For boys there is little conflict between their own valuation of their gender and societal valuation of it. For girls, however, although they may value being a girl and gender-linked activities, they very early recognize the differential societal valuation of male and female roles. Consequently, women have some incentive to attempt to raise their status by mastering activities and interests traditionally typed as masculine. Even at the preschool level, girls show greater modeling after the other gender than do boys.

In the social sphere, there are large gender differences in the modeling of aggression, which is widely regarded as a principal attribute of maleness. The heavy aggressive modeling by males is not lost on boys. Even at the very early age preschool boys are higher adopters of modeled styles of aggression than girls, and even more so if it is modeled by males than by females. In their spontaneous comments in the latter studies, the children expressed in no uncertain terms the inappropriateness of a woman behaving aggressively "Who is that lady. That's not the way for a lady to behave. Ladies are supposed to act like ladies..." "You should have seen what that girl did in there. She was just acting like a man. I never saw a girl act like that before. She was punching and fighting but no swearing." In contrast, the male's aggressiveness was admired by both the boys and the girls. It is not as though boys are preordained for aggressive modeling, however. When exposed to male models behaving nonaggressively in the presence of provocative cues, boys decrease their aggressiveness.

Although boys are more inclined than girls to adopt modeled aggressive styles of behaviour, the differences reflect primarily differential restraint rather than differential acquisition. When girls are offered positive incentives to reproduce the novel patterns of aggression they saw modeled, the results show that girls learn just about as much as boys from the aggressive models. In their analyses of the mass media, Gerbner and his colleagues document that televised dramas reflect the ideological orientations and power relations in the society. The basic messages they convey shape public images of reality. In the gendered portrayals of aggression in adult relationships, men are usually the aggressors, whereas women are more often helpless victims. When women do aggress, they are more likely to get punished for it than are men. Gerbner suggests that repeated exposure to such power scenarios reinforces public views that can contribute to the subordination of women.

In the televised world, men wield aggressive power extensively, but in the everyday world most people do not go around assaulting each other. Of those who resort to aggressive conduct, males are generally more directly aggressive than females, although the difference is much smaller than is commonly believed and further diminishes with age, under conditions of provocation, and in the presence of aggressive cues. In accord with social cognitive theory, gender differences vary depending on the anticipated consequences of aggression. Both the anticipated personal and social sanctions for aggression differ depending on sex status. Girls expect stronger parental and peer disapproval for aggression and greater self-censure for such conduct. As a consequence, girls make greater use than boys of indirect means of aggression. Gender differences in aggressiveness also partly reflect differences in perceived self-regulatory efficacy. Girls exhibit a significantly higher sense of efficacy to resist peer pressure to engage in untoward conduct, a difference that is replicated cross-nationally. Moreover, boys are more facile in disengaging moral self-sanctions from injurious conduct than are girls. The higher the moral disengagement and the weaker the self-regulatory efficacy, the heavier the involvement in antisocial conduct.

FROM SOCIAL SANCTIONS TO SELF-SANCTIONS

The developmental changes posited by social cognitive theory are concerned not only with attributes and activities that get gendered, but with the mechanisms through which such conduct is regulated. With development of self-reactive capabilities, the regulation of conduct gradually shifts from external direction and sanctions to self-sanctions governed by personal standards. Based on direct and vicarious experiences, young children gain increasing knowledge about the likely outcomes of gender-linked conduct and regulate their actions accordingly. Through the acquisitional processes reviewed earlier, children eventually adopt personal standards linked to self-reactive guides and motivators that enable them to exercise influence over their own conduct.

Research by Bussey and Bandura provides confirmatory evidence for socially guided control of gender-linked conduct in early development wiThemergence of self-regulatory control with increasing age. Nursery school children at four levels of gender conception were assessed for their gender knowledge, social reactions to gender-typed conduct by peers; personal standards and self- evaluative reactions to gender-typed conduct, and their actual gender-linked conduct under diverse situational conditions. They were tested for their spontaneous play when they had a variety of gender-typed toys to choose from and when only toys linked to the other gender were available. They were also tested for their approving and disapproving reactions to peers on videotape engaging in activities linked to the other gender; their judgments of how friends of the videotaped peers would respond to their conduct; and their self-approving and self-critical reactions to engaging in same-gender activities and those considered appropriate to the other gender.

Both 3- and 4-year old children reacted in a gender stereotypic manner to conduct by peers that did not conform to their gender. They disapproved of boys feeding, diapering and comforting dolls and girls driving dump trucks. They also expected the peer's friends to react in the same disapproving way. However, the 3-year olds did not exhibit differential self-evaluative reactions to engaging in masculine-typed and feminine-typed activities. Nor did their self-reactions predict their gender-linked conduct. By contrast, the 4-year olds exhibited substantial self-regulatory guidance based on personal standards. They expressed anticipatory self-approval for conduct linked to their gender but self-criticism for conduct deemed appropriate to the other gender. Moreover, their anticipatory self-sanctions predicted their actual gender-linked conduct.

The children's spontaneous comments when confined to a play environment containing only material considered appropriate for the other gender gives graphic testimony that stereotypic gender orientations are already ingrained at this early tender age. Some boys tried to have the stereotypic "feminine" toys promptly removed. For example, when it became apparent that they were being left only with "feminine" toys, one boy hastily announced to the departing experimenter, "No, I'm finished with those toys," even though he had completely shunned them during the prior period. They were not at all hesitant in expressing their displeasure with the selections they were left with: "I don't like baby dolls."

During the session they tried to do anything but play with the "feminine" toys. One boy flung the doll across the room and turned his back on it, getting it at least out of sight if not out of mind. Some sought to restructure their constrained options by sticking to moderately "feminine" toys and transforming them into masculinized tools, as, for example, using an eggbeater in the cooking set as guns or drills.

Although girls expressed much weaker self-evaluative reactions to "masculine" activities, some of their comments were most revealing. In expressing her self-sanctions against playing with a truck, one girl explained, "My mommy would want me to play with this, but I don't want to." In this case it would be interesting to know whether the mother was modeling a gender role that conflicted with the one she was prescribing, or whether the daughter's personal standards had come under the sway of extrafamilial influences.

The findings of this study also have important bearing on gender constancy and gender schema theories. Children who had not even attained gender identity, let alone gender constancy, demonstrated clear preference for engaging in same-gender rather than other-gender activities. Although they could not label objects as gender-linked, they were quite aware of the social standards associated with gender-linked objects and disapproved of peers' conduct that did not conform to their gender. Even the youngest children behaved towards peers in a gender-stereotypic manner, despite their limited gender-linked knowledge. They regulated their own conduct by the reactions they expected from others, pursuing same-gender activities but shunning activities linked to the other gender. Neither children's gender identity, stability, constancy, nor gender classificatory knowledge predicted gender-linked conduct.

FROM GENDER CATEGORIZATION TO GENDER-ROLE LEARNING

Gender-role learning requires broadening gender conceptions to include not only appearances, but clusters of behavioural attributes and interests that form lifestyle patterns and social and occupational roles. Knowledge about gender roles involves a higher level of organization and abstraction than simply categorization of persons, objects, and activities in terms of gender. To complicate matters further, the stylistic and role behaviours that traditionally typify male and female orientations are not uniformly gender-linked. Many men are mild mannered and some females are aggressive. As a result, children have to rely on the relative prevalence of exemplars and the extent to which given activities covary with gender. If children routinely see women performing homemaking activities, while males only occasionally try their hand at it, homemaking readily gets gender-typed as a woman's role. But if they often observe both men and women gardening, it is not as easily linked to gender.

As children mature not only are they more cognitively adept at discerning the gender linkage of interests and activities and integrating diverse information into more composite conceptions, but their social world expands. They are increasingly exposed to a broader range of social influences outside the home. Before examining how this expanded range of social influences affects children's gender development and functioning, we anlayse the changing role of parents in gender differentiation over the course of development.

PARENTAL IMPACT ON SUBSEQUENT GENDER DEVELOPMENT

We saw earlier that parents play an active role in setting the course of their children's gender development by structuring, channeling, modeling, labeling and reacting evaluatively to gender-linked conduct. As children's verbal and cognitive capabilities increase, parents broaden the conception of gender by instructing their children about gender-linked styles of conduct and roles that extend beyond merely classifying objects, people, and discrete activities into male and female categories. Behavioural styles represent clusters of attributes organized in a coherent way. Girls are encouraged to be nurturant and polite and boys to be adventuresome and independent.

Parental conversations with children are extended to emotions, and these discussions take different forms for sons and daughters. Not only do mothers talk more to their daughters than to their sons, but they use more supportive forms of speech with their daughters than with their sons. In addition, they are more likely to encourage daughters when they make affiliative and supportive remarks to others. In contrast, mothers are more likely to encourage autonomy and independence in their sons than their daughters. Mothers rarely discuss anger with their daughters but often do so with their sons and are quick to attribute this emotional state to them. It is interesting to note in passing that emotiveness is regarded as a prime characteristic of women but anger, which men emote freely quite often, gets ignored in the gender comparisons of emotional proneness. We have seen in the previous analysis that parents promote sharper differentiation of gendered conduct with boys than with girls. This gender dichotomization is stronger for fathers, who continue this differential treatment throughout childhood.

Despite the findings and the extensive ones reported earlier, the influence of parents on children's gender development and functioning has been the subject of empirical dispute. Maccoby and Jacklin concluded that there was little support for parents' differential treatment of boys and girls. More recently, Lytton and Romney came to the same view based on the findings of a meta-analysis. This conclusion did not go unchallenged by other theorists. The issue in contention requires conceptual, empirical and methodological analysis.

The claim that parents do not treat the gender-linked conduct of their sons and daughters differently is most puzzling given the substantial evidence cited that many parents, in fact, actively create highly gendered learning environments in the home. The studies documenting the early parental structuring and channeling of gender orientations were excluded, for unexplained reasons, from Lytton and Romney's meta-analysis. All too often, parental influence is treated as a homogenous monolith. Families, of course, differ in the types of gender attributes and roles they model and promote in their children. Similarly, children differ in the degree to which they adopt traditional or egalitarian styles of behaviour. Evaluation of parental influence requires tests of covariation between parental practices regarding gendered conduct and their children's gender conduct. If parents who practice equality in social, educational and other pursuits have children who are egalitarian in their gender orientation, the lack of parental gender differentiation does not mean that they have had no impact on their children. Quite the contrary. They have been highly successful in their egalitarian efforts. Parents who espouse traditional gender orientations actively encourage and reward traditional gender-linked activities and pursuits in their sons and daughters.

Lytton and Romney did not differentiate between parents who socialize their children along traditional gender lines from those who foster more egalitarian gender roles, nor did they test the linkage between parental practices regarding gendered conduct and offspring conduct. The benefits of egalitarian orientations, such as better mental health and adjustment, higher self-esteem, and more satisfactory personal relationships have been widely publicized. Cultural changes are easing sharp divisions in gender attributes and roles. Indeed, increasing numbers of parents are espousing an egalitarian ethic in their socialization practices. Another factor that is ignored in evaluating parental impact on gender development is the level of consensus between mothers and fathers in their socialization practices. Fathers are more active in differentiating gender attributes and roles and more demanding of male orientations in their sons that are mothers. To complicate matters further, gender encompasses a diverse array of attributes. Parents do not respond to all aspects of gender-linked conduct in the same way. The parent who is concerned about the gender-typedness of their child's clothing or hair style may be unconcerned about the gender typing of their academic pursuits. Within families, fathers and mothers often react differently to the same behaviour in their child. Yet, it is usually the mothers who are studied with methods relying heavily on retrospective self-reports. Such data often reflect the prevailing societal views about parenting practices rather than the actual practices used. Lumping interfamilial diversity, intrafamilial diversity and interdomain diversity in gender socialization into a homogeneous conglomerate can spawn a lot of misleading conclusions. In addition, parents' self-reports often underestimate the extent of their differential treatment of boys and girls. Observational studies of parent-infant interactions show that parents tend to treat male and female infants differently and offer them gender-linked toys even when they say they do not behave differently on the basis of gender. The infants enlisted for these studies are arbitrarily dressed either as a male or female and given a male or female name so it is the attributed gender not the infants' behaviour that activates the differential reactions in adults. Indeed, gender stereotypes are so deeply ingrained culturally that they can be activated automatically in people who profess gender nonbias.

To understand parental influences one must measure what they are modeling, teaching and evaluatively encouraging and whether these differential modes of influence operate in concert or counteractively. Studies of parental impact on gender orientation rarely do so. Failure to measure a constituent mode of influence through which the parental impact is exerted can yield misleading findings. Analyses must also factor in the conditional nature of a given influence process. Social modeling is a good case in point. Modeling is a complex process rather than simple mechanistic mimicry, as it is often portrayed under the label of "imitation." The extent to which exposure to an adult model will exert an effect on children is partly conditional on the quality of the relationship and the social status of the model, and the functional value of behaviour being modeled among other things. For example, children prefer to pattern their behaviour after models who are nurturant and those who possess social power. Analyses that ignore important conditional factors can be misleading in their conclusions.

Family structures vary and are changing rapidly with single-parent families on the rise. The types of gender attributes and roles that are modeled and encouraged in single-parent families differ from those modeled and cultivated in dual-parent families. By necessity, single-parent families model egalitarian gender roles to a greater extent than two-parent families because single parents have to assume both maternal and paternal functions. This is another familial factor that affects whether parents raise their sons and daughters similarly or differently. To lump families favouring egalitarian lifestyles with those promoting traditional differentiation as though they should all be earnest traditionalists confounds rather than clarifies issues concerning parental socialization practices.

Human development is influenced by the construed environment rather than mechanistically by the actual environment. For example, parents judge school to be more difficult for their daughters than for their sons even though they do not differ in actual academic achievement. Girls perceive their mothers as having lower academic expectations and lower achievement standards for them than for boys. In studies demonstrating that believing is seeing, children who had seen a female doctor working with a male nurse, produce stereotypically distorted remembrances in which they convert the male to the doctor and the female to the nurse. Such findings underscore the importance of assessing the family environment as perceived and retained in memory by children in evaluating the impact of parents on their children's gender development. An experimental analysis of modeling under different simulated family dynamics tested whether preschool children would pattern behaviour after an adult who possessed power over rewarding resources or after the consumer of these resources. The children modeled their behaviour after social power, except for the power constellation in which the female possessed the resources rather than the male. A number of the children dispossessed the female model of her power status by treating her as merely an intermediary of male ownership. As the preschoolers explained it in their unreserved way, "He's the man and it's all his because he's a daddy. Mommy never really has things belong to her"... "He's the daddy so it's his but he shares nice with the mommy"..."He's the man and the man always really has the money and he lets ladies play too. John's good and polite and he has very good manners". These children modeled their behaviour after attributed social power rather than actual power. In short, it is events as perceived that shape developmental courses. To clarify parental influences one should also assess children's perception of their parent's status and practices rather than rely solely on a mechanistic model of direct environmental effects.

The final factor concerns the temporal ordering of parental influence. Parents play an active role during the early phase of gender development. With further development, family management practices change in form and locus of influence. After children adopt personal standards parents lighten their socialization pressures because they are largely unnecessary. Without analysis of changes in the balance of parental and self-directive influence as self-regulatory capabilities are developed, children appear fully gendered under the control of peers with seemingly inactive parents. The view that parents exert no differential impact on their children's gender orientation is deeply problematic.

12

Scheduled Castes and Scheduled Tribes

This stage is arranged in six sections. After the introduction of the stage, the second section deals with the main features of the international covenants and the Indian Constitution; the third section delineates the context of this stage, that is, the status of Scheduled Castes and Scheduled Tribes as well as the denotified and nomadic tribes; the fourth section outlines the major human rights issues and the corresponding laws, rules and regulations; and the fifth section sets out the role and, to some extent, the specific responsibilities of the District Magistrates in relation to the human rights of the Scheduled Castes and Scheduled Tribes against the overall background set out in the earlier sections. The last section contains the concluding observations. It may be mentioned that the term Dalit is being increasingly used to denote the Scheduled Castes and, sometimes, the Scheduled Tribes as well. Though the original meaning of the word Dalit encompasses all the oppressed people, it has, over a period of time, become almost synonymous with the Constitutional category of Scheduled Castes, signifying an assertive expression of untouchable heritage and a rejection of oppression. However, in this stage, the terms Scheduled Castes and Scheduled Tribes have been adopted in conformity with the terminology adopted in the Constitution of India.

CONCEPTS, COVENANTS AND THE CONSTITUTION

A compendium of human rights has evolved, over time, emerging from a liberal humanist formulation at the time of the Universal Declaration of Human Rights 1948 to a comprehensive framework, reflecting the rise of democratic consciousness of people all over the world. The Universal Declaration of Human Rights adopted about half a century ago, was followed by two separate Covenants, namely, the International Covenant on Civil and Political Rights 1966 with entry into force on 23 March 1976; and the International Covenant on Economic, Social and Cultural Rights 1966 with entry into force on 3 January 1976, which were generally ratified by India in March 1979. The Universal Declaration of Human Rights along with the Covenants lays down universal standards, among others, in relation to freedom, equality, dignity, nondiscrimination, right to life and liberty, education, employment and remuneration, development, social security, equality before law, equal access to public service; and participation in social, political and cultural aspects of society.

A Convention on Elimination of All Forms of Discrimination Against Women (CEDAW) was adopted by the United Nations General Assembly in 1979 and ratified by India in June 1993. The International Convention on the Elimination of All Forms and Racial Discrimination (CERD) was ratified by India, thereby agreeing to principles of dignity and equality of all human beings irrespective of race and descent. India is also a signatory to Convention 107 of the International Labour organization concerning indigenous, tribal and semi-tribal people which places on the Government the primary responsibility for developing coordinated and systematic action for the protection of the tribal population and their progressive integration into the life of their respective communities fostering individual dignity.

A comprehensive concept of human rights thus forms part of a global compact and a large number of instruments of human rights have been evolved within the United Nations system and ratified and reaffirmed by India. Human rights are indivisible and interdependent. The Universal Declaration recognizes freedom from fear and freedom from want as two sides of the same coin. People cannot advance their economic, social and cultural rights without the political space and civil freedom to do so. Article 11.2 of the International Covenant on Economic, Social and Cultural Rights recognizes the fundamental right of everyone to be free from hunger.

It was recognized at the World Conference on Human Rights held at Vienna that the existence of widespread extreme poverty inhibits full and effective enjoyment of human rights and therefore its immediate alleviation and eventual elimination must remain a high priority for the international community. The World Conference on Human Rights also affirmed that extreme poverty and social exclusion constitute a violation of human dignity and urgent steps are necessary to promote the rights of the poorest. The emphasis in the Universal Declaration of Human Rights as well as the pronouncements at the various conferences of the United Nations has been on the obligation of the member States to promote and protect the human rights. The Vienna Declaration and Programme of Action adopted in June 1993 at the World Conference on Human Rights, reaffirmed the solemn commitment of all States to fulfil their obligations to promote universal respect for and observance and protection of all human rights. More specifically, it has been declared that the protection and promotion of human rights is the first responsibility of the Governments. In turn, this obligation and responsibility devolves on the agencies of the State. The Indian Constitution, as set out in its Preamble, is a testament to secure to all its citizens Justice, social, economic and political, Liberty of thought, expression, belief, faith and worship, equality of status and of opportunity and fraternity, assuring the dignity of the individual and integrity of the nation. The founding fathers of the Constitution were fully aware of the iniquitous forces embedded in the social systems, economic institutions and political organizations in India in relation to the weaker and vulnerable sections of the society and, therefore, considered it necessary to provide for specific corrective measures and mandates in the Constitution in their favour.

The safeguards for the members of the Scheduled Castes relate to the removal of the disabilities as well as positive measures to enable them to acquire a dignified position in the national life. The major concern about the members of the Scheduled Tribes has been that of protecting and preserving their command over resources and the best in their tradition. The Constitution incorporates a number of commands for the elimination of the inequities and inequalities prevalent in the Indian society and for promoting equality and social justice. Article 14 of the Constitution guarantees equality before law and equal protection of laws. Article 15 prohibits discrimination on the grounds of religion, caste, sex or place of birth as well as disabilities in regard to access to public places and also specifically provides that nothing shall prevent the State from making any special provision for the advancement of any socially and educationally backward classes of citizens or for the Scheduled Castes and the Scheduled Tribes.

Article 16 provides for equality of opportunity in the matter of public employment with specific provision for reservation of appointments or posts in respect of any backward class of citizens. Article 17 abolished untouchability forbidding its practice in any form and making the enforcement of any disability arising out of untouchability a punishable offence. Article 21A (recently added) lays down that the State shall provide free and compulsory education to all children of the age of six to fourteen years. Article 23 prohibited traffic in human beings and forced labour. Article 24 bars the employment of children below fourteen years in any factory or mine or hazardous occupations.

An important part of the Constitution and of great significance to the poor is the Directive Principles of State Policy which are fundamental in the governance of the country. Article 38 of the Constitution envisages a social order in which justice, social, economic and political shall inform all institutions of national life and requires the State to endeavour to minimize inequalities in income, status and opportunities. Article 39 visualizes, among others, the right to adequate means of livelihood; the equitable control and ownership of the material resources of the community and that the operation of the economic system does not result in concentration of wealth and means of production to the common detriment. It also envisages equal pay for equal work for men and women as well as opportunities for children to develop in a healthy manner and without exploitation. Article 41 stipulates that the State shall within the limits of its economic capacity and development make effective provisions for securing the right to work, to education and to public assistance in cases of unemployment, old age, sickness and disablement and in other cases of undeserved want. Article 43 calls upon the State to endeavour to secure a living wage to all the workers. Article 46 mandates the State to promote with special care the educational and economic interests of the weaker sections of the people and in particular of Scheduled Castes and Scheduled Tribes and protect them from injustice and all forms of exploitation.

The Indian Constitution thus provides for a comprehensive framework for the socio-economic advancement of the Scheduled Castes and the Scheduled Tribes in order to achieve the objective of a just and humane society. The Constitutional perspective combines both the positive notion of rights guaranteed through the State and law as well as the notion of natural rights and includes horizontal rights applicable to all citizens and vertical rights to enhance the life chances of vulnerable groups, such as Scheduled Castes and Scheduled Tribes.

The fundamental rights set out in Part III of the Constitution contain not merely a corpus of limitation on the power of the State, guaranteeing State free spaces for the pursuit of individual and collective life, but also as an onslaught on the entrenched intransigent attitudes and behaviour in society and culture. Through Article 17 (outlawing of untouchability) and Article 23 (proscription of many forms of serfdom and traffic in human beings) the Constitution directly addresses and confronts the oppressive formations in civil society and mandates State action in this respect to secure basic human rights. The Indian Constitution is unique in that it designates violation of these human rights of Scheduled castes and Scheduled Tribes as offences created by the Constitution itself and casts a Constitutional duty on Parliament to enact legislations, regardless of federal distribution of legislative powers provided in the Constitution. Special provisions were also incorporated in the Fifth Schedule and the Sixth Schedule of the Constitution for the Scheduled Tribes.

While the Sixth Schedule contains provisions as to the administration of tribal areas in the States of Assam, Meghalaya, Tripura and Mizoram, the Fifth Schedule sets out provisions as to the administration and control of Scheduled Areas and Scheduled Tribes in other States. It may be added that the division of rights and principles into Part III and Part IV of the Constitution has been substantially, though not wholly, erased over time by adjudication. The Supreme Court through its corpus of active jurisprudence has enunciated many judicially created fundamental rights such as the right to dignity; right to livelihood, right to compensation and rehabilitation for injuries caused by State agents or agencies, right to speedy trial, right to health; and right to gender equality. More recently Part IX and Part IXA of the Constitution based on the Seventy-third and the Seventy-fourth amendments of 1992 have, among other things, provided for the reservation of seats as well as reservation of the posts of Chairpersons in the Panchayats at all levels and the urban local bodies in favour of the Scheduled Castes and Scheduled Tribes. Following the provisions in the Seventy third amendment, the Provisions of the Panchayats (Extension to the Scheduled Areas) Act was also enacted by Parliament in December, 1996. The Protection of Human Rights Act, 1993 defines human rights as the rights relating to life, liberty, equality and dignity of individual guaranteed by the Constitution or embodied in the international covenants and enforceable by Courts in India. The expression human rights thus denotes and describes a wide range of rights, some of them enunciated.

International declarations and Covenants, some directly and specifically guaranteed in the Constitution of the country, some others incorporated in the laws, rules and regulations made by the Central and State Governments in accordance with the Constitution; some laid down by Courts through the elaboration of legal and Constitutional provisions and some that yet exist only at the level of a democratic value system.

SCHEDULED CASTES AND SCHEDULED TRIBES

The concept of universal human rights makes no exception or compromises in its appeal to an indivisible humanity bound together by a universal code of human rights. At the same time, it has to be recognized that while human rights are indeed universal and indivisible, in unequal and hierarchical societies as in India, equal treatment and protection are not available to all human rights nor are all human rights violations given equal attention. This is especially true of weaker and vulnerable sections of society such, as Scheduled Castes and Scheduled Tribes and hence the need for a proper understanding of the context in which human rights are available, safeguarded infringed or violated in relation to these sections of the people. Defining prominent features of human rights issues in relation to Scheduled Castes and Scheduled Tribes is difficult in as much as these do not often fall in the same categories as the kinds of human rights categories more commonly addressed in normal human rights discourse.

Even at the beginning of the twenty first century, the Scheduled Castes who constitute a substantial section of the Indian population suffer from varying degrees of denial of dignity, decency, equality, security and freedom. The Scheduled Castes represent a constitutionally declared collective of castes, communities or groups, their defining characteristic being the suffering from the traditional practice of untouchability. The Scheduled Castes are subjected to the inhuman practice of untouchability, which is the most extreme form of the denial of human dignity and social oppression. The discrimination against the Scheduled Castes is not merely the kind of treatment suffered by the poor in general but the unique kind of discrimination in the form of untouchability, and this is the primary basis for regarding them as a distinct grouping, even among the poor within India. In terms of the provisions in Article 341 of the Constitution, the Scheduled Castes have been specified separately in relation to each of the States and Union Territories. The population of Scheduled Castes in India just as to the 1991 Census is 13.82 crores which is about 16.48 per cent of the total population of the country. Eight States, namely Uttar Pradesh, West Bengal, Bihar, Tamil Nadu, Andhra Pradesh, Madhya Pradesh, Rajasthan and Karnataka account for more than 75 per cent of the total Scheduled Caste population of the nation. On the basis of the trend in decadal growth rates, the population of the Scheduled Castes is likely to be around 17.9 crores, representing 17.5 per cent of the population in 2001. The Scheduled Castes live mostly in rural areas, with only about 14 per cent of them living in urban agglomerations. The habitations of the Scheduled Castes are scattered all over the country, generally in parts of villages or small villages.

The proportion of poor among the Scheduled Castes and the Scheduled Tribes is higher than in the case of the rest of the society, indicating poor resource base and denial of access. Almost three fourths of the bonded labourers in the country are from Scheduled Castes and Scheduled Tribes. The observations of the Working Group on the Development of the Scheduled Castes (1980- 85) are worth recalling. "Notwithstanding this extremely adverse situation, the Scheduled Castes contribute significantly to the sustenance and growth of the production systems of the country and the nation's economy. The largest single group among the agricultural labourers in the country are the Scheduled Castes. Footwear and other leather products are mostly contributed by the Scheduled Castes. A variety of handicraft and handloom products are made by the Scheduled Castes. They have a considerable share in the fishing activity of the country. Moreover they are the people who keep the country clean. The Scheduled Castes constitute, in the main, the bedrock on which the society and economy rest.

Rarely has any section of the society contributed so much for so long in return for so little. Indian society owes to the Scheduled Castes a heavy moral and material debt yet to be discharged." The Scheduled Tribes were identified on the basis of certain well defined criteria, including the traditional domain of a definite geographical area, distinctive culture including shyness of contact, occupational traits, such as preagricultural modes of cultivation and general lack of development. The list of Scheduled Tribes was notified by the President of India in accordance with the provisions of Article 342 of the Constitution. About 350 tribal communities, besides a number of subgroups have been scheduled in India, whose population is 6.8 crores just as to 1991 census comprising 8.08 per cent of the population.

Six States-Bihar, Gujarat, Madhya Pradesh, Maharashtra, Orissa and Rajasthan-account for about 75 per cent of the total tribal population. On the basis of decadal growth rate, the population of Scheduled tribes is estimated at about 8.8 crores in 2001 representing 8.6 per cent of the total population. Special provisions have been incorporated in the Fifth and the Sixth Schedules of the Constitution for the administration of the tribal areas. For the tribal population, there has always been a close traditional association with a territory or a tribal domain, with the tribal community enjoying a collective command over the natural resources, mostly in hilly or forest regions. They are often self-governing and guided by their own customs and tradition. Many of them have their own languages. Their size may vary from just a few hundreds to a million and more, located at different stages-hunters and gatherers, pastorals, shifting cultivators and settled agriculture. While bulk of the tribals live in tribal majority tracts, a substantial population is dispersed. The tribal economy revolves largely around land and land based resources; but land is more than a source of livelihood for the Scheduled Tribes. A large number of tribal families dwell in the forests or live close to the forests and their economy is closely interlinked with the forest resources. The tribal tracts are often rich in minerals and natural resources. The Scheduled Castes and the Scheduled Tribes are at the bottom rungs of the society-in assets, social status, education, health or even in living conditions.

The welfare and development of the members of the Scheduled Castes and Scheduled Tribes should be viewed at not merely in terms of material needs but equally or even more so in relation to nonmaterial needs, such as the right to live with freedom, human dignity and selfrespect. The people belonging to Scheduled Castes and Scheduled Tribes, are indeed the labouring classes, on whose strength, sweat and toil the nation survives. But almost all of them suffered and continue to suffer from varying degrees of unfreedom denial of human dignity and human rights. Throughout the whole of rural India, Scheduled Caste habitations are, even today, usually segregated, mostly on the outskirts of a village. The Scheduled Caste families in many villages are in permissive possession of housesites or homesteads with constant threats of eviction by the landowners or even the State.

In the urban areas, the problem is of living space itself, with just token space in unhygienic conditions and perpetual insecurity. The low levels of literacy of the Scheduled Castes and Scheduled Tribes are a particularly potent indicator of the denial of access to education in the past, leaving its mark on the present and future social situation. They have little land and lose their land and even when title over a small piece of land has been conferred, they have, often, been prevented from occupying the land and cultivating it.

The social category, generally known as the Denotified and Nomadic Tribes (DNTs), covers a large number of communities spread over different States, such as Pardhis, Sansis, Kheria Sabars, Lodhas, Bedias, etc. The estimate of their population in the country varies from 2 crores to 6 crores. Many of them were notified as Criminal Tribes under the Criminal Tribes Act 1871 and were"denotified" when the Act was repealed in 1952 after Independence. It was rightly considered, to quote the words of Jawaharlal Nehru"The monstrous provisions of the Criminal Tribes Act constitute a negation of civil liberty. No tribe can be classed as criminal as such and the whole principle is out of consonance with all civilized principles". Most of these communities now figure in the list of Backward Classes or sometimes, even the list of Scheduled Castes and Scheduled Tribes in relation to specific States. But the schemes for economic upliftment do not seem to have benefited them. The rate of literacy among them is very low, malnutrition more frequent and provisions for education and health care almost negligible, since many of them have remained nomadic. Bereft of their earlier occupations, with very little assets, they are even today suspected of being desperate criminals by the administration and by public, subjected to atrocities by the State agencies and the society. Very often the Habitual offenders Act which was enacted in 1959 is invoked against them.

HUMAN RIGHTS ISSUES, INSTRUMENTS AND LAWS

RIGHT TO HUMAN DIGNITY AND EQUALITY

The defining characteristic for Scheduled Castes is untouchability which is the denial of human dignity in its most extreme form. It is a socially and economically exploitative practice, constituting a gross derogation of the very existence as a human being. But the fact remains that notwithstanding the Constitutional and legal provisions as well as some sociopolitical and administrative efforts, untouchability is still prevalent on a large scale, particularly in rural India, barring perhaps some of the north eastern parts of the country. Even the spread of education has not been able to reduce the scourge of untouchability. On the basis of untouchability, in tens of thousands of villages which comprise nearly 80 per cent of the population of the country, almost every village is segregated into a Scheduled Caste locality and the non-Scheduled Caste locality. The continued prevalence of this evil and inhuman practice of untouchability constitutes the denial of basic human dignity and equality. It is worth recalling in this context the words of Babasaheb Ambedkar, expressed many years ago, on the 25 December 1927, at the Conference of the Scheduled Caste people for asserting their right to take water from the Chowdwar tank in Mahad in Maharashtra."It is not as if drinking the water of Chowdwar lake will make us immortal. We have survived well enough all these days without drinking it. We are going to the tank to assert that we too are human beings like other.

It must be clear that this meeting has been called to set up norms of equality". The abolition of untouchability is a key Constitutional provision for securing basic human dignity to Scheduled Castes. Article 17 of the Constitution declared its abolition and criminalized its practice in any form whatsoever. Following the stipulation in Article 17 of the Constitution, the Untouchability (offences) Act was enacted in the year 1955. As this law was found to be inadequate, this was replaced by the comprehensive Protection of Civil Rights Act 1955 comprehensively amended in 1976 (19.11.76), a quarter of a century after the Constitution. The Protection of Civil Rights Rules were formulated in 1977. The Act defines Civil Rights as any right accruing to a person by reason of the abolition of untouchability under Article 17 of the Constitution. The Act aims to punish the preaching and practice of untouchability and the enforcement of any disability arising from untouchability.

Untouchability was made a cognizable and non-compoundable offence and a minimum punishment was stipulated for enforcing religious disabilities, social disabilities, refusal to sell goods or render services as well as other offences such as insult, molestation, obstruction, boycott, unlawful compulsory labour, to do scavenging or sweeping or removing carcass or job of similar nature on the ground of untouchability. The Act also provides for cancellation or suspension of licences of convicted persons under Section 6, as well as suspension of grants of land or money to a place of public worship or educational institution or hostel guilty of an offence. Section 10A empowers the Government to impose collective fines. Section 15A of the Act places a duty on the State Government to ensure that rights accruing from the abolition of untouchability are made available to and are availed of by the persons subjected to any disability arising out of untouchability including legal aid, setting up of special Courts, supervision of prosecution, periodic surveys, identification of untouchability prone areas and steps for removal of untouchability in such areas.

A special law-the Scheduled Castes and Scheduled Tribes (Prevention of Atrocities) Act was enacted in the year 1989 (which came into effect from 30 January 1990), necessitated by the continuing predicament and plight of the Scheduled Castes. The Statement of Objects and Reasons of the Act summed up the position of Scheduled Castes and Scheduled Tribes as follows.

- "Despite various measures to improve the socio-economic conditions of the Scheduled Castes and the Scheduled Tribes, they remain vulnerable. They are denied a number of civil rights. They are subjected to various offences, indignities, humiliations and harassment. They have, in several brutal incidents, been deprived of their life and property. Serious crimes are committed against them for various historical, social and economic reasons.... Because of the awareness created among the Scheduled Castes and Scheduled Tribes, through spread of education etc, they are trying to assert their rights and this is not being taken very kindly by others. Occupation and the cultivation of even the government allotted land by the Scheduled Castes and the Scheduled Tribes is resented and more often these people become victims of attacks by the vested interests. Under the circumstances, the existing laws like the Protection of Civil Rights Act 1955 and the normal provisions of Indian Penal Code have been found to be inadequate to check these crimes. A special legislation to check and deter crimes against them by non-Scheduled Castes and non-Scheduled Tribes has, therefore, become necessary".

The Scheduled Castes and Scheduled Tribes (Prevention of Atrocities) Act 1989 created, for the first time, a whole new range of offences termed as"atrocities" and provided for stiff sanctions. The underlying spirit of the Act and Rules (which were framed in 1995) is that the Scheduled Castes and Scheduled Tribes by their very location in the oppressive social system are extraordinarily vulnerable and that their human rights should be protected by law and its implementing agencies from the onslaught by others against them. The Act cast a statutory duty on Government to take concrete steps to prevent atrocities and ensure the feeling of security among the Scheduled groups.

As pointed out by the distinguished jurist Upendra Baxi, the bulk of these offences were directed against the patterns of behaviour which shatter the self image of the members of the Scheduled communities and related forms of public humiliation. First, there are the modes of destroying self esteem such as forced feeding of obnoxious matter, forcible public parades after stripping the victims, throwing obnoxious objects in the living spaces; forcing people to leave the places of residence; denying them traditional access to places of public resort and all other related forms of public humiliation. Under the Act, all these constitute atrocities. Second, atrocities have a clear economic dimension.

The Act therefore criminalizes beggar, bonded labour, wrongful occupation, possession, cultivation, transfer and dispossession of land belonging to or notified as such to the Scheduled groups. Gender based aggression forms the third group of offences. Assaulting the women of Scheduled groups with an intent to outrage or dishonour their modesty is an offence. So is their sexual exploitation by those in a dominant position. Deliberate abuse of legal and administrative processes constitutes the fourth class of atrocities. This includes false, malicious and vexatious legal proceeding and even laying a false information before a public servant (which includes the police).

Fifth, in a far-reaching addition to the Indian Penal Code, the Act prescribes that any offence carrying a sentence of ten years or more if carried out against the person or property of the member of Scheduled Caste or Tribe on the ground of her belonging to these communities will attract a life sentence. Sixth, the use of force or intimidation of any member of the Scheduled Caste or Tribes affecting the decision not to vote or vote for a particular candidate in a manner other than that provided by law is an atrocity. This provision restores the democratic honour of the Scheduled Caste and Tribes. Public servants are liable to punishment for atrocities and those who, including the police, who default in their statutory duties stand exposed to a substantial prison term. The Special Courts are empowered to presume abetment if the fact of rendering financial assistance to the perpetrators of such offence is proved. Also, if atrocities are committed in pursuance of conspiracy, The Act provides even for externment of anyone likely to commit an atrocity under the Scheduled and Tribal areas specified under Article 244 of the Constitution. The Act also provides for the appointment of special public prosecutors. The Act also provides for severe penalties-atrocities carry a minimum jail sentence of six months and a maximum of five years.

The Act provides for expeditious trial and disposal of cases pertainingo ST Communities through the agency of special Courts, denial of anticipatory bail, penalty for neglect of duties by public servant, as well as a duty to take concrete steps for preventive action against atrocities and restore the feeling of security among the Scheduled Castes and Scheduled Tribes. The Act is not only a penal policy measure; it envisages effective measures for the prevention of atrocities and for assistance in various ways to the victims of atrocities. The Scheduled Castes and Scheduled Tribes (Prevention of Atrocities) Rules were issued by Government of India in 1995.

The Rules are exhaustive and provide for precautionary and preventive measures, supervision and spot inspection by District Magistrate, setting up of Scheduled Castes and Schedule Tribes Protection Cell, Relief and Rehabilitation of victims, State Level and District Level Vigilance and Monitoring Committees. Rule 3 specifically provides for the identification of atrocity prone areas by the State Government and order to the District Magistrate, Superintendent of Police or any other officer to visit the area and review law and order situation, cancelling arms licences of non-Scheduled Caste and Scheduled Castes and Scheduled Tribes, constitution of High power State level Committee, District and divisional level Committees, setting up of Vigilance and monitoring Committees, setting up of awareness centers and organizing workshops to educate Scheduled Castes and Scheduled Tribes about their rights and protection, encouraging Non Governmental Organizations for establishing and maintaining awareness centers and deploying special police force in the identified area.

Rule 6 provides for spot inspection by District Magistrate and others. Rule 7 requires that the offences shall be investigated by a police officer not below the rank of a Deputy Superintendent of Police. Rule 8 envisages the setting up of the Scheduled Castes and Scheduled Tribes Protection Cell by the State Government. The Rules make provisions for travelling allowance, maintenance expenses, etc. to the victims or the dependents. Rule 12 lays down specific measures to be taken by the district administration, including mandatory visit by the District Magistrate and the Superintendent of Police, registration and investigation of the offence as well as relief and rehabilitation. Rules 16 and 17 provide for the setting up of State level Vigilance and Monitoring Committee and a District Level Vigilance and Monitoring Committee with the District Magistrate as the Chairman. The scales of relief for victims of atrocities have also been set out in detail in the Rules. As reported in Crime in India 2000 (National Crime Records Bureau, Ministry of Home Affairs, Government of India June 2002) the total number of crimes against Scheduled Castes was 25,638 in 1998; 25,093 in 1999 and 25,455 in 2000. The number of offences under Protection of Civil Rights Act in regard to Scheduled Castes was 724 in 1998; 678 in 1999 and 672 in 2000. The offences under Scheduled Castes and Scheduled Tribes (Prevention of Atrocities) Act were 7,443, 7,301 and 7,386 respectively. The total number of crimes against Scheduled Tribes was 4276 in 1998; 4450 in 1999; 4190 in 2000. The number of offences under the Protection of Civil Rights Act in relation to Scheduled Tribes was 50 in 1998, 45 in 1999 and 31 in 2000. The offences under Scheduled Castes and Scheduled Tribes (Prevention of Atrocities) Act was 709, 574 and 502 respectively. It is obvious that these numbers represent only the tip of the iceberg, as it is well known that a large number go unreported or unregistered. The rates of conviction by Courts are also very low.

The dehumanizing practice of manual scavenging is yet another blot on the Indian society and an affront to human dignity of the Scheduled Castes and the Scheduled Tribes. It is also interlinked to untouchability. Almost all those engaged in this occupation of manual scavenging-there are about 7 lakhs of them in the country-are from the Scheduled Castes and Scheduled Tribes. The continuance of manual scavenging constitutes a gross violation of human rights and worth of the human person that flies in the face of the Constitutional guarantee of a life with dignity for every human being in the country. A scheme known as National Scheme for Liberation and Rehabilitation of Scavengers and their Dependents was launched in 1991- 1992.

A special programme of scholarships for education of the children of those engaged in unclean occupations was also taken up. However, it was only four decades after the commencement of the Constitution that a statutory prohibition of manual scavenging was attempted through the enactment of the Employment of Manual Scavengers and Construction of Dry Latrines (Prohibition) Act in 1993. It took another four years to bring the Act into force in six States in 1997. Even now, some of the States are yet to adopt the law. The Statement of Objects and Reasons of this legislation is worth noting."Whereas fraternity assuring the dignity of the individual has been enshrined in the Preamble to the Constitution, and whereas the dehumanizing practice of manual scavenging of human excreta still continues in many parts of the country and whereas it is necessary to enact a uniform legislation for the whole of India for abolishing manual scavenging by declaring employment of manual scavengers for removal of human excreta an offence and thereby ban further proliferation of dry latrines in the country". Section 3 of the Act prohibits employment of manual scavengers as well as construction or maintenance of a dry latrine from a date to be notified by State Government. Under Section 5, the State Government is required to appoint a District

Magistrate or a Sub divisional Magistrate as the Executive Authority for the purpose of the Act. The Act provides for various powers and functions of the Executive Authority and penalties for contravention of the Act. A National Commission for Safai Karmacharis was also set up in August 1994 under the National Commission for Safai Karmacharis Act, 1993 to monitor and oversee the programmes. A National Safai Karmachari Finance Corporation was set up in 1997. The Tenth Five Year Plan aims at total eradication of manual scavenging by Mission Mode approach by 2007. In some of the States like Andhra Pradesh, a Mission for eradicating manual scavenging and rehabilitation of Safai Karmacharis has been initiated, with specific time frame for demolition of community dry latrines and conversion of private dry latrines.

RIGHT TO LIVELIHOOD AND EQUALITY-LAND

There were certain parts of India where, historically, the so called untouchable communities were prohibited from owning any landed property. A unique feature of the Indian rural situation is thus the close interrelationship between the caste hierarchy and the agrarian structure. While the large landowners invariably belonged to the so-called upper castes, the cultivators belonged to the middle castes and the agricultural workers largerly to the Scheduled Castes, Scheduled Tribes and other extremely backwared communities. The picture of the landless labourer continues to remain the dominant motif of Scheduled Castes even today. Their social position is inescapably bound up with their condition as a predominantly landless people working on the land of others. Land control is the basis of the agrarian hierarchy and often the caste hierarchy and, therefore, any scheme of development which fails to address the issue of land control is unlikely to produce any systemic transformation. It has been pointed out by perceptive observers that the small number of success stories of Scheduled Caste families often reveal the acquisition of a plot of land as the crucial asset which builds the base for advancement.

Small resources like a home site of ones own and even a very small part of productive land can operate as a powerful tool of liberation of the Scheduled Castes from total and arbitrary dependence on the dominant. Soon after Independence and during 1960s and 70s, there was widespread support to land reforms on grounds of both equity and efficiency. The first phase of land reforms after Independence consisted of the abolition of intermediaries and this brought about 20 million peasants, many of them belonging to the Scheduled Castes and Scheduled Tribes, in direct relationship with the State. Under the land ceiling laws enacted by various States, about 53.79 lakh acres of land have been distributed by the end of 2001 to 55.84 lakh beneficiaries; of these beneficiaries 36 per cent were from the Scheduled Castes and 15 per cent from the Scheduled Tribes to whom about 18 lakh acres and 7.8 lakh acres were assigned. In addition, in a number of States efforts were made to allot lands at the disposal of the Government to the Scheduled Castes and the Scheduled Tribes on a preferential basis. The tenancy reforms also resulted in the conferment of ownership rights for about 124.22 lakh cultivators in respect of 156.30 lakh acres of land and the tenants belonging to the Scheduled Castes and Scheduled Tribes benefited from this measure. Programmes such as Operation Barga in West Bengal resulted in the recording of sharecroppers and ensuring a fair share of produce to them. Since a majority of the poor Scheduled Castes and Scheduled Tribes live in rural areas, the issue of land is of fundamental importance to them. The distribution or redistribution of the land in favour of the poor frees them from exploitation, strengthens labour and credit markets, provides a source of sustenance and confers economic and social status. In short, it serves to empower the poor within the rural structure. The protection, preservation and enlargement of the control and command over land is thus one of the crucial issues in relation to the Scheduled Castes and the Scheduled Tribes in rural areas. It is land that is at the center of poverty, parasitism, exploitation, misery and iniquitous relationship and to the rural poor, ownership of land denotes enhanced social status and equality means equality in the ownership of land, endowing them with self-respect, self-confidence and a sense of equality.

The longing for a piece of land on the part of the rural poor is well known. There are a number of States where there is a legal prohibition on the transfer of lands belonging to members of the Scheduled Castes and Tribes to others. More specifically, for the Fifth Schedule areas, there are Regulations for protecting the lands of the Scheduled Tribes under the Fifth Schedule of the Constitution, prohibiting the transfer of land to non-tribals. The Sixth Schedule envisages a large measure of autonomy for the tribal areas, providing for the setting up of Autonomous District Councils which will exercise control and administration over land. The Panchayats (Extension to the Scheduled Areas) Act 1996, along with the conformity legislations of the States vests the Gram Sabhas in these areas with the power to prevent alienation of land and to take appropriate action to restore any unlawfully alienated land of a Scheduled Tribe.

RIGHT TO LIVELIHOOD- LABOUR

The most marginalized groups of poor in rural areas, the Scheduled Castes, consist of unorganized labourers located precariously on the brink of subsistence, depending on uncertain employment and wages. The largest segment of unorganized labour is engaged in agriculture and related activities. Out of about 369 million workers in the unorganized sector in 1999-2000, about 237 million were engaged in agriculture sector alone and nearly half of them belong to Scheduled Castes and Scheduled Tribes. Employment opportunities for members of agricultural labour households outside local agricultural sector are negligible. Social problems for them emanate from their low status in the rural hierarchy and economic problems arise due to inadequacy of employment opportunities, low income and inadequate diversification. One of the laws which is of great significance to the unorganized labour is Minimum Wages Act 1948.

The Act empowers both Central and State Governments to fix minimum wages for agriculture and other Scheduled employments and revise them periodically. So far about 1200 Schedule employments in the State sphere and 40 employments in the Central sphere have been brought with in the preview of the Act. Minimum wages can be fixed either by the Committee method or direct notification method. They are required, to be reviewed and revised once in five years. Clams can be filed with the competent authority for adjudication u/s 20 of the Act in the event of nonpayment or short payment. Advisory Boards have been given the power to assist the appropriate govt (Central and State) in the matter of fixation, review and revision of minimum wages.

The object of the Minimum Wages Act is to ensure that market forces and the laws of demand and supply are not allowed to depress wages of workmen in employments where the workers are poor, vulnerable, unorganized and without bargaining power. The Act helps unorganized workers in scheduled employments and if properly enforced, ensuring minimum wages can offer great potential for income transfers in favour of the poor. Experience shows that the nonpayment of minimum wages is widespread due to the absence of a proper mechanism for enforcement and the rates of minimum wages are not regularly revised within the specified period.

RIGHT TO FREEDOM AND LIBERTY

Slavery converging with landlessness and Scheduled Castes was deep rooted in Indian society. Slavery in its acute form declined in most regions in India and with the enactment of Anti-Slavery Act in 1843 and Sections 370 and 371 of the Indian Penal Code 1860, it stood abolished and became punishable. But hereditary or long-term servitude institutionalized as bondage continued to be the condition of large proportion of agricultural labour, a majority of them Scheduled Castes and Scheduled Tribes. It is possible that some of the orthodox forms of agrestic bondage have undergone changes over a period of time, but they have not been eliminated altogether. There are also large number of bonded labourers in brick kilns, stone quarries, limestone mines, match factories, carpet weaving, irrigation works and a variety of other occupations.

Nearly 75 per cent of the bonded labourers belong to Scheduled Castes and Tribes. Article 23 of the Constitution prohibits begar and other similar forms of forced labour and declares it a punishable offence. It was only in 1975 that the Bonded Labour System (Abolition) Ordinance was promulgated on 24 October 1975 followed by the Bonded Labour System (Abolition) Act 1976. The Bill was passed by both houses of Parliament on 9.2.76 but given retrospective effect from 24.10.75, the date when Bonded Labour System (Abolition) Ordinance had been promulgated. The Preamble to the Act mentions that the Act is to provide for the abolition of bonded labour system with a view to preventing the economic and physical exploitation of the weaker sections of the people. The Act abolishes bonded labour system and frees every bonded labourer, discharging the bonded labourer from any obligation to render any bonded labour. The liability to repay any bonded debt is also extinguished. While authorizing the State Government to confer powers on District Magistrates, the Act also specifically and directly lays down in Section 12 that it shall be the duty of every District Magistrate to enquire and take action to eradicate bonded labour.

Vigilance Committees with the District magistrate as chairman at the district level and SDM as chairman at the subdivisional level duly vested with powers have also been provided for. The cases under the Act can be tried by Executive Magistrates. It may be noted in this context that some States like Tamilnadu have brought out a detailed Manual on the identification, release and rehabilitation of Bonded Labour. It is also necessary to note that the provisions of the Scheduled Castes and Scheduled Tribes (Prevention of Atrocities) Act 1989 apply if the bonded labourer happens to belong to the Scheduled Castes or Tribes, as most of them are. Section 3 (vi) of this Act lays down"whoever compels or entices a member of the Scheduled Caste or a Scheduled Tribe to do begar or other similar forms of forced or bonded labour .... shall be punishable with imprisonment for a term which shall not be less than six months but may extend to five years and with fine."

RIGHTS OF CHILDREN

While estimates of the number of working children vary, a dependable estimate of that number can be arrived at if elimination of working children and primary education are taken together and it is considered that the children currently not attending school are working in some form or another. In 1991, there were as many as 72.9 million out of school children. It is the poorest and the most disadvantaged sectors of the society *i.e.* the Scheduled Castes and the Scheduled Tribes that supply the vast majority of working children. Eleven States, that is U.P., Bihar, Rajasthan, Gujarat, Maharashtra, Madhya Pradesh, Andhra Pradesh, Karnataka, Tamil Nadu, Orissa, West Bengal, account for more than 90 per cent of working children.

The largest number of working children are in agriculture and agriculture related activities. There is also a wealth of documentation of child labour in the diamond industry of Surat in Gujarat State, Carpet industry of Mirzapur, Bhadohi and Varanasi belt and glass units of Firozabad in Uttar Pradesh, match factories of Sivakasi in Tamilnadu, gemstone polishing units of Jaipur in Rajasthan, Slate industry of Markapur in Andhra Pradesh, etc. Children in domestic servitude may well be the most vulnerable and exploited children of all, as well as the most difficult to protect.

RIGHT TO EQUAL ACCESS

An important measure which has its origin in pre-independence days but pursued with greater vigour in independent India is the reservation in appointments in public services and in higher educational institutions in favour of the Scheduled Castes and Scheduled Tribes. Some of the States have legislations providing for such reservations, while in many States this has been done by executive orders.

It may be seen that in the case of the Scheduled Castes, there is still a significant shortfall in Group A and Group B posts. The position in regard to the Scheduled Tribes shows shortfalls in all categories. While this reflects the picture in respect of the posts under the Central Government, the position is similar in regard to the posts under the State Governments as well as the Central and the State public sector undertakings. The reservation in admission to higher educational institutions, such as engineering and medical colleges, has served to improve the opportunities of the Scheduled Castes and Scheduled Tribes to pursue professional careers. The issue of reservation has to be viewed one of equal access and equitable sharing in the public administration and emerging opportunities.

RIGHT TO DEVELOPMENT

Initially, the approach to the development of the Scheduled Castes and the Scheduled Tribes took the form of a few limited schemes of ameliorative nature by the Centre and the States. In the various States, in the first quarter of Independence, schemes for the Scheduled Castes and Scheduled Tribes consisted largely of programmes of education, housing, distribution of government waste land/Gair Mazrua land and opening of hostels for the students. Over the successive Five Year Plans, particularly from the beginning of the Fifth Five Year Plan (1974-79), the approach to the development of the Scheduled Castes and the Scheduled Tribes underwent a basic change with the emphasis shifting to ensuring of adequate flow of benefits from all the sectors of development in favour of the Scheduled Castes and the Scheduled Tribes. A systematic institutionalized effort in planning for the development of the Scheduled Castes was initiated late in the year 1978 in the nature of Special Component Plan (SCP) for Scheduled Castes.

The Special Component Plan (SCP) was designed to channelise the Plan outlays and benefits in all the sectors to the Scheduled Castes, at least in proportion to their population in order to secure their integrated development. It is intended to be a plan for the development of the Scheduled Castes in relation to their resource endowments and their needs in all the areas of social and economic activity including agriculture, animal husbandry, poultry, fisheries, education including scholarships, hostels, and midday meals, provision of drinking water, electrification of Scheduled Caste localities, development of sericulture, minor irrigation including construction and energisation of irrigation wells, programmes for specially vulnerable groups, housing and house sites, link roads, self employment schemes, social forestry, allotment of land as well as schemes for development of lands and allotment of shops and stalls in public places.

The Special Component Plan is an important and integral part of the planning process intended to secure the rapid socio-economic development of the Scheduled Castes. In the year 1980, the Special Central Assistance (SCA) was also introduced as an additive to the Special Component Plan. Thus, the strategy for the development of the Scheduled Castes is anchored on the Special Component Plan formulated and implemented by the Centre as well as the States supported by the central scheme of Special Central Assistance. It was also in the seventies that the State Governments created specific institutional mechanisms for providing assistance for economic development of the Scheduled Castes.

The Governments in the States with substantial Scheduled Caste population have set up the Scheduled Caste Development Corporations (SCDC) to enable the members of the Scheduled Castes to take up viable income generating activities. In the year 1979, the Government of India also introduced the centrally sponsored scheme of assistance to the State Governments for investing in the share capital of their corporations. The National Scheduled Caste Finance and Development Corporation (NSFDC) was established in 1989 to provide support to the economic development programmes for the Scheduled Castes. A National Safai Karamcharis Finance and Development Corporation was also set up in January 1997to facilitate all round socio economic development of Safai Karamcharis and their dependents and to extend financial assistance for the establishment of income generating viable projects. In respect of the Scheduled Tribes, the basic principles that should guide the approach to the development of the Scheduled Tribes were clearly set out by the Prime Minister Pandit Jawaharlal Nehru in the form of five principles known as'Tribal Panchsheel' which was later endorsed by the Renuka Ray team (1959), Dhebar Commission (1961) and the Shilu Ao Committee (1969).

The Panchsheel laid down specifically that:

- The tribal people should develop along the lines of their own genius and we should avoid imposing anything on them but rather try to encourage in every way their own traditional arts and culture.
- Tribal rights in lands and forests should be respected.
- We should try to train and build up a team of their own people to do administration and development.
- We should not overadminister these areas or overwhelm them with

multiplicity of schemes; we should rather work through and not in rivalry to their own social and cultural institutions.

- We should judge the results not by statistics or the amount of money spent but by the quality of human character that is evolved.

The tribal situation in the country was gone into indepth before the concept of Tribal Sub Plan was evolved in the year 1974-75. The Tribal Sub Plan (TSP) strategy took note of the fact that a clearer approach to the tribal problems was necessary in terms of their geographic and demographic concentration, if faster development was to take place. The tribal areas of the country were classified into three broad categories-first, the States and Union Territories having a majority of Scheduled Tribes population; second, the States and Union Territories having a substantial tribal population with major tribal population concentrated in particular administrative units such as Blocks and Tehsils; and thirdly, the States and Union Territories having dispersed tribal population. In the light of this approach, it was considered that tribal majority States like Arunanchal Pradesh, Meghalaya, Mizoram, Nagaland and Lakshadweep may not need a Tribal Sub Plan as the entire Plan of these States was meant for the Scheduled Tribe population.

For the second category of States and Union Territories, the Tribal Sub Plan strategy was adopted after delineating areas of tribal concentration. A similar approach was adopted in the case of States and Union Territories having dispersed tribal population by focusing special attention on the pockets of tribal concentration keeping in view the nature of their dispersal. In order to effectively administer the programmes, the Tribal Sub Plan strategy adopted the Integrated Tribal Development Projects (ITDP) for tribal areas with substantial tribal population, the Modified Tribal Development Approach (MADA) as well as clusters for pockets of tribal concentration and special projects for Primitive Tribal Groups (PTG) along with administrative, financial and functional integration and equally all necessary measures to eliminate exploitative relationships.

The Special Central Assistance supplements the Tribal Sub Plan. A number of States have set up Tribal Marketing Corporations for securing a fair price for the minor forest produce and the agricultural products procured and sold by the tribals. The Government of India also set up the Tribal Cooperative Marketing Development Federation (TRIFED) in 1987 as the apex coordinating body for the State Tribal Marketing Corporations in order to ensure remunerative prices for minor forest produce and agricultural items produced or collected by tribals and to protect them against exploitation by private trades and middlemen. A National Scheduled Tribe Finance and Development Corporation has also been set up to support the Scheduled Tribe Finance and Development Corporations in the States. The Government of India had also issued guidelines in 1975 in regard to excise policy in the tribal areas emphasizing the banning of commercial vending of the liquor in the tribal areas, while permitting the tribals to brew their own liquor for consumption at home and for religious and social occasions. The tribal communities particularly those who live within forests or in close proximity to them are victims of unimaginative application of forest laws and loss of traditional rights in forest produce, apart from being confronted with the problem of displacement.

The National Forest Policy 1988 reiterated the symbiotic relationship between the tribals and forests and stressed the need for associating the tribal people closely in the protection, regeneration and the development of forests as well as providing gainful employment to the people living in and around the forests. The policy also provided for the full protection of the traditional rights and concessions enjoyed by the tribals. In the year 1991, a series of policy instructions were issued by the Government of India to ensure harmony and to avoid conflict between the local tribal community and the forests, including regularization of occupations by landless poor and the tribal people, conversion of forest villages into revenue villages and joint forest management.

The Tenth Five Year Plan (1997-2002) envisages the continuance of the process of empowering the socially disadvantaged groups through a three-pronged strategy-social empowerment through removal of all the still existing inequalities, disparities and other persisting problems besides providing easy access to minimum services; economic empowerment through employment cum income generating activities with ultimate objective of making them economically independent and self-reliant; social justice through elimination of all types of discrimination with the strength of constitutional commitments, legislative support, affirmative action, awareness generation, conscientisation of target groups and change in the mindset of people through renewed commitment to a National Charter for Social Justice based on the principle of social harmony with social and gender justice and necessary legal measures.

RIGHT TO EDUCATION

Article 46 of the Constitution directs the State to promote with special care the educational and economic interests of the Scheduled Castes and Scheduled Tribes. Article 21 A of the Constitution has laid down the fundamental right to education for children in the age group of six to fourteen years. The National Policy on Education 1986 placed special emphasis on the removal of disparities and equalization of educational opportunities.

The Policy laid down that the central focus in the educational development of the Scheduled Castes is their equalization with the non-Scheduled Caste population at all levels and states of education in all areas and in all the four dimensions-rural male, rural female, urban male and urban female. The Programme of Action (POA) 1992 accorded priority to the opening of primary and upper primary schools to meet the needs of Scheduled Caste habitations and hamlets, provision of nonformal distance education, adequate incentives; coverage of the Scheduled Castes localities and tribal areas under the Operation Black Board and the programme of Universalization of Elementary Education. While there has been an increase in the percentage of literacy among the Scheduled Castes and Scheduled Tribes, the levels are still perilously low and there is a need for intensive efforts to achieve a reasonably high rate of literacy as also to remove the disparity in the levels of literacy in relation to the general population.

One of the earliest efforts of the State in regard to the development of Scheduled Castes and Tribes has been in the field of education. The schemes taken up include scholarships for prematric studies and post matric studies, free supply of school uniforms, stationery and text books, opening of hostels for the Scheduled Caste and the Scheduled Tribe students, establishment of residential schools as well as the setting up of Ashram Schools for the tribal students. The Post Matric Scholarship Scheme is particularly noteworthy, because of its open ended nature making all the eligible Scheduled Caste and Scheduled Tribe students entitled to scholarship at all levels of post matric education. The scheme has contributed significantly to the access and retention of Scheduled Caste and the Scheduled Tribe students in higher education.

RIGHT TO LIFE AND LIBERTY

It has to be said that, barring some exceptions, the role of the police in relation to human rights is widely perceived as being negative and as an institution, it turns out to be no respector of human rights, more particularly in relation to the poor and downtrodden Scheduled Castes and Scheduled Tribes. Nothing tarnishes the image of the police more than the brutality directed against the persons in their custody.

Deaths in police lockup and encounters occur frequently. The facts that the majority of the victims are from weaker sections of the society such as Scheduled Castes and Scheduled Tribes and these deaths are the outcome of third degree methods and flagrant violation of human rights of citizens are causing concern.

RIGHTS OF WOMEN

Almost all the women from Scheduled Castes and Scheduled Tribes are women workers. Taking women workers as a whole, they have an overwhelming presence only in unorganized sector-nearly 85 per cent of women work in primary sector-and women's share in organized sector employment is only about 17 per cent and mostly in lower rungs in hierarchy. Even though the Constitution lays down equal remuneration to men and women as part of the Directive Principles and the Equal Remuneration Act was enacted in 1976, it is well known that in a majority of instances women are being paid much lower remuneration than men for the same work. The position of women belonging to Scheduled Castes and Scheduled Tribes is all the more deplorable compared to their male counterparts, struggling, as they do, for basic survival and vulnerable as they are to various forms of sexual abuse. They are"thrice alienated" on the basis of class, caste and gender. Although sexual violence is a problem from which women in general suffer, in the case of women from Scheduled Castes and Scheduled Tribes, it is far more intense and widespread as, due to the lower social attitude towards women from these communities and their economic dependence, they become victims of the sexual violence on a larger scale.

The so called unclean occupations are performed mostly by women from the Scheduled Caste and Scheduled Tribe communities. Another social evil is that of dedicating girl children to local deities and letting them get sexually exploited as they grow up. This practice, which is a part of the wider Devadasi system, is widely prevalent in parts of the country, known by local names such as Jogin, Jogati, Basavi, Mathamma in Andhra Pradesh, Maharashtra and Karnataka. Most of the people subjected to such exploitation are from Scheduled Castes and Scheduled Tribes. Some of the States, such as Andhra Pradesh, have passed enactments prohibiting such practices and for punishment for those who abet such practices.

ROLES AND RESPONSIBILITY OF THE DISTRICT MAGISTRATES

The Indian Constitution has been based on the values of equality, human dignity and justice and incorporates most of the human rights embodied in the international covenants. The laws and policy prescriptions emanating from the Constitution provide form and content to these mandates. In countries such as India, the State has an overarching presence and there are areas of legal and administrative action where the State alone is called upon to act in public interest.

Illustrations of this nature are the Protection of Civil Rights Act or the Scheduled Castes and Scheduled Tribes (Prevention of Atrocities) Act or the Bonded Labour System (Abolition) Act, apart from the general laws. The State Governments and in a number of specific cases, the District Magistrates have been conferred with special and well defined powers and functions under such laws and rules to exercise them in public interest. Keeping in view, the situation in which the Scheduled Castes and Scheduled Tribes are located in the society and the range of human rights issues that arise in their context, the District Magistrate, as the legally empowered authority under the general laws as well as different specific statutes and as the Head of the district administration, has the duty and responsibility, not merely to prevent the violation or infringement of human rights of the Scheduled Castes and Tribes but to uphold promote, protect and preserve human dignity, decency, equality and freedom as well. The role and the responsibility of the District Magistrates in respect of the human rights of the members of the Scheduled Castes and the Scheduled Tribes are thus wide ranging.

UNTOUCHABILITY AND ATROCITIES

One of the inhuman forms of indignity and violation of human rights is the practice of untouchability. The different overt and covert manifestations of untouchability include denial of access to public places, places of worship, shops, fields, road and pathways, land and water, refusal of services, denial of seats in public transport, abuses in the name of caste and a variety of other acts of discrimination. The Scheduled Caste often depends on the mercy of the so called upper castes even to take drinking water from public water supply sources for their use. A common practice in hotels in rural areas is that they have to eat and drink from separate vessels in which they must wash themselves. In some schools, the children belonging to the Scheduled Caste are made to sit on the floor or at the back of the classroom. The practice of social boycott is a virulent form of untouchability, because of the economic vulnerability and dependence, social boycott operates as a devastatingly effective means for the dominant community to starve the Scheduled Castes into submission. Many District Magistrates assume or tend to believe that untouchability does not exist or that it is a thing of the past. On the other hand, the district Magistrate should be acutely conscious of the widespread and varied, open and covert, forms of untouchability in the district and make full use of the entire district machinery to put down this practice firmly and effectively. It is the duty of the District Magistrate to strive towards its eradication as mandated under Article 17 of the Constitution and as provided for in the Protection of Civil Rights Act 1955. The barbaric acts of atrocities is another crucial area which constitutes a gross violation of the right to life with dignity and equality of the Scheduled Castes. A special legislation, the Scheduled Caste and Scheduled Tribes (Prevention of Atrocities) Act was enacted in 1989 to supplement the existing laws.

The District Magistrate has been accorded specific powers, duties, functions and responsibilities under this statute. It is unfortunate that Governmental agencies, especially the magistracy and police authorities who are directly charged with the implementation of this Act do not have a proper understanding of the spirit and contents of the Act and Rules. It is seen that the police are unwilling to acknowledge that an atrocity has occurred or simply refuse to register a case or bring about a compromise on the terms dictated by the dominant people. Quite often, only trivial sections of the Act are invoked irrespective of the gravity of the crime.

The District Magistrate must ensure the proper and effective implementation of this Act in all its aspects and in the spirit in which it has been enacted. A prompt visit to the places of occurrence along with the Superintendent of police as mandated in the statute should be ensured. This will not only provide for proper action in specific cases but also generate a climate of confidence and adherence to human rights. The District Level Vigilance and Monitoring Committee with the District Magistrate as the

Chairman should be active and a close monitoring and review should be undertaken. The supervision of the investigation and prosecution as well as the review of the performance of the Special Public Prosecutors as provided for in Rule 4 should be regular and probing.

Immediate steps should be taken for providing relief and rehabilitation to the victims as set out in detail in the Rules. During the periodical elections to the local bodies, legislative assemblies or Parliament, the dominant sections intimidate and frighten the Scheduled Castes and Scheduled Tribes from voting just as to their free will. This has been specifically brought within the definition of Atrocities under the Scheduled Castes and Scheduled Tribes (Prevention of Atrocities) Act. As District Magistrates as well as returning officers, it is their duty to ensure that the voting rights of these sections of people are fully safeguarded. Yet another specific form of denial of human rights is the prevention of the Scheduled Caste and scheduled Tribe persons from availing of the elective positions in Panchayat institutions or to function as elected members or Sarpanches or heads of Panchayat bodies.

There are some Panchayats in some of the States where even nominations have not been allowed to be filed for the posts reserved for the Scheduled Castes. Firm and effective action has to be taken in all such cases under the normal criminal laws as well as the Scheduled Caste and Scheduled Tribe (Prevention of Atrocities) Act. The right of the Scheduled Castes and the Scheduled Tribes to participate in the Panchayati Raj and other democratic institutions should be fully protected. The Protection of Civil Rights Act 1955 as well as the Scheduled Castes and the Scheduled Tribes (Prevention of Atrocities) Act 1989 and Rules 1995 have to be read together and acted upon. These laws are powerful tools available to the District Magistrates to safeguard the human dignity and human rights of these Constitutional categories. Atrocities are a symptom of a deeper malady in the society and, therefore, simultaneously, efforts are needed to strengthen the overall socio economic position of the Scheduled Castes and the Scheduled Tribes through educational and economic development.

MANUAL SCAVENGING

The dehumanizing practice of manual scavenging continues in most parts of the country, particularly in urban and semi-urban areas. As pointed out earlier, the District Magistrates are the Executive Authorities for this purpose under the Employment of Manual Scavengers and Construction of Dry Latrines (Prohibition) Act 1993. Action should be taken by the District Magistrates to get the dry latrines demolished in a time bound manner. While doing so, it is necessary to see that this does not result in retrenchment and loss of livelihood to any one. As a large number of those engaged in this work are actually employed by the Municipalities or other local authorities, they should be reallocated to dignified work in the same organization. In respect of those who are private workers, suitable alternative means of livelihood should be worked out and implemented, utilizing various schemes which are available. The children of the Safai Karmacharis should be enrolled into the schools and hostels.

LAND-LAND REFORMS AND LAND DISTRIBUTION

The District Magistrates who are also District Collectors or Deputy Commissioners incharge of land administration enjoy enormous powers and functions in regard to land administration and hold a special responsibility in this respect. There are still large extents of lands available for allotment to the Scheduled Castes and Scheduled Tribes-whether it is Government wasteland/Gair Mazrua lands; lands declared surplus under land ceiling laws; Gram Sabha lands; Bhoodan lands; or temple lands. In some States like Madhya Pradesh, a part of the grazing (Charnoi) land has been released for assignment to the landless poor Scheduled Castes and Scheduled Tribes. In most of the States, there are rules for preferential allotment of land to them as they constitute the largest group of agricultural labour. The land ceiling laws in many States also provide for an overriding preference in the allotment of ceiling surplus land in favour of Scheduled Castes and Scheduled Tribes. The effective implementation of land reforms and the allotment of land at the disposal of Government and ensuring uninterrupted possession of such lands can secure a substantial improvement in the conditions of living of the rural Scheduled Castes and Scheduled Tribes. There is also scope for purchase of private lands and allotting them to landless Scheduled Castes and the Scheduled Tribe families under the Land Purchase Schemes introduced in many States. Selection and allotment of good cultivable land and supporting the land allotment with irrigation and other inputs would enable the landless to become independent cultivators. There are also a number of instances where the Scheduled Castes and Schedule Tribes who have acquired land through land reform laws or other legal means are harassed on this account. Many of them have lost their land due to acts of violence and intimidation by dominant communities who take forcible possession of land that legally belong to Scheduled Castes and Scheduled Tribes.

Physical attacks by dominant sections and denial of employment are also not uncommon. Where they are sharecroppers, there are severe problems faced by them in enjoying the fruits of their own labour. Hence, apart from formal allotment of land and issue of documents such as title deeds, it should be ensured that the allottees are placed in effective possession of the land. In case of any obstruction or threat by the dominant sections, necessary protection by police should be given to the allottee. As many of the atrocities against Scheduled Castes and Scheduled Tribes have their source in their struggle to obtain land, action should be taken in such cases under the provisions of Section 3 (iv) and 3 (v) the Scheduled Castes and the Scheduled Tribes Act.

LAND-LAND ALIENATION AND RESTORATION

Unfortunately, land alienation has been going on unchecked and restoration process remains feeble, thwarted by the propertied sections either through force or manipulation of law. Even the Survey and settlement of lands by Government agencies has caused large scale loss of tribal land due to unimaginative and sometimes motivated steps by the local persons. There are many States where the lands of both Scheduled Castes and Scheduled Tribes are protected from alienation by law. In certain States, lands had been reserved exclusively for the Scheduled Castes. In the States where tribal areas have been notified under the Fifth Schedule, there are specific Land Transfer Regulations relating to tribal lands promulgated under the schedule. In many States, the District Magistrates have been designated as Agents to Government in relation to the Scheduled Areas. It will be the responsibility of the District Magistrates to ensure the effective implementation of the Land Transfer Regulations and enactments to protect as well as restore the lands of the members of the Scheduled Castes and the Scheduled Tribes.

LAND-IRRIGATION AND INPUTS

The lands of the Scheduled Castes and the Scheduled Tribes and even the lands allotted to them are usually of low quality and bereft of irrigation facilities. Steps should be taken to provide irrigation facilities under various minor irrigation schemes.

LAND-LIVING SPACE

The poor Scheduled Caste and Scheduled Tribe people struggle for securing house sites. In many villages, they have been in permissive possession of housesites and homesteads with a constant threat of eviction. The allotment of a house site will go a long way to release them from the grip of the dominant rich. In urban areas, the problem is even more difficult. The term slum clearance or encroachment removal is often an euphemism for uprooting powerless migrants from their homes and shifting them to low value sites, usually at the periphery, leading to their virtual economic extinction. Most of them belong to the weaker sections, particularly Scheduled Castes and Scheduled Tribes. The District Magistrates should take care to safeguard the interests of these vulnerable people in adequate measure.

CONCLUSION

The District Magistrate has a leadership role in the district as the head of the district administration. A professional, competent and sensitive District magistrate can ensure justice, human rights and human dignity for all sections of the society but in particular, members of SC and ST. The least that can be done is to prevent injustice to the Scheduled Castes and the Scheduled Tribes-indeed all the poor in the society-in the various arenas of administration such as public offices, including police stations where they are often humiliated. It should be ensured that the law enforcing machinery itself respects the right giving legislation adequately and with earnestness. In all issues that concern the Scheduled Castes and Scheduled tribes, sensitization and motivation, providing proper guidelines, high level review and monitoring, a simple redressal mechanism, close supervision, regular flow of information and more than anything else, accessibility to these disadvantaged groups will serve to secure positive results.

The overall national and state policies are, no doubt, not amenable to changes at the district level. But they have to be creatively and imaginatively applied in actual implementation. Public servants such as District Magistrates to whom powers and functions are delegated in public interest have an area of relative autonomy and exercise considerable independence and freedom within the overall power structure. It is also open to the District Magistrates to suggest changes and seek modifications in laws and state policy in the interests of the weaker sections. Indeed, many policy changes have taken place on the basis of suggestions based on the experience of field level officials. The District Magistrates themselves should accept imbibe and internalize the values of human rights, equality, non discrimination, human dignity, justice and democratic practices and consider themselves as part of the mechanism for protection of human rights.

The urge to respect human rights should largely come from within District Magistrates, representing the State, should uphold and enhance human rights of the Scheduled Castes and the Scheduled Tribes; ensure there is no violation or infringement and take immediate remedial that measures as any such derogation takes place. As a general rule and practice, the District Magistrates must make efforts to visit and stay in the Scheduled Caste and Scheduled Tribe localities, thus reaching out to them and interacting with them to enable them to overcome their economic and social disabilities and to address their basic needs. They should win their trust, confidence, and respect. Finally, it should be kept in mind that the social and economic situation of the Scheduled Castes and the Scheduled Tribes varies from State to State and often, even within a State. The Constitution has made special provisions for the administration of the fifth Scheduled and the Sixth Schedule areas in view of their distinct features.

It is also to be noted that while the Constitution and Central laws prevail all over the country, there are, in addition, many State specific laws, regulations and rules which vary from State to State. In respect of development programmes also, there are nationwide schemes as well as State specific and local programmes. It is therefore necessary for the District Magistrates to act with a proper contextual understanding and analysis of the specific situation in each district.

13

Social Work and Human Rights of Disabled and Physically Challenged

This stage attempts to discuss social work and human rights of those persons with disabilities who, temporarily or permanently, experience physical, intellectual or psychological impairment of varying degrees. Most often, their lives are handicapped by social, cultural and attitudinal barriers which hamper their full participation and enjoyment of equal rights and opportunities.

DEFINITION OF DISABILITY

The Persons with Disabilities (Equal Opportunities, Protection of Rights and Full Participation) Act, 1995, while defining disability in Section 2(t) stipulates,"person with disability means a person suffering from not less than forty per cent of any disability as certified by a medical authority." The disabilities that have been listed in Section 2 include blindness, low vision, hearing impairment, locomotor disability/cerebral palsy, mental retardation, mental illness and persons cured of leprosy. In addition, autism and multiple disabilities have been covered under the National Trust for Welfare of Persons with Autism, Cerebral Palsy, Mental Retardation and Multiple Disabilities Act, 1999.

AUTHORITIES TO GIVE DISABILITY CERTIFICATE

As per rule 4.1 of the Implementing Rules of the Disabilities Act, 1995,"A Disability Certificate shall be issued by a Medical Board duly constituted by the Central and the State Government."

COMPOSITION OF THE MEDICAL BOARD

Rule 4.2 of the Implementing Rule lays down that,"The State Government may constitute a Medical Board consisting of atleast three members out of which atleast one shall be a specialist in the particular field for assessing Locomotor/Visual including low vision/hearing and speech disability, mental retardation and leprosy cured, as the case may be."

TYPES OF DISABILITY CERTIFICATE

The Rule 5(1) of the Implementing Rules of Persons with Disabilities Act, 1995 provides that,"The Medical Board shall, after due examination, give a Permanent Disability Certificate in cases of such permanent disabilities where there are no chances of variation in the degree of disability."

The Medical Board shall indicate the period of validity in the certificate, in case where there is any chance of variation in the degree of disability 5(2).

RELEVANCE OF A DISABILITY CERTIFICATE

Rule 6 of the Implementing Rules of the Disabilities Act, 1995 clearly states that,"The Certificate issued by the Medical Board under Rule 5 shall make a person eligible to apply for facilities, concessions and benefits admissible under the schemes of the Government or Non-Governmental organizations, subject to such conditions as the Central or the State Government may impose."

HUMAN RIGHTS ISSUES

A cursory analysis of the case law available and the reports of national and international organizations indicate that, worldwide, persons with disabilities arc subjcctcd to certain common forms of discrimination.

The most common ones are the following:

- Denial of equality of opportunities in earning livelihood.
- Denial of just and fair conditions of work.
- Denial of equal access to the programmes of education.
- Denial of access to public transport, built infrastructure and information systems.
- Denial of participation in family, social, cultural, and political life.
- Emotional, sexual and physical harassment.
- Denial of right in the family property and to own property

The stated forms of violations can be identified as violations of economic, social, cultural, civil and political rights of persons with disabilities. Disability tends to be couched within a medical model, identifying people with disabilities as ill, different from their non-disabled peers and in need of care. Because the emphasis is on the medical needs of persons with disabilities, there is a corresponding neglect of their wider social needs. This has resulted in their severe isolation.

In the UN Standard Rules on the Equalization of Opportunities for Persons With Disabilities, 1993,'disability' summarizes a large number of different functional limitations occurring in any population in any country of the world. People may be disabled by physical, intellectual or sensory impairment, but a distinction has been made between disability and handicap meaning"handicap is the loss or limitation of opportunities to take part in the life of the community on an equal level with others". The purpose of the term handicap is to emphasize the focus on the shortcomings in the environment and in many organized structures of society. A coherent programme of"equality of opportunity" entails tackling deeprooted social attitudes to disability. Besides that, equality entitles each person to equal membership in society. This calls for critical reorientation of all the structures and processes which have important implications in the lives of all citizens including those with disabilities."In essence, the human rights perspective on disability means viewing people as subjects and not as objects. It entails moving away from perceiving the disabled as problems towards viewing them as holders of rights. Importantly, it means locating problems outside the individual and addressing the manner in which various economic, social, cultural and political processes accommodate the difference of ability."

THE CONSTITUTION

DISABILITY: A STATE SUBJECT

The Constitution of India is premised on the human rights values which recognize that all persons are born free and equal in rights and dignity. The Preamble, the Directive Principles of State Policy and the Fundamental Rights enshrined in the Constitution, stand testimony to the commitment of the State to its people.

These provisions envisage a very positive role for the State towards its vulnerable citizens. As per Entry 9 in the List 11 of Schedule 7 of the Constitution, the subject of'Relief to the Disabled and Unemployable' is the responsibility of the State Governments. Despite the Constitutional mandate, most of the State Governments have neither introduced any law nor have introduced the State Policy on Disability so far. Some schemes have been introduced to provide scholarships, pensions, assistive devices, braille books, out of turn houses etc. But, their impact has been insignificant perhaps due to inadequacies in the scheme.

Article 41

This Article enjoins that,"The State shall, within the limits of its economic capacity and development make effective provision for securing the right to work, to education and to public assistance in cases of unemployment, old age, sickness and disablement." These provisions, to a certain extent, reflect the traditional values of Indian culture that accord great importance to organized response by the State towards its disadvantaged and vulnerable members.

Article 15

Article 15 of the Constitution enjoins that,"no citizen shall, on grounds only of religion, race, caste, sex, place of birth or any of them, be subject to any disability, liability, restriction or condition with regard to -

- Access to shops, public restaurants, hotels and places of public entertainment; or
- The use of wells, tanks, bathing ghats, roads and places of public resort maintained wholly or partly out of State funds or dedicated to the use of the general public".

The public facilities mentioned in this Article are designed on an assumption that all people can walk, see, hear, and can use hands, but may be discriminated on other grounds. It is recognized that people are handicapped not so much due to their disabilities as they are on account of environmental barriers and, therefore, it is necessary to create barrier-free facilities for persons with disabilities under Section 44 of the Disabilities Act 1995. It, therefore, enjoins on the establishments in the transport sector to adopt rail compartments, buses, vessels and aircrafts in such a way as to permit easy access to PWDs.

Section 45 calls for installation of auditory signals at intersections for the blind, curb cuts to be replaced with gentle slopes for wheel chair mobility, engravings on zebra crossing, railway platform etc for the safety of the blind and for persons with a low vision. Section 46 provides for ramps in public buildings, hospitals and schools, braille symbols and auditory signals in the elevators, etc. However, precious little has been done by the governments to translate these provisions into reality, so much so, that even necessary amendments in the light of the Disabilities Act have not been carried out in building bye-laws, fabrication standards for buses, rail coaches, vessels etc. As a result, barriers for equal participation in the mainstream systems and processes continue to persist.

Javed Abidi filed a Civil Writ petition bearing No 812 of 2001 Vs Union of India and Ors before the High Court of Delhi. He was aggrieved on the removal of temporary wooden ramps from the Red Fort, Qutub Minar, Humayan's Tomb, Jantar Mantar and other similar monuments of historic importance. These ramps were fabricated and fixed by the Ministry of Social Justice and Empowerment and Archaeological Survey of India during the visit of Mr. Stephen Hawkins, the renowned physicist (Wheelchair User), who wanted to see these monuments.

After his visit the Archaeological Survey of India decided to remove these ramps. Abidi filed the case seeking justice in accordance with Section 46 of the Disabilities Act, 1995, which mandates ramps in public places for wheelchair access. The petitioner urged the Court for directing the respondent not to remove the wooden ramps and instead to erect permanent ramps ensuring barrier-free access to persons with disabilities. Mahesh Sharma and Shivani Gupta Vs Ministry of Railways 2000 was a complaint case before the Chief Commissioner for Persons with Disabilities. Complainants were aggrieved on account of barriers to access trains and related facilities such as railway stations, waiting rooms and toilets. The relief was sought as per Section 44 of the Disabilities Act, 1995. The Chief Commissioner recommended

Ministry of Railways to evolve a longterm plan with short and medium term objectives for making railway stations, rail coaches and other facilities accessible for wheelchair users and for persons with other types of disabilities.

In pursuance of the recommendations, Ministry of Railways drew up a plan with a modest budget for:

- Making ramps at the major railway stations at 155 locations in the first phase.
- The Railways also decided to convert 20-proto-type Guard-cumsleeper coaches with wider doorways and modified toilets to permit direct access by wheelchair.
- For New Delhi, Hazarat Nizamudin and old Delhi railway stations, the respondent set aside a sum of Rupees 33.42 lakhs for providing ramps, accessible waiting rooms, accessible toilets, accessible parking space etc.

Article 16

This Article guarantees that"no citizen shall, on grounds only of religion, race, caste, sex, descent, place of birth, residence or any of them, be ineligible for, or discriminated against in respect of, any employment or office under the State."

- The silence of the Constitution regarding discrimination in employment on grounds of physical or sensory disability should not have caused exclusion of persons with disabilities in matters of employment and appointment to any public office; as most people with disabilities possess the capacity to productively contribute and be self-reliant provided the conditions of work are just and fair. However, people on grounds of disability have encountered rampant discrimination due to inadequate safeguards in the law. The medical fitness criteria for entry and retention of government service outrightly discriminates people on grounds of disabilities. A petition was filed under Article 32 in the Hon'ble Supreme Court of India by one Narendra Kumar Chandla vs State of Haryana and Ors. AIR 1995, S.C.519. Chandla was aggrieved on account of being reduced in rank on acquiring disability during service. The Supreme Court, however, at that stage refused to entertain the petition under Article 32. The petitioner, therefore, approached the Punjab and the Haryana High Court, which dismissed his petition. Chandla again filed a Special Leave petition in the Supreme Court. Though the Supreme Court by its Order appointed him as L.D.C. (clerk), which was lower in rank but protected his salary in the pay scale of `1,400-2,300. However, he was deprived of his right to promotion to the next higher grade forever. No doubt, to a great degree the Supreme Court removed the injustice and protected his livelihood but it did not lay down the law prohibiting discrimination in the matter of career enhancement on acquiring disability during service. In order to prevent discrimination on grounds of disability extra legal safeguards have now been provided, for example, Section 47 of Persons with Disabilities Act, 1995 lays down that"No establishment shall dispense with, or reduce in rank, an employee who acquires a disability during his service. Provided that, if an employee, after acquiring disability is not suitable for the post he was holding, could be shifted to some other post with the same pay scale and service benefit. Provided further that if it is not possible to adjust the employee against any post, he may be kept on a supernumerary post until a suitable post is available or he attains the age of superannuation, whichever is earlier. No promotion shall be denied to a person merely on ground of his disability."

- The medical fitness criteria for entry in the government service and in the public sector undertakings are so provided that it outright denies opportunity of entry in the service on grounds of disability even if the post in question is the one already identified for PWDs and the candidate in question has already qualified the selection criteria. In the case of Nandakumar Narayanarao Ghodmare Vs. State of Maharashtra and Ors., a physically handicapped candidate was rejected because of colour blindness. When it was pointed out to the Court that only 5 posts out of 35 posts required perfect vision, the Supreme Court directed the Government to consider the case of the appellant and to appoint him to any of the posts of the Agricultural Class II Service post, other than the posts which required perfect vision. But unfortunately, the medical fitness standards laid down by most governments and public sector undertakings still are unfair and are in violation of law.

INTERNATIONAL COVENANTS AND AGREEMENTS FOR PERSONS WITH DISABILITIES

DECLARATIONS

In the 1970s, the evolution in thinking on disability issues at the United Nations manifested itself in a number of UN initiatives, which embraced the growing international concept of human rights of persons with disabilities and equalization of opportunities for them. For instance, in Resolution 2856 (XXVI) of 20 December 1971, the General Assembly proclaimed the Declaration on the Rights of Mentally Retarded Persons.

The declaration"the mentally retarded person should enjoy the same rights as other human beings, including the right to proper medical care, economic security, the right to training and rehabilitation, and the right to live with his own family or with foster parents. Furthermore, the Assembly declared that there should be proper legal safeguards to protect the mentally retarded person against every form of abuse if it should become necessary to restrict or deny his or her rights". In 1975, the General Assembly of the UN adopted the Declaration on the Rights of Disabled Persons, which proclaimed that"disabled persons have the same civil and political rights as other human beings." The Declaration states," Disabled persons should receive equal treatment and services, which will enable them to develop their capabilities and skills to the maximum and will hasten the process of their social integration or reintegration". This Declaration is a comprehensive instrument with a clear focus on the rights of persons with disabilities.

RULES AND RESOLUTIONS

The world community observed 1981 as the International Year of the Disabled Persons. Its central theme was -"Full Participation and Equality." It set the trend of human rights in the disability arena, as the State was held responsible to guarantee enjoyment of full citizenship and fundamental rights by persons with disabilities.

Subsequently, the UN General Assembly adopted the World Programme of Action (1982-the most comprehensive global strategy which placed'equalization of opportunities' as a central theme and as its guiding principle for the achievement of full participation of persons with disabilities in all aspects of social and economic life. To give recognition to economic, social and cultural rights of PWDs the period 1983 -1993 was observed as the UN Decade of Disabled Persons. The Decade intensified debate on equal opportunities and non-discrimination. Recognition of the inherent equality of all human beings as well as the entitlement of each individual to all human rights forms the core of human rights law. In International Human Rights Law, equality is founded upon two complementary principles: non-discrimination and reasonable differentiation.

The principle of non-discrimination seeks to ensure that all persons can equally enjoy and exercise all their rights and freedoms. Discrimination occurs due to arbitrary denial of opportunities for equal participation. For example, when public facilities and services are set on standards out of the reach of persons with disabilities, it leads to exclusion and denial of rights. Such exclusion has several adverse consequences on the psyche, development and growth of the individual. It saps initiative. It cripples the will to contribute ones very best to any productive endeavor. It demoralizes and demotivates people to come up with the best of their imagination and ingenuity which would promote quality of work. Equality not only implies preventing discrimination (example, the protection of individuals against unfavourable treatment by introducing antidiscrimination laws), but goes much beyond in remedying discrimination against groups suffering systematic discrimination in society. In concrete terms, it means embracing the notion of positive rights, affirmative action and reasonable accommodation.

MATERIAL EQUALITY

Commonly, the notion of equality manifests in two distinct ways: legal equality and material equality. In the material equality perspective, society is obliged to modify those differences that deny or impair the right of each individual to be an equal member of society."Policy research demonstrates that building codes, principles of barrier-free design, adapted curricula, targeted policy and funding commitments are useful mechanisms to reduce discrimination and increase equal participation". The UN Standard Rules on the Equalization of Opportunities for People with Disabilities, 1993 is an instrument based on the principle of material equality. The principle of'equal rights' in the Standard Rules is described as implying"that the needs of each and every individual are of equal importance, that those needs must be made the basis for the planning of societies and that all resources must be employed in such a way as to ensure that every individual has equal opportunities for participation."

STANDARD RULES

The UN Standard Rules imply a strong moral and political commitment on behalf of States to take action for the equalization of opportunities for persons with disabilities. States are required under the Rules to remove obstacles to equal participation and to actively involve disability NGOs as partners in this process.

In the first operative paragraph of resolution, the Human Rights Commission recognizes the UN Standard Rules as an evaluative instrument to be used to assess the degree of compliance with human rights standards concerning disabled people. The Commission further recognizes that any violation of the fundamental principle of equality or any discrimination or other negative differential treatment of persons with disabilities inconsistent with the United Nations Standard Rules on the Equalization of Opportunities for Persons with Disabilities is an infringement of the human rights of persons with disabilities.

ASIAN AND PACIFIC DECADE

The Governments of the ESCAP region, proclaimed, the Asian and Pacific Decade of Disabled Persons, 1993-2002, by resolution 48/3 of 23 April 1992, at Beijing. The resolution was intended to strengthen regional cooperation in resolving issues affecting the achievement of the goals of the World Programme of Action concerning Disabled Persons, especially those concerning the full participation and equality of persons with disabilities.

The Meeting held at Bangkok in June 1995 examined the progress made since the introduction of the Decade and adopted 12 targets and 78 recommendations concerning the implementation of the Agenda for Action, including the gender dimensions of implementation. Of the 12 policy areas under the Agenda for Action, ESCAP has focused its efforts on areas that were not covered by the mandates of other United Nations instruments and bodies.

The policy areas include:

- Better coordination among various ministries at national and State level.
- Enactment of comprehensive legislations for the protection and promotion of rights of the disabled.
- Establishing accessible information systems for wider dissemination of critical knowledge.
- Removal of barriers from built environment, transport system and public facilities.
- Production, maintenance and distribution of assistive devices to overcome various impairments.
- Strengthening self-help organizations of persons with disabilities, their parents and of women with disabilities.

A comparative advantage of the ESCAP disability programme was the development of active inter-divisional collaboration, including the ESCAP Human Settlements Section, in the promotion of non-handicapping environments; the rural development section, in poverty alleviation among rural disabled persons; the general transport, coordination and communications section and the tourism unit, in the promotion of accessible public transport and the promotion of barrier-free tourism.

However, despite the achievements of the Decade, persons with disabilities remain the single largest sector of those least-served and most discriminated against in almost all States in the region. Much remains to be done to ensure the full participation and equality of status for persons with disabilities.

In May 2002, ESCAP adopted the Resolution"Promoting an inclusive, barrier-free and rights-based society for people with disabilities in the Asian and Pacific region in the twenty-first century". The Resolution also proclaimed the extension of the Asian and Pacific Decade of Disabled Persons, 1993-2002, for another decade, 2003- 2012. The Biwako Millennium Framework"outlines issues, action plans and strategies towards an inclusive, barrier-free and rights-based society for persons with disabilities." To achieve the goal, the framework identifies seven priority areas for action, in each of which critical issues and targets with specific time frames and actions follow. In all, eighteen targets and fifteen strategies supporting the achievement of all the targets are identified.

THE UN HUMAN RIGHTS INSTRUMENTS AND DISABILITY

There has been an increasing international recognition that disability is a human rights issue. There is also recognition that disability and disabilityrelated exclusion and marginalization is a concern for the UN human rights bodies. In August 1984, the Sub-Commission on Prevention of Discrimination and Protection of Minorities appointed a Special Rapporteur, Mr. Leandro Despouy, to conduct a comprehensive study on the relationship between human rights and disability.

In his report, Mr. Despouy made it clear that disability is a human rights concern, with which the UN monitoring bodies should be involved.

INTERNATIONAL COVENANT ON ECONOMIC, SOCIAL AND CULTURAL RIGHTS (ICESCR)

The Committee on Economic, Social and Cultural Rights under International Covenant on Economic, Social and Cultural Rights (ICESCR) in 1994 assumed the responsibility for disability rights by issuing a General Comment No 5, in which the Committee makes an analysis of disability as a human rights issue.

The General Comment states:"The Covenant does not refer explicitly to persons with disabilities. Nevertheless, the Universal Declaration of Human Rights recognizes that all human beings are born free and equal in dignity and rights and, since the Covenant's provisions apply fully to all members of society, persons with disabilities are clearly entitled to the full range of rights recognized in the Covenant.

Moreover, the requirement contained in Article 2 of the Covenant that the rights enunciated will be exercised without discrimination of any kind based on certain specified grounds or other status clearly applies to cover persons with disabilities". To illustrate the relevance of various provisions of ICESCR, a few articles can be examined.

For instance:

- Article 7 refers to the"right of everyone to the enjoyment of just and favourable conditions of work which ensures adequate remuneration". The just and favourable conditions of work have been interpreted and translated into the domestic labour standards by several governments. The concept of reasonable accommodation and barrier-free work environment is in fact premised on the notion set out in Article 7 of the Covenant. Reasonable accommodation can be defined as"providing or modifying devices, services, or facilities, or changing practices or procedures in order to afford participation on equal terms". Examples of"reasonable accommodation" include installation of a wheelchair ramp and elevators for people with mobility impairments, the introduction of part time work schedules for workers with severe conditions, availability of readers for visual impairments, and sign translation for people with hearing impairments.
- Article 11 recognizes that everyone has the"right to an adequate standard of living for himself and his family, including adequate food, clothing and housing". Available statistics show that world over this article is violated grossly in the case of persons with disabilities. High correlation between disability and poverty, and disproportionate number of disabled children in orphanages, visible presence of maimed, blinded and mentally ill persons amongst beggars are some examples.

INTERNATIONAL COVENANT ON CIVIL AND POLITICAL RIGHTS (ICCPR)

The Quinn and Degener study on the use of human rights instruments in the context of International Covenant on Civil and Political Rights, suggests that out of 114 States party reports reviewed, 76 (67 per cent) made some reference to disability. Other than addressing social welfare measures and equality laws, States party reports tend to refer to disabled persons in connection with civil commitment and the compulsory treatment of mentally ill or intellectually impaired persons. The State parties with reference to disabled persons do not extensively cover treatment of disabled defendants and prisoners, voting rights, marriage and divorce laws, and immigration laws and bioethics issues.

With the exception of the initial report of the Czech and the second periodic report of Ireland, which frankly acknowledge that State prisons are unable to accommodate disabled prisoners. Denmark reports that the State has established a training programme for police officers on how to deal with disabled prisoners. UK reports that a common standard of conduct has been laid down for all the staff working in prisons, which also refers to disabled inmates. These trends reflect greater respect for civil and political rights of PWDs in a much broader context.

The norms laid down in the International Standards are predominantly protective in nature and do not exclude any individual or class of individuals. In General Comment No 8, the Committee on Human Rights establishes that physical disability can never be a legitimate ground for restricting the right to vote. Neither may any intellectual disability be considered a reason for denying a person the right to vote or to hold office. The Comment further states that persons assisting disabled voters must be neutral, their only task being to preserve the independence of the voter. The Comment highlights the importance of participation in the political process by persons with disabilities who constitute a sizeable minority but have been an insignificant political constituency due to unfavorable circumstances. From the approach adopted by the Treaty Monitoring body, it is evident that people may be different from a physical and intellectual standpoint but so far as their civil and political rights are concerned, all people are the same.

CONVENTION ON RIGHTS OF THE CHILD (CRC)

There's yet another important international instrument *viz.* Convention on Rights of the Child (CRC) which establishes the rights of a disabled child to effective access and reception of education, training, health care services, rehabilitation services, preparation for employment and recreation opportunities in a manner conducive to the child's achieving the fullest possible social integration and individual development, including his or her cultural and spiritual development (Article 23). In fact, this is the only instrument, which has comprehensive and exclusive provisions regarding rights of the disabled children, although Article 2 of this Convention prohibits any discrimination in respect of the enjoyment of Convention rights on the ground of disability.

In paragraph 2 of Article 23, States parties are encouraged and required to ensure assistance to children with disabilities who are eligible and who apply for such services. The Committee on the Rights of the Child has identified four general principles that should guide the implementation of all Convention rights:

i. Non-discrimination,
ii. Best interests of the child,
iii. Right to survival and development,
iv. Right to be heard and to participate.

"The Committee on the Rights of the Child considers the self representation and full participation of children with disabilities as central to the fulfilment of their rights under the Convention. Article 12 may thus be viewed as the Convention's backbone. It encourages States parties to give a face to the invisible and a voice to the unheard, thereby enabling children with disabilities to enjoy a full and decent life in accordance with Article 23. Furthermore, the Committee has expressed its determination to do all it can to encourage governments to prioritize the rights of children with disabilities, and in line with Article 12 to ensure that disabled children participate in devising solutions to their problems." The CRC is unique in explicitly addressing the issue of disability, and it, therefore, has a great potential in advancing the rights of children with disabilities.

TORTURE CONVENTION

The Convention Against Torture and Other Cruel, Inhuman or Degrading Treatment or Punishment is of particular relevance to millions of people with disabilities, who are subjected to inhuman and degrading treatment in the institutions meant for their care and development. The imbalance of power is the root cause of such violations which happen due to poor supervision and arbitrary standards in the special institutions for PWDs. Mental health institutions, homes for severely and multiple disabled are the breeding grounds of such unlawful practices.

Torture has aroused profound concern in all quarters. Article 5 of the overarching Universal Declaration on Human Rights and Article 7 of ICCPR prevent inhuman and degrading treatment including medical treatment without the consent of the individual in question. The fact that the Convention only covers torture committed by or with the consent of public officials may be thought to limit its significance in the context of disability. Since, increasingly, countries in the developing world and some in the developed are routing services thorough private voluntary organizations, it becomes all the more necessary for the States to regulate standards and working of these institutions to check instances of abuse as States parties are under an obligation to prevent torture. Persons with disabilities, who are institutionalized, rarely take recourse to legal remedies.

It is mainly due to their total dependence for survival on these institutions and State sponsored care providers. In this respect, the disability related discrimination is an outcome of inadequate regulations and indifference to the problems faced by the disabled. Article 4 of the Convention requires each State party to ensure that all acts of torture and criminal offences are covered under the domestic law and their record is maintained category wise. Reports should, therefore, provide detailed information on criminal laws that prohibit torture. Emphasis should be placed on their applicability to persons with disabilities.

CONVENTION ON THE ELIMINATION OF ALL FORMS OF DISCRIMINATION AGAINST WOMEN

Convention on the Elimination of all Forms of Discrimination against Women (CEDAW) is a human rights treaty with the focus on women in general and marginalized and vulnerable women in particular. Recognizing that disability combined with gender stereotype causes multiple disadvantages, the Treaty Monitoring Body under this Convention adopted General Recommendation No 18, which urges State parties to include information on women with disabilities in their periodic reports with respect to their exercise of several rights contained in the Convention.

This makes it amply clear that all provisions contained in this Convention are very much applicable to women with disabilities as they are for other women. The purpose of adopting a General Comment is to assist State parties in fulfilling their reporting obligations.

The attention of the State parties thorough a General Comment is drawn to the insufficiencies and to the neglected areas. The Treaty Monitoring Body not only analyses the shortcomings in the report but also provides useful suggestions to stimulate appropriate response from the State parties. Most importantly, the General Comments offer authoritative interpretation of the Covenant and its application in domestic law.

DISABILITY CONVENTION

The UN General Assembly in its Resolution 56/168, 2001 recognizes that Governments, UN bodies and NGOs have not been successful in promoting full and effective participation and opportunities for persons with disabilities in economic, social, cultural and political life.

Expressing deep concern"about the disadvantages faced by 600 million disabled around the world" the General Assembly passed a resolution to establish an Ad-hoc Committee to consider a proposal for a comprehensive and integrated international Convention taking into account the recommendations of the Commission for Human Rights and the Commission for Social Development. While arguing for the Disability Convention, the Asian and Pacific forum of Human Rights institutions emphasize that"a coherent and integrated human rights approach to disability cannot be developed under the present treaty system" and an exclusive Convention would give"status, authority and visibility" to disability in the human rights area which cannot be achieved through the process of reform of existing instruments and monitoring mechanisms.

Adding a new treaty would also complement existing international standards for the rights of the disadvantaged. Favouring thematic treaty on disability rights Gerard Quinn states"It would make much more sense to encapsulate the relevant human rights standards in a single legal instrument.

It would clarify State parties obligations and it would give disability NGOs a clear target-one that is dedicated to disability rights in a holistic sense. This, in turn, could potentially enable international law to accelerate positive developments within states." A human rights and social justice approach enables the use of various categories of rights and also recognizes how rights have to be a concern in thinking about approaches to disability and social policy that enhance, rather than diminish, the status of those with disabilities.

In conclusion, international and domestic laws are a reliable vehicle that can aid transformation in material conditions and mental attitudes towards disabilities. The contemporary international law recognizes that all States have a duty under Article 56 of the Charter of the United Nations to ensure respect for and to observe human rights, including the incorporation of human rights standards in their national legislation. The Constitution of India empowers the government to take measures necessary to honour India's commitment to any international treaty or agreement. In the last 10 years government has adopted special laws, policies and schemes which are briefly analysed here.

LEGAL PROVISIONS

THE MENTAL HEALTH ACT OF INDIA, 1987

There is a general agreement that among persons with disabilities, those with intellectual and psychological impediments are most vulnerable and are discriminated both outside and within the families. To afford protection to the rights of this section, the Government of India repealed the outdated and inadequate Indian Lunacy Act, 1912 and the Lunacy Act, 1977 and enacted the Mental Health Act of 1987. Conditions conducive to protect autonomy, freedom and dignity of the mentally ill persons should have been created since the Act lays down comparatively rational criteria for admission in psychiatric hospitals and psychiatric nursing homes, and for the custody of his person, his property and its management. Under this Act, a District Mental Health Authority has been provided. Until 1995, many mentally ill persons were consigned to jails and those living in mental health institutions were no better as the conditions both in prisons and in mental institutions are far below the stipulated standards."In the Chandan Kumar Banik Vs State of West Bengal, 1995 Supp. SEE 505, the Supreme Court went into the inhuman conditions of the mentally ill patients in a mental hospital at Mankundu in the District of Hooghli.

The Supreme Court deprecated and discontinued the practice of tying up of inmates with the iron chain who were unruly or not physically controllable and ordered drug treatment for these patients. The administration of the Hospital was also removed from the Sub-Divisional Officer and replaced by a competent doctor with requisite administrative ability and powers. The Supreme Court gave directions to remove other deficiencies in the care to ensure that the patients now detained in the mental hospitals would receive appropriate attention in all respects in a humane manner." Due to deep-rooted prejudice and insufficient understanding of the Mental Health Act, the menace of committing people to jail did not stop for many years after the Mental Health Act became the law. Sheela Barse Vs. Union of India and Anr. 1993 4 SEE 204 was a case of detention of noncriminal mentally ill persons in the jails of West Bengal.

Their appalling condition were noted by the Supreme Court, which observed:

- That admission of non-criminal mentally ill persons to jails is illegal and unconstitutional.
- The Court directed that the function of getting mentally ill persons examined should vest with Judicial Magistrates and who, upon the advice of mental health psychiatrists, should assign the mentally ill person to the nearest place of treatment and care.

The NHRC has been deeply concerned with the unsatisfactory conditions prevailing in mental hospitals in the country, many of which function as custodial rather than therapeutic institutions. In the light of problems like overcrowding, lack of basic amenities, poor medical facilities, little or no effort at improving the awareness of family members about the nature of mental illness, or of the possibilities of medication and rehabilitation, the Commission came to the view that there was great need for it to take up this issue which, if not redressed, would result in the continuing violation of the rights of those greatly in need of understanding and support.

Subsequently, an operational research project was undertaken in collaboration with NIMHANS. Based on the findings of this project, a comprehensive set of guidelines has been developed and widely disseminated with a view to ensuring quality in the Mental Health Institutions. The Commission is monitoring the performance of State governments in the light of guidelines and directions of The Hon'ble Supreme Court Supreme Court of India.

THE REHABILITATION COUNCIL OF INDIA (RCI ACT)

The Rehabilitation Council of India was set up by the Government of India in 1986, initially as a society to regulate and standardize training policies and programmes in the field of rehabilitation of persons with disabilities. The need of minimum standards was felt urgent as majority of persons engaged in education, vocational training and counselling of PWDs were not professionally qualified. Poor academic and training standards adversely affect the chance of disabled in the world of work.

Therefore, an Act of Parliament in 1993 enhanced the status of the Council to a statutory body with an aim:

- To regulate the training policies and programmes in the field of rehabilitation of people with disabilities.
- To standardize training courses for professionals dealing with people with disabilities.
- To prescribe minimum standards of education and training of various categories of professionals dealing with people with disabilities
- To regulate these standards in all training institutions uniformly throughout the country.
- To recognize institutions/organizations/universities offering Certificate, Diploma, undergraduate and postgraduate degrees in the field of rehabilitation of persons with disabilities.
- To promote research in rehabilitation and special education.
- To maintain Central Rehabilitation Register for registration of professionals.

Sixteen categories of professionals and para-professionals are covered under the RCI Act. The Council has so far developed and standardized 85 different courses, which are offered by 203 academic institutions. The Council has accorded importance to both pre-service and in-service training, as inclusion of disability-perspective is vital to the integration of persons with disabilities in all facets of community life. In the Central Rehabilitation Register, about 21,000 professionals have been registered so far. The Manpower Development Report prepared by the RCI estimated that in the 9th plan period 3,63,000 trained persons would be needed. But the total output has not exceeded above 25,000. To accelerate the human resource development the distance education mode is now being explored.

THE NATIONAL TRUST ACT

The National Trust for Welfare of Persons with Autism, Cerebral Palsy, Mental Retardation and Multiple Disabilities Act was passed in 1999 and became operational in 2001. This Act provides for the constitution of a national body for the welfare of persons covered under this Act.

The main objectives of the Act are:

- To enable and empower persons with disability to live as independently and as fully as possible within and as close to the community to which they belong.

- To strengthen facilities to provide support to PWDs to live within their own families.
- To extend support to registered organizations to provide need based services during the period of crisis in the family of PWDs.
- To deal with problems of PWDs who do not have a family support.
- To promote measures for the care and protection of PWDs in the event of death of their parent or guardian.
- To evolve procedures for the appointment of guardians and trustees for PWDs requiring such protection.

The Act mandates the creation of Local Level Committees comprising District Magistrate or the District Commissioner along with one representative from a registered organization and one person with disability. The Local Level Committee is vested with the authority to decide upon the applications of legal guardianship received from parents, relatives or registered organizations duly authorized by the natural guardians of persons. The Committee is required to maintain inventory and annual accounts of the property and assets, claims and liabilities submitted by the legal guardians to it. The Local Level Committee can remove a guardian so appointed for negligence or for misappropriating the property of the person with disability.

Activities	Number	States	Union Territories
Formal awareness programmes	100	24	4
Local level committees formed	347	25	4
Organizations registered	277	25	1
State level master trainers trained	43	25	
District level master trainers trained		11	

DISABILITIES ACT, 1995

To give effect to India's commitment to the Proclamation on the Full Participation and Equality of Opportunity for the Persons with Disabilities 1993, in the Asian and Pacific Region the Parliament of India, enacted a very comprehensive piece of legislation known as"The Persons with Disabilities (Equal Opportunities, Protection of Rights and Full Participation) Act, 1995". The Act spells out the responsibilities of the various organs of the State and provides policy guidelines in the area of education, employment, manpower development, housing, social security, research and training.

It aims to promote creation of barrier free environment for persons with disabilities. The Act also lays down specific provisions for the development of specific services and programmes for equalizing the opportunity for the enjoyment of right to education, work, housing, mobility, communication and public assistance in case of severe disability and unemployment. For the translation of intended aims Central Coordination Committee and State Coordination Committees have been envisaged in a multi-sectoral mode with representation to persons with disabilities, Members of Parliament, professional bodies and eminent citizens. To counteract problems of discrimination, prejudice, neglect and non-compliance to mandated responsibilities the institution of Chief Commissioner in the Center and Commissioner for persons with disabilities in the States have been provided. These quasi-judicial bodies are vested with the powers of a civil Court. This mechanism has been quite effective in redressing individual grievances on account of deprivation of rights, facilities and guarantees.

The wide-ranging provisions of this Act are compiled under 14 different stages. The stage on Prevention and Early Detection of Disabilities, Education, Employment, Affirmative Action, Non-Discrimination, Research and Manpower Development, Institution for Persons with Severe Disabilities contain substantial provisions of the Act. Despite having a sound legal framework and a plethora of programmes, schemes, rules, regulations etc., corresponding improvements in the circumstances of persons with disabilities are not visible.

The rate of illiteracy, unemployment and poverty among persons with disabilities is alarming. The transport, buildings and information systems are designed on same old standards though the law demands creation of barrier-free facilities. The State governments, local authorities and panchayats have taken little care in fulfilling their obligations under various laws so much so that funds committed by the Central Government thorough a number of schemes have remained grossly underutilized. The recruitment rules and service regulations still have discriminatory provisions.

Some improvements could be achieved with Court interventions. Fifty Five per cent of the complaint cases before the Chief Commissioner for PWDs pertain to service matters. Similarly, the barriers to education are deep rooted. Many institutions, despite mandatory provision of 3 per cent reservation of seats in educational institutions, have denied admission to students on grounds of their disability. Hon'ble Supreme Court of India in the Rekha Tyagi versus All India Institute of Medical Sciences and Ors has given a clear verdict to the academic institutions to provide 3 per cent reservation to students with disabilities as per Section 39 of the Disabilities Act, 1995.

ENDEMIC AREAS AND IMPORTANT STATISTICS

POVERTY AND MALNOURISHMENT

In general, people with disabilities are estimated to make up 15 to 20 per cent of the poor in developing countries. Poor families often do not have sufficient income to meet their basic needs. Inadequate shelter, unhygienic living conditions, lack of sanitation and clean drinking water combined with poor access to health facilities breed disability. It is estimated that currently 515 million Asians are chronically undernourished, accounting for about two thirds of the world's hungry people.

Common micronutrient deficiencies that affect disability include:

- Vitamin A deficiency-blindness
- Vitamin B complex deficiency-beri-beri (inflammation or degeneration of the nerves, digestive system and heart), pellagra (central nervous system and gastro-intestinal disorders, skin inflammation) and anaemia
- Vitamin D deficiency-rickets (soft and deformed bones)
- Iodine deficiency-slow growth, learning difficulties, intellectual disabilities, goitre
- Iron deficiency-anaemia, which impedes learning and activity, and is a cause of maternal mortality
- Calcium deficiency-osteoporosis (fragile bones) (All Caps), 2002b)

Due to the lack of food and nutrition security for the poor, about 30 per cent of all infants born in India are born weighing less than 2,500 grams, which is the WHO cut-off level to determine low birth weight with a lower chance of survival and high risk of disability.

CRIME AND DISABILITIES

Violent crimes underline shortcomings in the social, political and economic arrangements. Such crimes not only leave people with a sense of insecurity and fear but also deprive them of their life and liberty. During 1999, the percentage share of the violent crimes reported in India was 13.5 per cent of the total 2,38,081 reported cases under IPC (Crime in India 1999). Many children and women are abducted to be used in prostitution, slavery and beggary. The risk of emotional, mental and physical disabilities increase manifold. In the mid nineties, the government of Saudi Arabia repatriated more than 500 maimed Indian children who were used for begging. The case of female domestic workers with amputed fingertips, nose and earlobes also surfaced during the same time. They too were smuggled into Arab countries by powerful mafia gangs operating in various parts of India, Philippines and other developing countries.

There are hardly any studies that have analysed the nexus between disability and crime, though at every nook and corner one can't escape the sight of maimed, blinded and mentally ill persons begging and wandering. Unfortunately, even the law enforcement agencies themselves commit acts of torture and inhuman treatment particularly to persons in detention. Custodial crimes, which include death, rape and disability, have drawn attention of public, media, legislature and human rights organizations. Bhagalpur blinding case is the illustration of this menace.

ACCIDENTS AND DISABILITY

As per the Central Bureau of Health Intelligence Report of 1997-98, the number of deaths due to road accidents was 69,800 and railroad accident deaths were approximately 15,000. An expert in the field, Dr Leslie G Norman of London, estimates that for every road accident death there are 30-40 light injuries and 10-15 serious injuries, which may lead to disability.

Improvements in vehicle design and medical facilities, as well as stronger enforcement of traffic regulations concerning the compulsory use of seat belts (car use) and helmets (motorcycle use), and restrictions on alcohol consumption and other intoxicants need to be treated more seriously than it has been."It is estimated that by 2020, road traffic accidents will be ranked as the third leading cause of disability in the Asian and the Pacific region. Quadriplegia, paraplegia, brain damage and behavioral disorders are some disabilities common among survivors of such accidents.

OCCUPATIONAL HAZARDS AND DISABILITY

To maximize profits, production is often located wherever costs are lowest, regulations are loose and workers least likely to organize for better working conditions and fairer wages. This often results in high rates of accidents, poisoning from toxins, loss of hearing and vision, and health deterioration.

Occupation-related health problems of workers employed in stone quarrying, leather industry, glasswork, weaving, diamond cutting, hand embroidery, etc. children employed in the carpet, cracker and match industry, have not received appropriate and sustained attention, as occupational health has not been perceived important enough both by the corporates and those responsible to regulate work standards. Even in the western countries, permanent disablement as a result of industrial and highway accidents outnumbers war causalities, for example, 44,000 people lost their limbs in industrial accidents, while 17,000 American soldiers became disabled in the Vietnam war.

Similarly, poor farmers and peasants are very vulnerable to disability as they work for long hours exposed to sunlight, dust and smoke. Wheat harvesting and amputations, paddy sowing and muscular diseases, coconut picking and spinal cord injuries are some common hazards associated with agricultural activities. The efforts to improve the design of agricultural implements have been quite successful in preventing disabilities. However, parallel improvements in the primary health system have not been achieved, as it lacks the capacity to deal with agricultural accidents which occur at the village level.

EMPLOYMENT OF THE DISABLED

Creation of opportunities for gainful employment is a task which governments all over the world perform. The development index is indicative of the employment in a given country. What makes a developed country different from a developing nation is its capacity to create and maintain unemployment as low as possible and on the other hand, sustain a level of growth which takes care of the employment needs of young adults. As per the 1991 National Sample Survey, there were over 70 lakh persons with disabilities in India in the employable age group.

The disabilitywise break-up is as follows:

Type of disability	Number of persons (in lakhs)
Locomotor disability	43.87
Visual disability	10.54
Hearing disability	12.48
Speech disability	10.47
Any other physical disability	68.81
Total	146.17

The employment scenario regarding PWDs presents a rather discouraging picture. Underemployment and unemployment continues to be rampant among the disabled, despite efforts made to improve employment opportunities for PWDs by the Government of India, State Governments and UT administrations.

As per the sample survey, conducted by NSSO in 1991, the rate of employment among the PWDs in rural areas was 29.1 per cent and in the urban areas 25.2 per cent. The table below gives classified information:

Sr. No.	Status	Rural	Urban	Total
1	Self-Empt. Agriculture	1.65	0.07	1.72
2	Self-Empt. Non-Agricultural	0.52	0.37	0.89
3	Regular Employee	0.25	0.28	0.53
4	Casual Labour	1.18	0.20	1.38
	Total	3.60	0.92	4.52

EDUCATION

The first school for hearing impaired children was established at Mumbai in 1884, and for the blind at Amritsar in 1887. Between then and now we have not been able to create an educational infrastructure that can cater to the needs of children with disabilities. As a result, more than 80 per cent of them remain deprived of educational opportunities, even lacking basic literacy skills.

Of the children dropped out in 1991 43 per cent are reported to have acquired disability. This highlights the inadequacies of the education system. The NSSO 1991 yielded 42 per cent are rate of education covering blind, hearing, speech and locomotor impaired persons. If 3 per cent population of mentally retarded and mentally ill persons is added to 1.9 per cent of other four disabilities, the coverage of 42 per cent comes down to approximately 20 per cent, in fact, even less.

TYPES OF VIOLATIONS

The nature of violations to the rights of persons with disabilities is also reflected in the annual reports of Chief Commissioner for Persons with Disabilities. Subject-wise complaints in the year 2000-2001 was as follows:

Sr. No.	Subject	Percentage
1	Employment	52
2	Education	14
3	Concession/Entitlement	9
4	Harassment	8
5	Housing and Property	4
6	Barrier-Free Environment	2
7	Miscellaneous	12

Coordination:

- The District Magistrates coordinate various development programmes in the district. Therefore, they can ensure that people with disabilities benefit from all the developmental schemes particularly those aimed at women, children, elderly persons, unemployed and socially disadvantaged sections.
- Better coordination among authorities in health, education, rural development, urban development, transport, traffic is vital to the translation of laws and policies and schemes for the disabled into reality.
- All the district committees, programme heads and officers in charge of schemes meant for persons with disabilities can form a District Coordination Committee. The District Magistrates can chair meetings of such a Coordination Committee and review its performance in a most effective and least time-consuming manner.

Affirmative Action:

- The competent authorities in urban development, rural development, revenue deptt. etc. may be advised to ensure that people with disabilities are given preference in the allotment of houses, shops, kiosks and agriculture and industrial land pattas including houses under Indira Awas Yojana and likewise as per Section 40 and 43 of the Disabilities Act, 1995.
- Scholarships to students with disabilities, pensions to the elderly disabled persons and unemployment allowance to those disabled whose names are registered for more than two years in the employment exchange must be given and any hurdles causing delay should be reduced by eliciting monthly progress report from the concerned authorities as per Section 30(d) and 68 of Disabilities Act, 1995.

Certificates:

- The District Chief Medical Officer and District Hospital should be advised to constitute a Medical Board which should meet on one fixed day atleast twice a month for looking after the need for the Disability Certificate as per rule 4, 5, and 6 of the Implementing Rules under Disabilities Act, 1995.

- Through a quarterly camp-approach at the block level, Disability Certificate, Income Certificate, Caste and Domicile Certificate, Free Bus Pass, Railway Concession Forms can be distributed to PWDs. Pension, scholarship and unemployment allowance can be disbursed in these camps to ensure efficiency, transparency and to check delay and malpractice.

Block level activities:

- Ensure that 3 per cent of JGSY works are allocated for the disabled in your block as per the Government of India directions and in accordance with Section 40 of the Disabilities Act, 1995.
- The BDOs can also ensure that each disabled person is given a house under Indira Awas Yojana.
- Credit assistance can be given for economic upliftment to a large number of disabled people under SGSY (Swarna Jayanthi Gram Swaraj Yojana) Scheme as 3 per cent budget is earmarked for PWDs in this scheme.
- The panchayats can be encouraged to facilitate creation of barrierfree school, post office, health center, rail and bus stand, panchayat building and religious shrines from the Swaran Jayanti funds.

Education:

- All the heads of the educational institutions at school, college, university, technical and professional level should be advised not to refuse admission on grounds of disability as per Section 26 of the Disabilities Act, 1995.
- All educational institutions, government and government aided, should reserve 3 per cent seats for students with disabilities as per section 39 of the Disabilities Act, 1995.
- All written tests, exams and interview procedures must be modified to ensure that persons with disabilities can participate without any discrimination and in accordance with the provisions referred to under the stage of Education in the Disabilities Act, 1995.
- The NGOs and district education authorities engaged in integrated education of disabled children must be helped in accessing funds under the scheme of Integrated Education of the Disabled Children (IEDC, Government of India, thorough the Ministry of HRD). Similarly, the schools covered under DPEP must be monitored closely to see the performance of disabled children and the teachers in these schools.
- Orientation and sensitization programmes should be introduced for the teachers, co-curricular staff and administrators of the regular school system, so that integration of the disabled children can be achieved more effectively. The Rehabilitation Council of India can provide assistance in this regard.
- The school authorities and medical authorities should coordinate the school health check-up programme to identify disabilities and for their prevention and treatment as per Section 25©.

- The District Social Welfare Officers should be encouraged to bring all the disabled children to the Balwadis and Anganwadis for early integration. Sensitization of the Balwadis and Anganwadis workers can be looked after by NIPSID.

Accessibility:

- All the educational institutions and health institutions can be advised to provide ramps, barrier-free toilets and other facilities as per Section 45 and 46 of the Disabilities Act, 1995.
- The Municipal Corporation and competent authorities should be advised to adopt model-building byelaws developed by the Ministry of Urban Affairs, Government of India. All the new buildings, private and for public use, thus, would be built on accessible norms as prescribed in Section 45 and 46 of the Disabilities Act, 1995.
- All the renovation activities and commissioning of new buses and other means of transport should be approved only if they comply with accessible standards laid down in Section 44, 45 and 46 of the Disabilities Act, 1995.
- The Municipal Commissioners can ensure that all the shops, commercial establishments, cinema theatres, bus stops etc. are provided with facilities like ramps, hand railings, barrier free toilets and accessible drinking water facility for the disabled people.

Employment:

- For starting a business enterprise like provision stores, tea shops, vegetable and fruit stalls, STD booth etc. the SC/ST unemployed disabled people can be covered under the schemes for SC/ST.
- Under PMRY (Prime Minister's Rozgar Yojana) Scheme a number of disabled youth can be helped to set up STD booths, Xerox centres, computer internet browsing centres etc.
- You can ensure that the Government local bodies and Government undertakings furnish information to employment exchanges about vacancies reserved for disabled people. This would ensure proper utilization of 3 per cent quota in jobs for the disabled as per Section 33 of the Disabilities Act, 1995. Government, public sector undertakings and all the institutions receiving aid from any government is obliged to appoint disabled persons on 3 per cent posts in all the categories as per Section 33 and 2(k) of the Disabilities Act, 1995.
- All the State Governments and the Government of India have compiled a list of identified jobs in various services and sectors for different categories of the disabled. This list is in pursuance of Section 32 of the Disabilities Act and thus can be used by the district authorities and all those requiring to employ PWDs.
- All the appointing authorities in the Government and governmentaided sectors must not dispense any employee from service, reduce in rank, deny promotion to an employee on merely

grounds of disability. Instructions to this effect must be issued as per Section 47 of the Disabilities Act, 1995.

Women with disabilities:

- You can ensure that all the disabled women are made members in the local self-help group of women (SHG) under the women development programme of the Government, so that they can become recipients of the Government assistance under the revolving fund and the economic activity assistance under SGSY.

The Nilgiri District in Tamil Nadu and Anantpur in Andhra Pradesh are examples of good practice and District Magistrates can always rely upon these model disability-friendly districts.

RIGHTS FOR SENIOR CITIZENS OF INDIA

We have started living in the age of ageing, but it is only the dawn of that Age. From 12 million in 1901, we rose to be 20 million in 1951, and there are now nearly 77 million older persons in India today. This figure is projected to be 177 million in 2025, about 11 per cent of these are above 80 years. By 2025, we would have 25 per cent of these who would be above 80 years. The population statistics do not mean anything useful unless we sufficiently consider what these numbers add up to.

About 90 per cent of older persons today are from the unorganized sector, that just means that at the age of 60, they have no regular source of income, no worthwhile form of social security, *i.e.* no provident fund, no gratuity, no medical insurance, after formally or informally retiring from active earning. About 80 per cent of the older persons live in rural areas and have limited access to health care and other services. Ageing has important implications, both at the macro and micro levels.

While at the micro level, it affects individuals and their families, at the macro level it affects the entire nation. With about 33 per cent of the elderly living just below the poverty line, and another 33 per cent just above it, but belonging to the lower income group, the financial situation of about 66 per cent of the older persons today is fragile. This relates to serious livelihood insecurities caused by factors including growing incidence of prolonged old age ailments, disabilities, dysfunctions, lack of opportunities in gainful activities and little or no familial support. Old age poverty in India would be a permanent feature, if today we don't cope with it by setting aside substantial resources and ensure that public health and social services are up to the task. Situation of Older Women is an area of serious concern. While 48.2 per cent of the older persons today are women, this proportion is likely to rise further and, in a few years, we would have a feminine India. This feminization of ageing has further consequences.

The older woman in India faces a triple jeopardy-being a woman in a largely patriarchal society, economically dependent and aged. And to add to that, if she is a widow, which is the case with 55 per cent of elderly women today, the world may not be a pleasant place to live. This is a situation very few perceived decades ago and, therefore, very little or no action was taken at various levels to correct it. We anticipate that ageing populations will drain our resources, but that cannot be a ground to throw them by the wayside for the simple reason that, when the old were young, they had made significant contribution to the family, society and the nation. Time has, therefore, come for the young to repay even a millionth part of that debt which they owe to the old. Family plays a major role in looking after the elderly. Family is viewed as one of the most unique entities; it holds together dynamic relationships of members of different ages and generations. The concept of respecting the elders was ingrained in children during their younger years of upbringing. However, the influence of demographic changes on the family is very evident today. With the shift of household platform from extended families to nuclear families, there is an increased demand on family resources, making it necessary for individual family members to have more than one job. This reduces the time family members spend together. With the migration of working members in search of employment, the older persons are left behind-alone too. This just means that they have to look after themselves. So, the welfare of older persons is gradually shifting for family to community and government.

LEGAL PROVISIONS

CODE OF CRIMINAL PROCEDURE, 1973

Section 125(1) (2) makes it incumbent for a person having sufficient means to maintain his father or mother who is unable to maintain himself or herself and, on getting proof of neglect or refusal, may be ordered by a first class magistrate to make a monthly allowance not exceeding ₹500/-. It is applicable to all, irrespective of their religious faith and religious persuasion, and includes adoptive parents. This section has been interpreted by the Supreme Court in its ruling, so as to make daughters and sons, married or unmarried, equally responsible to maintain their parents.

HINDU ADOPTION AND MAINTENANCE ACT, 1956

By Section 20(1) of the act, every Hindu son or daughter is under obligation to maintain aged and infirm parent. Amount is determined by the Court taking into consideration the position and status of the parties.

LEGISLATION BY THE HIMACHAL PRADESH GOVERNMENT

The Himachal Pradesh Mata-Pitah aur Arthrik Pariposhan Vidhayak 1996 passed by Himachal Pradesh Vidhan Sabha makes it mandatory for children to look after their aged parents and other dependents or pay a maintenance allowance. The amount of maintenance is to be commensurate with the family's status. The status of Government through this legislation has tried to bypass the Courts. Complainants can simply go to a Sub-Divisional Magistrate or any other appellate authority to seek redress of their grievances. The Government of Maharashtra has passed a Bill on similar lines.

INCOME TAX REBATE (SECTION 88B OF FINANCE ACT, 1992)

This provides for rebate in Income Tax to senior citizens. The rebate is available in the case of a resident individual (s/he may be an ordinary resident or a non-ordinary resident; he may be an Indian citizen or a foreign citizen) who has attained the age of 65 years at any time during the relevant previous year.

From the assessment year 2001-2002, tax rebate under section 88B shall be:

- The amount of income-tax before giving any rebate under sections 88, 88B and 89(a); or
- Additional tax rebate of 100 per cent of tax on total income subject to a maximum limit of ₹15,000 (men and women) under section 88B
- Tax rebate of 15 per cent is given under section 88 for income between ₹1.5 lakhs to ₹5 lakhs
- Ceiling on savings for tax rebate is now raised from ₹80,000/- to ₹1,00,000/-
- Investment of up to ₹2 lakhs in the Relief Bonds issued by RBI have been declared tax-exempt for Senior Citizens or employees retiring under VRS.

INCOME TAX REBATE (SECTION 88C)

This provision relates to the additional rebate of ₹5000/- to women taxpayers.

- Senior Citizens are excluded from"One by Six" scheme for filling income tax return under proviso to section 139(1), if they own immovable property exceeding a specified floor area, whether by way of ownership, tenancy or otherwise (clause 1) or are a subscriber to a telephone (clause 3). The conditions specified in both the clauses above do not apply to any senior citizen who has attained 65 years of age but is not engaged in any business or profession during the previous year.

Index